Not Just a Man's War

Contemporary Chinese Studies

This series provides new scholarship and perspectives on modern and contemporary China, including China's contested borderlands and minority peoples; ongoing social, cultural, and political changes; and the varied histories that animate China today.

Christopher G. Rea and Nicolai Volland, eds., *The Business of Culture: Cultural Entrepreneurs in China and Southeast Asia, 1900–65*

Eric Hyer, *The Pragmatic Dragon: China's Grand Strategy and Boundary Settlements*

Kelvin E.Y. Low, *Remembering the Samsui Women: Migration and Social Memory in Singapore and China*

Jennifer Y.J. Hsu, *State of Exchange: Migrant NGOs and the Chinese Government*

Ning Wang, *Banished to the Great Northern Wilderness: Political Exile and Re-education in Mao's China*

Norman Smith, ed., *Empire and Environment in the Making of Manchuria*

Joseph Lawson, *A Frontier Made Lawless: Violence in Upland Southwest China, 1800–1956*

Victor Zatsepine, *Beyond the Amur: Frontier Encounters Between China and Russia, 1850–1930*

Patrick Fuliang Shan, *Yuan Shikai: A Reappraisal*

Selina Gao, *Saving the Nation through Culture: The Folklore Movement in Republican China*

Andres Rodriguez, *Frontier Fieldwork: Building a Nation in China's Borderlands, 1919–45*

Yuxing Huang, *China's Asymmetric Statecraft: Alignments, Competitors, and Regional Diplomacy*

Elizabeth A. Littell-Lamb, *The YWCA in China: The Making of a Chinese Christian Women's Institution, 1899–1957*

For a complete list of the titles in the series, see the UBC Press website, www.ubcpress.ca.

Not Just a Man's War

Chinese Women's Memories of the War of Resistance against Japan, 1931–45

YIHONG PAN

© UBC Press 2024

All rights reserved. No part of this publication may be reproduced, stored in a retrieval system, or transmitted, in any form or by any means, without prior written permission of the publisher, or, in Canada, in the case of photocopying or other reprographic copying, a licence from Access Copyright, www.accesscopyright.ca.

Printed in Canada on FSC-certified ancient-forest-free paper (100% post-consumer recycled) that is processed chlorine and acid-free.

Library and Archives Canada Cataloguing in Publication

Title: Not just a man's war : Chinese women's memories of the war of resistance against Japan, 1931–45 / Yihong Pan.
Names: Pan, Yihong, author.
Series: Contemporary Chinese studies.
Description: Series statement: Contemporary Chinese studies | Includes bibliographical references and index.
Identifiers: Canadiana (print) 20240317866 | Canadiana (ebook) 20240317947 | ISBN 9780774870351 (hardcover) | ISBN 9780774870368 (softcover) | ISBN 9780774870382 (EPUB) | ISBN 9780774870375 (PDF)
Subjects: LCSH: Sino-Japanese War, 1937–1945—Women. | LCSH: World War, 1939–1945—Women—China—Manchuria. | LCSH: Women—China—Manchuria—History—20th century. | LCSH: Communists—China—Manchuria—History—20th century. | LCSH: Oral history—China—Manchuria. | LCSH: Manchuria (China)—History—1931–1945.
Classification: LCC DS777.533.W65 P36 2024 | DDC 940.53/518082—dc23

UBC Press gratefully acknowledges the financial support for our publishing program of the Government of Canada, the Canada Council for the Arts, and the British Columbia Arts Council.

This book has been published with the help of a grant from the Canadian Federation for the Humanities and Social Sciences, through the Scholarly Book Awards, using funds provided by the Social Sciences and Humanities Research Council of Canada.

Financial support from the Chiang Ching-kuo Foundation is also greatly appreciated.

UBC Press is situated on the traditional, ancestral, and unceded territory of the xʷməθkʷəy̓əm (Musqueam) people. This land has always been a place of learning for the xʷməθkʷəy̓əm, who have passed on their culture, history, and traditions for millennia, from one generation to the next.

UBC Press
The University of British Columbia
www.ubcpress.ca

To those women and men who told me their experiences, and those of their parents, about the War of Resistance.

Contents

Note on Romanization / ix

Acknowledgments / xi

List of Abbreviations / xv

Introduction / 3

1 Representations of Wartime Women in the People's Republic of China / 21

2 Self-Writing by the Women Soldiers of the Communist New Fourth Army / 42

3 My Journey of the Revolution: Oral Narratives of Five Communist Women / 66

4 Those Turbulent Years: Memories of Women Associated with the Nationalist Party / 98

5 Surviving under the Enemy: Oral Narratives of Middle-Class Women in Japanese-Occupied China / 125

6 I Want to Speak Up before I Die: The Testimonies of China's "Comfort Women" and the Oral Narratives of Working-Class Women / 153

Epilogue / 176

Appendix: Interviews / 187

Glossary / 192

Notes / 195

Bibliography / 226

Index / 247

Note on Romanization

I use the Pinyin Romanization system for Chinese names and places throughout the text except for the names of Chiang Kai-shek and Sun Yat-sen since both are widely known in the West spelled according to the Wade-Giles system. The names of authors and interviewees in Taiwan are in Pinyin except in the case of Chi Pang-yuan, as this spelling of her name is used in the English translation of her work, and in the case of Tsai Ing-wen.

Beijing has been the capital of China for most of the time since the tenth century. In 1928, it was named Beiping when it was not the capital of the Republic of China. From July 1937 to August 1945, it was renamed Beijing under the Japanese occupation. It became Beiping in 1945–49, and Beijing from 1949 onward. In the text, I use "Beiping" for the period 1928–49, and "Beijing" for other periods.

Acknowledgments

The research and writing of this book were never a solitary, lonely process. On each step forward, I had support from so many people. To them, I am deeply indebted.

I started this project for academic purposes. During the process, it became more of a personal endeavour because the self-narratives – written and published or obtained through my interviews – are by women that include my own mother, the mothers of my friends, and ordinary Chinese women. They all came of age during China's drastic transformation in the early twentieth century, lived through the War of Resistance against Japan (1931–45) and the Civil War (1946–49), and endured the turbulent events that followed in the twentieth century on mainland China and Taiwan. Having gotten to know these women, I now have a deeper understanding of what their generation endured and have come to greatly admire them all. Their stories have personalized the historical record of China. My deepest gratitude goes to those women I interviewed, who trusted me with these stories and gave me their consent to tell them, as well as to those who have published their memories. This work would not have been possible were it not for their collective memory as a whole. They left a valuable legacy that has served to connect me more deeply with the history of China and of Chinese women in particular.

I want to express my sincere thanks to my colleague, Dr. Jeffrey Kimball, for introducing me to the peace conference that prompted my research of Chinese women during the Resistance War. Deep gratitude goes to my colleague and dear friend, Dr. Mary Frederickson, for her intellectual input, encouragement, and for reading early drafts of this work. It was her words – "these women's stories are waiting to be told" – that made me persist with this project. I am also deeply grateful for my colleague and dear friend, Dr. Judith P. Zinsser. Her undying support at every step of the project included many intellectual conversations on women's history; many careful readings and re-readings; insightful comments; and strong moral support that kept me moving forward, especially during times of difficulty.

I would like to thank all of the scholars whose works listed in the bibliography informed this work and kept me engaged in it. In particular, I would like to thank Dr. Bian Lingling for inviting me to publish a paper on Communist New Fourth women in the journal *Research on Women in Modern Chinese History* (published by the Institute of Modern History, Academia Sinica in Taiwan), and the peer reviewers whose comments on that paper encouraged me to examine my viewpoints from broader angles. My thanks also go to Dr. Sophia Lee for her detailed comments on my paper about the middle-class women under the Japanese occupation in the war. A conversation with Dr. Su Zhiliang on China's former "comfort women" and his dedication to this important topic were also a source of inspiration to me. Lastly, my deep and sincere gratitude goes to the three readers of this manuscript whom UBC Press coordinated prior to publication. Their long lists of suggestions, including insightful comments for revision – such as the need to cut and condense sections, add new references, and discuss new issues – and their corrections of errors in the text, have significantly improved the book. Any remaining errors in the book are my own.

I would like to also offer my deep gratitude to all my siblings Zhenwei, Zhenying, Yiling, Yifei, Yiti, and Qixin; and to my relatives Pan Ziyang, Liu Jiren, and Liu Zhijian. They helped in so many different ways: in accessing primary sources in libraries or through private venues, in finding people for me to interview; or by accompanying me on field trips to mountainous areas. My heartfelt gratitude also goes to my friends Haung Ce, Guo Shuhua, Li Xingyan, Lu Min, Tong Yu (Jade Morton), Wang Qing and her husband, and Teresa Yu. Not only did they facilitate me meeting their mothers or relatives for interviews, they also provided a variety of other support that made my research possible.

In addition, my special thanks go to a number of people who contributed in significant ways to the book during its various stages: to freelance editors Dr. Jeanne Barker-Nunn, Aaron M. Gilkison, and Pam Messer for their careful and excellent work; to the editors at UBC Press in the production of the book: Senior Editor Randy Schmidt, Production Editor Megan Brand, and Copy Editor Frank Chow, who have provided professional assistance and were always there to address any concerns I may have had. It was such a pleasure to work with them.

The libraries that were of enormous assistance in facilitating my research are at the University of Michigan, the University of British Columbia, Miami University with Interlibrary Loan section and OhioLink network, and the National Library of China in Beijing. Early research was supported by funding from the Asia Library Travel Grant from the University of Michigan and from the Hampton Fund of Miami University. The publication of the book was also made possible by financial support from the Government of Canada, the Canada Council for the Arts, and the British Columbia Arts Council.

My thanks also go to the journals for permitting me to include revised versions of the following previously published papers in the book: "Feminism and Nationalism in China's War of Resistance against Japan" in *The International History Review*, 19, 1 (February 1997), 115–30; "Their 'Quiet' Devotion: Communist Women in the War of Resistance against Japan (1937–1945)" in *The Chinese Historical Review*, 16, 1 (spring 2009), 1–26; "Never a Man's War: The Self-Reflections of the Women Soldiers of the New Fourth Army in the Resistance War against Japan (1937–45)" (in Chinese) in *Research on Women in Modern Chinese History*, 24 (December 2014), 83–131; "Surviving under the Enemy: Oral Narratives of Middle-Class Women in Japanese-Occupied China (1931–45)" in *Frontiers of History in China* 14, 3(2019), 323–52.

Abbreviations

ACWF	All-China Women's Federation
CCP	Chinese Communist Party
GMD	Guomindang (the Nationalist Party)
N4A	New Fourth Army
PRC	People's Republic of China

Not Just a Man's War

Introduction

Sitting in the living room of her Beijing apartment, eighty-eight-year-old Wang Yao (1913–2008) recalled the night of September 18, 1931. She had been a high school student in the city of Shenyang. That evening, a Friday, she and her friends

> went to school to watch a play called "A Patriotic Heart." It was about a student with a Japanese mother and a Chinese father. The mother had to leave China for Japan because of the tensions between the two countries. The play was put on to raise funds to help the victims of the Yellow River flood. We were so excited that we wanted to go to another show the following night ...
>
> Then we heard the sound of cannons. Within one night, Shenyang was no longer ours ... The war changed my life.[1]

That night, the Japanese Kwantung Army staged what came to be known as the Manchurian (Mukden) Incident near the city of Shenyang, in which the Japanese Army blew up a section of the Japan-controlled railway, blamed it on the Chinese army, and then used it as a pretext for attack. The Chinese garrison resisted but was forced to retreat. Shenyang and Changchun were occupied by the Japanese. Soon the Japanese Imperial Army occupied all of Manchuria (comprising three of China's most northeasterly provinces) and established a puppet state, Manchukuo, in February 1932. In July 1937, China and Japan entered a full-scale war that ended with Japan's defeat in 1945.

Known in its short form as *Kangzhan* in Chinese (the Resistance War, or the War of Resistance), China's war against Japan lasted from 1931 to 1945 and was one of the principal theatres of the Second World War. The War of Resistance transformed China. By the end of the war, China had nullified all unequal treaties with Western powers that had previously reduced China to a semi-colonial status. China then became one of the great powers as a permanent member of the United Nations Security Council. Domestically, the Chinese Communist Party (CCP) had grown much stronger than before in terms of territory, number of adherents, and military force. In contrast, the Nationalist Party (Guomindang, or GMD), the ruling party of China, had been devastated by the war and its own corruption. Postwar negotiations, mediated by the United States, sought a coalition government in which both parties would have participated, but failed to bear fruit. China descended into a civil war (1946–49) from which the Communists emerged as victors. On October 1, 1949, CCP chairman Mao Zedong proclaimed the founding of the People's Republic of China (PRC). The Nationalist government fled to Taiwan and China became a Communist country. Tensions on both sides of the Taiwan Strait and between China and Japan have persisted to this day, a potential source of crisis in East Asia.

The complex impact of the War of Resistance on the Chinese people has lasted far beyond the war and into the Cold War and after. This book is an interpretation of Chinese women's memories of the war. It is based on memoirs, oral histories, and collections of reminiscences published on mainland China and Taiwan, plus nineteen interviews I conducted personally. During the war, China was fragmented. The urban areas in the coastal east were mostly under Japanese occupation. The Nationalist government, with its war capital in Chongqing, exercised control over southwest China, while the Chinese Communist Party, headquartered in Yan'an, controlled the northwest and some rural areas in north and central China. The war left people with different experiences and memories as they lived in various places in wartime China in which the levels of violence, suffering, and resistance varied.[2] This book uncovers the diverse gendered, political, military, social, economic, and psychological experiences of ordinary women who lived in different geographical regions: in the Chinese Communist Party, with the Nationalist Party, and of the privileged middle class, the victims of sexual violence at the hands of the Japanese Imperial Army, and the working poor under the Japanese occupation. It inquires into how the war was experienced by them, what these women want to remember, and what they wish to convey with their narratives; it explores how they, as social actors, exerted their own agency under social, economic, and political constraints to survive and to effect change for themselves and for Chinese women in general.

For decades, the history and the public memories of the War of Resistance was monopolized by the PRC government during the Mao Zedong era (1949–76). The master narrative of the twentieth century was a history of the political evolution of the Communist Party centring on Mao. To build the cult of Mao, the roles of other Communist male leaders remained secondary. Communist women's history was marginalized, and their images were stereotyped. The PRC historical discourse demonized the Nationalists and distorted their roles. From the early 1980s, with the reform and the opening up of China to the world, the war has become more of a central part of the official discourse for a new nationalism. The political relaxation and the end of the Cold War led to remarkable developments in the reinterpretations and remembrance of the war in China and overseas. On September 3, 2015, under Xi Jinping's government, Beijing staged the first national parade in commemoration of the seventieth anniversary of the end of the war, marking "a major milestone" in the changes in the collective memory. The war became more of a political tool in Xi's efforts to assert China's role on the world stage.[3]

Since 2012, Xi Jinping's government has tightened up political and social control, with greater concentration of power and more intense penetration of society by the state.[4] In spite of the political closing down, there have already appeared in China and overseas a rich body of in-depth studies on the military, political, economic, and diplomatic aspects of wartime China, the experiences of various regions, and the important role of the Nationalist government and army in the resistance. Studies on China's war memory have investigated how memories were politicized, distorted, and suppressed, and how they remained in the shadows in the Cold War climate. Since the 1980s, there has been a new remembering, and retrieval of the memories of survivors of the war has grown.[5]

For this book, I have chosen a range of mostly ordinary women for analysis. A series of "great" women – those prominent in politics, literature, and religion, and as professionals – played important roles in history that will be addressed here where relevant, but this book focuses on stories of mostly ordinary women and their self-writings and narrations.

Feminist studies based on official documents have explored the Chinese women's movement and offered a series of critiques on the mixed, mostly damaging effects on women of the policies of political parties and governments. Since the 1990s, there has been a shift in research into women's personal experiences and perspectives, and their tactics and approaches with regard to patriarchy. This shift is shown in the extant English scholarly works on Chinese women's war experiences. Placing women on centre stage, they deal mostly with a specific geographical region or a specific category of women. This book also has women's personal experiences as a focus for analysis. Each group of stories has enriched the narrative of the war history, making the history more inclusive. It stresses women's agency in history. More importantly, it connects diverse groups of ordinary women to address how different socio-economic and educational backgrounds, political inclinations, and geographical locations shaped their lives and informed their choices during the war in terrible, sometimes life-or-death circumstances and put them on different trajectories of experiences.

The book not only treats women's memories as sources for a deeper understanding of the war but also takes them as a subject for critical analysis and interpretation.[6] As memories were collected or written down when the women were in their later years, they could be fragmented or faulty, given the passage of time; they might exhibit distortion due to the restraint demanded by cultural values and social norms and/or the women's inability to clearly articulate long-ago experiences. Political and historical changes can lead one to be selective, restrained, or exaggerated when relating memories, or even to conflate some memories with others. In addition, these women's gender consciousness or subconsciousness may also have had the effect of "(muting) their own thoughts and feelings when they try to describe their lives" in publicly acceptable terms.[7]

Feminist studies have established theories and approaches for examining women's personal experiences. They have addressed both the limitations and effectiveness of oral history, biography, autobiography, testimonies, and memory. They answer basic questions: Why did women accept positions of inferiority? Why and how did they refuse such positions?[8] How can we use women's history to write a war history?[9] History is made by memories. Oral histories let women speak for themselves.[10] Women's personal narratives, written or oral, form a vital part of the recovery of women's hidden history. The self-narratives of women shed light on subjective meanings to women themselves.[11] As Gail Hershatter has shown in her oral history study of Chinese rural women in the 1950s, women's memories would provide rich details, gendered perspectives, and specific ways of describing the past that may not be found in archival sources.[12] What matters most in my work are the memories of ordinary women of different backgrounds. Their self-writing and narration reveal the strong inner urge of this war generation to remember the war toward the end of their lives because the past was meaningful in shaping their lives and the history of China. In their own words, with their own logic, these women present a women's war, a war in which women underwent multiple types of suffering, made contributions to the war effort at home and at the front, and more importantly, found ways to effect changes in everyday lives, whether as soldiers or students, whether working outside the home or as homemakers.

The book demonstrates that the self-articulation of the past empowered women. It validated the importance of their life experiences. We see how the Communist women soldiers argue that their "quiet" devotion and heroic efforts contributed to the party's rise to power, and that the revolutionary wars were never just a man's cause. The War of Resistance was not just a man's war, thus the title of this book. The self-writing and narrations of the women associated with the Nationalist Party and government make us see how they paid tribute to the human spirit in the war of suffering. The stories of middle-class and working-poor women bring us into a deep understanding of how they refused to be ignored as passive beings in all the hardships they shared in the face of Japanese aggression, and why the victims of the sexual violence perpetrated by the Japanese Imperial Army wanted to speak before they died.

The book is a micro-history, with a small selection of women's memories. Their stories demonstrate the texture and rhythm of everyday life during the war. Although the word "feminism" rarely came up when they reflected on their past, these women demonstrated autonomy and courage in their search for strength. One could change one's life and those of others regardless of one's political association, socio-economic status, or education. Their incremental efforts made social changes.

The Struggles for National Liberation and Women's Liberation: The Chinese Women's Movement (1890s–1945)

The women who lived through the War of Resistance were born and grew up in the early twentieth century of a China in transformation, when the Chinese women's movement grew and evolved. In the 1898 "Hundred Days of Reform" during which leading male reformers Kang Youwei and Liang Qichao campaigned for gender equality, women reformists themselves asserted that women's liberation needed to be closely connected with the fate of the country. Referring to the well-known phrase "The rise and fall of all-under-heaven is the responsibility of every man" (*tianxia xingwang, pifu youze*),¹³ reformist women raised the slogan "the rise and fall of all-under-heaven is also the responsibility of every woman."¹⁴ The women's movement from then on played an undeniable role in all major events of the Chinese nation: the 1911 Revolution, the May Fourth Movement (New Culture Movement) (1915–20s), the Northern Expedition (1926–28), and the War of Resistance against Japan. In accordance with the Third World women's movements, the Chinese women's movement could never be independent of the nationalist movement: it was first of all motivated by the desire to save the country. In her exploration of women's subjectivity in the early 1900s, Joan Judge has pointed out that when nationalism was the dominant political priority in China's transformation, women activists used nationalism to "carve out new subjectivities and act on them in society and politics," although nationalism also yoked them to the demands of the larger national project.¹⁵ Although the extent of the enabling and yoking effects of nationalism on women striving for equality is debatable, women activists within the two political parties, the Nationalist and Communist, and outside them had functioned as a collective political force invoking national liberation as a means of advancing women's status in the early twentieth century.¹⁶

The New Life Movement

From the Manchurian Incident in 1931 to early 1937, faced with escalating Japanese aggression, the Nationalist government under Chiang Kai-shek insisted on a policy of "first internal pacification, then external resistance." This involved the subduing of regional warlords and elimination of the Communist Party, and the building of a strong China. The government, in its social engineering, implemented the New Life Movement (NLM) beginning in 1934. Directly opposing the radical anti-Confucian and liberal feminist tendencies of the May Fourth Movement that began in 1915, the NLM aimed to restore the Confucian ethical concepts of *li, yi, lian,* and *chi,* rendered as propriety, righteousness, integrity, and a sense of shame, so as to lead China to a spiritual rejuvenation. Chiang Kai-shek and his wife, Song Meiling, were dominant leaders of the NLM. Song called upon Chinese women to reform the family and serve the broader Chinese society. She maintained that the nation's problems needed to be solved by the citizens themselves, and, in the same way, women's inferior status needed to be rectified by women citizens.[17]

Feminist critics have pointed out the limited effects of the NLM on gender equality.[18] Once dismissed as a frivolous, useless, and reactionary project, the NLM in recent scholarship has, on the contrary, come to be seen as a prominent vehicle for instilling in the population a sense of Chinese citizenship in the face of Japanese aggression and battling against the Communist ideology of class warfare.[19] The NLM invoked a concept of citizenship that emphasized more responsibility in the fight for China's survival against foreign imperialism than individual rights from the state.[20] Its social engineering strongly espoused the belief that social stability was closely related to the family, that managing the family well would contribute to a stronger China.[21]

In its own journal, *Women's New Life Movement Monthly* (*Funü xin shenghuo yuekan*), which ran from November 1936 to June 1937, the NLM for women had essays discussing the roles of women in saving the nation. It linked nationalism closely with motherhood and created for Chinese women an ideal image of the "super wise wife and good mother" (*chao xianqi liangmu*).[22] Author Zhenzhuang reiterated that restoring old virtues did not mean that women would have to return to their previously submissive status; rather, the "super wise wives and good mothers" were those who would actualize their own potential and assume their own duties as wife and mother, and, as the national crisis intensified, shoulder the mission to save the nation.[23]

Within the Nationalist Party, a group of women activists advocated for women's interests. Their journal, *Women's Resonance* (*Funü gongming*), took a strong feminist stance on the issues of women's self-liberation. Amid the national crisis triggered by the Japanese invasion, the journal called for the emancipation of women as part of national salvation.[24] When the NLM for women created the notion of "super wise wife and good mother," the journal proposed "new-wise-wife-good mother-ism" (*xin xianqi liangmu zhuyi*), which demanded reciprocity, the basic principle of Confucianism that both women *and* men should cultivate the virtues and ethics necessary for successful families and a resilient society.[25]

The NLM worked to revive Confucian values, as women throughout the ages had followed Confucianism since its core values could benefit them. Recent scholarly works argue that Confucianism lent important responsibilities to women in the family as educators of children, as moral custodians of the family, and as the force keeping the household intact.[26] Women's domestic, private spaces were closely connected with outside, public spaces. Women in the historical past used the domestic power to exert their influence.[27] As in the societies of other developing countries, where the domestic sphere is one in which women "may have ultimate control" and where the woman's role in the home is "a means of empowerment,"[28] Chinese women's experiences in the early twentieth century affirmed the importance of the domestic.

The Chinese Communist Party: The Radical Ideology and the Pragmatic Strategy

The Chinese Communist Party, born in 1921 during the anti-traditional, iconoclastic, anti-imperialist May Fourth era, had its theory on women's liberation grounded in the Marxist ideology that class rather than gender was the fundamental source of gender oppression. Women's liberation could be realized only in a proletarian-dominated socialist society that had eliminated private ownership and all traditional views and practices that had placed women in an inferior status. The Chinese Communist Party considered liberal feminism "elitist," "bourgeois," and "narrow and one-sided,"[29] and as a negative term to be combined with the adjective "western."[30] In reality, the party exhibited both ideological rigidity as well as pragmatic flexibility when working with other women's organizations. It utilized established venues for advancing its own cause.

After the Manchurian Incident in 1931, the Chinese Communist Party called for immediate armed resistance against the Japanese imperialists.[31] On August 1, 1935, it issued what was famously known as the August First Declaration, departing from its previous policy of overthrowing the Nationalist government. Instead, it called for an end to civil war and the establishment of a united front of all parties, organizations, and people of all circles, including overseas Chinese and ethnic minorities, for the cause of national salvation. Although it was still weak in political and military power, the Communist Party's anti-Japanese stance galvanized public support for the party, while Chiang Kai-shek's continued policy of non-resistance alienated many. In occupied Manchuria, the August First Declaration resulted in the formation of the Northeast Anti-Japanese Allied Forces (*Dongbei KangRi lianjun*), which included men and women, the non-Communist anti-Japanese forces, and the Communists.[32] In Shanghai, the Communists developed a pragmatic policy of working collectively with organizations disgruntled by Chiang's nonresistance to Japanese aggression. This approach enabled the party to create a space for its own influence and development.[33]

In urban areas, the Communists infiltrated schools and factories and radicalized women. As part of the Communist strategy to employ art as a medium for political messages, the party penetrated the Shanghai film industry, producing films addressing women's conditions as well as the question of national salvation. One such film was *Sons and Daughters of the Time of Storm* (*Fengyun ernü*, 1935). The theme song of the film, "The March of the Volunteers," written by Tian Han, an underground Communist Party member, and set to music by Nie Er, a member of the Communist Youth League from 1928, soon gained popularity in calling for resistance against Japan. It became the national anthem of the People's Republic of China in 1949.[34]

The Communist and pro-Communist women contributors made their voices heard in the realm of publishing. The journal *Women's Life* (*Funü shenghuo*) took the lead in reporting on activities related to national salvation and in consolidating a united front for women.[35] It was strongly opposed to the NLM's image of the "wise wife and good mother." One of its authors, Junhui, condemned the ideology as a Hitlerian attempt to control women,[36] while another, Shen Zijiu, condemned this image as serving foreign imperialists since this ideology was aimed at pushing women back into their homes at a time of national crisis.[37]

Female Activism in the Movement for National Salvation

A dynamic national salvation movement emerged that involved women of the Nationalist Party, the Communist Party, and forces outside the two parties – women's organizations, students, and the Chinese Young Women's Christian Association (YWCA), making women a vital force for social, political, and public activism. The Nationalist government's policy of appeasement aroused strong public indignation. Motivated by patriotism, these differing forces formed strong centres of public opinion that played an important role in mitigating Chiang Kai-shek's policy of internal pacification before external resistance and in providing opportunities for the Communists to increase their influence.[38]

Prominent women in the left wing of the Nationalist Party, such as Song Qingling (1893–1981) and He Xiangning (1878–1972), were the national voices and leaders in this broader salvation movement. Song Qingling, the widow of the founder of the Nationalist Party, Sun Yat-sen, denounced Chiang's government for stifling people's resistance.[39] From the early 1930s until the end of the war in 1945, she remained a strong symbol and voice in China's human rights movement and in the war.[40] He Xiangning, who joined Sun Yat-sen's Revolutionary Alliance (Tongmenghui) in 1905, worked often in cooperation with Song in support of national human rights and resistance to the Japanese.[41] Female students, a new social collective, had emerged as one of the outcomes of the modernized educational system instituted in the early 1900s. Exposed to the outside world and informed of national history and politics, they had become very active in China's political scene and in the national salvation movement.[42] The Chinese YWCA was another important force in the movement. Since its establishment in Shanghai in 1899, it had played an important role in the transformation of Chinese women. It evolved into an organization that cut through class distinctions and brought together women from various social strata: students, clerks, those in businesses, professionals, housewives, and the working-class poor in both urban and rural areas.[43] Its programs dealt with social ills and stressed self-cultivation and self-liberation instead of devotion to radical political revolution.[44] Through its night classes for women factory workers, the YWCA spread the ideas of patriotism, nationalism, and anti-imperialism.[45]

CHINA'S BITTER WAR: 1937–45

The Marco Polo Bridge Incident on July 7, 1937, when Japanese and Chinese troops exchanged fire near the bridge, marked the beginning of all-out war between China and Japan. The war unified China. The Nationalist Party and the Communist Party, previously enemies, established the United Front in September to fight against the Japanese aggressors.[46] Commitment to national salvation also led to a women's united front. In May 1938, Song Meiling invited fifty women from across the nation – social activists, women professionals, educators, leaders of the YWCA and of the Communist Party – to a five-day conference at Lushan in Jiangxi to discuss women's work for the war effort. They decided that the Women's Advisory Committee (WAC) (Funü zhidao weiyuanhui) of the New Life Movement under Song Meiling would be the coordinating agency for all women's organizations. The WAC had since functioned as the leadership responsible for mobilizing Chinese women for war efforts in the Nationalist-controlled areas.[47] The Lushan conference initiated the Work Program to Mobilize Women for Participating in the War of Resistance and National Construction (Dongyuan funü canjia kangzhan jianguo dagang), which outlined the organization and training of women from all backgrounds – peasants, workers, professionals, students, housewives, refugees, and military dependents – with the primary goal of mobilizing women to participate in the "sacred war of resistance and national construction." The program was not feminist since addressing women's interests was only a prerequisite to harnessing the enthusiasm and energy of women rather than a goal in itself. It was reformist in its calls for change geared exclusively toward women, including increasing literacy, improving occupational skills, increasing opportunities to work in industry and government, and improving working conditions. It also called for social reform and for changes in customs that had oppressed women for centuries: female infanticide, foot-binding, child marriage, polygamy, physical abuse, and the selling of women as housemaids and concubines.[48]

In October 1937, the Nationalist government moved China's capital from Nanjing first to Wuhan in Hubei Province and then to Chongqing in Sichuan by the end of the year. A port city on the Yangtze River, in the mountainous terrain of southwestern China, Chongqing would be the wartime capital of China until May 1946. The Nationalist-controlled provinces of southwestern China became "Free China," referred to as the "Great Rear Area" (*da houfang*).

THE NATIONALIST GOVERNMENT: FULFILLING GENDERED DUTIES AS GOOD CITIZENS

Under the slogan "Resistance above all" (*kangzhan gaoyu yiqie*), the Nationalist government continued the notion that a wise wife and a good mother should also be a good citizen. To be a good citizen, men should fight on the front lines and women should devote themselves to the home front by participating in production, propaganda, rescue work, child care, and the provision of battlefield services. Song Meiling held that

> if a woman wishes to make an actual personal contribution to the nation's advancement, she must be a wise wife and a good mother as well as a good citizen. If she cannot be a good citizen, she cannot be a good mother or a wise wife. If she cannot be a good mother or a wise wife, she then cannot be a good citizen. Her children could not have much confidence in her or in their country.[49]

In "The Mission of Chinese Women in the Resistance War," published on July 1, 1941, in the *Chongqing Daily*, Song affirmed that in the war, the central issue for the Chinese women's movement was not demanding political equality from the state, as the law had already accorded them that. Rather, women should demand opportunities from the state to offer their service and devotion to maximize their potential. Song added that women should not strive for individual rights as the European women of the nineteenth century had done. "Our greater mission is to unite women nationwide to stand side by side with men, and make concerted efforts to achieve the freedom, equality, and independence of our nation."[50]

Critics of the Nationalist Party's gender policy in the war point out its ambivalence and limitations. The government encouraged women to organize and participate in the war effort, and yet feared women's growing influence. The Nationalist women's organizations left out peasants and working women.[51] The emphasis on women serving on the home front held a biased, traditional view of gender that treated women as less physically strong and resilient than men. Demanding that women contribute would not automatically lead to a higher status for women.[52] Careful research has also documented how, in Nationalist-controlled areas, the resistance brought out the potential of Chinese women in their service to the nation, and how educated women worked to extend the mobilization from urban Chinese to the rural poor, a group that had been previously overlooked.[53] China's women's movement in the War of Resistance, Lü Fangshang notes, broke away from the "old and conservative" way of focusing on women's individual rights and on men-women conflicts, embraced women of all strata nationwide, and broadened its mission to encompass not just women's equality but also national resistance and reconstruction. During the war, more than eighty women's journals were published.[54] Over 800 women's organizations existed.[55] Song Meiling, herself a Christian, had continued to work closely with such important Christian women educators as Wu Yifang, president of the Jinling Women's College (1928–51), the first female college president in China.[56] Both the YWCA and the YMCA, their headquarters relocated to Sichuan, actively provided services in propaganda mobilization, fundraising, and assistance to the Chinese military, wounded soldiers, war refugees, and students who evacuated into the country's interior. The organizations were an active link with the outside world, obtaining moral and material support from overseas.[57] Studies by Isabel Crook show that the reforms carried out in the Nationalist-controlled areas stimulated local changes.[58] In her study of the Chinese suffrage campaign in the first half of the twentieth century, Louise Edwards argues that Chinese suffragists were pragmatic in appropriating nationalism in their own cause and in invoking both the logic of gender equality and gender differences for women's political rights.⁵⁹ She holds that during the war, the Chinese women suffragists, both Nationalists and Communists as well as those from nonaligned parties, invoked nationalism to lobby on behalf of feminist issues and continued to fight for women's political rights. The War of Resistance did not restrict the Chinese women's movement.⁶⁰

Recent studies on women's personal experiences have attached more importance to women's own agency. Danke Li's oral history of women of diverse backgrounds in wartime Chongqing tells stories of women as activists in the resistance, as victims of wartime suffering, and as "innovators of survival strategies and managers of survival for the family and community."⁶¹ Joshua Howard's study of women workers in the cotton mills of wartime Chongqing explains how these workers became politicized and active in the labour movement.⁶² Helen Schneider demonstrates that during the war, the Nationalists engaged in the dual project of resistance and state reconstruction through social reforms to enhance family education and women's role in managing the family as mothers and homemakers for strengthening China. She observes that women reformers were empowered by participating in the project.⁶³

The Communist Party: The United Front as a Powerful Weapon

The Chinese Communist Party, under the United Front during the war, expanded its base areas behind enemy lines with the Shanxi-Chahar-Hebei (abbreviated as Jin-Cha-Ji) Border Region government and in rural central and southern China. Similar to the Nationalists, the Communists subordinated the women's movement to their broader political agenda. Kay Ann Johnson argues that the party's women's policy sacrificed women's rights in the name of a united resistance against Japan: "Its policies, by the early 1940s, were aimed at hindering the development of a women's movement."⁶⁴ One particularly well-known case is that of Ding Ling, who openly raised questions of gendered problems in the Communist Party during the war and was therefore attacked by the party.⁶⁵

Ding Ling (1904–86) gained fame as a young writer during the May Fourth era. An anarchist with a feminist mind, she eventually turned to communism and joined the Communist Party in 1932. In November

1936, she went to Yan'an, where Mao Zedong greeted this nationally famous writer with a poem, describing her with the phrase "yesterday's civilian lady, today's military general."[66] Distraught by the discrimination against women that she witnessed in Yan'an, she wrote two stories that exposed the gender problems of Communist rule: "When I Was in Xia Village" and "In the Hospital."[67] In her essay "Thoughts on March 8" ("Sanbajie yougan") of 1942, Ding Ling describes the problems that a liberated woman in Yan'an had to face. Women could not freely socialize with men before marriage without inciting gossip. If a married woman had to stay home to take care of her children, she would be slandered as "a Nora who returned home."[68] In addition, men divorced their wives on the grounds that they were backward, even though what caused their "backwardness" was the heavy burden of child care. To avoid this burden, women resorted to having abortions or begging orphanages to take in their babies.[69] During the Rectification Movement (1942–44), the party criticized Ding and those who agreed with her.[70] On Ding's feminist tendencies, the party maintained that "full sex equality had already been established" in the Communist-controlled areas, and that feminism was outdated and harmful.[71] Ding subsequently admitted that she had been wrong to stand on the side of the few and not that of the party. Even in her later years, after decades of reflection, she still believed that her "Thoughts on March 8" had a major flaw in its biased women's perspective that failed to consider the larger political situation.[72]

In February 1943, the Central Committee of the Communist Party issued a resolution on women that criticized the women's movement in the Communist base areas for its neglect of economic production as the most suitable mode for women's contribution, and its overemphasis on such slogans as "free choice in marriage," "economic independence," and "down with the four women's oppressions" (the four oppressions imposed by political, religious, clan, and husband authorities). It insisted that women's economic independence was fundamental to women's liberation, and therefore "encouraging them to participate in production was of the utmost importance in protecting women's interests."[73]

Feminist studies based on official documents have offered a series of critiques on the mixed but mostly damaging effects of the Communist Party policy on women. Elisabeth Croll concludes that, under pressure for unity against the Japanese invaders, it proved impossible to completely eliminate the inequalities between the sexes, generations, and classes.[74] Patricia Stranahan argues that the party's priority was not a revolutionary transformation of gender inequality but political survival and growth.[75]

While working under the United Front, the party scaled back all social revolutionary programs in the areas it controlled.[76] Judith Stacey contends that in its efforts to mobilize a people's war, the Communist Party had to retain the support of the Chinese peasants, and therefore its economic, military, and family policies in the base areas were effectively a "democratic patriarchy" that empowered peasant men and sustained patriarchy in the family.[77] Within the party, the party positioned itself as a benevolent father, echoing the concept of the "Confucian patriarch" from Chinese tradition.[78] Its intervention in the personal lives of its members with regard to their choice of marriage partners followed traditional "Chinese familial patterns."[79] As radical feminists see women's entry into the military as representing women's potential for power,[80] the party's exclusion of women from combat meant that women still engaged mostly in traditional domestic work during the war.[81]

By contrast, Communist top women leaders in charge of "women's work" – Cai Chang (1900–90), Deng Yingchao (1904–92), and Kang Keqing (1912–92) – concluded that as a result of the collective efforts made by Chinese women during the war, women raised their own consciousness and political and social status.[82] Postwar research published in China also emphasizes that the Communist Party implemented a policy of gender equality and mobilized women into a broad anti-Japanese democratic movement that increased women's status.[83]

By shifting from party policy to focus on women's own experiences, Christina Gilmartin, in her analysis of the dynamism between the party's patriarchy and Communist women's agency from 1921 to 1927, argues that Communist women tolerated unequal treatment within the party partly because these women "had created their own space, culture, and lives within this political organization." At the same time, their complicity with the party's gender hierarchy also perpetuated patriarchal patterns within the party.[84] By letting women speak for themselves, Helen Young's oral history of the Communist women soldiers of the Red Army reveals that they maintain a more positive view of their experiences in their own stories than feelings of oppression by the party's patriarchy.[85] Nicola Spakowski shows that during the War of Resistance, although the Communist Party mostly placed women in supporting roles and political work, some women challenged the exclusionary policy of the party: "they raised the question of women's 'right to fight.'"[86] David Goodman illuminates how women of different social backgrounds within and outside of the Communist-controlled Taihang region struggled for gender equality.[87] In exploring marriage in revolutionary regions during the 1940s, Cong

Xiaoping shows how rural women used the legal system in changing their lives.[88] By examining the lives and careers of some Communist women and men during the Communist revolution, the War of Resistance, and after 1949, Wang Zheng maintains that Communist women and men fought strenuously against sexism and male dominance in society and in the party.[89]

How did Chinese women themselves perceive the Nationalist and Communist ideologies and their own lived experiences during the War of Resistance? The following chapters will examine this topic.

Description of Chapters

Chapter 1 discusses how representations of women in the War of Resistance have evolved in the People's Republic of China from a state monopoly to a multi-faceted, diverse, new way of remembering. The master narrative of the War of Resistance during the Mao era reinforced the cult of Mao Zedong and the domination of males, and the concomitant marginalization of females in the party. Women were not erased, however. The government under the All-China Women's Federation (ACWF) and mass media publicized exemplary Communist heroines in the war to serve Communist Party's ideological and political purposes. Since the 1980s, with China entering the era of reform and opening to the outside world, there have been remarkable developments in terms of the reinterpretation of China's history in the twentieth century. Women themselves have played crucial roles in researching Chinese women's history, writing reminiscences, and carrying out and participating in oral history interviews, all of which have provided rich sources for my study of the women's war experience.

Chapter 2 is a critical analysis and interpretation of the reminiscences of the war years published by women soldiers of the Communist New Fourth Army. It examines how their gendered perspectives shaped their stories, and how the publication of their memories has reclaimed the crucial roles of the New Fourth Army and the women in that army, both of which were neglected in the history writing under Mao. Their memories prove that the war was not just a man's cause.

Chapter 3 captures the voices of five Communist women, plus the interview of the son of a Communist woman. The thematic analysis of those memories offers insights into each person about how they, as young female students of relatively well-to-do families, decided to embark on the Communist revolutionary path, what the war experience meant for them, and why they perceived the war era as a time "full of youth and idealism," in the words of Luo Ying, one of the women interviewed.

Chapter 4 switches to an examination of the perspectives of women associated with the Nationalist Party based on publications in Taiwan and two unpublished oral narratives I collected. These women were of the wealthy and privileged class or of prominent local families who supported the Nationalist establishment. The chapter explains why Chi Pang-yuan (a student in the war) and other women associated with the Nationalists saw the war and postwar time of 1945–49 as years of suffering, loss, and exile as they fled from Japanese aggression and then from mainland China after the Nationalists' defeat in the civil war. It shows that they did not present themselves as passive victims because each in her own way functioned as a historical actor for the improvement of her own situation.

Chapter 5 offers a discussion of my interviews with six middle-class women who lived in Japanese-occupied areas. During the war, although many chose to go to the Nationalist or Communist-controlled areas, the rest of the people remained under Japanese occupation. In the public perception, their life was seen then as pathetic. One of the women, Wang Yao, said that her life was too ordinary to remember, and yet her story and those of the others show that they refused to give in to despair in the harsh conditions of the occupation. Apolitical though they were, their war experiences had political significance.

The last chapter has a discussion of the Chinese "comfort women," those who were sexually enslaved by the Japanese Imperial Army. It makes a special point that in the process of speaking up, these women were transformed into "survivor activists."[90] The chapter also brings in the voices of five ordinary working-class women I interviewed. Working from childhood to support their families, they lived under Japanese aggression and patriarchal oppression. The war was full of bitterness, "was no life for humans," in the words of Wang Hong, one of the five interviewees. Yet, they survived and persevered with fortitude and courage.

These women's stories provide insight into their war lives and demonstrate that women's experiences matter in the writing of the history of the war. They address the many ways women are related to war, how they suffer and respond. They testify to the fact that war has unique effects on women; it is crueller for women than for men worldwide throughout history.⁹¹ Also, as Robert Gildea's *Marianne in Chains* shows that the history of occupied France was not a simple story of cold, hunger, and fear, nor of good French and bad French, but rather one of multiple experiences,⁹² so the Chinese story similarly consists of different people having different experiences under different circumstances. My book is about the women's war, which "has its own colors, its own smells, its own lighting, and its own range of feelings."⁹³ It has its own words – women's words.

1
Representations of Wartime Women in the People's Republic of China

On the eve of the founding of the People's Republic of China (PRC), Deng Yingchao (1904–92), the vice director of the All-China Democratic Women's Federation, spoke about the crucial role women had played in the Communist revolution. For thirty years from 1919,

> Chinese women, together with the Chinese people, participated in the struggles against imperialism, feudalism, bureaucratic capitalism, and the Nationalist reactionary regime ... In the great struggle for national independence, for democracy and freedom, and for women's liberation, the working class and revolutionary intellectual women in particular sacrificed their lives ... Women formed an indispensable force in the Chinese revolution for victory over enemies and for a new China.[1]

The birth of the new China in 1949 was celebrated by films featuring not just Communist heroes but, in recognition of the contributions Deng Yingchao had pointed out, also heroines from the revolution and from the War of Resistance against Japan. The 1949 film, *Daughters of China* (*Zhonghua nüer*), retells the actual story of eight women martyrs from the Northeast Anti-Japanese Allied Forces (Kanglian) in Manchuria who, to avoid being captured by the Japanese, drowned themselves in a river in 1938.[2] *Zhao Yiman*, released in 1950 and also based on a true story, follows the eponymous heroine in her career as a political mobilizer for workers and peasants in Japanese-occupied Manchuria, as a military commander in the Kanglian, and as an indomitable prisoner of the Japanese, and her eventual execution by them in 1936.[3]

Since these early works, historical representations of women in the War of Resistance have evolved. This chapter illustrates the dynamism in the evolution and explains how the historical representations of women in the War of Resistance have evolved in the PRC from a state monopoly on historical narrative to multi-faceted, diverse, new forms of remembrance, along with the radical shifts in domestic and international politics in the history of the PRC.

Exemplary Communist Women in the War of Resistance

During the War of Resistance against Japan, the documents and publications of the Chinese Communist Party, such as *Chinese Women* (*Zhongguo funü*) and *Liberation Daily* (*Jiefang ribao*), as well as Western journalists who visited Communist areas, carried reports on women's heroic deeds.[4] The growth and expansion of the Communists during the War of Resistance and the civil war with the Nationalists in 1946–49 were largely due to the mobilization ability of villagers and the socio-economic reforms the Communist Party implemented in rural China.[5] Communist cadres, both men and women, played important roles in these reforms at various levels, engaged in propaganda and organization among the peasantry, and mobilized rural populations for the war effort. The official stance soon after the war, exemplified in a *Reader for New Women*, published in 1949, asserted that during the war the Communist Party had implemented a policy of gender equality and mobilized Chinese women into a broad anti-Japanese democratic movement. This had enabled women in the liberated areas to gain equality with men.[6]

During the Mao Zedong era (1949–76), the party leadership laid down guidelines for historians on what to study, how to research, and what conclusions to reach.[7] The master narrative of the twentieth century became a history of the political evolution of the Communist Party, centred on Mao.[8] In the Cold War context, the history of the War of Resistance needed to serve the purpose of national mythmaking: it glorified the Communist Party while condemning the Nationalist Party, government, and military as incompetent, corrupt, and at odds with the Communists in terms of governance and war aims. Moreover, the role of the United States in Japan's defeat was suppressed. The myth of the Chinese Communist Party fighting alone and triumphing against Japanese imperialism became hegemonic national memory.[9] In this history, the roles of other Communist male leaders and Communist base areas aside from Yan'an remained marginalized. The history of the New Fourth Army, active in central and southeastern China, was subject to a historical "blackout."[10] The suffering of the common people and atrocities committed by the Japanese military were remembered primarily to serve the political needs of the Communist-led government.[11] The Communist Party's dominated propaganda, and its control of information "prevented the vast majority of Chinese from narrating their experiences during the war."[12]

Women's roles were marginalized in the history of the War of Resistance. Although woman-focused work had been an integral part of the Communist Party's political activities from early in the Jiangxi Soviet era and through the War of Resistance, official party histories of the Mao era gave little attention to gender issues. As was the case in the Soviet Union, the Chinese Communist Party portrayed the war as a male experience.[13] In *A Single Spark Starts a Prairie Fire* (*Xinghuo liaoyuan*) and *Red Flag Floating in the Sky* (*Hongqi piaopiao*), both published as series consisting of personal recollections and oral accounts for the pre-1949 era, most of the essays are of a political and military nature. Most of the contributors were men.

In its constitution, the PRC fully embraced gender equality. Part of this embrace was the implementation of state-led women's liberation, in which the government issued laws to reinforce gender equality in the political, economic, cultural, educational, social, and family realms. It instituted a state bureaucracy of women at the national level – the All-China Women's Federation (ACWF), with branches down to the local level – to ensure the implementation of laws and policies regarding women and to represent women's interests. Critics argue that China's state feminism as practised from 1949 to 1976 resulted in the erasure of gender. By insisting that women become the equals of men, state feminism made it difficult for women to assert their independence vis-à-vis the male-dominated state apparatus; it deprived women of their own voice in the male-dominated state discourse; it desexualized women. What equality meant in this context was really masculinization.[14]

In contrast, however, others argue that PRC state feminism did not erase gender but rather intended to submerge gendered issues such as love, marriage, family, or sexuality in class theory so that the authorities could direct these aspects of individual lives from a "proletarian" perspective.[15] Communist works and rhetoric in fact justified feminine qualities as long as these represented the proletarian standpoint and served higher revolutionary purposes.[16] Along this same line of thinking, instead of being a bureaucratic tool for the government and serving the PRC state patriarchy, the ACWF engaged in feminist interventions for women's interests.[17] The state models of socialist new women did not all subject women to the state, but "often empowered subalterns who chose to identify with the socialist state."[18] Young women growing up in Maoist China were not desexualized, and a gender-free identity promoted by the state could also be empowering for women.[19]

Indeed, the marginalization of Chinese women in histories written about the Communist revolution did not erase women's roles, but it did intend to subordinate women's issues to the ideological and political agenda of the party. Women's history had to accord with party history. Thus, in 1964 the ACWF initiated a research project with the aim of compiling a history of the Chinese women's movement. Fundamentally political in nature, its purpose was to affirm the Communist Party's leading role in China's revolution and in the transformation of Chinese women. In her speech to members of the research project on December 8, 1964, Deng Yingchao instructed that they carry out research according to Mao Zedong Thought. She reiterated the claim that only the Communist-led women's movement could ensure women's liberation, and therefore the research must have as its central theme the women's movement as led by the proletariat and should criticize the "erroneous" approaches of the bourgeois suffrage campaign and the feminist movement. The research project focused on the period from the May Fourth Movement to the early 1930s. It did not include the period after 1937 for reasons not mentioned.[20] This was perhaps due to the complexity in party politics and the difficulty of identifying and locating relevant primary sources. In the 1950s and 1960s, the Shanghai Women's Federation had twice organized projects to collect materials on the women's movement, and had even drafted outlines for writing the history of the Shanghai women's movement. The Cultural Revolution (1966–76), however, cut all these efforts short.[21] As a result, the complex, rich, and dynamic history of Chinese women in the first half of the twentieth century remained largely unknown.[22]

Stories of Communist women were not erased from the public space, however. China has a long tradition of female biographies written for didactic purposes in the historical genre *lienü zhuan*, or "biographies of women." The tradition of writing biographies of "exemplary women" continued after the turn of the twentieth century and reflected a desire to hold on to traditional morals in the midst of the drastic transformation China had been undergoing.[23] This classical *lienü zhuan* tradition also found a place in the Mao era. The party-controlled mass media publicized exemplary Communist women, and school textbooks had stories of heroic Communist women. Film was probably the most effective medium by which the stories of positive female examples reached the masses. As a powerful propaganda tool in the creation and dissemination of Communist values, the film enjoyed huge popularity.[24] In the pre–Cultural Revolution era from 1949 to 1966, among the 110 films that belonged to the genre of "revolutionary history" set in the period from 1921 to 1949,[25] many featured women involved in the War of Resistance. *Women of China* (*Zhongguo funü*), the official journal of the ACWF and the only magazine on women during the Mao era, was widely circulated through the federation's local branch offices nationwide. One of its principal missions was to report on "new persons and new deeds": women who through their actions served as models in the new China. The magazine also published stories of women's struggles during the revolution and short biographies of famous women in recent history, such as Xiang Jingyu (1895–1928), a Communist veteran and theorist of women's liberation,[26] as well as stories of historically famous Confucian women, such as the mother of Mencius (fourth century BCE), Ban Zhao (c. 40–c. 120), and the legendary woman warrior general Mu Guiying of the late twelfth century who fought against foreign invaders.[27] School textbooks before 1966 included the *Ballad of Mulan* (sixth century) about the legendary woman warrior Mulan who fought for her country.[28]

Presented not in complete life stories but in sketches, with selections of their deeds and activities, the stories of the Communist women embodied the party's moral standards and, through them, the party disseminated its ideology, educated the people on Communist tradition, and fostered Communist values. While it shared a similarity with Confucian ethics, the ethos of the Communist heroines undermined the traditional Chinese family by championing labour carried out beyond the home in the cause of national transformation and in service to the Chinese Communist Party.

Communist Heroines in the War of Resistance

The party-controlled mass media recreated several types of Communist heroines from the War of Resistance, the most celebrated being Communist martyrs. These heroines embodied endurance, frugality, and ultimately self-denial and self-sacrifice. All of these superior moral virtues had been those expected of the model Confucian woman as well. Where the female Communist martyrs went beyond the traditional model was in their struggle for national liberation from Japanese imperialism, their unyielding faith in, and unquestionable loyalty and total devotion to the party, their revolutionary optimism, and their willingness to sacrifice their families for the nation. Famous in this category was Zhao Yiman (1905–36), an "immortalized" woman warrior featured in films, textbooks, museums, and comics series.[29] The film *Zhao Yiman* (1950), based on her last three years of life from 1933 to 1936, portrays her as a physically strong, married but childless middle-aged woman who is courageous in whatever dangerous situation she finds herself. Working underground with her husband, Zhao leads the workers' movement in the Japanese-occupied city of Harbin. When the Japanese suppress the workers' strike and imprison her husband, Zhao takes the patriotic workers to join a rural anti-Japanese guerrilla force. It is there that the film reveals her gendered side, showing her working among peasant women sewing clothes for resistance forces. After she becomes the commander of anti-Japanese military forces in the forested mountains, Zhao fights in several battles and the newspapers bestow on her the colourful epithet "the white horse-mounted Communist bandit in red." She sheds no tears upon learning of her husband's death at the hands of the Japanese, and after she herself is taken prisoner, she never yields to the torture to which the Japanese subject her. Given her knowledge of important military intelligence, the Japanese place her in a hospital instead of killing her, hoping she will eventually relent. There, Zhao Yiman encourages a young nurse to fight. "Can a young girl fight?" the nurse asks, to which Zhao replies in the affirmative: "Look at me, am I a man?" Finally, she persuades the nurse and the male guard to help her escape, but the attempt fails and she is recaptured and executed. The images of her raising a gun under the red flag and walking to the execution ground holding her head high, shouting anti-Japanese slogans while surrounded by Japanese soldiers and Chinese collaborators depicted in a pseudo-bestial manner, became standard representations in movies of the War of Resistance made during the Mao era.

Famous also were the eight women martyrs in the Northeast Anti-Japanese Allied Forces (Kanglian) depicted in the film *Daughters of China*. The film portrays these women soldiers fighting as a collective alongside men as their equals. Notably, six of the women's names are incomplete, the film omitting either their given names or their surnames, perhaps to de-emphasize their individualities. This is changed in a more recent remake of the film, as discussed below. The film's main character, Leng Yun, is the embodiment of a Communist female leader. She cares for others, gives speeches, and leads her soldiers into battle as a military commander. The film also has a gentle touch: when Leng Yun and her husband are forced to part ways to take on different missions, they say goodbye to each other in a walk through flowers, and her husband expresses himself in soft tones and gestures.

Another woman soldier in the film, Hu Xiuzhi, is a poor peasant who lost her home and husband to Japanese artillery and volunteers to join the Kanglian. Her story shows how a "feudal little daughter-in-law" grows into a Communist martyr.[30] Cutting her hair short and donning an army cap mark her ritualistic break from tradition and her entrance into the revolutionary collective. She grows in the collective through the hard daily life of the military, with drills and live combat, often without adequate food or medicine. Throughout the film, the main characters share the camaraderie of the battlefield, develop close ties with the local peasants, and celebrate their victories with song and dance. It is not the cruelty of the war but rather revolutionary optimism that dominates the film, an element placing it alongside the vast majority of other revolutionary war films produced during the Mao era that express revolutionary romanticism and glorify the final victory of the Communist Party.[31]

The climax of the film comes after Leng Yun dies under Japanese guns, when Hu Xiuzhi carries her body and leads six other women walking into a raging river to avoid capture by the Japanese army. Under enemy gunfire, they disappear into the roaring torrent. The film ends with their portraits and deeds immortalized in the Northeast China Revolutionary Martyrs Memorial Hall in Harbin with Mao Zedong's inscription "Long live the martyrs." Their deaths remind people of inspiring stories of traditional women warriors as well as the long-esteemed practice of defying capture by suicide. Dying by suicide in order to preserve one's honour in times of calamity is celebrated throughout the classical dynastic histories. Indeed, the prescriptive cults of female fidelity and loyalty have made their perennial appearance whenever China has been threatened by foreign invasion.[32]

Hu Xiuzhi belongs to the category of "slaves to fighters under the guidance of the Communist Party,"[33] the second type of Communist war heroine. One of the few booklets about women soldiers published in the Mao era, *Heroic Sisters: Recollections of the Kanglian*, narrated by Xu Yunqing, exemplifies this type.[34] From a poor peasant family, Xu joined the women's corps of the Fifth Army of the Kanglian in July 1936 after her fellow villagers had killed Japanese soldiers and collaborationist policemen. Joining the resistance forces meant survival for her, enabling her to attain a liberated identity and to transform herself into a revolutionary fighter. Illiterate and too shy to even eat with men at the beginning, Xu learned to read and write, learned about socialism and communism, and became an effective public speaker, mobilizing peasants in support of the army. In February 1937, she became a Communist Party member. In her words, "the party transformed me from an ignorant peasant girl into a Kanglian soldier with political consciousness, showing me the bright future of our motherland, and making me a Communist soldier. The party is truly dearer than my mother."[35] The book includes her accounts of how other peasant women replaced their traditional concept of female inferiority with a sense of a fighter for a higher purpose: "Once we drive away the Japanese, we will have a good life. Women will no longer be trampled underneath and will be like women soldiers in this regiment, equal to men."[36]

The third type of Communist war heroine is the bourgeois-miss-turned-Communist-fighter. While a large number of educated women joined the Communist-led resistance against Japan, this type of heroine was represented only in a fictional figure, Lin Daojing from the novel *The Song of Youth* (*Qingchun zhi ge*, 1958)[37] and the film of the same title, released in 1959.[38] The novel was the first in the PRC to present a young female student's road to revolution.[39] After several major revisions, it became a virtual textbook illustrating how a young bourgeois lady becomes a Communist fighter.[40] The character Lin Daojing is actually based on the experiences of the author herself, Yang Mo (1915–95), one of the few published women writers of the Mao era. The story addresses femininity, romantic love, and marriage while describing Lin Daojing's path to becoming a revolutionary. In the novel, she is a young, beautiful, educated girl from a bourgeois family. During her journey from rebellion against her conservative family to her growth into a Communist soldier, she falls in love with three men. The first becomes her husband but turns out to be a selfish, superficial man. The next two, being Communists, guide her onto the path of revolution. When Lin is imprisoned, a Communist woman further inspires her to fight against Japanese invaders by joining the masses. The film version eliminates any romantic and mutual attractions between Lin and the leading male Communist and adds more revolutionary propagandistic messages.

Although feminist scholar Meng Yue argues that *The Song of Youth* subjects a woman to male Communists and intellectuals to the Communist Party, demonstrating how educated women sacrificed their gendered subjectivity to the nation,[41] the novel and film enjoyed enormous and long-lasting popularity during the Mao era and beyond. To audiences, the rebellion against family and the novel's descriptions of romantic love and a woman's search for self-fulfillment were appealing. Not seeking to subvert party dogma, Yang Mo offered an alternative to the formerly simplistic heroic model. When the government gave writers some leeway to pursue their personal artistic expression, she took the opportunity to offer her own interpretations, asserting her own voice and attempting to express her own artistic vision. Evidence of the complex reception of the novel during the Mao era was the inclusion of one of its sections in a reader for senior middle school students, and the editor's commentary on the section gave cautionary advice to students that Lin Daojing should not be looked upon as a heroine but rather as simply a youth who took the road of revolution under the guidance of the party.[42]

The fourth type of war heroine is the heroic mother. As in Confucianism, where the mother enjoyed prestige and power, the quintessential ideal feminine figure in the Communist tradition was the all-embracing, nurturing, and caring mother. Indeed, of all the women in wartime Chinese Communist literature and art works, only the mother figure was permitted to maintain a feminine body.[43] One widely publicized heroic mother was Rong Guanxiu (1896–1989) of Hebei Province, who joined the Communist Party in 1938 and devoted herself to the War of Resistance. She led the local women's anti-Japanese salvation association, cared for wounded soldiers, and sent all three of her sons to the front. In 1944, the Communist Shanxi-Chahar-Hebei (Jin-Cha-Ji) Border Region government honoured her as the "Mother of the Army."[44] Another famous mother was Bai Wenguan (1873–1941), the mother of Ma Benzhai (1902–44), of Muslim Hui ethnicity from Hebei. To resist the Japanese, Ma Benzhai found and led a Hui army in an alliance with Communist forces. When the Japanese held his mother hostage to force Ma's surrender, she died by suicide to relieve her son of the burden of choosing between filial duty to his mother and loyalty to the nation. The film, *The Hui Muslim Detachment* (*Huimin zhidui*, 1959), made her famous nationwide.[45] Like mothers in many other cultures, these mothers possessed a maternal ethos of accepting the death of their sons in sacrifice for a greater cause.[46] A third mother figure, Sister Four (Si Saozi), presented in a short fictional story of 1957, is a young peasant and wife of a local Communist during the War of Resistance in Hebei. She sacrifices her own baby boy to save a wounded soldier, and nourishes the soldier with her own breast milk as there is no water to be found in the mountains.[47] A virgin mother is depicted in the 1958 story "An Unwed Mother" ("Wei chujia de mama"). After the widower Huang leaves for the front to fight the Japanese, Yang Xiu, a peasant and Communist cadre, proposes to be his wife in order to care for his two young children and elderly father. Even after his death at the front, she remains a member of the family to fulfill her wifely duty.[48] The virtues of chastity and wifely devotion depicted in these narratives resemble those of so many exemplary women represented throughout the premodern Chinese tradition.

During the decade of the Cultural Revolution, the ACWF and its magazine closed down. Most revolutionary art and literature produced during the pre–Cultural Revolution days, including *The Song of Youth,* suffered condemnation and were banned as "poisonous weeds." Following the Maoist mantras of "class struggle as the key," "politics in command," and "art serving the workers, peasants, and soldiers," Mao's wife, Jiang Qing (1914–91), and her associates took charge of cultural activities and insisted on the dominance of political ideology in creating new literary and artistic works. Stages and screens came to be dominated by the eight model theatrical productions and a few additional works.[49] Some films followed in the period from 1970 to 1976. In all of these works, Communist heroes and heroines became more stereotyped and one-dimensional, beholden to the strictures of the "three prominences," namely, that characters be "tall, great, and perfect" (*gao, da, quan*).

For Communist heroines during the War of Resistance, the ultra-leftists of the Cultural Revolution eliminated the trope of the bourgeois-miss-turned-Communist. The Cultural Revolution criminalized intellectuals, and therefore their transformation into Communists disappeared from artistic works. The heroic categories of martyrs, slaves-to-fighters, and heroic mothers remained. Compared with the period before the Cultural Revolution, the ultra-leftists stereotyped Communist women as superwomen, which further erased their feminine gender and masculinized them. Of the eight model plays that dominated Cultural Revolution stages and screens, two were set during the War of Resistance.[50] Women in these works were essentially without family ties. Sister A Qing in the opera *Sha Village* (*Shajiabang*), for example, has a Communist husband who is mentioned only in passing. Grandma Sha in the same work and Grandma Li in *The Red Lantern* (*Hongdeng ji*) are both widows, defined mostly by their class status and political views as strong supporters of the Communist cause. These model plays attributed all social evils to class disparities while ignoring the gender oppression women had suffered.[51]

Feminization and Commercialization of Communist Women in the Reform Era's "Red"-Themed Art

In 1978, China under Deng Xiaoping entered a period of economic reforms and opening to the West. Economic growth and political relaxation have led to drastic changes throughout Chinese society. A significant change in the memory of the War of Resistance has taken place, from Communist Party-centred to more diverse narratives due to the influence of both domestic and international conditions.[52] Waves of new ways of remembering have seen the establishment of memorial museums and mass media productions. Academic studies have recognized the positive role the Nationalists played in the war and addressed how the war affected China across a range of aspects.[53] The reformist government and the public have felt the need to turn back to history to reach a deeper understanding of how that history has shaped China's place in the world. Rana Mitter's recent work *China's Good War* traces such changes in understanding of the war through interpretation of academic studies and of productions of various genres in print, online, and onscreen. It illustrates how the loosening of the state monopoly on history writing has enabled many historical actors, including those who lived through the war, to advance their own agendas.[54]

With a general population eager for alternative perspectives in historical accounts, "mass media historians" – writers, journalists, and film and TV documentary producers and directors – have participated in the project of reclaiming and reinterpreting history. Their works have changed public historical consciousness.[55] The works of literature, film, music, and theatre produced after Mao's *Talk at the Yan'an Forum on Art and Literature in 1942* with the purpose of establishing cultural hegemony for revolutionary ideology have come to be called "red classics." The state promoted red classics to reinforce class consciousness, patriotism, and nationalist sentiment for legitimizing Communist ideals and the Communist Party as serving the nation.[56] Audiences in the reform era showed enthusiasm and fascination for red themes. Such red nostalgia appeals to the war generation and the generation that lived through the Mao era. The appeal ranges widely: from such remade classics of a revolutionary Chinese identity as a bulwark against rising individualism engendered by the capitalist economy,[57] to serious attempts by some works to subvert the Communist hero myths,[58] to the commercialization and sexualization of Communist men and women for the market economy. What these various forms of appeal share is their attempt to bring Communist men and women back down to the level of the average citizen and the depiction of their humanness.[59] Indeed, the complicated and rich history of early twentieth-century China seems a fertile ground for the dramatization of human moral conflict, retribution, and redemption from the entire range of human pathos.

Humanization as a common feature in red topics and in remakes of red classics has come about in the context of the relaxation of the party's political dominance and ideological obsession, economic commercialization, liberalization of cultural expression, and what has been termed a "sexual revolution." Although such open space was increasingly closed with the intensifying state control under the Xi Jinping's government since 2012, the openness in the pre-Xi era led to the official and popular discourses on femininity, sexuality, female bodies, and desire. It opened up new spaces for the discussion of gender and women.[60] Works of varying quality range from the exploration of individuals' deeper emotional lives to the resexualization of the female body, using "revolutionary eroticism" for commercial purposes.

The remakes of the red classics retain the original works' basic plots, main characters, "classic" scenes, and music, but offer different interpretations, embellish some contents, provide more realistic settings, and employ up-to-date technologies and popular movie and TV stars. The long list of TV series remakes of red classics featuring the War of Resistance includes *The Song of Youth* (2006; twenty-five episodes), *Shajiabang* (2006; thirty episodes), and *The Red Lantern* (2007; thirty-one episodes). A 1987 remake of the 1949 film *Daughters of China* was released with a new title, *Eight Women Walking into the River* (*Banü toujiang*). Whereas the original version abbreviated the female characters' names, the new version includes the complete names of all eight women and portrays them more from their feminine side: they fall in love, give birth, have children, cook and sew, and love flowers and beauty. The remake retains the revolutionary optimism of the originals and portrays the war as China's heroic resistance under the Communist Party.

The 1950 film *Zhao Yiman* was remade in 2005 as *My Mother Zhao Yiman*. In the original version, Zhao Yiman was a legendary heroine mainly for transmitting political messages for the Communist Party.[61] The makers had little idea of Zhao's background. It was only through the efforts of Zhao's elder sister in the 1950s that more of her story became known. A short biography was published in 1989 by the Party History Office and the Women's Federation of Yibin, Sichuan, her birthplace. Born into a landlord family, Zhao Yiman rebelled against foot-binding and fought for the right to go to school. She joined the Communist Party in 1926 and enrolled as one of two hundred female students at the Central Academy of Military and Political Studies in Wuhan. She was subsequently sent by the Chinese Communist Party to study in Moscow and married a fellow Communist member in 1928. According to the biography, she regretted her marriage and childbirth, since they interfered with her work. Leaving her two-year-old son with her in-laws, Zhao left for Manchuria in 1931, where she engaged in intelligence work and guerrilla warfare. After her capture by the Japanese, she was executed on August 2, 1936, at the age of thirty-one. The biography contains Zhao's own writings, including her farewell letters to her son before her execution, one of which entreats him: "I hope you will not forget that your mother sacrificed herself for the nation." The book also includes excerpts of official police documents of the Manchukuo regime.[62]

In the original 1950 version of *Zhao Yiman,* Zhao, played by Shi Lianxing, is a born heroine and a middle-aged, tough-looking woman. In the 2005 remake, *My Mother Zhao Yiman,* Zhao (played by Zhang Han) appears much younger and more feminine and beautiful than her previous incarnation. The remake also tells the story of her last few years in Manchuria, but, unlike the original, it has many flashbacks of her early years.[63] The new version tells the story through the background narration of her son from a point in time when she is already a recognized heroic Communist mother-soldier. Dialogues between mother and son across time and space add dramatic depth to the narrative and allow a more feminine, motherly image of the woman to come to the fore; for example, when she is held prisoner as a patient in the hospital, she waters flowers and enjoys church bells. Through the eyes of her son, Zhao Yiman is depicted as a mother who fought and sacrificed her life for the happiness of his generation; it was love for her son that gave her strength and courage. At the time of her execution by the Japanese, what is in her mind's eye is not the Communist red flag as in the 1950 version, but her son.

At another level, her feminine and sexualized image is constructed through the perspective of the Japanese officer Ono. Unlike the animal-like creature of the 1950 film, this officer played by a Japanese actor is clean-cut and gentlemanly. When he first meets her, Zhao is seriously wounded and a prisoner. Ono then appears so taken by her youth and beauty that he takes out a handkerchief to wipe the bloodstains off her face and hands, in spite of being in front of other Japanese soldiers. Whereas the ninety-minute-long 1950 version includes approximately thirty minutes on Zhao's life in prison, the 2005 film devotes a much larger proportion of time, around sixty out of its ninety minutes, to prison scenes, which centre on Ono's sadistic attempts to break Zhao's will. Ono wants to overpower her not just because she is a Communist but also because she is a young woman. In one encounter, he twists her face toward him in an intimidating gesture to get her to reveal information about the anti-Japanese forces. When she refuses, he channels his sexually charged rage into a desire for physical abuse, giving his subordinate the order to lash her with a whip but at the same time exhorting him "not [to] touch her face." Ono does not hide his admiration of Zhao's strength, nor does he hide his wish to conquer her, telling her that "a woman should not feel ashamed when she tells a man that she is afraid."

Newly created red-themed TV drama series have featured femininity. The multi-episode TV drama *Women Soldiers of the New Fourth Army*, which first aired in 2011, depicts "red youth" and their "red romance" in the Communist army during the War of Resistance. It centres on student-soldiers and tells the stories of five pairs of lovers in the army.[64]

"Red second-generation" (*hong erdai*), children of Communist veterans, have participated in history reclamation projects. The first documentary on the women of the New Fourth Army, *My Mother: The Stories of Three Women Soldiers of the N4A*, which first aired in 2010, was created by children of New Fourth Army veterans and deals with their mothers. It traces the three women's life experiences from childhood to old age. It has interviews with other women veterans along with commentary by historians.[65] A book memorializing the three mothers featured in the documentary was published in 2011.[66]

The ACWF (1978–): No Success in the Revolution without Women; No Women's Liberation without the Chinese Communist Party

In all the resurgence of remembering women from the War of Resistance, the ACWF has taken a leading role. In 1979, it established its History of Chinese Women's Movement Compilation Committee and Research Office under instructions from the Central Committee of the Chinese Communist Party. From 1981 to 1986, it issued an internally circulated journal on the history of the women's movement (*Fuyunshi yanjiu ziliao*), which published speeches, talks, research reports, short biographies, and historical documents. The journal called for submissions of reminiscences, historical photos, memorabilia, and documents. All government units could subscribe to it.⁶⁷ It promulgated the official line that the history of the Chinese women's movement must demonstrate that there would have been no new China, and no women's liberation, if not for the leadership of the Chinese Communist Party, and that the revolution could not have succeeded without women's participation.⁶⁸

During this era, out of the shadow of Mao Zedong and in the spirit of "righting past wrongs" and "seeking truth from facts," the ACWF expressed the pressing need to resume writing the history of the women's movement, a project that had begun in 1964 only to be disrupted by the Cultural Revolution. Deng Yingchao, as the honorary director of the ACWF and a member of the Communist Politburo, gave a speech in December 1979 at the first meeting of the committee overseeing compilation of the history. She recognized that during the Cultural Revolution, "feudalistic ideas were stronger than bourgeois ideas" – that is, many Communist women cadres were implicated in the political problems of their husbands, but men were not as often suspect in the problems of their wives.⁶⁹ Deng must have felt strongly that the ACWF was finally able to begin the history project. In another speech, in September 1981, she remarked that "the opportunity did not come easily. We could now hold such a meeting only after our party underwent extremely hard and complex struggles and hard and complex work."⁷⁰

Writing the history of the Chinese women's movement would consolidate the legitimacy of the Communist Party, whose prestige had been seriously damaged by the Cultural Revolution. The party was faced with a crisis of faith among the general population in the early 1980s. As historian Wang Youqiao has pointed out, lack of understanding about the history of the revolution was one of the main causes of the crisis. To him, many Chinese, the youth in particular, had lost faith in Marxism and the party's leadership, but were interested in bourgeois liberalism. The history project was therefore one of the most urgent political tasks for the nation at the time.⁷¹ The history of the Chinese women's movement, Deng Yingchao and others reiterated, needed to show that only the Communist-led women's movement held the correct approach since its struggle was not demanding rights from men, unlike the feminist movement.⁷² The bourgeois women's movement might be useful in some ways but it would not solve fundamental gender issues, and it might even lead women into "evil ways."⁷³

A history of the women's movement would publicize the Communist women's spirit of struggle, their devotion, and their sacrifice of the interests of their own families and children for those of the children of millions of others.⁷⁴ In the China of the 1980s, the double burden of domestic housework and working outside the home was an issue women were keen to address. The ACWF felt that it needed to promote the spirit of self-sacrifice as demonstrated through the history of the women's movement in order to inspire women in managing their heavy burdens.⁷⁵

China's opening to the world and the knowledge of research on Chinese women done by overseas scholars also amplified the need for research inside China.⁷⁶ A political agenda fed this need as well. Concerned that some of the works on the Chinese women's movement produced overseas were "friendly and serious" whereas some others "distort and smear the women's movement," the vice director of the ACWF, Luo Qiong, felt it necessary to write the history of the movement from a Marxist-Leninist standpoint in order to dispute the "wrong ideas and historical facts."⁷⁷

Adopting what amounted to a "military campaign strategy," the ACWF mobilized research teams consisting of women and men in Beijing and in various provinces, municipalities, autonomous regions, and counties, often in collaboration with local and party history research offices. These research teams painstakingly collected source materials from archives, newspapers, magazines, and photographs. What they were looking for was not just information about work carried out by Communist women but also information about women's movements led by the "middle and reactionary women organizations" – feminists and women's groups affiliated with the Nationalists. Research teams conducted interviews in rural and urban areas. Group discussion seminars were held to collect oral accounts. All this was done with the intent to rescue "live materials" from revolutionary veteran men and women as well as from "enemies."⁷⁸

The result was impressive. In 1989, the ACWF published *The History of the Chinese Women's Movement, New Democratic Period*.⁷⁹ This official, "master" narrative of the women's movement for the pre-1949 period recognizes to a certain extent women's activism under liberal feminist and Christian organizations as well as the Nationalist Party. With regard to Chinese women in the War of Resistance, it highlights the great contributions women made, their patriotic, self-sacrificing spirit, and their loyalty to the Chinese Communist Party. The work's conclusion is that women improved their social and political status through the efforts they made in the war with the leadership of the Communist Party. Underlying the argument is a basic claim: women were able to liberate themselves only by participating in the struggle to liberate the whole nation from foreign imperialists.

A series of collections of archival materials and documents has been published by the ACWF and associated research teams.[80] In 1991, given the continued development of gender studies in China and the announcement that the Fourth World Conference on Women would be held in Beijing in 1995, the ACWF established the Women's Studies Institute of China, which began publication of the *Journal of Women's Studies* in 1992. An open forum, the journal's coverage has broken out of the confines of the women's movement under the Communist Party and the ideological bounds of Marxism to address a wider array of gender issues and theories.

Let Women Speak for Themselves

Parallel to the ACWF's efforts, a remarkable development is the emergence of gender studies in the academic fields and of a new generation of feminist scholars. From the mid-1980s, Li Xiaojiang published feminist critiques of the Chinese revolutionary modernity, and pioneered the first of China's women's and gender studies.[81] Since 1985, women's studies have become a new and vibrant academic field. Gender and women's theoretical studies rather than party ideology has become a dominant framework in the study of Chinese women. Thousands of research papers and hundreds of books have appeared dealing with women's history from political, social, cultural, and/or economic perspectives, and with the development of feminism in China.[82] Li Xiaojiang's oral history project, initiated in 1992, brought out the voices of women about their experiences and perceptions. The resultant work, titled *Let women speak for themselves*, records oral accounts of women's experiences in the Communist revolution, the War of Resistance, and the civil war.[83]

In gendering Chinese history, research on women in the War of Resistance has expanded beyond Communist-centred narratives to address different geographical regions, various social groups, non-Communist women, and different aspects of their involvement. Gendered and feminist viewpoints have challenged the master narrative, and have also provided fresh insights into the suffering of women during the war.

Historian Su Zhiliang and his team have been a driving force in the study of Chinese "comfort women," the sex slaves of the Japanese Imperial Army.[84] The first history monograph devoted solely to the women's movement during the War of Resistance was published in 1999 by Ding Weiping. Affirming that the Communist Party was the leading force in the movement and that Nationalist government's policies on women in the regions under its control restricted women's demands for freedom and democracy, her work demonstrates how the women's united front of the Communists, the Nationalists, and other women's organizations facilitated the release of the huge potential of women and enabled them to play decisive roles in the war effort. Ding explores how women activists affiliated with the Nationalists and those not aligned with any particular political party spoke out publicly against gender discrimination in government employment.[85] Zhou Lei and Liu Ningyuan's 2016 monograph on the women's movement during the War of Resistance goes beyond the conventional periodization of the war back to 1931, the year of the Manchurian Incident, which marked the actual start of the conflict. The work reverses the Communists' earlier negative portraits of the Nationalists and argues that the Nationalist government's policies for women played a critical role in enhancing their efforts in the war. The book devotes a large section to the roles of women activists of the upper and middle classes, and of such organizations as the Service Group for the Front that consisted of members of different parties, demonstrating how they were devoted to the resistance and to raising women's status.[86] Xia Rong's work about the Women's Advisory Committee of the New Life Movement examines this highest organ of the Nationalist government in the women's movement from 1936 to 1945. She argues that the committee was effective in promoting a spirit of service to the nation in areas controlled by the Nationalists. Its involvement in the constitutional movement and women's struggle for independence paved the way for the further development of women's rights.[87] Through the lens of feminism, Chen Yan's *Gender and War* moves away from political history to the social and cultural study of women's experiences in Shanghai from 1932 to 1945. She analyzes the war's effects on traditional gender dynamics through the examination of writers, career women, housewives, and those wrongly accused as "traitors."[88]

The resurgence of women studies has led to the publication of biographies, reminiscences, and memoirs by the Communist women themselves. In China's long literary tradition, women wrote about themselves and some left autobiographical works. However, the concept of autobiographical writing – writing about the self as an individual – came into being in China only in the late nineteenth century. From the 1920s to 1940s, women's first-person narration in literature and autobiographical writings grew in importance in the public sphere.[89] In the Mao era, however, individuals in general were prohibited from publishing autobiographies although Jiang Qing, Mao's wife, tried to defy this rule. Jiang Qing, a movie actress, joined the Communist Party in 1934 and went to Yan'an in 1937, where she soon became Mao's wife. In 1972, during the Cultural Revolution and at the height of her power, she gave lengthy narrations of her life to an American scholar. These were her attempts to gain "historical recognition, to record her past as she alone knows it, and to be remembered in the future for her beliefs and accomplishment."[90]

In the post-Mao reform era, biographies of veteran Communist women have appeared,[91] and some of these women have published memoirs of their experiences as life-long revolutionaries.[92] Collections of such self-narratives have laid claim to the women's place in history.[93] Women of the generation of the War of Resistance also published their reminiscences.[94] These works reflect Communist women's collective memory, which celebrates their commitment to Communist ideology and the virtues of courage and self-sacrifice. At the same time, beneath collective memory one can discern women's individual voices and perspectives. Publication of their memoirs was intended to stress their agency in effecting changes. The Chinese Communist women "fought wherever the party directed them, with quiet devotion," says the editor of *Women Soldiers of the Central Plain* (*Zhongyuan nüzhanshi*), a collection of reminiscences by women soldiers of the New Fourth Army.[95] "Quiet," because most of them worked away from the battlefield; "quiet" also because they asked for neither recognition nor reward in return for their devotion. The publication of their reminiscences has been their way to break the silence and prove that the war was never just a man's cause.

Oral history has been a strong tool for studies centred on women's voices. Historian Jin Yihong offers an analysis of the written and oral memories of women born in the early twentieth century through the 1980s. Her work illustrates how the lives of ordinary women have been transformed over the course of the long century.[96] Writer Zhang Xi's reportage includes stories based on interviews with more than twenty female soldiers from the Communist Eighth Route Army.[97] Liu Ying, the daughter of a Kanglian woman soldier, authored a work of reportage based on interviews of other Kanglian female soldiers.[98]

In the mid-1980s, historian Qi Hongshen began an oral history project on colonial education during the Japanese occupation of China that included a few narratives by women.[99] In 2002, the team of nationally renowned TV host Cui Yongyuan began making visual recordings of interviews of the Chinese civilians and veterans, including soldiers of the Nationalist army. A derivative production, the thirty-two-episode TV documentary *My War of Resistance* (*Wode kangzhan*), was aired in 2010. More than three hundred veterans were interviewed for this documentary. The documentary provides a public space to display the formerly suppressed memories of these Nationalist soldiers. It also gives voice to some women.[100] Cui Yongyuan's oral history research centre, founded in 2012, published a collection of twenty-one oral accounts of the war generation in 2016. Notably, only one of these accounts is that of a woman.[101]

To rescue historical evidence, the PRC government has organized projects that collect archival materials and oral accounts of men and women who had witnessed war atrocities committed by the Japanese Imperial Army.[102] In 2004, the government initiated a project that would be carried out by all party history offices at the provincial level nationwide. It involved the collection of historical sources on China's casualties and loss of property during the War of Resistance. Notably, it also included sources on sexual violence against women.[103]

Since the late 1980s, museums featuring wartime suffering have become important sites of memories. The most famous among them are the Memorial Museum of the Resistance War in Beijing and the Nanjing Massacre Memorial Museum. The Nanjing Museum of the Site of the Lijixiang Comfort Stations (opened in 2015) and Chinese Comfort Women History Museum (opened in 2016) have revealed the hidden history of the victims of Japanese atrocities. They keep alive collective traumatic memory and invite visitors to participate in these emotional experiences to heighten their sense of social responsibility.[104]

******

During the Mao era, in the context of the Cold War, the master narrative of the history of the Communist revolution and the War of Resistance centred on Mao Zedong and the male-dominated Communist leadership. The important roles women had played in the revolution were marginalized. At the same time, state feminism, under the aegis of the All-China Women's Federation and through mass media in general, created images of ideal women who embodied Communist ethos for the didactic purpose of propagating Communist values.

Since 1978, when China embarked on the path of reform and opening up, drastic social and economic changes and political relaxation have led to rapid growth in the reinterpretations of twentieth-century history. In the remembering of the War of Resistance, the mass media has played a significant role through the remaking of red classics and the production of red-themed pop art. Works in both of these realms have tended to sexualize the Communists and revolutionary culture. The ACWF has taken the leadership role in compiling primary documents and in writing histories of the Chinese women's movement, largely insisting that the revolution could not have succeeded without women's participation. With the remarkable growth of gender studies in China, academic scholarship has shifted focus from the role of the Communist-led women's movement to social, cultural, and economic aspects of women's history, and women's general sufferings and struggles throughout the years of war and revolution. Although the tightening up of the public space under Xi Jinping has restricted public voices, what has already appeared in women's own writing and oral history interviews provides valuable sources for research on gendering China's war experience.

2

Self-Writing by the Women Soldiers of the Communist New Fourth Army

In the early winter of 1938, American journalist Agnes Smedley arrived at Yunling, southern Anhui, the headquarters of the New Fourth Army (N4A), the Chinese Communist army in the War of Resistance. In her interviews of women soldiers, Smedley asked seventeen-year-old Wang Yugeng (1921–93) and another N4A woman a series of questions: Why did you want to be a woman soldier? Why did you stop going to school? Are you homesick? As a woman soldier, why don't you go to the front for combat?

Wang and her comrade responded that they wanted to become soldiers because the country was in danger of becoming extinct and the people were suffering; everyone had a duty to save the country. The N4A was in fact a great school, and the War of Resistance provided a "special education" for these young people. "How could we not miss home but homes were under the iron hoof of the Japanese. Wait and see, we will fight to get our home back ... The army is a family; ours is a revolutionary family." To the question of why they did not participate in combat, they replied: "Ms. Smedley, aren't you also participating in China's resistance but do not take up weapons to go to the front either?" The war of national liberation needed people to politicize and mobilize the masses, Wang said, and it was the women soldiers who did these important jobs.[1]

Born into a well-to-do family in Baoding, Hebei Province, Wang Yugeng was a student at the Baoding Women's Normal School in the summer of 1937. During the Japanese bombing of the city, she left home without saying goodbye for fear of causing her parents to worry, and joined the Communist Eighth Route Army Student Soldiers Detachment in Linfen, Shanxi. After a short period of training, she joined the N4A in early 1938. She married General Ye Fei of the N4A in 1940.[2] During the war, many educated youths like Wang Yugeng joined the Communist-led resistance in the N4A and the Eighth Route Army and at Yan'an. Many others joined the Nationalist-led cadre training programs, engaged in service for the front and for mobilization under the leadership of the Nationalist government.

As discussed above, the master narratives in China stressed the positive effects of the Communist Party's women policy and publicized stereotypes of Communist heroines during the Mao era, while feminist critics have argued that the military nature of the war reinforced the patriarchy within the party. This chapter offers a thematic analysis of the published reminiscences by women soldiers of the N4A to explain what the memories of their political, military, social, and gendered experiences mean for the history of the Communist Party and the war, and for the women themselves.

The analysis is based on several sources. N4A women published their own collections: *Women Soldiers of the Central Plain* (*Zhongyuan nüzhanshi*, hereafter ZYNZS) by veterans in the fifth division of the N4A[3]; *Iron Currents: Accounts of Heroines of the Ironsides* [*Tieliu: tiejun jinguopu*, hereafter TL], a collection of accounts of the N4A women in Jiangsu, Anhui, Fujian, and other areas[4]; and Wang Yugeng's individual work, *Brilliant Moments in Memories* (*Wangshi zhuozhuo*).[5] Wang's personal recollections inspired a fictional TV series of thirty forty-one-minute episodes, *Women Soldiers of the New Fourth Army*, which first aired in 2011.[6] As the "red second generation" (*hong erdai*), her daughter and the son of General Chen Yi (1901–72) of the N4A co-planned a documentary, *My Mother: The Stories of Three Women Soldiers of the N4A*, which first aired in 2010 on a China Central TV station. This is the first documentary ever on the women of the N4A. It traces the dramatic stories of Wang Yugeng, Zhang Qian (1922–74; wife of General Chen Yi), and Ling Ben (1920–86; wife of General Zhong Qiguang of the N4A) from the time they were teenagers to the war era, to the post-1949 years through the Cultural Revolution (1966–76) and after. It has interviews of women veterans and comments by historians.[7] The makers of the documentary also published a book commemorating the three mothers.[8] A realistic piece of literature (*jishi wenxue*), *The Women Soldiers of the New Fourth Army*, contains archival materials and personal recollections of the women soldiers describing how they worked harder and sacrificed more than men during the war.[9]

The chapter does not intend an in-depth comparison of the N4A women with those of the Red Army (the Communist army before 1937) or with women in the Eighth Route Army and in Yan'an. Such a comparison deserves a longer and more comprehensive study since it would address different geographical and physical environments, varied cohorts, and political, military, and social complexities.

Reclaiming the Roles of N4A Women in the War History

Japanese aggression after the Marco Polo Bridge Incident on July 7, 1937, led to the formation of the United Front between the Nationalist Party and Communist Party against the common Japanese enemy. In August 1937, the Communist Red Army (totalling 41,000) was incorporated into the Nationalist Revolutionary Army as the Eighth Route Army, and in 1938 as the Eighteenth Group Army.[10] In October 1937, the Red Army in the south (with a combat force of over 10,000) was reorganized as the New Fourth Army of the Nationalist Revolutionary Army. In reality, both the Eighth Route Army and the N4A operated independently under the Communist Party.

The N4A soon attracted a large number of urban and rural educated youths, technical professional staff, and members of local military forces and secret societies. Although the N4A suffered great losses in early January 1941 in what is known as the Wan'nan Incident or the N4A Incident, when the conflicts between the Nationalists and the Communists led the Nationalist army to open fire on the N4A headquarters in southern Anhui,[11] the N4A reestablished itself in Jiangsu soon after and continued to expand. During the eight years of the war, it was active in central and southern China and fought and tied down 160,000 Japanese troops and 230,000 members of the puppet army, engaging in 22,000 battles. By 1945, the N4A had grown to a total of 215,000 plus the local military force of 97,000. It founded base areas that covered 253,000 square kilometres with a population of three million.[12] Its important roles contributed to the victory over Japan and laid the foundation for the triumph of the Communists over the Nationalists in 1949. However, under the Communist rule from 1949, in the party's efforts to build the cult of Mao Zedong in the 1960s, the N4A in the south during the war, away from Mao's Yan'an base, received insufficient attention in the study of the war history.[13]

The reminiscences of the N4A women aim to reaffirm the important status of the N4A in the history of the War of Resistance and the civil war, and, more important, the roles played by the women soldiers. They want people to see that "in the various sections of the N4A and on several fronts women were present and left their footprints ... [They] went through life-and-death situations and shed their blood of youth in the development of the anti-Japanese military force, in the building of the revolutionary base areas, and in the national salvation."[14] Underlying these words is an urgent sense that the N4A as well as its women soldiers should have a legitimate place in history. In the 1980s, when the Communist Party's reputation was suffering as a result of the Cultural Revolution and when all kinds of Western ideas flooding into China were, as Wang Yugeng believed, confusing the younger generation, she felt it her responsibility to inform the Chinese youth of how the Communists had spent their youth. She not only wrote her own reminiscences but also encouraged her husband, General Ye Fei, to publish his memoirs.[15]

Zhu Hong, editor-in-chief of the ZYNZS and herself a veteran of the N4A, organized the commemoration project as part of her mission to publicize the N4A and advance women's liberation. Born in 1924 into a traditional Chinese medical doctor's family, and schooled in Wuhan and then Chongqing, Zhu Hong joined the Communist cause in July 1938. She transferred to the N4A in 1944 and worked as a teacher in the Communist-operated schools and as a journalist for the party's newspapers. After 1949, she continued to work in journalism and participated in the compilation of the history of the War of Resistance following the end of the Cultural Revolution. Shortly after her retirement in 1988, she initiated the project of organizing N4A women to write their recollections. By then, most veteran N4A women were seventy years or older. Their names and roles in the war history were unknown to the public. Initially, Zhu collected the names of around 300 N4A women; by 1994, the list had grown to 980.[16] Although not all could tell their stories, these women have at least left their names in Zhu's collection.

Zhu Hong has pointed out an important, gendered motive in the publication of the reminiscences. As the post-Mao commercialization and consumerization of Chinese society has led to the resurgence of gender inequality, women and their bodies are being commodified and objectified. The profit-driven mass media and popular publications have become vulgar, produced for amazement and entertainment. Zhu Hong therefore strongly feels the need to remind the public of the Communist ideals of the revolutionary generation – to tell these stories to remind people of the revolutionary morality of the older generation and inspire self-respect and self-strength among the younger generation. She believes that the stories of women soldiers contain more value and vitality than works that are prevalent in contemporary China, which are about material desires and are cynical, decadent, escapist, or simply just about sex and violence.[17] She concludes that the N4A women have proved that "revolution and revolutionary wars were never just a man's cause. Chinese women have always participated in them and stood at the front ... The fate of Chinese women has been an integral part of the Chinese national and class liberation and social transformation. One could not understand China's revolution without understanding the struggles of revolutionary women."[18]

The N4A women's reminiscences point out that the war was crueller for women than for men. Women had to endure more hardships and sufferings than men in the military. Not only did they have to live a military, unsettled life like men, or work as administrators or political mobilizers like men, but they also had to overcome physical hardships, cope with social prejudice against women, and "fulfill their duties as wives and mothers."[19] Being marginalized or forgotten by history is another cruelty women had to endure. According to their children, their mothers "joined the revolution in their early youth, made selfless devotions to the national liberation and the birth and growth of the new China, lived at the side of the founding fathers, shared their difficulties and hardships, and sometimes experienced more sufferings. However, because of their special position, few books or articles are about them."[20]

Of great significance in N4A women's self-remembrance is their gendered perspectives and voices, enabling us to use female gender as an independent category for analysis. From such writings, we see how these Communists, at seventy to eighty years of age, expressed and confirmed their own values while the Chinese Communist Party was carrying out a "capitalist" revolution. In contrast to the Mao era's deification and stereotyping of Communist heroines, the works by the former women soldiers have brought us closer to an understanding of Communist women and their gendered and physiological experiences during wartime.

Their self-writings do not form a distinctive, independent voice separate from the party's ideology on Marxist feminism, which insists that the women's movement should be subordinate to the Communist revolution. The writings of the N4A women emphasize self-sacrifice for Communist ideals and the national interest. The women decided on the title *Women Soldiers of the Central Plain* for their collection of reminiscences because being a soldier was an ordinary, simple identity: a soldier's daily life was not all heroic, but a soldier's life is related to a heroic cause. The task of women soldiers was fighting against invaders and feudal forces, and against their own weakness, for if "they failed to overcome one's weakness they would not triumph over enemies."[21] Despite all adversities, they believe that they have gained "self-dignity, self-esteem, self-confidence, self-respect, self-strength" on their journey to "self-reliance."[22]

Selected Memories

Due to the limited space, authors in *Women Soldiers of the Central Plain* usually choose one unforgettable event or a person or a moment to write about. Their highly selective memories demonstrate revolutionary optimism, heroism, deep comradeship formed through horrific hardships, and the close ties between the army and the people. The authors refrain from revealing many personal conflicts, anxiety, or confusion about politics. If they write about any feelings that were deemed contrary to the revolutionary optimism, the intention is to demonstrate how they overcame their negative feelings. They were victors of the War of Resistance and of the civil war, defeating the Nationalists by 1949. What should be remembered is the heroic spirit and desire for the liberation of the nation that was brought out by cruelty and suffering. In the political climate of the 1990s, China's censorship and self-censorship would have directed them toward more positive portraits of their experiences in China's "good war" against Japanese invaders. The official narrative of the War of Resistance against Japan as a good war has been powerful in presenting China as strong, victorious, and "morally righteous."[23]

The women's selective memories avoid sharp criticism and the mention about the dark side of politics. If they refer to the 1942 Rectification Movement or to the Cultural Revolution, in which many party members had suffered persecution, they tend to express forgiveness of the mistakes the Communist Party made after these women had the wrong accusations rectified, had their reputations restored, and had their privileged treatment resumed. A common analogy is that, just as children should forgive any mistakes made by their parents, they should forgive the party. Zeng Zhi (1911–98), who joined the party in 1927 and worked in the N4A, wrote: "In my long revolutionary career, I made mistakes, received criticisms and disciplinary penalty: warning, serious warning, and probation within the party, every kind of disciplinary measure and more than once ... In the Yan'an Rectification, I was locked-up for one year and four months." Yet she remained loyal to the party: "It was the individual leaders not the party organization that wrongly gave me the penalty ... The Communist organization has been the one I have followed all my life. The Communist cause, the party had led its members to carry out, has been the faith of my life."²⁴ Such faith is shared by many other Communist members.

The selective memories also avoid politically sensitive topics in the party's history. The silence might be due to the too complicated entanglements, uncertainties in facts, and involvement of too many people. One obvious example of such avoidance involves the responsibilities of deputy commander Xiang Ying in the Wan'nan Incident. Xiang Ying (1898–1941), who was killed in an event related to the incident, had been a Communist member since 1922 and a founder of the N4A, and had had political disagreements with Mao Zedong even before the War of Resistance.²⁵ The Communist Central Committee blamed the destruction of the N4A on him, and party propaganda made him the scapegoat.²⁶ The ZYNZS refers to the Wan'nan Incident according to the official line, as having been caused by the Nationalists. In the TL, Mao Weiqing, a survivor of the Wan'na Incident, states: "The rightist tendency of deputy Commander Xiang Ying caused the loss of time that led [the troop] into the encirclement."²⁷ Several essays in TL were written by survivors of the Wan'nan Incident about their experiences in the Nationalist concentration camp after being captured by the Nationalist army.²⁸ The Chinese Communist Party suspected anyone who was imprisoned or lost contact. It required that they prove their innocence and loyalty by undergoing investigations and writing explanations of their activities for the time period in question.²⁹ Those who wrote about the incident must have felt that they had the responsibility and obligation to explain what they did, to prove their loyalty as Communists and demonstrate their belief in the Communist cause.

The children of the N4A veterans have a more open approach to the political issues in history. In TL, Zeng Kehong recalls how his mother, Zhou Linbing, escaped from the siege of the Nationalist army in the Wan'nan Incident. He writes that from the 1980s his mother had been active in writing the history of the N4A and in commemorating Xiang Ying with deep feelings, and had raised funds to make a TV series of the N4A "in order to educate the later generations and to reflect the true spirit of the N4A."³⁰ Also in TL, Yuan Zhenwei recalls how his mother, Qiu Yihan, a Red Army veteran, devoted her life to the revolution as an ordinary soldier. His father, Yuan Guoping (1906–41), was another N4A leader whom the Communist Party's Central Committee held responsible for the losses in the Wan'nan Incident. Yuan Zhenwei's essay praises his father's revolutionary spirit and refers to the "fair evaluation" given by the Communist Party after 1978, which rectified Yuan Guoping's name.[31]

Not all avoided negative subjects. Wang Yugeng revealed the darkness of the Communist Party in her essay of 1991 about her comrade Yang Ruinian (1916–42). Yang had graduated from the prestigious Suzhou All Women's Normal School (Suzhou nüshi) and worked as a teacher before joining the resistance cause in 1937. An outspoken and bright young woman, she often expressed opinions that contradicted her party superiors. When she and a Red Army veteran became close, even though to her this was just friendship, both were subjected to gossip and criticism by the party because this implied romantic love, a bourgeois sentimentality, and was therefore unacceptable. In her agony, Yang thought of "women's rights" and "women's liberation," as she felt her freedom and rights infringed. Further, from early on she was suspected by the party of being associated with the faction of Trotskyites, an ideological enemy of the Chinese Communist Party. In spite of this, Yang Ruinian remained loyal to the anti-Japanese cause, and encouraged her younger brother to join the N4A. In the Wan'nan Incident, she was imprisoned by the Nationalists and executed in 1942 despite never having been a Communist Party member.[32] Wang Yugeng's account contributed to the creation of the TV drama *Women Soldiers of the New Fourth Army*.[33] The protagonist in the drama series, Xiang Ruiyun, is based on Yang Ruinian. The drama features "red youth" and "red romance," and challenges the values of the Mao era. In the series, Xiang's antagonist is a dogmatic woman of the era of the Red Army, who distrusts the educated and has a twisted personality. The drama also tells the stories of five pairs of lovers. In the story of Xiang Ruiyun, it depicts another type of Communist heroine – an educated youth who has been wronged by the party but remains firm in her belief in the party and in communism.

The selective memories reflect the reality that the enemies the women soldiers had to fight were the Japanese and the anti-Communist Nationalists. The conflict between the Chinese Communist Party and the Nationalist Party was a major theme. As Hans van de Ven argues, the War of Resistance was for China not just "a war with Japan, but also with itself."[34] The fighting between the two political parties before, during, and after the War of Resistance determined the fate of China. Even in the United Front against the Japanese, deep ideological conflicts and power struggles remained. Chiang Kai-shek never gave up his anti-Communist stance and his policy of restricting the Communist Party.

The Communist Party, for its part, never abandoned its independence and efforts to expand. After the first phase of the war, with heavy fighting, in which the Nationalist military suffered great losses whereas the Communist Eighth Route Army developed from an army of about 40,000 to one of 250,000, the Nationalists decided to restrict the Communists. The conflict intensified although the United Front still existed.[35] The N4A, in particular, was caught in the struggle. It existed in areas where it had to wage war against the hostile Nationalist army, the Japanese, and Chinese collaborator regimes with the Japanese.[36]

In line with the Communist Party's terminologies, the reminiscences of the N4A women often refer to the conflicts with the Nationalists: that the Nationalists implemented the policy of "guarding against, restricting, and combating the Communists" (*fanggong, xiangong, fangong*); that the N4A had to survive in between the Japanese, the puppet troops, and the *wanjun,* that is, the anti-Communist army; that "the Nationalist fought the Japanese on the surface but attacked the Communists in reality"; and that the Chinese Communist army was for the people, the true force that shouldered the mission of fighting against the Japanese and destroying the old system to establish a new socialist China. They describe how the women underwent great dangers surviving the Nationalist military attacks in such major events as the "Zhugou tragedy" (*Zhugou can'an*) in November 1939, in Zhugou, Henan[37]; in the Wan'nan Incident and the Nationalist imprisonment and killing of Communist members in concentration camps[38]; and the Nationalist army's encirclement of the N4A base in Hubei in 1943–44.[39] These descriptions are intended to demonstrate the women's courage, the bloody nature of the Nationalists, and women's contribution to the war – and the fact that it was the Communist Party that was victorious in 1949.

BECOMING A COMMUNIST FIGHTER AGAINST THE JAPANESE

The War of Resistance disrupted the normal life of the Chinese people. Many Chinese youth, men and women, voluntarily joined the resistance out of idealism, patriotism, and a desire to save the nation. Young idealistic women such as Ding Ling and Chen Lian (daughter of Chiang Kai-shek's secretary, Chen Bulei) joined the Communists in Yan'an in fighting for the motherland.[40] For the working class, who were suffering severe economic misery, joining the resistance offered a way of release. For the middle class, the war worsened economic conditions and there seemed to be no personal future. For all those who lost homes, schools, jobs, and family members, it offered a viable alternative to passive suffering.[41]

Although brief and focusing on one or two episodes, the self-writings of N4A women enable us to trace the life course of family influence, radicalization, motives for joining the resistance, and transformation into Communist members. From the N4A women's reminiscences, we see that the non-resistance policy of Chiang Kai-shek from 1931 made them turn to the Communists. The early failures in the Nationalist army's battles against the Japanese from late 1937 made them even more frustrated with the Nationalist government. In contrast, the Communists represented hope as real fighters against the Japanese. Many joined the Communists also because of the influence of their families, relatives, friends, teachers, or schoolmates. Many were radicalized toward the Communists in their school days.

Schools had been an underground operation for the Communist Party from the 1920s. One such school was the Kaifeng Beicang All-Women's Middle School, founded in 1921. As a private school, it was outside the heavy political influence of the Nationalist government. The school hired several socially progressive teachers.[42] In their reminiscences, students recalled how their teachers taught them about the intrusion of foreign imperialism in China, the 1911 Revolution, and the May Fourth Movement, and how they would discuss in class the meaning and purpose of life, the concept of citizenship and social and gender inequalities. The school became an active site of patriotic anti-Japanese activities. In late 1935, inspired by the student movement in Beiping demanding the Nationalist government for resistance against Japanese aggressions, the Beicang students joined other schools in Kaifeng in staging their petitions. In 1936, they formed their own branch of the National Liberation Pioneers (Zhonghua minzu jiefang xianfengdui), a pro-Communist organization, and in August 1937, the school established its first branch of the Chinese Communist Party.[43] Around the time of the outbreak of the war in July 1937, over a hundred students at this school joined the war effort, most of them to the Communists.[44] In a class of forty-three students, forty joined the Eighth Route Army, the New Fourth Army, and local patriotic organizations.[45]

Class struggle resonated strongly among those of working-class backgrounds, driving them to join the war effort. Li Xi (1921–46), a child-labourer from the age of twelve in a small stocking factory in Shanghai, gained knowledge of anti-Japanese efforts from her underground Communist teachers at the YWCA night school. The school was tuition-free for workers. She became involved in anti-Japanese activities as a member of the night school's drama group in 1935. In the early days of the war, she worked among the refugees and the wounded, and in 1940 the Communist Party sent her to the N4A.[46] From refugee camps, a fertile ground for anti-Japanese propaganda and Communist agitation, the Shanghai Communist Party recruited some 3,000 into the New Fourth Army in the first two years after 1937.[47]

The CCP provided women with social legitimacy and the opportunity to change their lives, which attracted many women. Helen Young's study of Red Army women shows that gender equality was a motivating force[48]; it was also an important driving force for women during the War of Resistance. For women of all social strata, China's patriarchal system "planted [the] seeds" of their desire for social justice and gender equality. Joining the Communist-led resistance gave women a new identity, a sense of self-worth. TL has accounts that explain how gendered oppression led many to break away from family confines. In ZYNZS, at least nine women had been child-wives. Joining the Communist collective freed them from old, oppressive families, and turned their personal resistance into collective action against patriarchy. Some women turned to the Communists out of resentment against arranged marriages. Zhang Ming, who came from a poor peasant family, had run away from her husband to become a factory worker in Nanjing before she joined the Communists.[49] Yang Zheng (b. 1910 in Anhui) was from a landlord family that supported her education all the way to graduation from the Anhui Provincial Normal School, but then she had to enter into an arranged marriage. After six years of unhappy married life, she left her husband, taking her daughter (b. 1928) with her. In 1938, Yang and her daughter became war refugees; two years later, they joined the Communist-led anti-Japanese propaganda team. Yang joined the party in 1941, followed by her daughter a year later.[50]

Established in the economically and culturally advanced areas of central and southeastern China, the N4A attracted a considerable number of intellectuals, students, skilled workers, and overseas Chinese from its inception. During the war, the Communist Party's underground organization transferred these people from Shanghai to the N4A. It took only a couple of days via the underground route to go from Shanghai to the N4A base in northern Jiangsu.[51] The N4A was "China's youngest, most female, and most cosmopolitan army,"[52] unlike the Eighth Route Army, which filled its ranks mostly with peasants.[53] TL has seventy-four essays. Over forty authors mention that at the time they joined the Communists, they had education of middle school or higher levels. One was Luo Qiong (1911–2006), an activist of the women's movement. She went with her husband, the economist Xue Muqiao, from Shanghai to the N4A in 1938, and joined the Communist Party that year. She worked as a political instructor until 1940, when she and her husband left for Yan'an.[54]

ZYNZS has 194 essays. A striking feature is that many of those N4A women came from well-to-do families – ranging from landlord, rich peasant, capitalist, bureaucratic, old army officer, gentry to middle-class peasant, and small businessman to teacher, intellectual, clerk, and Chinese medicine doctor. Such family backgrounds enabled them to receive an education. Many were young, born mostly between 1915 and 1925. In 1937, they were between the ages of twelve and twenty-two. Their youth contributed to their passion for the cause. Their unmarried status made them less hesitant to leave their parents to join the anti-Japanese force.

The Chinese Communist Party's class theory claimed that one's socioeconomic status determined one's attitudes toward revolution. One must break away from one's family of the exploitative class in order to become a Communist Party member. Faced with Japanese aggression, however, the N4A urgently needed to recruit educated youth to expand its force, and class purity was not always a priority for the party membership.[55] The N4A pragmatically recruited educated people and promoted them to leading positions. By October 1941, 60 percent of its cadres at battalion level or lower were intellectuals, and 80 to 90 percent of its political instructors at company level or lower had a middle school or college education.[56] Under the policy of "uniting the intellectuals," Li Landing, a seventeen-year-old graduate from a Shanghai school of obstetrics, was promoted to an administrative position soon after she joined the N4A in December 1941.[57] In the case of one such woman, Hua Yixia, the probation period was reduced from three months to one.[58]

In their narratives, women from non-proletarian families do not attach much importance to criticizing their wealthy families. Only when they were applying to join the Communist Party did they need to demonstrate that they had "betrayed" their families.[59] Wang Jinwen recalled that when she was strict about not granting party membership to a woman of "complicated social experience," she was chastised by the party's minister of organization in Hubei in 1938 for her "excessive caution" in recruiting intellectuals. Her leader reminded her that intellectuals would play important roles in the revolution.[60]

In complying with party ideology, young women from well-do-do families underwent a transformation from being a bourgeois miss to being a

Communist. Joining the Communist-led resistance distinguished them from their old selves or other women. According to their narratives, it marked "an end of searching in the dark," "a beginning of a new life," and "taking on a new path," and it meant "growing up in a revolutionary cradle."

The transformation usually began with changing of personal names in order to protect families in the occupied and Nationalist areas. This implied taking up a new, revolutionary, identity. Zhang Zhangzhu, who joined the N4A at the age of fifteen, took *qian* as her new name. The word means red, indicating her determination to make the whole world revolutionary red. As Zhang Qian, she later married General Chen Yi of the N4A.[61] Yang Ti remembers how she left Shanghai without informing her parents and arrived in Anhui with five friends in the spring of 1939. By taking off her long gown (*qipao*) and leather shoes and donning a military uniform, she undertook the ritual of transformation of identity. She then learned "how to be a revolutionary" by taking classes that discussed Communist revolution, political economy, philosophy, women's issues, the policy of the united front, international issues, history of social evolution, and techniques of mass organization, and undergoing military training.[62] Transformation meant the establishment of a new identity – a soldier and a Communist, a member of a revolutionary community with a shared purpose. If women joined the Communist revolution with the aim of breaking away from the feudal bondage of their patriarchal families, once in the Communist revolution, they were to transcend their own personal liberation agenda to embrace the Communist ideology that women's emancipation was and should be part of the emancipation of the whole human race.

To Qian Zhengying, a university student from Shanghai who joined the N4A in 1942, transformation meant "rebirth" into a soldier and the replacement of academic learning by learning from the peasants.[63] Similarly, Luo Qiong believed that intellectuals must integrate with peasants and workers in order to transform into revolutionaries. Working as a political instructor in the N4A, Luo Qiong had as students veteran Communist men of peasant background who initially looked down on her as a young petty bourgeois miss. Eventually, she gained their respect by training to be a soldier in military drills, living like an ordinary soldier, and trying to understand them and their backgrounds. To her, teaching these men about Marxism and socialism was also a process "to learn from the soldiers of peasant-and-worker backgrounds."[64]

A large number of progressive intellectuals and students joined the Communists during the war, and the Communist Party attached great importance to training them to become cadres. Yan'an was the most important centre, with different schools enrolling women students.[65] In July 1939, the Chinese Communist Party's Central Committee established the Chinese Women's University (Zhongguo nüzi daxue). In its two years of operation, it had over a thousand students from various backgrounds. Eighty percent were intellectuals and students who had fled from the Japanese-occupied areas to Yan'an. The rest were Red Army veterans and cadres from a working-class background at the grassroots level in the Communist base area. The curricula consisted of revolutionary theories, revolutionary methods, leadership skills in the women's movement, and professional skills for the anti-Japanese cause and national reconstruction. Mao Zedong spoke of the importance of such training at the opening ceremony of the university: "China's War of Resistance will not succeed without the awakening of Chinese women who take up half of China's population."[66]

The N4A also had branches of the Anti-Japanese Military and Political University, its colleges and schools, and the Education Brigade (Jiaodao zongdui) for political education and military training for the purpose of cultivating students into cadres to work among the people.[67]

In many of the N4A narratives, the major theme is not about the transformation of a bourgeois miss or an ignorant poor woman into a Communist soldier. Rather, it is about how patriotism, voluntarism, idealism, and gender and social equality drove them into the war efforts; it is about their contributions to the anti-Japanese cause. The emphasis is on women's own agency in their daily work.

A New Fourth Army Woman Soldier's Daily Work

During the war, women of the N4A performed jobs related to conventionally feminine responsibilities – doctors and nurses, secretaries, clerks, art and cultural propaganda workers, teachers, and political instructors – and in women's work and mass movements. Evaluated from a feminist perspective, confining women to gendered work perpetuated the Communist Party's patriarchal characteristics. In general, however, the Communist women themselves did not identify with this view. They perceived their work as profoundly significant, as an integral part of the revolutionary work.

By 1940, the N4A had 10 field hospitals, 8 detachment hospitals, 20 regimental receiving stations, 200 battalion medical teams, and 300 first-aid groups.⁶⁸ Zhang Yangfen graduated from the National Shanghai Medical College in the summer of 1937. She left her position at the Nanjing central hospital to join the N4A in early 1938. The military hospital in Yunling, Anhui, that she and her comrades operated maintained high quality, as Agnes Smedley noted during her visit in 1938. In the fall of 1939, Zhang returned to Shanghai for a family visit. She turned down the opportunity for further medical studies in the United States, where her older brother lived, and returned to the N4A because, in her words, the "rise and fall of the nation is the responsibility of every one," and because "the people are fighting hard for the independence and freedom of the nation, and for the happiness of the people. That place needs me; it is where I should be; that place represents my values of life."⁶⁹

In the highly mobile guerrilla warfare, N4A women health workers were often responsible for caring for the wounded, treating the local peasants, and protecting patients in emergencies.⁷⁰ Yi Qiping, a graduate of the Wuhan nursing school, worked at a field hospital in Hubei from late 1938; she was in charge of obstetrics for the N4A women. In the war, these women "fell in love, married, and got pregnant with the new generation." Located in the mountains, the hospital used caves as medical wards. In October 1942, during the Japanese mopping-up campaigns, Yi led a team of 30 staff, mostly young women, in transferring over 100 patients, including 7 or 8 pregnant women, to safety deeper into the mountain valley. She herself had to care for her own baby girl. One pregnant woman died of complications. Another gave birth to a baby, whom she named "Dongsheng," meaning "born in a cave." They survived with the help of the local people.⁷¹

During wartime, the power of art was invaluable in mobilization and in transmission of ideas and messages, as well as for inspiration and entertainment. Using art for politics' sake, the Communist Party was more successful in the military and in its base areas than the Nationalists in regions they controlled, in mobilizing people, propagating ideals, and bringing about profound social and political changes.⁷² Women were a major force in this line of work. Ye Hua, a member of an art company in Shanghai, later worked as a playwright for the N4A. She wrote tens of plays from 1940 to 1945, mostly about battles or events that had taken place in the war. These plays functioned as "weapons" against enemies and as "heroic songs" for the resistance.⁷³ The power of her plays was "worth many bullets" aimed at enemies.⁷⁴

In January 1938, the N4A formed its Battlefield Service Troupe (*zhandi fuwu tuan*), first in Nanchang and then moving to Anhui and Jiangsu.

At its peak, its members totalled 400; half were female and many were students from art schools. The troupe consisted of work groups of mass movements, dramas, songs, fine arts, and dance. Members lived a military life, engaging in morning drills and regular military training and serving as sentries. Their major daily routines were studies of Communist ideas and lectures by Communist veterans on specific policies; propaganda among soldiers, peasants, and locals; and teaching songs and performing on streets, in theatres, and on temporary stages, and sometimes for the Nationalist army.[75] After the N4A's major victory over the Japanese in Fanchang, Anhui, in November 1939, Wang Yugeng and two male members wrote a three-act play, *The Battle of Fanchang* (*Fanchang zhi zhan*). The play had seven or eight shows for the local military, the civilians, and the governments and drew highly enthusiastic responses. According to a 1940 report, it began drizzling during one show but

> the audience still remained enthusiastic, kept on singing and shouting slogans. No one paid attention to the rain ... When it showed the battle between the Chinese and Japanese soldiers, the young women and children (as a chorus group) sang again: "... Rise, fellow countrymen; kill the Japanese devils! ... " One thousand voices of the audience shouted together. An elderly woman of 79 years old joined the shouts too.
>
> The play ended, and it rained heavily. People were still lingering around; their singing continued.
>
> This is "sharing the bitter hatred against the enemy" (*tongchou dikai*); this is "one million hearts beating as one" (*wanzhong yixin*)![76]

In February 1940, to celebrate the upcoming March 8 International Women's Day, Wang Yugeng and another woman wrote another play titled *Women of the Great Times* (*Dashidai de nüxing*), based on interviews of over twenty N4A women soldiers. Many actors performed as themselves, depicting their journey in the revolution and their contributions. The performance was received enthusiastically by the audience.[77]

The growth of the N4A from an army of 10,000 to almost 300,000 would have been impossible without mass mobilization. Communist women contributed to this success.[78] In the mass movement, women's work laid the foundation for the expansion and final victory of the Communists. In the spring of 1938, Wang Yugeng and her group of five (three women and two men) worked among the peasants in northern Anhui. They moved in with the locals, women into peasant households and men with single poor peasants. In her "family," Wang performed all sorts of chores, "like a newly married daughter-in-law." Sharing the same bed with the women, she talked with them about daily life. The work group investigated local conditions, organized associations of peasants, women, children, and the militia, and taught at night school for literacy. By implanting a rent-interest reduction policy, the N4A won the support of the locals.[79]

In the gender segregated social environment of rural China, the young, educated N4A women worked specifically with rural women. Following local customs, they often formed a sworn sisterhood with local young women, and established a mother-daughter relationship with the elder women to gain their trust and support. They explained to the locals about gendered sufferings under the Japanese invasion and under China's patriarchy. The trust and emotional ties encouraged local women to establish women's associations, deal with gendered issues such as child-wives or domestic violence, and support the N4A by washing uniforms, making shoes, carrying out agricultural production and urging their men to join the N4A. Inspired by the N4A women as models of gender equality, many young peasant women would also join the army.[80]

Many N4A women worked in gender-neutral positions – as mobilizers, teachers, journalists, propaganda workers, or underground agents in occupied areas. Some assumed male-dominated leadership positions at various levels. Chen Shaomin (1902–77), a Communist Party member from 1928 was a co-founder of the E-Yu-Wan (Hubei, Henan, and Anhui) Anti-Japanese Border Region, and held the top position as party secretary there. Other women held positions as head of the county and district.[81] Bao Yousun, a Communist Party member from 1932, helped develop an anti-Japanese guerrilla force in 1937 in Shucheng, Anhui, which had grown from 60 to 700 by 1938. She and two other women led the Communist Party's committee in Shucheng, gaining it the nickname the "women's party committee."[82]

In 1940, Xiang Ying, the commander of the N4A, claimed that women of the N4A had gained equality, although he condemned women's requests to go to the front as a demand for false equality.[83] In reality, participation in combat was not uncommon for N4A women. Some veteran Red Army women assumed leadership roles in the military conflicts in the War of Resistance, such as Chen Shaomin, who took command in a series of battles and was known among the locals as Mulan (the legendary woman warrior).[84] Li Jianzhen (1907–92), commanding a guerrilla force in 1943, became known as the "Mu Guiying [legendary woman warrior] heroine." Xie Fei (1913–2013) led more than twenty battles against the

Japanese and collaboration armies when she was the party secretary of Yushang County in Zhejiang.[85] As the only woman and the top leader of a guerrilla force of forty members, Liu Jie engaged in military actions against hostile Nationalist troops in a crucial battle in March 1940 the result of which expanded the N4A's influence. This "demonstrated fully her leadership ability equal to that of a man,"[86] in the words of a phrase commonly used to praise a woman.

Having a gun was what it meant to be a soldier. Soon after joining the N4A, Wang Yugeng received a rifle that "to a female student-soldier not aged twenty yet, was heavy but was so precious. Whenever I touched it, I would think of how I would use it to shoot the enemy."[87] In 1941, she received a pistol for her work. Carrying it on her waist belt, she "felt handsome and tall." Engaging in military encounters was part of her guerrilla style of work. That "political power grows from the barrel of a gun" became her strong belief.[88]

As the N4A was situated in pockets among the Japanese, the collaboration regimes, and the anti-CCP Nationalist forces, it had to move often, engaging with hostile forces and coping with Japanese mopping-up campaigns. Women were part of all these hardships. In 1942, Li Landing graduated at the age of seventeen from an obstetrics school in Shanghai, and left home to join the N4A in Jiangsu without letting her mother know. The job of her medical group of four was to care for wounded soldiers who were staying with the peasants. She often had to transfer medicines to different places through enemy lines. When the combat troop had to leave during Japanese raids, Li Landing and her medical group were responsible for the safety of the wounded.[89] When the Japanese came, pregnant women and young mothers with babies had to take shelter with peasants. They had to depend on the support of peasants to deal with difficulties and when encountering the enemy.[90]

Belonging to the Revolutionary Family: Sisters, Wives, Mothers

The war was more taxing for women than for men, for they lived an unsettled life, worked at various jobs, faced special challenges in marriage, maternity, and child care, and had to fulfill their duties as wives and mothers. Women joined the revolution to be free from their traditional responsibilities – but were they?[91] Feminist scholars have pointed out the patriarchal nature of the Communist Party during the war (discussed in the Introduction). Christina Gilmartin concludes that early Communist women activists accepted their "second-class" status within the party, taking up work in subordination to men's leadership and carrying out childrearing responsibilities unquestioningly. "Most women revolutionaries at that time could not break through the psychological and tangible barriers to their assuming more egalitarian political roles inside the party. They did not seem to question the extent to which they assumed child-rearing responsibilities, which they saw as an extension of their biologically determined reproductive roles."[92] Traditional exemplary women were to be models for the Communist women. In his speech at the opening ceremony for Chinese Women's University at Yan'an, Wang Ming, the first president of the university, claimed that the university would train women to be independent, revolutionary women, and to be "models of the new good mother, new virtuous wife, new filial daughter of the new time." What he meant by "new good mother" was that women should be like the mother of Yue Fei (1103–42), who taught her son to die for his country; the new virtuous wife should be similar to Liang Hongyu of the twelfth century, who assisted her husband in the battle against northern invaders; the new filial daughter should be like Mulan, a legendary woman in a sixth-century ballad, who joined the army in her father's place.[93]

How did the N4A women explain their status? How did they explain their acceptance of an "arranged" marriage by the party and their large share of family responsibilities in married life? In his study of daily life in Yan'an, Zhu Hongzhao has concluded that the Communist women rebelled against the traditional family and joined the revolution. Their marriage in the revolution gave them pride as well as misery but "they did not make open complaints or noises. Instead, they wrapped up their hearts that had been hurt and bled with more revolutionary covers."[94] In reality, Ding Ling, in her essay "Thoughts on March 8," published in 1942 at Yan'an, criticized the gender inequality in Yan'an, as mentioned in the Introduction. In her memoir, Zeng Zhi reveals her resentment of and resistance to the patriarchal behaviour of male Communist cadres, particularly her husband, Tao Zhu (1908–69), a high-ranking party veteran. After she gave birth at Yan'an, Tao Zhu would not take time off to visit her at the hospital or help with child care at home:

> Similar to the majority of men in China at the time, many male comrades in Yan'an were concerned that they would be laughed at as "hen pecked" or "wife-centred." Simply put, that was a legacy of male-superiority, male dominance, or patriarchy. Such an old idea existed in every page and every

chapter of Chinese feudal civilization of thousands of years. For the influence of patriarchy idea, the question was not whether who had it or not, but it was to what extent one had. A firm revolutionary as Tao Zhu was not an exception.[95]

In their collective narratives, however, the N4A women mostly refrain from discussing gender inequality within the party itself, perhaps due to self-censorship; they felt that there was a gender difference but that women were equal in the revolutionary community. They do recall their marriages, the pains and dangers of childbirth, and the difficulties of rearing their children. In relating their experiences, they employ revolutionary rhetoric and logic to emphasize their sense of belonging to a big revolutionary family and the meaning of self-sacrifice. The sense of solidarity, of belonging to a large revolutionary community, with all fighting for the same goals, was psychologically empowering to them.

In the narratives of the N4A women veterans, the metaphor of belonging to a revolutionary family and concepts associated with family abound. Joining the Communist resistance against the Japanese invasion meant "joining the revolutionary family" or "going into the embrace of the party"; "the party is like parents," comrades are "brothers and sisters," and are "dearer than family members." Family had been a basic unit of Chinese society, and family values a basic component of Confucian moral ethics. Family embodied many levels of meaning to these women. In a practical sense, many women joined the party under the influence of relatives and siblings. Breaking away from their family of origin to achieve independence, the youth needed another source of support, which they found in the Communist community. The community provided them with shelter, security, and a sense of belonging. Veteran N4A soldier, Lin Ke, who joined the Communist resistance at the age of fourteen, said: "I lost my mother at the age of seven; had known no maternal love since childhood. The friendship in the revolutionary family gave me the warm care I'd never had; made me happy and joyful. The love in camaraderie and the hatred of the Japanese imperialism gave me the strength to overcome all the difficulties and hardships."[96] In this revolutionary family, women found shared care and formed a sisterhood. While hardly any male leaders were addressed as elder brothers by their subordinates, it was common for female leaders to be referred to as elder sisters by their subordinates, male or female. Many student soldiers looked up to senior female leaders as their role models who embodied the party's ideals, and whose care and guidance were big-sisterly or "motherly."[97] The deep friendship would continue to the next generation.

To the N4A women, the most important concept in the revolutionary family was "revolutionary," referring to national independence, realization of socialism and communism, and Communist moral ethics. Identifying with these ideals would provide one with a strong sense of the moral high ground. Such identification would also make one accept self-sacrifice and comply with the party in the name of revolution. Revolution should be above all. It should be above romantic love. As a Red Army woman veteran, Wei Gongzhi (1905–73), said to Qin Yun when they worked together in the N4A:

> It is harder for women to engage in revolution than for men because women participate in the revolution not only for national liberation but also for their own liberation – a twofold task. Chinese women's liberation is inseparable from the Chinese revolution. A revolutionary woman must not only have a strong revolutionary will but also a correct concept of love. It is often a mistake to attach much importance to one's appearance. A woman comrade must place revolution first, striving for self-strength so as to be independent in the society. Love should be secondary.[98]

Romantic love was not much of a theme in the reminiscences of the N4A, whereas marriage and childbirth were.

Regarding marriage, whereas the Chinese tradition was to follow "the order of the parents and the words of the match-maker," many N4A women followed "the order of the party organization and the words of the leaders." The general rule for marriage in the Communist armies is known as "25-8-*tuan*": one spouse should be twenty-five years of age or older, have served in the army for eight years, and hold a position of at least the head of a regiment (*tuan*) before one could marry.[99] However, in ZYNZS, the age or rank restrictions are hardly mentioned. The wartime Communist Party had more men than women. If the situation permitted, the party encouraged marriage. Often, supervisors assumed responsibility for making marriage possible for cadres and army officers. Initially, many female students in the N4A did not intend to marry until victory in the anti-Japanese war had been won. Pressured by their leaders, however, they accepted the idea that a revolutionary needed a revolutionary spouse for the sake of the revolution, so they agreed to arranged marriages, often to male cadres many years their senior. As a contemporary saying went: "The resistance against Japan is a protracted war. Courtship is a quick battle."¹⁰⁰ When Zhou Zhifang (b. 1919) was asked by her "elder sister" supervisor to consider a marriage prospect, she hesitated because she felt she was too young and "too immature," with too many differences between her and the prospect, but her supervisor persuaded her.¹⁰¹ Lin Juxian, a college student from Beiping who joined the Communist Party in late 1937, was assigned to work underground in a city in Hubei Province together with a much older Red Army veteran whom she did not know. They would live as a couple. When Lin questioned whether they were compatible, her "big sister," the party leader, responded: "As long as being compatible with the same purpose and in devotion to the party, what else should you ask? Don't be so petty bourgeois and emotional. Make up your mind. In the current war situation, there has to be a quick battle and quick finish." Lin felt that "a party member should follow party's order, and therefore I agreed." She moved in with him the following afternoon. That was her marriage.¹⁰²

Some women sought marriage as a way of improving living conditions. They "went after cadres of high rank so as to ride on mules and horses. They did not intend to join the revolution but wanted to become a madam officer (*guan taitai*)."¹⁰³ In their reminiscences, however, the emphasis is on the idea that marriage did not deprive married women of their independence as revolutionaries. They still lived separately from their husbands most of the time. Fan Li commented: "Those with prospects for marriage and a few who married were all proud that they had their own independent work, were unwilling to rely on their men, and all demonstrated spirit of hard working, activism, and strive for political progress."¹⁰⁴ She married a Red Army veteran in 1941 at the age of twenty-three. She recalled that hardship in the revolution and separation from her widowed mother never made her shed any tears, but pregnancy and childbirth did. She did not explain what exactly caused her to cry – whether the pains of childbirth, separation from her children, or possibly an unwanted pregnancy that would hinder her work. Her first baby was born in 1942, when the N4A was under attack by the Nationalist army and she had to move twenty-one times in twenty-three days for safety. Her second baby was born under Japanese bombing. Her babies survived but had to be left in the care of local peasants.¹⁰⁵

The commemoration project of the N4A female veterans offered them a public space to reflect and explain the complexities of motherhood during the war. Implied in the stories were the anxieties, agonies, and emotions of child care or loss, and the self-sacrifice of women for the sake of the revolution. "In the bordering region of constant battle, pregnancy and childbirth were the hardest," Wu Zhiying wrote. "I witnessed quite a few women comrades who paid a heavy price." They had to leave the army to take shelter with the locals.[106] Contraceptive devices were hardly available, and even the rhythm method was not widely known.[107] These women "were so young, so brave and tough and determined in revolution. It seems they could learn to do anything, except to be a mother! Not ready in mind or experience," an N4A doctor recalled.[108] In her ward, a young mother accidentally suffocated her baby son in her sleep. Another mother was so tired fleeing from the enemy that she accidentally dropped her baby into a deep river. The baby was rescued but died soon after.[109] Some cared for their babies on their own with the help of the orderly if their husbands were in a position to have one. Many had to leave their babies in the care of local peasants, getting them back later only if they could find them. The death of babies due to starvation, sickness, and lack of care was common. Like women in wartime conditions elsewhere, the maternal ethos of these N4A mothers saw the death of their children as inevitable, acceptable, and meaningful.[110] There was a moral meaning in death. When she found herself pregnant, Xue Ping decided to abort by jumping and running, with no success. She gave birth while hiding in a peasant's house. A midwife "simply dragged the baby out." The baby, left in care of a local peasant family, died at the age of three due to smallpox. Xue Ping wrote: "Are there any parents worldwide who don't love their babies? But during the time of the war, all decisions had to be made to serve the larger purpose of the war."[111] In 1940, at the age of nineteen, Niu Luogui married a comrade, and by 1945 she had given birth to three babies. She tried to take care of the first, taking him with her wherever she went for work, but a year later, during the Japanese mopping-up campaign, she had to leave the baby in the care of a peasant family. Both her second and third babies were left with the locals. Fortunately, all three survived the war. She wrote: "As a revolutionary woman soldier and a young mother, I had to endure the separation from close comrades and my own flesh and blood again and again; had to endure the emotional distress again and again." She was grateful to those locals for their support and love.[112] Both of Zhu Wenhua's babies were given to the locals, and both died. She wrote: "No mother in the world does not love her baby, but for the liberation of the nation and the happiness of the people, so many revolutionary mothers have sacrificed their own flesh and blood!"[113] To these Communist women the sacrifice was a worthy act.

******

As the most female, most educated Communist army in the revolutionary era, the New Fourth Army played a crucial role in the victory of the Communist revolution. Through their publication of war reminiscences, its female veterans have created a collective memory, asserted women's place, and gendered the history of the War of Resistance in the context of a reinterpretation of revolutionary history in the post-Mao reform era. The memories redress the marginalization of women's history in the Mao era and add a collective gendered perspective to the male-dominated narrative.

Compared with the stereotypical anti-Japanese super-heroines publicized in the Mao era, the N4A women's accounts describe more realistic Communist women. Their self-writings draw us close to understanding how women were radicalized and chose to join the Communist-led resistance driven by nationalism, idealism, and voluntarism, motivated by the search for gender and social equality. Their selective memories avoid sharp criticisms and the dark sides of Communist Party politics. What is important to them is the belief that as N4A soldiers, these young women worked in the mobilization, propaganda, and medical fields, and were essential in the building and expansion of the Communist rural base areas, and in the growth of the party among the Chinese peasants. As women living a military, unsettled life, they endured physical hardships and social prejudice, and performed their duties as wives and mothers at extreme personal sacrifice. The concept of belonging to a revolutionary family and the revolutionary rhetoric gave them a sense of solidarity and psychologically empowered them. Their stories are told as Communists, soldiers, wives, and mothers, emphasizing that the war was crueller to women soldiers than to men while also demonstrating their sense of empowerment within the collective and their own agency in contributing to the success of the Communist Party in the War against Japan and in the civil war with the Nationalists. They believe that through their contribution to the war, they gained self-dignity and self-reliance.

3
My Journey of the Revolution: Oral Narratives of Five Communist Women

"Let me tell you about my journey of revolution," Luo Ying (1924–2019) began her conversation with me in her two-bedroom apartment in Beijing. She was born in Weinan County, Shaanxi Province, to a father who worked as a senior staff member in a business firm in Sichuan, and a mother who stayed at home taking care of the family. In the summer of 1937, Luo, still an elementary school student, participated in the school's anti-Japanese propaganda work. This activism continued into her middle school years; she joined the Chinese Communist Party in March 1940 and conducted underground work. In the spring of 1942, she went to Yan'an and worked as a nurse in the Central Hospital. She revisited Yan'an sixty years later, in 2002, and recalled that "riding in a large jeep from Xi'an to Yan'an ... I felt we were victorious."[1] To her, "those war years were full of hardships and dangers as well as were the times of our youth, filled with solidarity, camaraderie, and idealism."

Through the introduction of friends and relatives, I had interviews with Luo Ying and four other women who joined the Communist-led resistance against Japan soon after the war broke out in the summer of 1937. All were of relatively wealthy families and went to modern schools, where they were radicalized.[2] I also talked with the only son of a Communist woman who was an activist of women's issues in publication and organization before going to Yan'an, where she was accused of being an anti-party element in the Rectification Movement.[3]

This chapter invites readers into the stories of these women. In contrast to the reminiscences of the New Fourth Army women soldiers discussed in the previous chapter, with contributors limited to writing about one event or person or moment and publication of the collection for a large audience, the oral narratives of these five Communist women, while sharing similar generational characteristics, had more vivid, individual stories about their families in both urban and rural settings, relationships with parents, and education; about how they embarked on the road of the revolution; and what their wartime experiences meant to them as party members and as women. There was an inner urge to claim the truth of their lives as individuals. To them, the interviews were a process of gendered self-identification.[4]

More than the written, published, narratives, the oral narratives of these women reveal deeper emotions. The sparks and sadness in their eyes, facial expressions, hand gestures, and body language helped their narrations, accompanied by inflection of voice and change of tempo, high and low tones, laughing, and weeping. Sometimes, a pause lasts for a minute. In remembering the past, each woman goes into herself as she "remembers not the war but her youth."[5] The interviews convey a strong sense of immediacy and add depth and emotion to the understanding of events.[6] In the interviews, I would first let them tell their stories and then ask them follow-up questions. The face-to-face dialogues led me into a greater understanding of their views and feelings. In reflecting on their past, they echoed the rhetoric of idealism, patriotism, and devotion to communism. Underneath that, when in their private homes, alone, talking to an attentive listener around the age of their daughters, they assumed a position of authority, of knowledge, as the sole centre of attention. Their self-censorship was relaxed, more inner feelings and ambiguities were revealed, and more candid comments with critical views of party politics were offered. They never forgot the mistakes the party had made in history, yet the war experience was, to a large extent, liberating for these Communist women.

Stories Waiting to Be Told

What struck me from the start was how eager Luo Ying was to tell her story. Her inner urge for self-articulation of her life was obvious. "I want to write it all down, story by story. I am no good at writing, have no knowledge of literature. I just want to write it down to pass it on to the next generation. This is history." Among the women I interviewed, she was the most emotional in her remembrance. Tears and laughter mingled in her telling of the past. As with the others, dates, names, and places flowed forth easily, because "many things were carved into my memory." In 2016, at the age of ninety-two, three years before her death, her self-published collection of short essays and poems was released, as "a souvenir for my children and friends."[7] The urgency to write it all down also stemmed from the fact that one of her daughters, a friend of mine who had introduced me to her, by then had serious doubts about the Communist Party's legitimacy and thought her mother was too much of a revolutionary who had never cared about family.

The revolutionary career paths of each of these women was so precious to them that they all want their respective paths to be remembered by others. Li Guang (b. 1922) mentioned that if not for my request for an interview, she would not have tried to remember the past. Once she started, however, she did not seem to want to stop. The most articulate among the five, she gave the longest account, covering her family history from her grandparents, the local geographical environment and social transformation, and the details of her daily work and life till the end of the war in 1945. The microphone attached to her blouse near her chest recorded her heartbeat beneath her calm and rational tones. The past lived on in her old photos and her elementary school homework on geography and hygiene with her careful and elegant Chinese brush writing, which she showed me. The notebook of her homework was in good condition. Through all the years of instability and moving around, she had kept these memories of the past. Her poems from long ago have remained with her, and a collection of them has been published.

Lu Nan (1923–2006) initially hesitated to have the interviews recorded on tape. She was cautious about what she had to say, and concerned that she would not make herself clear. Once she started, however, she let down all guards and lost her hesitancy, and she agreed to be taped. The narration followed a clear sequence with spontaneous enthusiasm.

Self-censored, Guo Lian (1921–2012) was concerned about the interview for fear of violating the Communist Party's prohibition. She agreed to be interviewed only after a telephone consultation with her work unit, which reassured her that the interview would be okay as long as she did not discuss her work after 1949. "I have not thought much about the past especially in retirement ... It is just an ordinary life." It seems that her hesitation to talk was not because such an ordinary life was not worthy of remembering, but because deep down it was a story of complexity and related so closely to party politics. It was too much and too difficult to explain. "People like us, we have been through the war alive, have not starved to death in the natural disasters of the great famine (of 1959–62, following the Great Leap Forward of 1958), have not been killed by diseases, and have survived all kinds of mass campaigns. Life has not been easy." This was the life path for all five of the Communist women interviewed. Once she began, Guo Lian's narratives were vivid and lively, full of candour. In remembering the past, she often mentioned the names and experiences of other comrades; places were not hard for her to recall. Why such clear memory? She explained that during the Cultural Revolution (1966–76), when a large number of Communist cadres in middle to senior positions were accused of being traitors, anti-party elements, or "capitalist roaders," they had to undergo investigations of their family backgrounds and pre-1949 activities, and she had to write "confessions" about past events to prove her political innocence. Those investigations and self-writing had refreshed and reinforced her memory. They also added new information to her life story. Her father was an officer in the old military. By "old," Guo Lian meant the military under the warlord in her region which, in the party's class theory, was bullying the people. The investigations during the Cultural Revolution concluded, however, that her father was in fact involved in anti-Japanese activities in the Northeast in the early 1930s. If not for the investigations, she would not have known that her father was an anti-Japanese fighter. "Thanks for that!" she laughed. Her sense of humour brought out the ironies and absurdities in politics.

These women's memories of the past were clear regarding names, places, dates, and events also because self-writing was not unfamiliar to Communist Party members. As early as the 1940s, the party required its cadres to write their autobiography (*zizhuan*). The autobiography followed a standard outline: 1) self-introduction: family background, level of education, personal names used, skills and interest, and name of spouse; 2) curriculum vitae: education, political activities, work experience, memberships in organizations; 3) family conditions and social relations: class and economic status of the family, one's relationship with the family, location of the family, detailed information about family members and relatives; 4) changes in views at each stage of educational and political life, including details of any arrest, release, loss of contact with the Communist Party, and re-establishment of the contact; 5) self-evaluation of one's understanding of the party's ideology and of work performance.[8] This type of writing was political – it had to show one's transformation to the party's approved ideology. It would also provide valuable resources for remembrance.

Gu Mei (1923–2011) did not want me to record on tape what she had to say. Instead, she let me first read her political autobiography, written by hand in 1953. It was in chronological order from childhood (her father ran a small fabric shop in Shanghai, while her mother was a factory worker), to her schooling and her underground work for the Communist Party in Shanghai, and later in the New Fourth Army. For each historical period, there were self-evaluations of her understanding of the party's ideology and policy and her activities. Then she had a long conversation with me during which I took notes. As she talked, her reservations fell away. Breaking out of the constraints of that political autobiography, and moving away from the Communist rhetoric, she began to speak from her heart, driven by her inner urge to tell me about her real self. She laughed at herself: "I gave too many self-criticisms in the autobiography!" Her restrained manner loosened up. At one point, when talking about sources of inspiration for anti-Japanese activities, she started singing the "Graduation Song" ("Biye ge") with no difficulty remembering the lyrics: "Fellow students, arise. Bear the rise and fall of the world! ... We are going to be the masters to die in the battle field. We don't want to be slaves to get promotion." This was the theme song in a 1934 film, *Plunder of Peach and Plum* (*Taoli jie*). The song was extremely popular with her generation, calling on the youth to fight against the Japanese invaders.

One Communist veteran refused my request for an interview. She was the mother of an elementary schoolmate of mine in Beijing. Around 1964, her mother gave us pupils a talk about how she, as a student of Yanjing University in Beijing majoring in sociology, participated in the student demonstration on December 9, 1935. This famous December Ninth student movement further stimulated the national salvation movement. I still remember her singing a song during the talk. Now in her old age, she did not wish to see me. I learned from others that in 1937 she went to Yan'an. In the Rectification Movement, she was accused of being a Nationalist secret agent. Her husband divorced her because of this. She later remarried and had two children, one of whom was my schoolmate. My schoolmate informed me that her mother had given quite a few interviews before, but no longer wanted to discuss her past because she did not want people to dwell on her personal matters, especially the divorce (her former husband became a well-known senior diplomat in the People's Republic of China). She also did not want her story to be "misused," especially by a professor at a university in the United States. "My mum is a Marxist old lady," her daughter told me. By "Marxist old lady," she meant a stereotypical Communist woman, one who was dogmatic and would defend the Communist Party in any way she could. It seems that to this Communist veteran, the past mattered so much that she would rather keep it to herself and her children, and did not want her experience in the Rectification to smear the party's image.

The Rectification Movement in 1942–44 began as a thought-reform process but soon devolved into a campaign in which many young students and intellectuals who had joined the Communists were falsely accused of being hidden traitors, secret agents, or spies of the Nationalists and therefore needed to be rescued. It was a terrifying "witch hunt," with forced confessions, coercion, and violence.[9] The campaign was not intended to purge but to "reconstruct and reincorporate" those accused.[10] It ended with Mao Zedong's open apology at several public meetings for the campaign's being out of hand and causing wrong to some comrades, without any admission that the campaign was wrong.[11] The movement left dark shadows and scars on many.

Growing Up, I Want to Save the Country; I Must Make My Mother Proud

Luo Ying, mentioned at the beginning of this chapter, believed that "our generation had its own idealism. China's sufferings made us have such consciousness." Her generation, educated in modern schools, had learned about China's humiliation from the mid-nineteenth century at the hands of Western imperialists, about the 1911 Revolution, and about China's civil wars during the warlord era. For her, it was the historical circumstances, the place of her native home, and her mother that had started her on the road of revolution. Luo Ying's father worked as a senior staff member in a business firm in Sichuan. He died in 1938 when Ying was only fourteen years old. A remote father figure, he did not have much influence on her. It was her mother who was the first to awaken her gender consciousness, and who gave her all her support when she was active in the resistance. With tears, Luo Ying spoke of her mother: "I changed my surname in 1947 to Luo in order to honour her [mother's surname]. Even though she had little education, she had sustained our family, managed it independently and raised us up. She walked to Yan'an in 1947 to see me. With her bound feet and strong willpower … She made a lot of contributions. Her influence on me was enormous."

Luo Ying grew up with her mother and elder sister in an extended family in the county seat of Weinan. "In the days when men were superior and women inferior, my elder and younger brothers both died in infancy. Mother as a sonless woman was looked down upon and discriminated against in the lineage. She wished her daughter to be independent and rely on herself, not on family or on any men. So, she sent me to school." The early education, first in an old style, taught her about Confucianism and a sense of morality, and about Mulan, a legendary heroine who disguised herself as a man in order to join the military against the invaders. Luo's open-minded teacher discussed gender equality with his pupils. This made her feel that "I was not a boy but I was sure I was as capable as boys." In 1935, the local temple was torn down and replaced by a modern school. Luo Ying was the only girl enrolled there during the new school's first year. "Often when I was back from school, I would teach my elder sister what I had learned."

Her home county, Weinan, is not far, sixty-four kilometres, from Xi'an, a politically important city. In December 1936, news of the Xi'an Incident spread to her school. In this incident, the Nationalist general Zhang Xueliang put Chiang Kai-shek under house arrest to compel him to fight against the Japanese. The Nationalist troops under Zhang were "stationed in our village; some stayed in our house. They were anti-Japanese but as the old army, the soldiers were badly disciplined, stealing things from us ... Young women, unmarried, in the village all had to go into hiding [for fear of sexual assault]." The old army of the Nationalists in contrast to the Communist propaganda of resistance against the Japanese affected the young Luo Ying and soon caused her to turn to the Communist Party.

"I was a girl of the mountains," Li Guang began her narrative with a strong sense of location. The mountains, however, did not forbid contact with the outside world. She was from Wan County (present-day Shunping), Hebei Province. A member of the local gentry, her grandfather owned land, a drugstore, and two inns in a town that was on an important transportation route, about eighty kilometres from the city of Baoding, an old city exposed to modern ideas. In a detailed account, she described how her progressive family cultivated in her an outgoing personality and a deep interest in politics from a tender age. Influenced by new ideas of reform that constantly flew in from outside, Guang's mother unbound her own feet with the encouragement of her father-in-law. Using the family's financial resources, Guang's father established the first new-style school for boys in the village, and later a school for girls. He and Guang's uncle were the teachers, and among the first group of female pupils were Guang's mother and elder sister.

At elementary school, Li Guang became particularly interested in new ideas, new literature produced by Chinese writers in the early 1910s to 1920s, and current affairs. The history of foreign imperialism in China, unequal treaties imposed by foreign powers on China, Dr. Sun Yat-sen's ideas of national reconstruction, and the Manchurian Incident and Chiang Kai-shek's non-resistance all aroused her concerns. School education taught her about gender equality but "family influenced me too, especially my mam." Mother was a strong character. "She told me the stories of the 'Red Lanterns' of all these teenaged girls [an unmarried women's organization in the Boxer movement against foreigners around 1900]. She was in her forties. When telling me the story, Mother showed us how the Boxers were fighting." Her mother's personal sufferings demonstrated to Li Guang gendered oppression. In order to gain any status, women in traditional China were expected to give birth to boys to preserve the patrilineal line. Of her mother's six babies, however, five were girls (one died at the age of three) and the only son died within a month. Death in infancy was common in those days due to lack of medical care. "Having girls only, Mother felt she failed to continue the family line so she suggested Father take a concubine … He took one, even a year younger than my eldest sister." Her mother did what a "virtuous" woman was supposed to do. Later however, Guang's mother "became aware that women and men should be equal … Often she would talk about gender equality. When getting into a fight with my dad, she would say men and women were equal; you can't bully me! I helped her too, even when I was six or seven years old. Father asked Mother to get lost. She would say: what right do you have to let me go! I am a master of this family too!"

School education was important in nurturing her progressive ideas. At the Baoding Women's Normal School, where Li Guang enrolled in 1936, she furthered her passion for reading all sorts of books and her interest in political affairs. In class, "I am also number one (like in elementary school), known as 'firsty' [she spoke this English word here]." At one school debate, the topic was which would benefit the nation more: novels or books on social science. Her side, social science, won. That was truly her belief. In the reading club organized by the underground Communists, she became more interested in political affairs and socially progressive literary works and magazines. "I learned about the Communist Party, and the party was good … In elementary school, I used to think that if I could become a schoolteacher after middle school, and work hard, I might become a writer, but seeing the country was more and more in trouble, I thought I should dedicate myself to the country. One should have higher ideals," she related.

Gu Mei had a complex analysis of her relations with her family. In her autobiography, written in 1953 under the political circumstances of the time, she criticized her early aspiration to be a medical doctor as "a naïve belief in a reformist way to change society." To a real Communist, only a revolution, not reforms, could save China. She labelled her own family as belonging to an "exploitative" class, admitted her lack of courage to completely draw a class line with her petty bourgeois family, and blamed herself for having "too much" emotional attachment to her mother when joining the revolution. In her conversation with me, however, she abandoned the political rhetoric and had a different story to tell. She pointed out that her father owned a small shop of fabrics as a result of his hard work and the help of relatives, implying that his wealth was not acquired through exploitation of the poor as the party's rhetoric would have it. She revealed a deep sympathy toward her mother:

> Mother suffered so much in her life. A factory worker, after marriage, she bore no son and that meant a low status within the family ... Father took a mistress. Mam had to work to support the family. Later she adopted a boy when I was ten ... I was her only daughter and could not pass on the family name. I always felt guilty, seeing how hard her life was. Mother wanted me to be strong, to get an education. With little schooling herself, she had always supported my going to school ... I thought I must study hard, and make a living like a man ... I must make my mother proud.

Her gender consciousness and her determination to make her mother proud are clearly expressed in this extract.

Nationalistic consciousness came naturally to Gu Mei: "No need for any education about nationalism or patriotism." The Japanese invasion of Shanghai taught her what it meant to be patriotic. Her father's store and their home were burned down under the Japanese bombing of Shanghai on August 13, 1937. China was the first country to suffer systematic bombing of civilians during the Second World War. To the Chinese, the first signal of the war was the bombing.[12] The family had to take refuge in the French concession with many other Shanghainese. The business was damaged and the family suffered serious losses. Gu Mei's grandmother lived in Wusong, at the mouth of the Yangtze River, where the Japanese army landed. Like many elderly people, Grandma did not want to flee but

> who could know that the Japanese wouldn't let go of them. They were tied up and shot down. Grandma was killed. In the hot weather, their bodies quickly became decomposed. The Chinese had sympathy for Chinese, so they placed each body in a black box. Hard to tell who was who. My aunty looked at teeth and hair and recognized my grandma.

The loss of Grandma and home, the constant fear of bombing and needing to take refuge, drove Gu Mei into the resistance with her mother's understanding: "Mum asked me: 'Why must you go into the activities when there are so many others?' Even so she tried to cover for me at work."

As with Gu Mei, Guo Lian's nationalistic feelings arose naturally. "We Northeasterners are the most resolute in resistance against Japan," she repeated several times in her narrative. Her nationalist identity began with the Japanese occupation in 1931 of China's Northeast, or Manchuria, where her home was. The family was directly affected since her father was a military officer; he joined the resistance at first but went into hiding when the Japanese aggression intensified and resistance became more dangerous. Guo Lian was ten years old: "I had no idea what was going on. The Northeasterners were very feudalistic in that they did not want girls to learn much." However, she remembered clearly: "Father sighed all the time and lamented: 'We have become slaves in a lost nation [*wangguo nu*]. The Japanese devils became the supreme emperor.'" The feeling of being a slave in a lost nation hurt the young Guo Lian deeply:

> When I was little, I was so scared of the household-checkup. The interpreters, followed by the Japanese, often came during the night when we were sleeping. They were so rude. They would kick the door open and come in to check everything. So scary I would simply hide under the cover in bed ... Once we had to flee from our house again, our dog stayed behind and tried to guard the home but was killed by a Japanese motorcycle. I hated those Japanese devils!

Under the Manchukuo regime, Guo Lian's school education, administered for the purpose of "enslaving" the Chinese, aroused strong resentment in her: "At school pupils had to learn the Japanese language. We would hide under the desk not wanting to go to the Japanese class. Teachers had to drag us out ... Later if you didn't pass the Japanese language test you wouldn't be allowed to go on to the next grade so we had to learn."

Although Guo Lian claimed that nationalism and voluntarism were the most important driving force for her to join the Communists, her story shows strongly that gender discrimination pushed her onto the revolutionary path. She was an unwanted daughter: "Mother gave birth to four girls. I am number three ... When I was born, again a girl, she was seriously disappointed. No son meant no status. Mother even wanted to find a concubine for my dad ... When she had my little brother, she often made me skip school to take care of him." In her words, Mother was "feudal," "a housewife [a term with negative connotation]," "didn't influence me much." It was her eldest sister who was her role model for a "new woman." Having graduated from a teachers' training school, the eldest sister became a middle school teacher of music and physical education. Her earnings supported the family. Lian wanted to be like her.

In September 1936, her parents sent Guo Lian to join her second elder sister, who was married and living in Beiping. She was so happy to escape from home: "I couldn't wait to leave!" In unoccupied Beiping, she enrolled in a night school run by Beijing University for workers, urban poor, and young women. During her year in this progressive school, Guo Lian learned about the Red Army, the Communist Party, current affairs, and the meaning of patriotism.

Lu Nan, of Kaifeng, Henan Province, began her narrative with her participation in the student salvation movement in the winter of 1935. For her, filled with nationalist passion, this was the most memorable event of her war years.

> I participated in the student movement. Who was responsible for this? The Henan University organized all the schools' students (in Kaifeng) to go to Nanjing for petitioning the government to fight. Not easy. (When denied to get on the train), we blocked the railway and stopped trains from running ... We were patriotic and wanted to fight against the Japanese ...
>
> My grandpa tried to prevent me and asked me to "study hard. Go to university in the future. Don't go around causing trouble." I replied: "No way, grandpa. China is about to become extinct. There would be no universities to go to. We must fight against the Japanese!"

Lu Nan was then a student at the Kaifeng All-Girls Middle School. The school had socially progressive teachers who taught about the concept of the nation and the humiliation of China under foreign aggression. Inspired by the Beiping student movement against Chiang Kai-shek's nonresistance policy, students in Kaifeng organized petitions for resistance as well. When the Kaifeng railway authorities forbade the students to take the train to Nanjing, students staged a blockade at the Kaifeng station from December 26 – four days and nights of sitting on the snow-covered ground. She was courageous:

> Was I scared? No, what's there to be scared of? We wanted to fight against Japan! ... Male students were at the front and we girls were behind them.

No one looked down on us (girls) ... Mother brought new quilts so we spread them under ourselves in the snow. She was educated so that made a difference. She said: "China is to be lost. We should let her stay there. There are so many of them."

As she talked, her whole person was back reliving exciting times. Her memories of these days were the most detailed, more so than her description of life in Yan'an. Only when I asked did she begin to talk about her family. She recalled with a sense of pride her family in Kaifeng, a medium-sized city in Henan, located along the railway line. Mother was from a big landowner's family and attended an old-style private school. She stubbornly refused foot-binding, and at the age of twenty-six was known as an "old maid" in the area. When Father, a mechanical engineer from a wealthy family, was looking for a wife with education and "big" feet, she was introduced to him. The two exchanged letters and poems before they married. They had two daughters and a son. Lu Nan was the youngest. Mother insisted that she go to a modern school, for she understood that the old traditional teaching was "useless." Lu Nan entered the elementary school when she was only five years old. In her middle school, underground Communist teachers were active and students were exposed to progressive ideas. When the Nationalist government replaced the progressive school principal, radical students protested, even resorting to violence against the new principal. "I joined them too but I could not bear to beat the principal," Lu Nan said. The political climate in her school aroused her activism from a young age.

The Beginning of a New Life in Joining the Communist-Led Resistance

Following the Marco Polo Bridge Incident on July 7, 1937, full-scale war broke out between China and Japan, changing the lives of these five teenagers. They embarked on the path of the Communist-led resistance, determined to save the country and holding on to the hope of living a better life than their mothers. The Communist Party's political identity in a collective empowered them with a sense of belonging and a higher purpose in life.

Luo Ying recalled that in the summer of 1937, many students returned from schools and colleges in other cities to their home in Weinan, Shaanxi. They called upon people to fight against Japanese aggression, putting up slogans and teaching people to sing patriotic songs. Luo Ying was a fourth grader at the elementary school:

> Our school was no exception. It also went into propaganda for the resistance against Japan. The school organized students for military training. As a fourth grader, I learned to understand that to liberate oneself we must liberate the nation. This was under the influence of some teachers. At that time, "The Marching Song of the Volunteers," "The Sword March," and "La Marseillaise" were all inspiring. The school also performed street plays, anti-Japanese plays. I participated in such plays as *Guiying Joining the Military* and *Laying Down Your Whip*.

Some students went to the Communist-organized training program for resistance against Japan. Luo Ying wanted to go too, but was turned down because of her young age. "I began reading anti-Japanese essays, many of them." From 1938, her co-ed Weiyang Middle School was a place where both the Communists and the Nationalists operated to influence students. Her elder cousin was a student there, and an underground Communist member, and he lent Ying works about anti-Japanese ideas. Several teachers were Communist members too. The reading club she joined was led by underground Communists, and offered books and organized discussions that helped raise her political consciousness even more. Luo Ying explained her choice of the Communist line:

> I remember I wrote an essay ... titled "Family" ... I believed that in the time of the War of Resistance, no one could have a family. You may have one today. It may be gone tomorrow. Look at those war refugees on the street. They had to beg for food ...
> The teachers who were on the side of the Nationalist Party said that students should not care much about politics and should focus on study. The Communist teachers would say to students that it was not that students did not want to study. It was the political situation that did not allow students to study. The frequent air raids forced students to take class outside ...

Corruption in the Nationalist army turned her away from the Nationalist government:

> I also witnessed the corruption of the Nationalists. In our town, restaurants had the notice: "In chatting, no mention about anti-Japanese." [This

referred to the time before July 1937]. How could we not when the war was all around us? That winter [in 1938], in our school were stationed newly enlisted soldiers of the Nationalist army. They had only thin clothes on, and were tied up by a rope for fear they would run away. After the army left, there was a huge graveyard outside the town with the bodies of those soldiers frozen to death.

The coming of the war, the death of her father in 1938, and the financial hardships the family had to endure further pushed her toward the Communists. "Father returned home but died in 1938. We were in financial difficulties. My mother still owned some land but she had to pawn many things in order to send me to school [Luo Ying's voice cracked]." Luo Ying joined the Communist Party in 1940. This marked a transformation to a new identity. A party membership meant the beginning of a new political life. "I bought a notebook and wrote on the first page: March 19, 1940. This is a day I would never forget; it is the new beginning of my life."

For Li Guang, the outbreak of the war meant that she had to leave school and return to her village. For a few months, the family often fled deep into the mountains away from the defeated Nationalist armies who came to harass people. "In those days, soldiers and bandits were the same. We had to run whenever soldiers came ... The Japanese had not arrived, the Nationalist army came, who retreated after defeat, enlisting people and animals for them, and taking away stuff from the households of common people." In contrast, the Communist army's arrival at her home village in November 1937 brought hope to the young Li Guang:

> The Communist Eighth Route Army came. A battalion of cavalry arrived in our village. Those soldiers on horses, common people liked them. In the past, soldiers were just like bandits but this time it was different. They helped people with fetching water, chopping firewood, and cleaning yards ... Never seen such good soldiers ... These young men sang songs everyday ...

An outgoing young woman, she decided to join the Communist army:

> The headquarters of the cavalry battalion was in the village school. I went there. I was brave. Often winning school debates with no fear. I said I want to speak to your leader. I want to join the resistance ... Political instructor Li came ... He encouraged me and praised me, and said they would go to talk to my family. My dad would not interfere. I had not told dad before

I went to apply. Mum would not stop me either. It would be useless even if they tried.

The next day, a male cadre came to her home and told her: "We will organize the women's association of salvation, and you would be the director in your district. The office will be at your local school." She began working for the organization right away.

Half a year later, in April 1938, sixteen-year-old Li Guang became a member of the Communist Party. Before she was accepted into the party, "I had read a pamphlet entitled 'The Construction of the Party,' and had remembered these clearly: First, the party was the vanguard of the proletarian class. Second, the party was the highest organization of the vanguard of the proletarian class. Third, the party grew in the two-line struggles. Six items altogether, plus the disciplines." "There was no ceremony. A form had to be filled out [for applying for membership]. For the question, why are you joining the party, based on my reading I wrote down: 'to strive for the realization of communism.'" Thus began her new life.

Guo Lian was in Beiping with her sister in the fateful summer of 1937 when the war broke out: "I was then studying hard in preparation of the entrance examination for a public school ... The people in the neighbourhood remarked that the Japanese arrived in the Red Gate. On July 28 they entered the city of Beiping." She had already participated in anti-Japanese activities: "We put up slogans and raised funds for supporting the 29th Nationalist Army under Song Zheyuan [in resisting the Japanese] organized by our teachers." But when school stopped, Guo Lian felt lost:

> After the Incident of July 7, the teachers left school. I was worried and anxious, uncertain what to do. Father wrote letters and telegrammed us worrying about the situation and urging us to return home to the Northeast. In August, we took a train to Tianjin [on the way to the Northeast]. Under the Japanese air bombing, no more train was available. My sister, one year older than I, and I stayed in a hotel. The manager asked us to leave the hotel for fear that the Japanese would come to check. He was worried for us. We went to stay in a teacher's house in the concession of Tianjin.

Guo Lian did not want to return home: "They just wanted to marry me off." To her, marriage was a dead end. In Tianjin, she met her night school teacher, who encouraged her to join the resistance. "The Northeasterners were different from others. They were active in the resistance. Of course, I was willing." Rejecting an arranged marriage like that of her sister, and with strong nationalist feelings, Guo Lian followed a group of teachers and students, one of whom later became her husband, on a journey that eventually led them to Taiyuan, a centre of anti-Japanese activities. From there, as part of a group of twenty-six students and professors (six of them women), she went to the Taihang mountainous region in northern China. Under the United Front, the Nationalist general Yan Xishan allocated funding to the Communists, and the Communists developed their resistance base areas in the Taihang mountainous region.

On December 23, 1937, Guo Lian became a Communist Party member at the age of sixteen. No ceremony was held since the party recruited members clandestinely under the United Front. Guo Lian remembered clearly her feelings of enthusiasm and devotion: "I was so excited that I couldn't sleep for several nights ... At that time if it was for the revolution, death was a worthy end. Death was nothing. We were brave in the War of Resistance. Death would be heroic and an honour for resisting against the Japanese. Had no fear for death."

In Gu Mei's hometown of Shanghai, the heavy fighting in August eventually brought the city under the control of the Japanese in November 1937, except for the foreign concessions, which were taken over by the Japanese only after the Pacific war started in December 1941. Gu Mei joined the Communist-affiliated student organization in 1939, when she was a student of the Minli All-Girls Middle School. The reading group was where they gathered to discuss political and literary works and to organize various resistance activities:

> A group of youth with hatred of collaborators and with no fear, we distributed flyers of resistance and salvation and fighting against collaborators. I didn't know much about the Communist Party. Had heard about it, but had little knowledge of it ... We raised funds to help the needy and participated in the boycott of Japanese goods. Our school had this resistance organization, it was clandestine ... We had meetings sometimes in the evenings. There were spies or some bad people, who would follow us on or off the bus. I had no fear.

Not just the Japanese and the collaboration regime but also the Nationalists, even under the United Front, still monitored Communist activities. Gu Mei's activism drew the suspicion of the school authorities and she was dismissed in June 1940. The notice was sent to her home. "I told my parents that I was dismissed because of my resistance. They understood." Her parents gave her their support.

In August 1940, Gu Mei joined the Communist Party. Her eyes sparkled as she recalled her pledging ceremony. The ceremony was held in secret in a room in her father's shop. Before a paper flag of the party the size of a matchbox, she pledged her loyalty:

> At the pledge, I was asked if you were arrested and forced to give information about the party, what would you do? I replied, I would bite my tongue off ... What if the enemy arrested your parents, would you give in? I said, absolutely not. Asked, what if they torture your parents but not you? I said, I would not yield. The party organization thought so much and asked so much because the enemies wanted to get information about the party ... We had to be ready to sacrifice our lives when joining the party.

Being ready to sacrifice not just herself but also her family demanded great courage and integrity. This gave her a sense of moral superiority and the spiritual power that she needed in the resistance. The Communist ideology gave her a clear sense of purpose and devotion.

By the time war broke out in the summer of 1937, both of Lu Nan's parents had died. Sad as it was, it seems that being orphaned gave her more freedom to choose her own life path. That summer, her grandfather gave her forty silver dollars for her to go to school, which had evacuated to a location in Henan not directly affected by the war. "Grandpa was sad for me to leave. We cried together. He thought I would go to school, and was sad that he would not see me again." Little did he know that Lu Nan had already applied to become a nurse in a military hospital under the Nationalist army. This was the last time they said goodbye to each other: when the Japanese bombed Kaifeng, her grandfather was killed just at the entrance of a bomb shelter.

After a short period of training, Lu Nan worked as a nurse caring for wounded Nationalist soldiers in Kaifeng. One soldier bled to death when she treated him. The fourteen-year-old girl was terrified:

> I went to the doctor. He said, don't tell anyone. I cried and said, he didn't die at the front, but now he died in my hand! The doctor said who said that? Don't say such a thing. But that was true, I said. He asked me to stop saying that: If you go on, we will fire you ... Later the hospital still received that soldier's quota of fund ... I felt this was too much. He died and you still got his money. They didn't allow me to mention this; said I would be locked up if I made this known to others.

This kind of corruption was common, and Lu Nan was deeply disappointed and disillusioned. When she evacuated with the hospital south to Wuhan later that year, she and three other young women ran away, looking for the Communists. The city of Wuhan had been an important centre for China's resistance under the Nationalist government from late 1937 to October 1938, before its capture by the Japanese. The United Front enabled the Communist Eighth Routh Army to set up its liaison office there. The Communists tried to recruit young people. With the guidance and assistance of the liaison office, Lu Nan and her friends went to Yan'an. On the way, one of them became homesick and left. Lu Nan and the two others continued the long, difficult journey, which her narrative described in detail.

Lu Nan became a Communist Party member at the age of fifteen during her three months of training at the Communist-run North Shaanxi Public School (Shaanbei gongxue) in 1938, with classes in politics and in telecommunication skills. The party accepted her because, in her words: "I worked very hard. After just one month of training, I was accepted into the Communist Party. I worked even more actively. I donated the gold bracelet that was the one and only thing my mother had left for me … I wanted to donate all my silver dollars but the advisor did not want them." At the secret pledging ceremony, she said: "I pledged that I would serve the people wholeheartedly and sacrifice all my life. All for the people. To die for the people." To join the resistance against Japan, one should of course be ready to die. It was as simple as that.

Finding Nationalist, Revolutionary, and Gendered Meanings

For these women, joining the Communist Party meant a new political identity and a revolutionary purpose in life. None had to take up weapons on the battlefields. To each, as to New Fourth Army women soldiers, the wartime days were full of hardship, and their devotion was wholehearted, with deep meaning.

After joining the party, Gu Mei was assigned by the party organization to work as the underground party secretary at two schools, disguised as a student. After the Japanese attack on Pearl Harbor in December 1941, the foreign concessions in Shanghai were no longer safe. The Japanese takeover of the entire city made underground resistance more dangerous. As a messenger, Gu Mei passed information between the Shanghai Communist Party organization and the New Fourth Army. She could not stay at home for fear of being followed by spies or police. Her parents were deeply worried for her safety: "I was disturbed … but I refused to surrender to fear."

In the summer of 1942, Gu Mei passed the entrance examination to the prestigious Fudan University, majoring in education. The party organization permitted this and her overjoyed parents raised the required tuition. However, when her activities aroused the suspicion of the authorities, the party instructed her to leave Shanghai for the New Fourth Army area. She had to leave without telling her parents but she wrote them a note: "I have to leave to take care of some matters. Please do not worry about me. I would be the same person outside as I am at home." "The same person" meant the same good and kind daughter she was taught to be by her parents. In her written autobiography, Gu Mei critiqued her sadness at leaving her mother: "I knew this feeling was backward. I had been working hard for the party, and the party trusted me very much. I must not show any weakness, so I made up my mind to leave." A Communist but also a daughter, during our interview Gu Mei showed her emotional agony and a sense of inadequate fulfillment of her filial duty: "After I left, my parents were looking for me everywhere ... mother cried till her tears dried up." She did not see her mother until seven years later, after the founding of the People's Republic of China in 1949.

In the New Fourth Army, Gu Mei worked first among the peasants in the Huainan Base Area, providing disaster relief and organizing peasants in the anti-Japanese mopping-up. "Life was hard. Living among the peasants, we had fleas. We also learnt a lot from the peasants, had our meals at peasants' houses and had very good relations with them." Later she worked in the army's political and personnel departments and as a literary instructor.

Gu Mei's autobiography written for the party organization in 1953 is valuable in recording her self-criticisms and showing her transformation from a petty bourgeois student into a Communist. In contrast, in their oral narratives, what the other four women reflected was not so much thought reform but more how they grew tough and matured through their work, which not only contributed to the liberation of China but also enhanced their own sense of power and equality to men.

Luo Ying worked as an underground Communist Party member at her Weiyang Middle School after joining the party in 1940. Her home province, Shaanxi, for the most part was not occupied during the war. Northern Shaanxi was controlled by the Communists with Yan'an as its centre, while the rest of the province was under the Nationalists. The city of Xi'an was bombed by the Japanese but never occupied. In Luo Ying's county, the Nationalists and the Communists competed to win over the youth. Despite the formation of the United Front, conflicts never disappeared. Several of Luo Ying's schoolteachers were arrested by the Nationalist government. Her work was to spread Communist ideas and recruit members from among the young people. She remembered one risky assignment: in the winter of 1940, she and four other comrades went to the Eighth Route Army office in Xi'an to pick up Communist pamphlets to bring back to their area. Ying hid these under her overcoat, while the others were covering her. They were able to pass the checkpoints of the Nationalist military police.

Luo Ying did not hesitate to talk about the deep fears she felt as an underground Communist worker: "That life gave me nightmares – even today. I often dream that they come to arrest me. At that young age, we were forced into an abnormal environment." In the spring of 1941, her name was on the Nationalists' watchlist. Fearing exposure of her Communist identity, the provincial party leadership approved her request to be transferred to Yan'an. Passing through three Nationalist blockades and risking arrest, she and several others arrived in Yan'an in the spring of 1942. With a tremendous sense of relief and safety, they shouted, "We are home!"

During the war, Yan'an was a target of Japanese bombing from November 1938 to October 1941, but on the whole it was relatively safe. In the early 1940s, the city had a population of 37,000–38,000, among whom were over 30,000 Communist cadres. They lived under a military communal system of food rationing. The Nationalist government had provided financial support to the Communists, but it later implemented an economic blockade and cut off supplies to the party. By 1940, material life had become very difficult.[13]

Luo Ying was given a set of uniforms and assigned to a nurse training program. This was not what she had hoped to do: "I felt I should go to study in the Marxist-Leninist College or go to the service group at the front." But obedience to the party's orders was required. After training for three months, she worked at the Central Hospital as a nurse, and was later promoted to head nurse. She was proud of how professional the hospital was, and prouder still of the role of women: "In our hospital, women held up half the sky. More than half of the sky! And many in the hospital were intellectuals, professionals. No such problems [as gender inequality]."

For Lu Nan, arriving at Yan'an in 1938 meant leaving dangers behind and finding a place of safety. She was happy: "Once in Yan'an it was a place of safety and security. No one would bully you anymore ... We were all equals ... We shared everything. No distinction of what is yours or mine." She worked as a stenographer, then became an elementary school teacher for the children of the Communist army and party cadres. Teaching materials for Chinese language and other subjects were lacking, so she composed them herself.

When Guo Lian arrived at the Taihang mountainous region in late 1937, the primary tasks were to mobilize the people for the war effort, establish the anti-Japanese local administration, and build up an anti-Japanese base area. As a cadre, her life fell under the rationing system. Each person was distributed a set of clothes every two years.

> We lived among the peasants and ate with them [the peasants would be offered financial compensation] ... I would carry my own quilt, a pair of shoes. I got sick with typhoid and malaria, and scabies caused by lice. We had no clothes for changing. In the winter, just a cotton-padded coat over the body with nothing underneath, a waist-belt over it. In the summer we got the cotton out of the coat.

One of her jobs was as head of a children's propaganda troupe for a year and a half: "All these kids were from eleven to fourteen years of age. They would sing and dance, do propaganda, and put slogans up on the walls." The troupe expanded from a dozen or so to eighty members. The propaganda greatly energized people. Guo Lian was proud: "In our Taihang Base Area, the sound of songs is louder than the gunshot."[14] Later, she received training at the Lu Xun Art College in Taihang for half a year.

Another job was related to women, involving women's literacy, gender equality, and efforts to help the war effort. "Organizing women into women's associations and encouraging women to go out to work ... not easy. Some women were forbidden by their husbands or mothers-in-law to go. We had to persuade them ... In our base area, the work was successful in promoting gender equality ... At that time, men could not beat their wives. If a man did, there would not be a struggle meeting [against him] but he would be criticized."

In 1942, her job took her into a male-dominated field. She became the vice director of a district below county level in the eastern part of Shanxi Province, and was in charge of leading the peasants in increasing production and in anti-Japanese mopping-up campaigns. Throughout her work, Guo Lian enjoyed political prestige and the respect of the locals, men and women. Well aware of many inequalities persisting in rural China among the peasants, she considered them unavoidable, requiring time to reform. Compared with peasant men and women, she herself attained a much higher social and political status and found meaning in work that was directly linked to the liberation of the Chinese peasantry.

As shown in Chapter 2, Communist women cadres played a significant role in mobilization at the grassroots level. During her eight-year resistance career, Li Guang was in charge of the work among peasant women. In Hebei, the Nationalist government was soon paralyzed by the war, which left room for the Communists to develop their regime and mass organizations into part of the party-controlled Jin-Cha-Ji Border Region. Being a local, Li Guang had the advantage of speaking the local dialect, knowing the customs, and having social connections in the area. Starting at the grassroots level, she went from village to village, explaining the notion of the nation and organizing women into associations to support the Communist army. In a remote mountainous village called Huapen, "there was this woman in her twenties holding a newborn baby. A woman of the deep mountains. I asked her: do you know which country are you from? 'What country? I am from the Huapen country.' She had no notion of her country, did not know to which province, or county her village belonged." From such a beginning, Li Guang persuaded her female relatives and those who were educated – who enjoyed local prestige and influence – or were matchmakers or "dispute settlers" to take the lead in forming women's associations. One effective way of gaining support was to form a relationship of daughter and mother with the peasants. Li Guang had more than one such a mother. These tactics helped to form women's associations, which mobilized women's support in making shoes and clothes for the Communist army and in sending their men to the join the Eighth Route Army. It was these peasant women who clothed the army and their sons who supplied its manpower.

As the chief editor of a local newspaper, *Rural Women,* Li Guang wrote stories, drew pictures, mimeographed copies, and distributed the paper to each village. The literate people would read aloud to the villagers. She was proud that people were interested in her newspaper. In her propaganda work, she revised folksongs with anti-Japanese lyrics, using the local, peasant language to explain the significance of anti-Japanese ideas. "At a mass meeting I would talk about why we should fight ... using words they would understand." People also wanted to listen because they knew that she was the granddaughter of old Mr. Li, a well-respected local man. At meetings, she would say to the villagers: "When an enemy is about to kill you, placing a sword on your neck, would you wrest the sword from him to fight or would you just wait to be killed? ... Peasants would understand that losing one's country is tragic. No one wanted to be a slave in a lost nation." In mobilizing women, she believed that "if you just talk about resisting against Japan but do not deal with their own problems, women could not be mobilized. We should aim at struggling for the nation's liberation and changing social customs and women's oppressed status to that of being equal to men ... We must protect the interests of women and children."

From 1939 onward, Li Guang held positions at the county level, then at the divisional level of the Jin-Cha-Ji Border Regional government, in charge of women and propaganda work. Working as a cadre of the party and government, she won the respect not just of women but also of men, who looked up to her as person of authority.

Working in her local area, Li Guang had not much time for being with her parents. As a Communist cadre, she was busy going to different places for work. On one home visit, "I cried when I was home to see my mum but she supported me." Self-sacrifice was necessary. Her mother died of the plague along with almost a hundred other villagers following the 1942 Japanese mopping-up campaign. When other villagers fled during the 1943 Japanese mopping-up campaign, her father, who had suffered a stroke, had to stay behind. He died soon after the Japanese left. "Many villagers died. So sad. Our house was in ruins, with only the foundations remaining." The family pains were part of the nation's sufferings that made her sacrifice worthwhile for the cause of saving the nation.

Believe in the Party; Believe in Communism

In their late seventies, these elderly Communist war veterans were excited to tell stories of their youth and their courage in overcoming the hardships and cruelty of the war years. With the end of the Cultural Revolution in 1976 and the more relaxed political and social climate in the post-Mao reform era, they were more open about party politics than the New Fourth Army women were in their published reminiscences.

Guo Lian felt strongly about the Mao-era marginalization of the important roles played by the Taihang Base Area: "What to praise and what to promote depended on the Central Committee. This is not fair. The Taihang Base Area made great contributions." It was unfair that some senior leaders in the Taihang did not receive the positions they deserved after 1949. The Rectification Movement also left deep scars on her. The campaign carried out by the Central Committee in 1942–44 targeted the Communist own members and supporters for fear that they were traitors, spies, and secret agents of the Nationalist government. Only after the death of Mao Zedong in 1976, did people in mainland China begin to openly discuss the complexity and the terror of the movement, which had Yan'an as its centre and was carried out in other Communist areas except Shandong. In the Taihang Base Area, the campaign began as a study of documents but escalated into one that falsely accused many cadres as secret agents or spies of the Nationalists.[15] When asked what her worst experience in the war was, Guo Lian paused for over a minute. Finally, she replied:

> Politically, the hardest was in the Rectification Movement. This one was [accused as] a secret agent, and that one a spy ... Many young intellectuals joined the revolution; they were all sincere. They were single-mindedly wishing to devote to the revolution. How did they have those filthy connections? To be honest, I didn't understand what was going on back then. At the time of the Rectification, people were forced to confess. Many committed suicide; many divorced because of this ... It was so tragic.

Tragic because she had to divorce her husband, who was accused of anti-party activities. She remembered: "He said to me back then: 'The party abandoned me, and so did you.'" The sad experience cast a dark shadow. In our interview, she did not tell me about the divorce initially, but revealed it later. The worst experience in the war was not the Japanese crimes, since one expected cruelty from the invaders; it was not the hardships in life she had suffered, since during wartime one expected such things; the worst was when you were not trusted by your comrades. However, this did not shatter her devotion to the party.

In 1944, Mao apologized for the Rectification campaign at several public meetings, admitting that the campaign went out of control and people were wronged.[16] In her written reminiscence, Li Jinzhao remembers that when working in the Chinese Women's University in Yan'an, she was accused of being a secret agent based on the fact that her father was a Nationalist general. However, when she saw Mao making apologies, and

> when he took off his hat and bowed to us ... the invisible walls between the party and us youth crumbled ... Hearing that Chairman Mao called us "comrades," I felt so touched and emotional at being wrongly blamed, as if parents had wronged their children but then held them in their arms to comfort them ... The great leader Chairman Mao personally reversed the verdicts for us. What more can we ask? Just there and then I made up my

mind: I would do whatever the party asked from now on ... to show my absolute loyalty to the party and to the revolution."[17]

Ge Yu, another Communist woman in Yan'an during the war, wrote that when she suffered the tough attacks in the Rectification campaign, she contemplated suicide. In 1944, when Li Fuchun, the general secretary of the Central Women's Committee, where Ge Yu worked, came to apologize, she openly expressed her resentment: "I came all the way from Guangdong to Yan'an to join the revolution around the age of sixteen or seventeen without telling my parents, having to endure all kinds of hardships along the way. I take the party as a strict father and a kind mother." Li responded that the party was neither a strict father nor a kind mother, but a political organization, and one should be ready to undergo any test and investigation by the party at any time. His talk made Ge Yu feel that "right at that moment, I grew up and matured. I understood what a party member should be like, and what the relationships between the party and its members and between comrades should be."[18] Despite having a commonly shared sense of indignation at the party's wrong policy, she also understood that the wrong policies and abuse of power should be differentiated from Communist ideals.

The movement began at different times in different Communist-controlled areas. When the movement began in February 1944 at her New Fourth Army area, Gu Mei was subjected to a screening and examination of her personal history. She admitted: "I had to offer analyses of my history and made up some facts so that I could pass the investigation ... although I did not have any resentment to the party organization." In the Jin-Cha-Ji Border Region, the full-scale of the Rectification Movement began only in 1944 when the wartime situation stabilized.[19] Li Guang was not negatively affected. When she arrived at Yan'an in 1944 to study at the party school, she recalled, "the Rectification Campaign was over. At the first public speech I ever attended by Chairman Mao, he made apologies to the wrongly accused and mistreated in the rescuing movement – the last stage of the Rectification Movement. Chairman Mao took off his hat and bowed on the stage. This was the first time I listened to his speech in person. I was excited." Recognizing the errors in the movement, she concluded: "Chairman Mao was a rare, brilliant leader for his greatness, intelligence, and wisdom." However, the Cultural Revolution "was a total mistake."

Lu Nan was not negatively affected by the Rectification Movement either, but she concluded that it "was a dark shadow of Yan'an." During the campaign, she was assigned to investigate others. She persuaded a young woman suspected of being a Nationalist secret agent to tell the truth rather than succumb to pressure by making a false confession, and she helped her clear her name.

Of the five women, Luo Ying was the most outspoken on party politics. In Yan'an, "I was too liberal (*ziyou zhuyi*)." By "liberal" she meant holding views different from that of the party. Liberalism and criticism of party leaders were two "crimes" in the Rectification Movement.[20] Her Yan'an phase showed her "rebellious" attitude toward the obedience required by the party. In 1943, she was accused of being a member of the Nationalist Party. In her words:

> The radical-leftist wind was irresistible. Every day people confessed. Under heavy compulsion and pressure, even our model doctor made up a story to confess that he was a secret agent. Extortions and forced confessions. Almost no one was good any more ... All went to the Central Auditorium to confess. If you had good behaviour, they would say you were sent by the Nationalists to "catch big fish with a long fishing line"; if you did not behave well, they would say you were sent to engage in sabotage activity. In fact, many of us were just teenagers from occupied areas ... full of patriotic enthusiasm for the resistance cause; most worked hard and had a good education ... they risked their lives to go to Yan'an. They were wronged ... When I was asked to confess how I joined the Nationalist Party, I said: give me your evidence ... Fortunately, this did not last long.

Commenting on herself, Luo Ying said half-jokingly:

> All my life in my dossier [an official record] I had the record of being too liberal, saying whatever I wanted, not willing to put up with the wrong accusations; complained if I was wrongly accused, but gradually I learned to be "smart"; I just shut up. You have sympathy for the common people, but who has sympathy for you? Those above might persecute you! And you suffer ... I tried not to get involved in the mass movements later on.

After 1949, Luo Ying worked most of the time in the medical field. She focused on professional skills because "I believe in humanitarianism; the spirit of healing the wounded and rescuing the dying." Like many, she felt strong resentment against those Communist cadres who abused their power and damaged the party's authority. "But I still have ideals ... Communism is a good ideal."

In the Yan'an Rectification Movement, the most famous target was the so-called Wang Shiwei anti-party group of five, including Wang, Pan Fang (Pan Huitian) and his wife, Zong Zheng (Guo Zhenyi), and Cheng Quan (Chen Chuangang) and his wife, Wang Li (Wang Ruqi). Wang Shiwei was executed by the party in 1947.[21] Historical studies of his clique have not had much to say about the other four. The two women, Guo Zhenyi (1902–76) and Wang Ruqi (1912–90), had graduated from the prestigious Fudan University in Shanghai, both activists in gender equality as essayists in women's journals, and in women's suffrage before they arrived in Yan'an.[22] Guo Zhenyi's book on Chinese women published in 1937 was one of a dozen books on women before 1949. It introduces the studies of women in Europe and in China, and examines the different approaches in the Chinese women's movement.[23] A liberal feminist who became a Communist Party member around 1939, Guo and her husband were senior research staff members at the Yan'an Central Research Institute when they were accused of being members of Wang's anti-party group. They were Wang's colleagues and lived as neighbours in Yan'an.

In the summer of 2021, I had the opportunity to converse with the only child of Guo Zhenyi. Unfortunately, he does not know much about his mother's political career. Born in 1937, he was sent around the age of three to live with his maternal grandmother, who belonged to a wealthy family in Hubei Province, and did not see his parents until 1949. As in many other families, his parents did not talk much about party politics in front of him, since the topic was too complicated. What he knows is that, unlike his father, his mother stubbornly refused to admit her "wrongs" during the Rectification Movement, and again in the early 1950s when the party re-examined the case. For this reason, her party membership was not reinstated. She was not assigned any jobs from then on, unlike her husband and Wang Ruqi and her husband, who held important positions in the PRC. Guo Zhenyi's son recalled: "I clearly remember two pieces of advice Mother gave me. One is: live a simple, frugal life. The other is: 'trust the party, trust the people.'" In her own case, what did she mean by trust? A phrase prevalent in Communist Party's terminology, it could mean many things under various circumstances. No alternatives, no choice, so one had to trust. Or it could mean she believed that one day the party would see that she was not anti-party. Without a job, Guo wrote poems and essays from the early 1950s. Unfortunately, nothing was left. We will never know what she really meant by "trust the party."

In her published works in the post-Mao era, Wei Junyi (1917–2002), a prominent editor and author who held a series of positions in propaganda work, such as chief editor of *China's Youth* and *The People's Literature,* explains what is meant by "trust the party." Born of a wealthy family, she was an activist in the student movement in December 1935 while studying at the prestigious Qinghua University. She joined the Communist Party in May 1936 and went to Yan'an in 1939. During the Rectification Movement, she felt deep doubt, agony, and resentment when her husband was accused of being a secret agent of the Nationalist government, but when Mao made his public apologies "we forgave and forgot all because we believed that we came to Yan'an for revolution, and the revolution was still ongoing. The Central Party committee wronged us but Chairman Mao personally offered apologies. How could we not forgive? We are one family."[24] Her memoir was written as a self-examination of her own ambiguities and conduct. To her, it was also meant to be a record to expose the darkness and absurdities of the party's mass campaigns that followed one after another from 1942, and to ensure that "our party would remember the historical lessons forever so as not to repeat the erroneous road in the past."[25]

NEGOTIATING IDENTITIES AS WOMEN AND COMMUNIST PARTY MEMBERS IN LOVE, MARRIAGE, AND FAMILY

No matter how cruel the war was, love was always present. Romantic love and marriage are themes in Wei Junyi's autobiographical novel, *The Road of Lu Sha.*[26] For the five Communist women I interviewed, Luo Ying's story of her first love was told in tears. During anti-Japanese activities in middle school, she and a schoolmate fell in love. Both were young and idealistic, and love and common belief gave them strength. When she became a party member, he gave her a notebook as a token of his love. They went to Yan'an together. One day, she suffered heat stroke and was hospitalized. He walked over ten miles to see her, and brought her one strawberry he had "stolen" from a farm on the way. "I swallowed it at once." That was the first time she had ever tasted one. The smell, the taste, the love it embodied remained in her body. The young couple married soon after the Japanese surrender in August 1945. Two years later, her twenty-five-year-old husband was killed by the Nationalists in the civil war. Luo Ying remarried sometime later; her new husband was a senior Communist cadre. As an elderly widow, she told me: "I want to write 'Strawberry love,' 'Friends in the sufferings,' one by one as stories ... I just want to write it down to pass on to the next generation." Her first love and her wartime experiences would be part of her legacy.

Li Guang married her husband, a senior Communist cadre, in 1940 in the Hebei Base Area. "Nothing special to say on this. He is the first and the only man I have ever loved," she told me. She was more eager to talk about her revolutionary work, but in her narrative she turned to the topic of love and marriage:

> I read some stories in primary school [by contemporary writers] ... They all have romantic love ... Also, I was interested in traditional literature ... such as *Romance of the Western Chamber* ... I believed that in man-woman relationships, a woman must keep her self-esteem ... read the *Dream of the Red Chamber,* I liked Tanchun, she is a thorny rose. A rose must have thorns ...
>
> Back then, those who joined the revolution, both men and women, were young. Thirty years of age was considered old. Naturally, people showed admiration and pursued love, but women [comrades] all had self-esteem and self-respect, holding on to the traditional value of chastity. Many were like this.

She met her future husband in late 1938: "Thin and tall, light complexion." He held a senior position, was well educated and liked reading, and he was a good singer. Singing revolutionary songs was a popular activity in the base area. Working together for two years, they developed good impressions, especially on his part. One day in 1940, when she was at the county seat for a meeting, the party supervisors announced that this would be their wedding day: "I was taken by surprise, but they said you told us that you had a good impression of him so there!" A simple banquet followed. Among the dishes was a doll made of wheat, a traditional auspicious symbol of childbirth. "I didn't want to get married, let alone childbirth, so I threw it onto the floor!" she laughed. Having been dragged into marriage, she told the tale to show her desire for independence, but she had no regrets, and the wedding was now an amusing story for her to tell.

Two years later she became a mother.

> I had no milk for the baby, and I had malaria with a high fever ... Then came the enemies ... I was carried on a stretcher with my baby. Do not remember how many villages we went through. After the retreat of the enemies, we got to the village where the party committee was. The baby was so starved that he could not even cry.

She decided to leave her baby son in the care of a peasant household since "work was priority." Her second child, a daughter, was born in 1944.

When she was assigned to study in Yan'an, Li Guang could take only the eldest with her, and she had to leave her four-month-old daughter with a peasant family. "I was heartbroken. For the eldest, I was young and was afraid that people would criticize me for being too sentimental about family so when I left him even though I felt sad I did not dare to show any emotions; had to prove I was strong. For leaving this younger one, I could not bear any more. I cried a lot when leaving her." Not until 1946 was her family of four reunited.

Marriage and responsibility for child care were not simply private matters for the Communist women – they directly affected their work outside the home. The responsibility made Gu Mei (from Shanghai) reluctant to marry. Like many others in the war generation, she viewed romantic love as a petty bourgeois, sentimental, and individualistic notion or behaviour. She did not want marriage because it meant childbirth, a hindrance to revolutionary work, and a burden to a revolutionary woman. "I thought I would wait until after we had defeated the Japanese to consider marriage. The war was too cruel [to think of marriage]," and when the party supervisor tried to persuade her into a relationship with a senior cadre in the army, Gu refused: "I had a somewhat 'rebellious' spirit and didn't agree. I thought people must have some feelings for each other before they marry." Later she fell in love with a young man but he died in the civil war. She married a senior cadre around her age in 1948.

Lu Nan (from Henan) married in 1940 in Yan'an. Her husband had been educated in both China and abroad, joined the Communist Party in the early 1920s, and participated in the Long March. He had had a wife and children in his home province in the south before the Long March but had lost contact with them. Now in Yan'an, Long March veterans such as he wished to establish new families. This was not uncommon. At the end of the Long March, when the Communists set up their headquarters at Yan'an, quite a few veteran Communists remarried because they had lost contact with wives who had remained at home or they had become separated from wives who were performing different tasks in the Communist cause. Some men left their less educated or illiterate wives for younger, educated women who came to join the Communist Party at Yan'an.[27] Lu Nan felt both love and care from her husband. Marriage to a senior cadre had no bearing on her own independent Communist career. She did not want to talk much about him, and insisted: "I am myself ... Let's concentrate on my career and my work." The marriage did give her a sense of security. Yan'an gave her a family. A year later, she became a "little mother" at the age of seventeen. She would have four babies (one of whom died at birth) by March 1947. "People had tried to persuade me to leave the child care to peasant families. I could not bear to do so ... I would be with them; live or die, we would be together." Fortunately, with the help of an orderly of her husband's and the daycare facilities in Yan'an, she was able to care for the children while continuing to work as an elementary school teacher.

Guo Lian mentioned that in those days, young women students admired the older revolutionary veterans, looking upon them as war heroes, but one issue was the incompatibility between soldiers of a worker-peasant background and young, educated women. She told a joke that was popular back then: when a military veteran was courting a young urban student who had already been a party member, she invited him to go for a moonlight walk, but he snapped: "What is there to see? A full moon only makes us a target for an enemy's attack!" In another joke, a young woman sent a note to an older veteran, her prospective marriage partner, saying "send you a sweet kiss," with the word "kiss" written in English. When his bodyguard delivered the note, the veteran asked: "She also sent me something sweet. Where is it?" The bodyguard was clueless. The veteran then accused him of stealing something sweet on his way to deliver the note.[28]

Initially, Guo Lian did not want to mention her first marriage, but she changed her mind: "I was young and naive, and wished to have someone to rely on." After leaving her Manchuria home for Beiping, at night school "I listened to my teacher all the time, and I depended on him. He was nice to me." She followed him into the Communist resistance and they got married while working in the Taihang Base Area; as mentioned above, however, the marriage ended in divorce when he was accused during the Rectification Movement of being a Nationalist secret agent. Her second marriage was to a fellow Communist in Taihang, and her first baby was born in 1944. In Chinese tradition, the mother would stay in bed during the first month following the birth, with good nutritious food, but in the challenging economic situation, all she had to eat was cornmeal with tree leaves: "We chopped into pieces the leaves, boiled them and then soaked them in the cold water so the bitterness would be gone. There was a shortage of salt. My unit leader sent me some." The salt made that kind of food taste alright. Like Li Guang, she left her son in the care of a peasant family:

> How did we take care of the babies in those war days? All babies had to be left to the locals ... then be collected back after the Liberation [in 1949] ... To tell you the truth, all we were thinking was making the revolution; everything was to serve the revolution. Children belong to a private matter. Personal sacrifice did not matter.

She got her son back after the war.

Luo Ying had her first child in 1949 and did not have to leave the baby since the situation was better, but she felt a need to explain: "My daughter asked me: why did those Communist women abandon their babies? I responded 'in order to give them a chance to live.'" It was the cruelty of the war that caused the separation of families. Women were forced to reconcile with the reality.

******

From 1949, all five women continued working and all their husbands held senior positions. Like many others, neither they nor their husbands were spared from attacks of varying degrees during the Cultural Revolution, but all survived. By the time they retired, Li Guang had held a senior position in a provincial government and in the All-China Women's Federation. Gu Mei had worked mostly in the court system in Nanjing. Guo Lian had been a senior cadre of personnel in a ministry in Beijing. Lu Nan had been a senior cadre in another ministry in Beijing, and Luo Ying had for the most part continued her medical work in Beijing.

Sitting alone in their living rooms, the five Communist women shared tender memories of their families, especially mothers or, in Guo Lian's case, an elder sister. Nationalist consciousness and an inner desire for gender equality was developed early at school. Once they joined the party, they assumed a multi-faceted identity, as a woman, a Communist, a daughter, wife, and mother. The war and the party provided them with an opportunity to have a public role, offering them both a new identity as a fighter for the nation and the promise of gender equality. Their war experiences were rich in meaning. In their advanced years, reflecting on their wartime experiences, they never forgot the cruelties and sufferings of the war or in party politics, but what they stressed was how they were young and idealistic and worked hard for the nation. What seems strong is the wish to look back with pride on their participation in the great cause of saving the nation, on working for the benefit of the common people.

4
Those Turbulent Years: Memories of Women Associated with the Nationalist Party

At the age of eighty, Professor Emerita Chi Pang-yuan (b. 1924) of the National Taiwan University began writing her memoirs. Since its publication in 2009, it has become a bestseller in Taiwan and gained wide acclaim in mainland China and in the Chinese-speaking world.[1] Her preface to the English edition begins:

> Since I came to Taiwan in 1947, the memories of the twenty-four years of my life lived in war-torn China have haunted me like a second reality. I came of age during a historic time when my country was united to resist the Japanese invasion.
>
> The twentieth century is not too long ago. Gigantic human griefs were buried with it. Its indescribable sufferings have lingered for three generations now. There still are some middle-aged grandchildren looking for the graves or bones of the missing soldiers. After the 1949 national divide, remembrances were mostly smothered; the blood of the martyrs and the tears of the exiled have gradually become untraceable.
>
> All these seventy years I spent my time reading and teaching, trying to push the overbearing nostalgia to the corner of my mind, but my heart rebels. It still bears the invisible scars of war. My soul sometimes still trembles with the fathomless sorrows of a lifelong exile.[2]

Professor Chi's wartime memories are from the perspective of women associated with the Nationalist Party and government. To her, the war caused great suffering and yet, since the memory of the war was suppressed, she has to write. Hers is a story of the cruelties of war and exile from her old home in Manchuria under Japanese aggression to Nanjing, and then to the Nationalist-controlled interior, and from the mainland to Taiwan in the civil war (1946–49). This is not a tribute to the "losers" of politics – the Nationalist Party. Instead, it is a sublimation of individual wills,[3] a tribute to her heroes: her father, who imbued her with a profound idealism; her mother, whose folklores and memories connected her with home in Manchuria; her first love, the young pilot Zhang Dafei of the Chinese air force, who died in the air battle with the Japanese; and the Chinese intellectuals who persisted in education during the war, fully convinced that "with me, China shall not perish."

This chapter is devoted to the war memories of Chi and other women associated with the Nationalists. It is about Nationalist perspectives, based on memories[4] and the life stories collected through interviews and published in the Oral History Series by the Institute of Modern History, Academia Sinica, in Taiwan. More than just war memories, the life stories trace family history, local environment, childhood (usually in an extended family), education, marriage, work experience, all the way to old age, which reveal more how wars affect women.[5] Also discussed are my interviews with Huang Yun (1922–2006) about her life during the war, and a videotaped short reminiscence by Zhang Wei (1915–2002), both of whom remained on the mainland in spite of family connections with the Nationalists.[6]

During the Mao era, the People's Republic of China treated the Nationalist Party and government as deadly rivals. The Nationalists' roles in the War of Resistance were either erased or negatively portrayed. Since the 1990s, the Chinese Communist Party's rejection of any significant role of the Nationalists in the War of Resistance has been reversed. Oral history projects have turned to Nationalist veterans on the mainland, transforming them from enemies to heroes. Women's studies have addressed activities of the Nationalist women, and a few published memoirs by women associated with the Nationalists who remained on the mainland are available for analysis.[7]

The war generation of these Nationalist-associated women belonged to wealthy and privileged or prominent local families. Their fathers worked as government officials, as civil servants, or as professionals, businessmen, and landowners in support of the Nationalist establishment. The women received education at modern schools, ranging from basic literacy and elementary school to university. The Japanese aggressions and the political and military conflicts between the Nationalists and the Communists that dominated the early half of twentieth-century Chinese history deeply affected their personal lives. Those who remained on the mainland suffered persecution under the Communist rule in the Mao era. Those who moved to Taiwan with the Nationalist government, as "mainlanders" on Taiwan, kept deep memories of the war's sufferings of fleeing from the Japanese and the Communists, with a sense of dislocation. Historian Yu Chien-ming notes that many of these women tend to attribute their bitter experience to "fate" – the notion of fate being a coping mechanism.[8] It was fate that caused them to be born and to grow up in a time of chaos. No matter what fate imposed on them, however, these women persevered by offering services to the nation when they could, by continuing on with their education, and by holding on to their families.

Resisting the Japanese and Saving the Nation

The Nationalist government had women in the military from its early stage before the war. The enrollment of women in the Central Academy of Military and Political Studies in Wuhan was a well-known event. One of these women, Xie Bingying (1906–2000), in her autobiography published in 1936, reflected on her path to a military and political career. During the war, she was active in work at the front and as a writer.[9] Faced with Japanese aggression, the women's battalion of Zhejiang formed under the local Nationalist leadership in May 1938. Its more than two hundred members fought against the Japanese behind enemy lines.[10] More famous was the women students army in Guangxi. From the early 1930s, the Guangxi military leaders, who demanded resistance against Japan, implemented policies to strengthen self-defence, self-governance, and self-sufficiency.[11] From 1933, Guangxi established a military training program for senior high school students, both male and female, in public schools. The training extended to lower middle school students starting in the latter half of 1934. Women aged sixteen to forty-five who had no schooling would receive literacy education and military training as well. After the war broke out, the Guangxi women students army was formed.[12] Aged twenty to twenty-five, they were expected to be "double fighters" against the external Japanese aggressors and against domestic gendered oppression.[13] Starting on foot from Guangxi in December 1937 and arriving at Wuhan in early January the following year, carrying their own bedding and equipment on their backs, these young women conducted propaganda work through public rallies and street drama performances on the way. Their images had a powerful effect, shaming soldiers into more action and inspiring common men and women to contribute to national salvation.[14] Under General Li Zongren (1890–1969), the women students army would go to the battlefield to rescue the wounded and take up weapons when called upon.[15] Li's wife, Guo Dejie (1906–66), was an enthusiastic supporter of the army. In a speech to these young women, she insisted that women could be more effective in mobilization among the populace. She urged them "to claim a place for women in the history of national salvation as well as to write a chapter in the history of the world's women's movement with own sweat and blood."[16]

Jiang Zhonglin, at the age of eighty-nine, in her home in Guilin, Guangxi, recalled that she and her younger sister, aged nineteen and sixteen, respectively, joined the students army of Guangxi in October 1937. As they left Guilin on December 14 that year, their mother said to them: "Come back alive. Mom will be waiting for you at home." The two sisters faced life-or-death situations from the Japanese air raids, at the battle front, and through the enemy siege. Jiang Zhonglin was proud that the students army was "tough as iron."[17]

Women joined the Nationalist expeditionary army to Burma in the early 1940s as secretaries, office staff, nurses, and interpreters.[18] In November 1944, in the campaign of "a hundred thousand youths as a hundred thousand soldiers," 5,714 students in Sichuan Province applied. In April 1945, a female student army of 1,200 was established. Although they did not go to the battlefield because the war ended in August, the enlistment was inspiring.[19] It also indicated a change in the Nationalist government's policy on the exemption of students and women from the army.[20]

At the age of fourteen, Cao Jingyi (b. 1926 in Linyi, Shandong) joined a local guerilla group against the Japanese invaders.[21] Guerilla forces organized spontaneously by locals were common soon after 1937. Most would join either the Nationalists or the Communists. In his *Red Sorghum* series, Mo Yan (b. 1955), the Nobel laureate for literature in 2012, tells a story of how one such guerilla group, whose members included women, established a power base in Shandong while intending to exercise independence from both political parties.[22] Cao Jingyi's guerilla force soon turned to the Nationalist military. She described those days with emotion, in language popularly used in talking about the military life in wartime:

> In my home area there was a group of patriots who refused to be "traitors to the Han Chinese [*hanjian*]" or slaves in a lost nation. Led by the local Mr. Wang Hongjiu, they raised the flag of resisting Japan and saving the

nation, and called upon others to form a guerrilla. My father, older brothers, and relatives all answered the call and joined one after another.

Under the circumstances of the time, and also of my own will, I joined the guerilla in June 1940 following my father and brothers. From then on, forests and streams were our camping grounds. Bread of coarse grain was our daily feast. In battles mixed with sounds of guns and bullets, we sang songs to inspire soldiers. In other times, we gave enthusiastic and sincere public speeches to the common people, awakening them from confusion and making them understand: "The rise and fall of all-under-heaven is the responsibility of everyone."[23]

The politics of her home county of Linyi was complicated, with the Japanese, the Nationalists, and the Communists contending against each other. Her first battle was with the Communist army in June 1940. Both sides suffered losses. As with the Communist women, the war memories of Cao and other Nationalist-associated women could not avoid the topic of the conflicts between the two parties even under the United Front. On days of relative stability during the war, Cao and other youth attended a school operated by the guerrilla force. On January 12, 1942, a Japanese army of 3,000 attacked with cannons and tanks. The Nationalist soldiers escaped, but Cao and other students were captured by the Japanese and taken to the city of Linyi: "Soon after entering the city gate, we, united as one, began to sing anti-Japanese songs with passion and enthusiasm. The onlookers of local residents all cheered for us."[24] After two months in prison, they were released on bail, and Cao continued her anti-Japanese activities.

Wang Ke (b. 1925 in Dongtai, Jiangsu) also lived in a strategically complex region contested by the Japanese and their collaborators, the Nationalists, and the Communists. Not yet sixteen years of age, Wang joined the Nationalist-run training program and then worked as a clerk in the military.[25] Her first battle was with the Communist New Fourth Army at Huangqiao, Jiangsu, from late September to early October 1940, because "these communists tried to expand control."[26] The second life-or-death encounter was with the Japanese. In the autumn of 1941, her Nationalist army unit was surrounded by Japanese gunboats and forced to retreat: "The Japanese implemented terrorism by bombing and burning villages in order to terrify the Chinese into submission to the Japanese supreme ruler and bowing to them. I felt so sad to see all this. Sad also because as a soldier I could not save the common people."[27] In another attack by the Japanese in February 1943, her boyfriend, a Nationalist army officer, was killed. Wang Ke was so enraged that she wanted to assassinate the Japanese and had to be dissuaded by her comrades. The desire for revenge spurred her to be active until the end of the War of Resistance.

As a woman in the military, Wang Ke was outspoken about the negative treatment the Nationalist women experienced:

> Living under the guns, one could die at any time. People had the mentality of living for the day ... Women soldiers would easily be misled if they met bad officers or bad men. Many of them were forced, seduced, or tricked into this. Officers used women soldiers as tools for releasing tensions. Some married them, who were then called "resistance war wives" [*kangzhan furen*, a term referring to those women who married men who had wives at home]. These women got into this involuntarily and then were accused of going into the army in order to snatch others' husbands. This is not fair to them ... In fact, women soldiers were as patriotic, hard-working, and courageous as men. Being in the military where men are dominant, they are easily neglected, and even seen as just a decoration.[28]

Many served in the auxiliary realm. Zhou Meiyu (1910–2001) worked in the military medical field during the war. It was part of her job to care for those on the battlefields and those who were sacrificing their lives for the country.[29] She never married, and nursing became her life's mission.[30] Her memoirs offer few details about her own life but devote many pages to the evolution of China's nursing in the twentieth century. Born and raised in Beiping, Zhou received her education in nursing at the Rockefeller-sponsored Peking Union Medical College (PUMC), the top medical school in China, and went to the United States on a Rockefeller scholarship, receiving a BA degree from the Massachusetts Institute of Technology in 1933. In 1938, she declined an invitation to become the first Chinese dean of the nursing program at PUMC, and instead joined the Medical Relief Corps (MRC) under the Chinese Red Cross (an agency of the Nationalist government).[31] The military front needed nurses, and "I wanted to contribute to the nation."[32] The MRC attracted many patriotic professionals and hundreds of medical students in China and abroad. It also attracted unmarried female students to join the mobile medical aid teams. Zhou noted that "among those volunteers were many young women. It is not that young men did not want to volunteer, they had families which they could not neglect. In wartime, singles have no attachment, and are relatively free to move."[33]

During the war, Zhou served as director of the nursing department in the Emergency Medical Service Training School (Zhanshi weisheng renyuan xunliansuo) under the Nationalist government. Moving with the school from Changsha to Guangxi and then to Nationalist-controlled areas in Guizhou, she taught and made regular inspection tours of the military hospitals, offering on-the-spot training. She remembered that in one of her inspections in Guangxi, she saw that the sick had to be put on the floor with only a thin layer of rice straw underneath them. More than a hundred died each day due to dysentery and typhoid fever; many lay in their own excrement. So she trained the staff about triage, sanitation, nutrition, and nursing, which helped reduce the number of deaths.[34] It was through such training that she and others developed and improved the Nationalist army medical system and trained over 400,000 medical staff.[35] She played an important part in transforming Chinese nursing from mostly "a form of Christian and professional service administered by foreigners into a patriotic, nationalized service administered by highly qualified Chinese nurses."[36]

Gender equality does not seem to be a specific topic in her accounts of her wartime experience. Although she was on the guest list of Song Meiling's May 1938 Lushan conference on mobilization of Chinese women for the war effort,[37] Zhou made no mention of this in her reminiscences. It is not clear why. Her independent, professional life path showed a woman striving for equality by doing what she could to improve women's status. Her memoirs indicate that her mother was her first and foremost role model. Her mother's moral traits were not the traditional ones that Chinese women were valued for, such as filial duty toward the in-laws, chastity, and silent service to the family, but were gender-neutral: "Mother was a great woman. Although she had only a primary school education, she loved reading. She possessed a strong sense of the nation, was rational, strong, with extraordinary courage; had faith in Buddhism, and never complained about any sufferings."[38] Western women missionaries in China were also exemplars for Zhou Meiyu. She remembered fondly how they inspired her with the ideals of compassion and humanitarian dedication. She did not convert to Christianity until much later, after moving to Taiwan, but from her early days at missionary schools, she believed in Christian ideals of compassion and service to society.

In her wartime life of non-combat military service, Guo Wencui (b. 1921) gained a strong sense of fulfillment and pride. In 1937, while an upper middle school student at the Kaifeng All-Girls Middle School in Henan Province, she enrolled in the Nationalist-run wartime training corps, which offered six programs: political work, mass organization, accountancy, service at the front, intelligence, and medical rescue. She chose political work. Next, she enrolled in the military school for army officer training at Chengdu for a year and a half. Her first assignment after graduation was working among the Yi ethnic people from late 1939 to 1941 on the construction of the Leshan-to-Xichang road in Sichuan, in the high mountains and difficult terrain. The road would connect Sichuan to the Yunnan-Burma highway, the transportation lifeline between the wartime Nationalist government in Chongqing and the Allied Forces. The Yi people were an important source of guides and construction labourers.[39] Guo's work team consisted of over a dozen army school graduates, six of them being women because "it would be easier for women to win the trust of the Yi people" and women were thought to be "a non-aggressive gender." Guo and her colleagues learned to speak the Yi language, made friends with the children and their mothers, and gave public speeches on the importance of unity between the Han and Yi peoples. A school was founded to teach Chinese to the Yi children. In the evenings, after a day of hard work at the construction sites, Guo and her comrades would drink, sing, and dance with the Yi around campfires. In these years, she felt, "life was hard, but it was interesting and fun."[40]

"In resistance, there is no difference between men and women and between the old and young," wrote Yang Huimin (1915–92) in her memoir of the war.[41] In the summer of 1937, at the age of twenty-two, she joined the Shanghai Girl Scouts. On October 26, the Nationalist army was forced to retreat after over seventy days of intense battles fought street by street with the loss of tens of thousands of soldiers. Shanghai was occupied by the Japanese. The 524 Regiment of the 88th Division was ordered to remain in the Sihang Warehouse to cover the withdrawal. The lone army of about 400, whose number was exaggerated as 800 in order to confuse and pose a threat to the enemy, was determined to defend their position to the last. They received enthusiastic moral and material support from the people of Shanghai. At the risk of being killed by the Japanese, Yang Huimin delivered a national flag of the Republic of China to the soldiers. Reaching the warehouse,

> I took off the outer jacket and placed the national flag soaked with my sweat in front of them. These nation-defending heroes were moved to tears ...
>
> In the morning light, about ten to twenty scattered on the rooftop all raised hands in earnest salute to the national flag. No music, no ceremony but the sacred, sombre atmosphere at that simple but solemn space was deeply touching. I will never forget it for the rest of my life.[42]

Reuters in Shanghai reported to the world the heroic deeds of "the 800" and Yang Huimin, the Chinese Girl Scout, who became national heroes. Yang appeared in the news and magazines as a national image of resistance. Her photograph, in uniform with the national flag, represented the heroic Battle of Shanghai.[43] On October 31, the Chinese soldiers moved into the foreign concession with the intervention of the British, and remained as prisoners. After the Japanese placed a bounty on her head of 10,000 silver yuan, Yang fled Shanghai for the Nationalist interior to continue working for the resistance. She received honours from Chiang Kai-shek and his wife, Madam Song Meiling. In August 1938, she represented China at the World Youth Peace Conference in the United States, made public speeches, and raised funds. She met President and Mrs. Roosevelt. In her travels to Europe and India, she also met Hitler as well as Gandhi.[44]

Movies have been made featuring the 800 and Yang Huimin,[45] in Hong Kong in 1938, in Taiwan in 1975,[46] and on the mainland in 2020.[47] The 800 heroes and Yang became a legend. There are different versions and conflicting accounts of the event. In one of Yang's own writings published in 1938, she delivered the flag on the afternoon of October 27, and the flag was raised that same day.[48] In her memoirs, the delivery took place during the night, with no specific date. According to *Li bao,* a newspaper published in Shanghai, she delivered the flag on the evening of October 28 and the flag was raised on the morning of October 29.[49] A few studies have discussed the confusion and recognized the political necessity for propaganda at the time to boost the image of Yang and the 800 in order to galvanize the people to resist the Japanese.[50] The fact remains that Yang Huimin presented the national flag at the risk of her life. Her act played an important ritualistic role to demonstrate to the world that behind this young woman and the lone army stood the people of Shanghai, millions of Chinese, and the nation.

The war took a disastrous turn for Yang, however. In September 1942, she was imprisoned by the same Nationalist government that had honoured her only a few years earlier, on the charge of colluding with the enemy.[51] In January 1946, she was acquitted by the Ministry of Defence.[52] After years of silence in Taiwan, she published her memoir to commemorate the lone army of 800 and to tell the truth as she saw it.[53]

Unlike the abovementioned women, Zhu Su'e (b. 1901), who joined the Nationalist Party in 1928, chose to remain on the mainland because of her disillusionment with the Nationalists by 1949.[54] Her oral narrative clearly demonstrates her feminist consciousness, reflected in such phrases as "equality between men and women," "promoting women's rights," "women are human beings," "self-reliance," "feudal oppression should be overthrown," and "to liberate women." Zhu was one of the early generation of women lawyers in China. She joined the Nationalist Party while at college because she held that the Nationalists overthrew the last imperial dynasty and was a ruling party. Married at the age of thirty (late for conventional Chinese women of the time), she worked hard at her profession, handling mainly cases involving women in property disputes. During the war, she stayed in Shanghai, running the magazine *Chinese Women* (*Zhongguo funü*) in 1938–41, and working in the Nationalist government-led salvation movement, training front-line rescue staff, helping refugees, and conducting fundraising, charity, and volunteer activities. "Originally, I wanted to pursue *nüquan* [women's rights] for myself. Then the nation faced crisis, and I became involved with the national salvation. But later the two could not be separated. *Nüquan* and patriotic national salvation merged into one movement."[55]

"The Country Destroyed; the Family Shattered"

"The country destroyed; the family shattered" (*guopo jiawang*), a phrase used by Chi Pang-yuan in her memoir, reflected a deeply shared feeling of many Chinese about wartime China.[56] The horrific war caused human grief and suffering to all, although in different ways and to varying degrees. The disrupted order, the death of loved ones, the loss of ancient homes, the separation of families, the social dislocations, the Japanese air raids, and hardships in daily life left painful psychological scars in the memories of Nationalist-associated women. The war shattered their privileged, sheltered life.

In tears, Zhang Yuqin (b. 1928) recalled the horror of her grandmother's disappearance in the Nanjing Massacre committed by the Japanese Imperial Army in late 1937 to early 1938. Before the Japanese captured the city, her parents fled in search of safety, but her grandparents refused to leave. Many elderly Chinese did likewise – they had no idea how cruelly the conquerors would behave. When the situation stabilized, Zhang returned to the city with her father:

> I could hardly believe what I saw. Dead bodies were everywhere, it was unbearable to look. Grandpa and grandma had been separated in chaos. Grandpa had been almost killed and grandma had disappeared. For days

grandpa and I were searching for her body among the corpses, often picking up skulls with hair ... I was not in fear but full of sadness and anguish. My poor grandma vanished from this world, never to be seen again."⁵⁷

During the war years, Pei-Wang Zhihong (b. 1928) lived in occupied Beiping with her family, who were of Manchu ethnicity. Aged nine in 1937, she recalled that upon occupying Beiping, "the Japanese were seeking young women everywhere, in every household. Neighbouring girls of seventeen or eighteen years of age all shaved their heads like men for fear of being caught ... The Chinese were so enraged that they killed some [Japanese]."⁵⁸ During the Japanese occupation, there was compulsory learning of the Japanese language at school. Food was rationed, with potatoes and cakes of soybean dregs. Due to her father's ill health, the family business was on the decline. At the age of sixteen, Zhihong had to work at low-paying jobs to help the family.⁵⁹

Li Zhen (b. 1933) was from a prominent family. Her father, Li Hanhun (1895–87) was a Nationalist general and the governor of Guangdong Province from 1938 to 1945; her mother, Wu Jufang (1911–99), was in charge of assisting war refugees and children in the province. Still a small child during the war, Li Zhen learned about death, loneliness, worries, and sense of duty. Whenever the Japanese bombed the city, Li Zhen was "always worried about my mother and father because most of the time they were at meetings away from home ... Many bombs were dropped in Shaoguan, killing people and setting the city on fire."⁶⁰ Through her visits with her mother to the refugee children's centres and schools, she grew up quickly: "I knew I was a very privileged person. These visits undoubtedly taught me something about duty and service, watching the dedication with which my mother went about her tasks."⁶¹

He Junnan (b. 1920 in Anhui) summarized her life as "fleeing from bandits as a child, fleeing from the Japanese growing up and then fleeing from the Communists."⁶² The war in 1937–45 led to an estimated ninety-five million refugees. Refugee problems occurred in twenty-one provinces, involving wealthy middle-class families as well as the urban and rural poor.⁶³ The psychological impact was profound.⁶⁴ Zhu Juyi (b. 1924) noted: "Our generation had a hard life. In youth, we encountered the War of Resistance followed by the war with the Communists. We had to be on run and had no regular education."⁶⁵ In the summer of 1937, when Zhu was just about to begin her first year in a missionary middle school in Wuchang, the Japanese began bombing the city. The family was split. Two brothers went to Chongqing under the Nationalists to continue school. Zhu's mother took her and a little brother to Hong Kong for safety. Her father, the manager of the Central Bank, stayed behind. In 1938, when her mother took them back to Shanghai by ship, she suffered a heart attack and died on the ship with only the fourteen-year-old Juyi and her brother at her bedside. In her calm and controlled tone, Zhu recalled that her mother was well educated, was married at the age of twenty, and gave birth to seven babies, three of whom died in infancy. She lived only till thirty-eight. Underneath Zhu's tone were buried sorrows and scars. The fleeing continued. After a few years in Shanghai, Zhu and her little brother went on the road again, passing through the Japanese blockades to unoccupied Jiangxi for school, and then to Fujian to join their father. In 1948, as a teacher in the kindergarten of the Nationalist air force, she moved to Taiwan.[66]

The exodus to China's southwestern interior involved long travel on land and rivers, and millions of Chinese. After the war broke out, the Nationalist government fled Nanjing to Hankou, Hubei, in October, and then established China's wartime capital in Chongqing. Military and civil offices of the central government, universities, schools, and factories went with the government. This move was presented as "a defiant retreat" by the Nationalist government, even though there were no specific plans for evacuation of the wider population, transportation was lacking, the roads were hard, and Japanese aggression and occupation in eastern and central China created dangerous obstacles.[67] To many, the flight meant cutting off the roots of ancient homes and a treacherous journey. It also signified their refusal to live under Japanese occupation.

Wu Weijing (b. 1931) remembered the move as a constant flight from Japanese bombing. Anticipating the coming of the Japanese, the family left Nanjing for Wuhan, where her father found a job with the Legal Committee under the Nationalist government but then had to leave for Changsha, and then Chongqing. On the way, "the enemy planes followed us wherever we went." Once they were in Chongqing, Japanese air raids became a regular part of life.[68]

Huang Yun (1922–2006) was the only woman associated with the Nationalists whom I interviewed on mainland China. In her early eighties and with her memory failing, she was not very articulate and was often confused about details. However, she was prepared with a short outline on a small piece of paper under the general title "Do not forget history," with six clear subtitles: 1) the loss of grandma; 2) fled to the foreign concession of Shanghai; 3) fled to Chongqing; 4) the Japanese bombing of Chongqing; 5) senior high school, taking flashlight to the shelter to study;

and 6) enrolled in the Northeast University in 1940. Huang Yun's grandmother died in the Japanese invasion of her hometown, Baoshan, located near the mouth of the Huangpu River near Shanghai. Her father was a writer and owned a bookstore in Shanghai. Her mother died of cholera when Yun was about five years old, so she lived in the care of her grandmother. Her father remarried. In August 1937, Baoshan suffered heavy bombing. Huang Yun's father took the whole family to safety in the crowded British-American concession, but her grandmother refused to leave her old home in Baoshan, thinking the bombing would be over soon.

> My dad and older and younger brothers and I fled during the mixed gunshots at midnight. Bullets flew beside my ears. Could see nothing in the dark.
> Later my elder brother went back home with others in a vehicle of the Red Cross to look for grandma, no one there ... Went to grandma's sister's home but found no one.

Grandma and her sister both perished. "Heartbroken. Grandma brought us up." The family had to move. "Shanghai was no longer safe. We wanted to go to Chongqing. So worried. Then we got to Hankou. Stayed there for over a month, and to Chongqing by boat." In the Nationalist-controlled interior in Sichuan, her father found a job with China Airlines. Huang Yun, like many refugee students, continued her education in a national middle school. However, Chongqing was no safe haven. The Japanese dropped 20,000 bombs from February 1938 to August 1943. The bombing did not stop until December 1944. The most terrible incident occurred on May 4, 1939, when 4,400 people were killed and 3,100 were injured.[69] Huang Yun recalled: "Back then, siren alerts for enemy air raids were often, twice a week. We had to walk a half kilometre to the shelter. Often, we would take flashlights with us to continue our schoolwork in the shelter." Persisting in her schoolwork under the Japanese air raids was a memory dear to her. The danger from the raids was ever-present:

> One day, a classmate came to me and said let's not go to the shelter, not run. We hid under the desks ... When the school supervisor saw us, she rushed us out ... About ten minutes later ... a bomb was dropped just six or seven metres away from us. A deafening sound. Fortunately, we were not killed.

She laughed when she told this story. So many years had passed, and the moment of danger would now have meant a triumph over death.

Unlike many others, Zhang-Wang Mingxin (b. 1918) did not think that the war caused much hardship to her wealthy family, with land and a hardware store in Wuhan, Hubei Province, but the family had been robbed:

> Come to think of it, perhaps because my family's financial situation was not too bad, and because I never cared much about political parties or factional issues, even though we had to flee, our flight was alright. Whenever there came disturbing news, we would rent a boat and leave. So, except that one time of leaving Hengyang, when the family suffered [from a robbery], I didn't know much about the battles, did not suffer, did not see a single Japanese soldier.[70]

Although fleeing did not seem so hard to Mingxin, once she was settled in Sichuan and married to a man who worked in a college while she worked as a clerk in a women's middle school, the couple had to deal with the constant Japanese bombing. Usually, several tens of families would put money together to build a shelter. The school shelter was built with money from the students. During the air raids, "teachers would bring the textbooks with them and would continue class in the shelter. It is as if teachers must take students into the shelter while fleeing for their own lives. If death comes, they would die together."[71]

In her memoirs, Chi Pang-yuan used the title "A Journey of Blood and Tears" (*xuelei liuli*) for the eight years of the War of Resistance.[72] While fleeing from Nanjing to Sichuan, Chi's eighteen-month-old sister died of an illness. In Chongqing, where her father worked in the central government, regular air raids were part of daily life. During one raid, their house had half its roof blown off:

> That night, a torrential rain fell, and our entire family, half sitting and half reclining, squeezed into the half of the house where the roof remained. My mother was sick and had to lie in her own bed, over which was spread a large oilcloth to keep the rain off. My father sat at the head of the bed, holding an oilpaper umbrella in one hand to cover his head and my mother's, waiting for day to break.[73]

The cruelty of the war accompanied Chi Pang-yuan also through the life of her friend Zhang Dafei (1918–45). Zhang's father, a police chief in Shenyang, had been burned to death by the Japanese for his anti-Japanese activities. In late 1937, Zhang became a pilot with China's air force. As a family friend, his visits to Chi's family and his more than a hundred letters to Chi brought the war closer to her. Chi recalled one of his "letters from the clouds":

> He told me that two days previously he had taken to the skies to track the enemy when suddenly, through a break in the clouds ahead, he saw a plane on which was emblazoned the rising sun! He clearly saw the face of the pilot in the cockpit, a face filled with fear. He didn't have time to think – all he knew was that if he didn't shoot first, it would be all over for him. Since returning, he couldn't forget the face of the pilot he had shot down.[74]

Zhang, a Christian since 1932, wrote to her in another letter:

> How will God judge me for being a devout Christian while having spent years killing? ... But the Japanese not only struck my cheek, they also killed my father and exterminated my family and to this day have not left off killing the people of my country in their own land. Every time I shoot down one of their planes, I could save many people from dying under Japanese bombing.[75]

Romantic feelings developed between them, but as a pilot who could be killed at any time, Zhang did not think he was able to truly love her. He was killed in an air battle with the Japanese on May 18, 1945, at the age of twenty-seven, just three months before the Japanese surrender.[76]

Wartime sufferings and especially the Japanese bombing caused mental anxiety, fear, and horrific trauma to all.[77] The Japanese bombing is also a common theme in the oral narratives of the poor, working-class women who lived in Chongqing. It did have discriminatory effects. In contrast to the Nationalist-associated women of the middle or upper class, the poor, due to lack of resources, were more vulnerable.[78] They remembered more of the social inequality. Many did not know about the bombing initially.[79] Unlike the privileged, they had no money to build private shelters. During air raids, even though cooking was impossible, the wealthy could bring prepared food into their shelters, but for the poor, hiding in crowded air raid shelters with crying babies simply meant hunger and thirst.[80]

XIANGE BUCHUO: EDUCATION MUST CONTINUE WITH NO INTERRUPTION

From the start, the Japanese targeted China's institutions of higher education, which were a major centre of anti-Japanese ideas and of Chinese culture. Soon after entering the city of Beiping in late July, they occupied university campuses. In Tianjin, the government buildings, communication centres, and Nankai University were their targets.[81] Many Chinese students rejected the idea of "saving the country by book learning" (*dushu jiuguo*) and chose to participate in organized resistance. However, even while giving top priority to national salvation, both the Nationalists and the Communists still considered education crucial for wartime training and for the long-term goal of building a new nation. In the areas they controlled, the Communists operated literacy classes, night schools, and regular schools, all with the effect of transforming social life.[82] To train cadres, the party established schools in Yan'an, such as the Central Party School, the Anti-Japanese Military and Political University, the Chinese Women's University, and Lu Xun Art College.

Meanwhile, the Nationalist government established various programs to train war staff. By the end of 1940, more than 41,000 educated women had received cadre training to help in the war effort and in woman-focused work.[83] The government kept China's educational system going, and maintained that China had enough manpower so college and middle school students were not expected to serve in the military.[84] On what should be the priority in wartime education in late 1937, the more radical-minded wished to transform the peacetime curriculum to serve national defence, whereas the Nationalist Ministry of Education and educators at large rejected major changes, adding only political indoctrination and Resistance to the curriculum.[85]

China's higher education continued. In August 1937, the Ministry of Education combined the National Beijing University (the centre of China's cultural renaissance), the National Qinghua University in Beiping (China's leading institution for science and technology), and Nankai University in Tianjin (China's most outstanding private university) into one university and relocated it into the interior. The university was formally named the National Southwest Associated University, or "Xi'nan Lianda" for short in Chinese. Setting up a campus in Changsha initially, driven out by Japanese bombs, and finally settling in Kunming, Yunnan Province, deep in the south in April 1938, Lianda took on the mission of preserving the national heritage as the Japanese threatened to destroy Chinese culture. The best university in China, it played important roles in China's intellectual, cultural, and political history.[86] Other universities relocated as well. By early 1941, 77 of the 114 prewar colleges and universities had moved into the Nationalist-controlled interior.[87]

China's middle schools also continued operation. The Nationalist government relocated 500,000 refugee students from middle schools, both men and women, to safety from the occupied areas. In the non-occupied areas of China, the number of middle schools grew from 3,200 on the eve of the war to 4,500 in 1945. Education advanced at all levels even as the Ministry of Education exerted stronger control over the curriculum and the indoctrination of patriotism, moral values, and especially Sun Yat-sen's Three Principles of the People – the political ideology of nationalism, democracy, and livelihood.[88]

The determination to continue education during the war is a major theme in Chi Pang-yuan's memoir, often expressed in the phrase *xiange buchuo*, rendered in her book's English version as "schooling must go on without interruption." Yet these four Chinese characters embody much more poetic and richer meanings than contained in the English phrase. Tracing its deep origin to Confucius, the phrase invokes the story of Confucius, who, even when surrounded by hostile people, continued playing his lute and singing nonstop, a symbolic gesture for remaining calm as a scholar, for he believed that "to see the bare blades clashing before him and to look upon death as though it were life – this is the courage of the man of ardor. To understand that hardship is a matter of fate, that success is a matter of the time, and to face great difficulty without fear – this is the courage of the sage."[89] And the courage of a scholar, according to Confucius, was to continue education even in great distress. *Xiange buchuo* represented the conviction that China would not perish if its culture was not lost. Chi Pang-yuan's memoir provides powerful testimony of this. In December 1937, when her father evacuated with the government from Nanjing, she and her mother and siblings fled from Nanjing to Sichuan with students of the National Northeast Zhongshan Middle School, which her father had established in 1934 with the financial support of the government. On the road, life was "filled with untold hardships, but whenever possible the teachers would hold class. The school carried enough textbooks in all subjects, lab instruments, and basic school equipment."[90]

Settled in Sichuan, Chi went to the Nankai Middle School, founded in Tianjin in 1904 by Zhang Boling (1876–1951), a reformer and also the founder of Nankai University, and then relocated to Chongqing. For her, the six years there were full of high-quality academic learning as well as the patriotic spirit embodied by Zhang Boling's words: "With me, China shall not perish."[91] The Nankai teachers assumed a mission of stimulating students' creativity and cultivating the spirit of internationalism through English-language learning and world cultural geography. Among various extracurricular activities, Chi joined the student debating club. In September 1941, one topic she participated in was "Will America enter the war?" She was on the pro side and won. Three months later, the Japanese attacked Pearl Harbor and the United States declared war on Japan.

Her university days began in the fall of 1943, and she majored in English literature from the second year onward at Wuhan University, which had relocated to Leshan, Sichuan. A first-rate Chinese university, it had transported more books to the interior than any other university. The main library was in the local Confucian temple – a hall to honour China's foremost educator continued to serve its function during the war. Chi immersed herself in English literature. The war raging around her made all the more keen her contemplation of all the human emotions in life and death. She was not disconnected from politics. Her correspondence with Zhang Dafei reminded her daily that people were fighting and dying. She held fast to the conviction that education, too, could be a way to save the nation.

"Whether a woman had education or not would determine how much her contribution would be to her family and to her country," Zhang Wei (1915–2001), who graduated from the famous Lianda, stated in her reminiscences. University education was her path to independence. In 1990, at the age of seventy-five, Zhang made a video recording for her children. Thanks to her son, I obtained a copy as well as some details of her life. Her two-hour oral reminiscence covers only two topics: education and marriage. A large part centres on her striving for education. Zhang was from Baoshan County, near Shanghai. Her father managed the family land and ran a small shop. Her mother, with bound feet and no education, took care of the family. After three years of traditional education in the Confucian classics, her father wanted her to quit: "This came like a thunder strike. I wept daily. Every day when he was back home from work, I would beg him to send me to school. He agreed but only because he wanted me to accompany my younger brother there." Education continued in the local school but her father did not want her to go on to middle school. She did not give up: "Often I carried my baby sister on my back and stood outside the classroom to listen to the teaching. Bit by bit, I could follow but whenever my little sister started crying, I had to leave." Zhang Wei's major source of support was her mother, who encouraged her: "It would be best if you could be [financially] independent, unlike me, living a pathetic life because I didn't make money." By borrowing money, Zhang Wei finished teacher training school. She found a teaching position at a kindergarten and then an elementary school. This was not enough for her. In 1936, she passed the entrance exam and enrolled in the Shanghai College of Commerce. A year later, the Japanese bombing of Shanghai in August destroyed the campus.

By this time, Zhang had gotten to know a young man, a teacher in the National School of Fine Arts, through the introduction of her middle school principal. Not long after the two met, he proposed, but she turned him down because "marriage is not the only way to gain happiness ... I was not interested in marriage, and said no. Look at my mom, she became a slave after marriage. The most important thing for anyone is financial independence." He did not give up. After relocating to Kunming with his school, he wrote to ask her to come to Kunming and continue university there. In 1938, Zhang Wei took a long shipboard journey alone from Shanghai to Hanoi, Vietnam, and arrived in Kunming by train. Her son later liked to say that it was romantic love that made her take the journey, but she insisted that it was her determination to continue her higher education. Her hopes were fulfilled. She enrolled in Lianda and majored in education. She did marry the art teacher in August 1939 while continuing her studies, because, she said, he would never give up. He often visited her at her student dorm: "So sweet. Whenever he came, he would bring braised pork or something ... My dorm mates all told me how wonderful he was ... So I married." A year later, their first baby was born: "The Japanese bombing was horrible. Several alerts for air raids a day ... One day I was alone in the house, the roof collapsed under the bombing ... I was holding my baby hiding under the wooden bed. All covered with dust when we came out." Wei worked at several jobs after the university, although her husband had a position in the Ministry of Propaganda. One was running a small workshop making children's clothes. In 1949, she and her husband decided not to flee to Taiwan with the Nationalists as they felt the Communist Party was more democratic. In 1951 in Shanghai, however, Wei's husband was imprisoned and sent by the Communist government to labour camp for over five years for his "crimes of working for the counterrevolutionary government." Wei taught at a middle school. She and her husband survived the devastating Cultural Revolution. Her story ends with a sense of pride stemming from her devotion to her four children and to all her students: "People have had different life paths. I deeply believe that we must strive." Had she not, life would have been a waste, she believed.

In the oral history collections *20th Century Wartime Experiences of Chinese Women* (*Fenghuo suiyue xia de Zhongguo funü fangwen jilu*) and

The Reminiscences of Women's Corps (*Nü qingnian dadui fangwen jilu*), most women recalled how they continued their education during wartime in spite of frequent disruptions. Yu Guofang (b. 1932 in Anhui) remembered that because the family had to constantly flee from the Japanese, she went to over twenty elementary schools before she had graduated. The hardships made her grow up and "cultivated in me a decisive personality in my adulthood, and a sense of independence and self-responsibility."[92]

In provinces partly occupied by the Japanese, local educators continued school by moving to non-occupied areas within the provinces. In Zhejiang, for example, many schools held "guerrilla" education in temporary classrooms in temples and lineage halls, constantly evading the Japanese. At night, students did homework under an oil lamp on poor-quality paper.[93] Shao Menglan (1910–2000) worked as an educator under these circumstances throughout the war years.[94] Of a wealthy and scholarly family in Zhejiang, and with a political science degree from the prestigious Fudan University in Shanghai, she firmly believed that women should not just be daughters, wives, or mothers but should be independent human beings equal to men. During the war years, her husband relocated with his Tongji University to Nationalist-controlled Yunnan and died of an illness in 1944. She remained in Zhejiang and taught at several schools there and then one in Jiangxi. Her only daughter and two sons were sometimes under her care, but mostly in the care of her mother and house servants. In taking refuge, her school would take desks and chairs and set up classrooms wherever possible. "Sometimes we would hold classes in the open field, and hang the blackboard on a tree. Students sat on the ground. All shared a bitter hatred of the enemy, and everyone wanted to fulfill their responsibility. Studying hard was also a way of assuming the responsibility so all were attentive."[95] For extracurricular activities, students performed plays to inspire patriotism among the locals. Concerts featured patriotic songs: "Back then the song we sang the most was 'Stand up! Those who refuse to be slaves!'"[96] This was the "The March of the Volunteers," which became the national anthem of the People's Republic of China in 1949. In the Number Three Wartime Middle School in Shangrao, Jiangxi, where she was an administrator and taught Chinese for a year, most students were refugees from different places. All had tuition and room and board provided by the government. All were given uniforms. The school was under the protection of an army platoon to ensure that it could operate.[97]

In the remembrance of Lu Lihua (1900–97), attempting to ensure the survival of her private school during the war was a difficult, unsuccessful struggle under the Nationalists. Lu was the principal of the private Liangjiang Women's Physical Education Normal School, which she had founded in 1922 in Shanghai and relocated to Chongqing. The school relied on a private donation for the land. The students numbered 500 at their peak, and studied and worked the land to support themselves. At the time of her interviews in Shanghai in the 1990s, Lu recalled that the Nationalist government suspected her school of being a peripheral organization of the Communists and required her to comply with the curriculum stipulated by the Ministry of Education. She agreed on the condition that the government fund her school. This did not work out, and the school closed within two years. A nonpartisan, "sandwiched" between the Nationalists and Communists, Lu Lihua lost her teaching position after 1949.[98]

In my interview with Huang Yun, she recalled that her university days were a time of relative stability. In 1940, she enrolled at Northeast University, which had relocated from Shenyang, Manchuria, to Santai, Sichuan. "We were on the government supply for food and accommodation, clothing, and a stipend of three *yuan* a month ... All was free. Otherwise, how could I afford to go to university!" This was the Nationalist government policy of student loans, which were considered loans initially, but later the government did not require they be repaid, her husband added.[99] Huang Yun majored in economics in the hope that it would enable her to find a job relatively easily. Economic independence was her ideal. At the university, morning drills started at six every weekday. Simple meals of vegetables and rice mixed with sand were barely enough. Life was exciting, however. Among a variety of student organizations, she served as an accountant for the student choirs. At the university, she met her future husband, a bright young man two years her senior. Like many other students, they joined the Three People's Principles Youth Corps (*sanqing tuan*), the youth organization of the Nationalist government. After graduating in 1944, they got married and found jobs, and remained on the mainland after 1949. Their earlier membership in the Youth Corps caused them political troubles during the Cultural Revolution, but they survived.

Responsibility to the Family; Conflicts with the Communists

In her oral narrative published as a monograph, Chen Meiquan (b. 1914 in Liaoning), stressed her sense of responsibility and how this sustained her in her service to her family and to society: "I had a strong sense of responsibility for the family even in my early teens."[100] This sense of responsibility began with her parents and siblings and her husband, and extended to her job and to the service of society. Inspired by her father, a police officer, she enrolled in the first class of female police of the Ministry of Interior's Senior Police College in Beiping in 1933. A female instructor lectured to them: "You are the first class of women students. You must engage in no courtship; must abide by discipline. If you succeed, there will be a next class for women. Otherwise, there will be none. You must open a new path for women!"[101] Chen and other women underwent the same rigorous curriculum as the men, with drills and military training. At school, she joined the Nationalist Party but was not very active in it. In 1936, seventeen out of twenty-seven female students graduated. The other ten quit. She was assigned a position in the police force in Nanjing and married a schoolmate a few years her senior who was a top official in the Nationalist government, with a position in the Ministry of Interior.

The outbreak of the War of Resistance in 1937 disrupted her police career. The existence of policewomen was "forgotten by the government."[102] Of the 191 pages of her reminiscences, only 16 are about the war, mostly describing her husband's work.[103] She performed her duty as a good supporting wife, constantly moving with him regardless of any dangers. In the face of Japanese air raids, she helped him with paperwork and took care of his needs. In Henan, on his inspection tours of air defence, they moved with simple luggage: one quilt, one bedding, two sets of clothing for each of them, two cooking pots, two bowls, two spoons, two pairs of chopsticks, and a wash basin. Twice she held clerical positions in the government, but neither lasted long because she had to move with her husband. "I believed in life and death together."[104] There is no mention of childbirth. Toward the end of the war, in early 1945, when conditions in Chongqing were relatively stable, she took a position as an officer in the recently established female student army. She recalled that, as director of personnel, "the position gave me the power of hiring, an opportunity to right the wrongs [of discriminatory practices against women]. Previously when a woman was looking for a job, they [the men] turned them down with the excuse: 'a woman? inconvenient even for toilet!' Now I hired only women for the office. Young women are as capable as men."[105]

Responsibility to the family was important to many Nationalist-associated women. The domestic sphere was a place where women could exercise dominant influence. When the country was fragmented, they tried to keep families together. In *20th Century Wartime Experiences of Chinese Women,* the nine women narrators' life stories convey a sense of nostalgia for family roots on the mainland and a sense of interconnectedness with family and with themselves as key links in the continuation of a long family history. To them, taking care of the family was an important service.

In her narrative, Xu Liuyun (b. 1917) portrayed herself as a dutiful but equal partner in marriage in a life of exile. In June 1938, she trekked from Shanghai across half of China to join her fiancé, a skilled worker in a Nationalist air force factory that had relocated to Sichuan.[106] By then, he was already cohabitating with another woman. This was common during wartime.[107] He told her this in a letter, but she decided to go to join him anyway. A woman of strong personality who began working at the age of twelve, she was tough: "If he marries another woman, I will be free ... I would return to Shanghai ... I am not upset. Useless to be mad."[108] With arrangements made by the China Travel Service, she and a female friend left Shanghai for Hong Kong and Vietnam by ship, then proceeded to Kunming by train, to Guizhou and Chongqing by truck, and finally by boat to Yibin, where her husband was. The journey took two months. Xu got married in October 1939 after the other woman left. For the next six years, until the end of the war, she was a homemaker and kept her husband and their two children well fed through her intelligence and resilience. Faced with the scarcity of daily necessities, she spent her husband's wages carefully: one-third for nutrition pills, one-third for house rent, and the rest for daily necessities. She knitted sweaters, made shoes, and did needlework to earn cash, and leased a house to rent out to others. During the frequent Japanese bombing, "after the planes dropped the bombs, my husband and I would go pick up bomb shells near the airport to sell for cash. The shells were still hot."[109] No matter what happened in life, she would toughen herself to deal with it.

Yu Wenxiu (b. 1921), who came from a landlord family in Anhui and whose father was a county official, also held on to the importance of family. She had an arranged marriage from childhood. In 1940, when her home area came under Japanese attacks, she followed her fiancé, a university student, to a Nationalist-run training program in Anhui, where she and forty other women performed military drills and received training in skills for working behind enemy lines. Three months later, her fiancé was assigned to work for the Nationalist government in Anhui. She worked as a schoolteacher and then as a clerk in a government office before giving birth to their first baby. When her father-in-law was arrested by the Japanese, she and her husband quit their jobs in order to rescue him, for this "was more important." Only after 1945 did her husband again find a job with the Nationalist government.[110]

Mang Yuqin (b. 1918) believed in being a virtuous wife and a good mother. She was from a wealthy family of Mongolian and Manchu ethnicities in the city of Jilin, in the province of the same name, which was occupied by the Japanese in 1931–45. With upper middle school credentials, she worked as a clerk in the railway bureau of Jilin until July 1939, when her first baby was born. She recalled: "Although I didn't want to give up my job, I had to return home to be a housewife and to take care of the baby."[111] She had no idea that her husband had joined a Nationalist-led underground resistance group until he was exposed and went into hiding for two years, from 1943 to 1945. During these two years, she and their three children stayed at her mother's place under the watchful eyes of the police. Often special agents would come to the door asking for information; often she was followed when she went out. Despite worry and fear, she forced herself to be strong. Once, she went out her house for the family business by disguising herself as a man. She commented: "Never expected that as a weak and timid person from childhood, I could have changed so completely due to the adversity."[112] She recalled even more hardships during the civil war and her flight to Taiwan in 1951 with her two children while leaving the youngest on the mainland to join her husband there. During her interview in 2000, she reflected on her sixty years of married life:

> I grew up in a conservative family … I think that for a young woman, marriage should be for life. No matter how hard the circumstances are, she should have no complaints or regrets, and always stand by her husband's side. This is the old teaching of Three Obediences and Four Virtues – obey parents at home, be filial to parents-in-law, and follow husband.[113]

Underneath lay her inner strength: "In my life of over eighty years, I have been through so much, the fickleness of human relations, separations and reunions, joys and sorrows. In loneliness and helplessness, I had no space to retreat, only had to toughen myself and press ahead."[114]

"If not for the war of 1937, my life may have been different. If not for getting married that early due to the Resistance War, I may have gone to Italy to study singing," Zhang Rongzhen (b. 1915) recalled. Her narrative describes how the war transformed her from a student dreaming of a brilliant career to a dutiful housewife. A graduate of the Shanghai Conservatory of Music in soprano, she wished to be a singer but had to give it up when the war broke out. She married on November 9, 1937, in occupied Shanghai after her school was destroyed in the Japanese bombing; the family was about to flee, and she needed some protection: "Our marriage was made possible by the Japanese."[115] Her husband had studied abroad and then worked as a chemical engineer for a Nationalist military factory. Their married life during the eight years of the war was a constant move in search of safety: first to Chongqing, where their first baby was born, then back to Shanghai in order to escape from the Japanese air raids in Chongqing, and then to Nationalist-controlled Guilin in the southwest after the Pacific War broke out. When the second baby was born, "we did not have any help. Everything was done by me. The next day after getting home [from the hospital], I cooked and washed diapers."[116] Zhang stayed at home taking care of the family until after they arrived in Taiwan, when she started working. In the interview, when she was in her late eighties, she reflected: "Now I have a family of four generations, every grandchild is smart, excellent, lively, and cute. Even though there are small regrets, I am very content. I feel fortunate for the whole of my life."[117] One editor of the *20th Century Wartime Experiences of Chinese Women,* Luo Jiurong, comments that for these women who went through the war,

> their bravery is not in fighting battles; their perseverance has nothing to do with killing enemies and shedding blood, but when the war destroyed normality of life, they made efforts in taking up their responsibilities ... Once into marriage, these women exerted themselves to fulfill the roles of wives and mothers. In the life of scarcity, they persisted in creating some order in life, providing for herself and her family an anchor of safety.[118]

In the Communist women's reminiscences, family should not be a priority in life; the revolutionary career was. The two parties, the Chinese Communist Party and the Nationalist, had been in conflict over ideology and national power. In the Communist women's reminiscences, direct military conflict with the Nationalists was part of wartime life. Similarly, military conflict seriously affected the Nationalist-associated women. Despite her lack of interest in party politics, as shown in her reminiscences, Zhou Meiyu was not spared. She was accused of being a Communist around 1940, and was even in danger of assassination. She laughed this off: "In those days some people were so narrow-minded and ignorant; they believed that people who worked hard, demanded nothing must be Communists. A huge joke, indeed."[119] As mentioned earlier, Cao Jingyi and Wang Ke battled with the Communists. Wang Ke reflected: "Come to think of us in the Nationalist army we were so pathetic. We had to fight the Japanese and the Communists, and had to deal with collaboration, and politicians who worked with the Communists. We were surrounded by enemies, so hard."[120] She shared the general Nationalist view that the Communists' priority was in fighting against the Nationalist government, that resistance against Japan was the least important part of their mission whereas "most Nationalists saw the Japanese as the number one enemy."[121]

Family was an important factor in shaping political affiliations, as in the case of Huang Yu (b. 1928). Her mother, Wu Jiaying, had been a political activist, a member of the Xinmin xuehui (study association of the new people), which Mao Zedong formed in 1914. Also a feminist and an educator, Wu was a friend of Xiang Jingyu, a Communist woman activist. She became anti-Communist, however, for she disagreed with those Communists on many issues.[122]

In an interview in the 1990s, Yang Xianzhi (b. 1920), who lived in Sichuan, reflected on how party conflicts have affected wartime memories. A middle school student in early 1938, she enrolled in Wuhan in the wartime staff training program. Before the fall of Wuhan, she and 400 women trainees retreated on foot to Chongqing, where she worked as a teacher of the Wartime Child Welfare Protection Association until 1944, when she went to study at a university.[123] Yang had remained in Sichuan since then. In the 1990s, when it was politically safe on the mainland to discuss the positive roles of the Nationalists in the War of Resistance, she gave her views:

> Madam Jiang [Madame Chiang Kai-shek, Song Meiling] played an important role in the establishment of ZZEB [the Wartime Child Welfare Protection Association] homes and was crucial in safeguarding their existence during the war years. However, after 1949, nobody dared to say anything positive about Madam Jiang and her role in the war. We former students and teachers of the ZZEB had to conceal our association with the ZZEB and Madam Jiang. Before the 1980s, no one paid any attention to the history and contributions made by the ZZEB until Deng Yingchao, wife of Zhou Enlai, said in a 1988 speech that the ZZEB had made great contributions in saving more than thirty thousand refugee children during the war years. After her speech, we were allowed to organize an alumni association. Now going to the annual meeting of the association became a highlight of my life.[124]

******

After moving to Taiwan, the women discussed in this chapter persisted in their efforts to build a fulfilling life. Both Chi Pang-yuan and Shao

Menglan continued to be educators. Zhou Meiyu played an important role in developing the nursing professions and in elevating the status of female nurses to equal that of men in the military. She was promoted to the rank of major general in 1958, the first woman general in Nationalist China after 1949. She concluded: "These step-by-step improvements within the system encountered so many obstacles back then. It is hard to establish a new system, and even harder in the military. Thanks to the enlightened leadership, our efforts have not been in vain."[125] Chen Meiquan's career took off after the defeat of the Japanese. In 1947, both she and her husband were elected to the National Assembly (Guomin dahui) among 301 female members and 2,744 males,[126] a position she held until 1991. In 1951, she and other women succeeded in their proposal for the establishment of a female police force in Taiwan. She held: "For women issues, women themselves must advocate, manage, and fight so as to gain public sympathy and support and to bring about real accomplishments."[127] Guo Wencui first served as an officer in the Women's Corps in Taiwan, and then for almost two decades as a military training officer in a university. She summarized: "[My] students in a disciplined life have cultivated proper manners of respected families, and have made achievements after school. Some became women leaders abroad. I feel honored too."[128]

In contrast to the Communist discourse that China's wealthy and powerful were local tyrants, corrupt or filthy bullies, and ruthless exploiters of working-class people, for the Nationalist-associated women their families connected them with a deep root and offered them a strong sense of belonging, stability, and strength. The family also seriously impacted them in the ideological, political, and military conflicts between the Nationalists and the Communists that dominated early twentieth-century Chinese history. The foreign invasions as well as domestic military conflicts shaped and reshaped their lives.

In their reflections on their wartime experiences, suffering and exile emerge as major themes. The War of Resistance was not "a good war." However, the Nationalist women chose not to be victimized by the war. A large number of them joined the Nationalist-led resistance in the military, in the medical field, and in the mobilization and various other capacities. Many more pursued education in spite of wartime chaos and disruption. What anchored them was the belief that education must go on with no interruption; education had the potential to save them as well as the nation. Many held on to their families, performing family obligations as daughter, wife, and mother, and rendering service to society when they could. Throughout all this, they overcame many obstacles, and triumph in adversity gave them a sense of accomplishment.

5
Surviving under the Enemy: Oral Narratives of Middle-Class Women in Japanese-Occupied China

After the Japanese occupied Manchuria in September 1931, their aggression continued and eventually led to an all-out war between China and Japan. At the height of the war, Japanese forces occupied almost all the urban eastern half of China's territory. The Nationalist government controlled "Free China," provinces in the mountainous interior in the southwest. The Communists maintained their headquarters in Yan'an in the northwest and rural base areas in north and central China. Collaboration regimes emerged in occupied areas. While many Chinese joined resistance forces led by the Nationalists or the Communists and many others retreated with the Nationalist government into the interior, the vast majority remained in their homes. Some collaborated with the Japanese out of self-interest or in order to survive. Most simply remained for they lacked economic resources and political connections with the Nationalists.[1] For this great mass of people, about 200 million, "there was no alternative to living with the enemy."[2] Following the war, their memories were buried for a long time. They themselves did not want to bring those memories out into the open.[3]

The Chinese master narrative of the war in the Mao era centred around how the Communist Party led heroic resistance against Japan. In reality, however, there were "multi-faceted experiences of war" across class, gender, and ethnicity as well as time and space.[4] The life stories of women in occupied China are the focus of this chapter, based on my interviews with six women.[5] One was Wang Yao (1913–2008). Initially, she was reluctant to tell her stories, saying that she was too timid to join any resistance so her experience was too mundane and too ordinary, yet she told a story full of meanings.

These six women were representatives of an important group that has been marginalized and ignored by the mainstream narrative – relatively privileged, middle-class women who survived the Japanese occupation. All six received a modern education in the new schools instead of being taught traditional Confucian values at home. The new schools had the effect of creating a new social class of female students. Unlike the Communist veterans discussed in Chapter 2, they were not radicalized at school; rather, education cultivated in them an aspiration to financial independence. Of the six, only Wang Bo had experienced foot-binding. Three professed the Christian faith. None showed much interest in politics at school or after. All held a strong belief in education as a means of self-improvement. None was affiliated with any political party during wartime. Analysis of their personal experiences serves as a case study, shedding light on the ways in which middle-class women negotiated gendered survival and loyalty to family and nation. Their personal stories demonstrate the evolution of Chinese women undergoing drastic changes in the twentieth century in the awakening of gender consciousness and in their determination to pursue education in order to attain independence and self-reliance.

In the Grey Zone of Occupation

At the time of the War of Resistance and in the histories written afterwards, several terms were used to refer to people in occupied China. The most condemnatory terms were "traitors to the Han Chinese" (*hanjian*), who acted immorally and betrayed both the nation and the people, and "puppets" (*kuilei*), those who worked actively with or for the Japanese. Less emotion-laden terms included "people consorting with the enemy" (*tongdi fenzi*), and "those who were close to the Japanese" (*qin Ri*). Most of the people in the occupied areas who were struggling to survive were designated as "slaves in a lost nation" (*wangguo nu*), a term that suggests "varying degrees of pity and condemnation."[6]

During the war, the Nationalists and Communists executed a large number of *hanjian*. In 1944–47, the Nationalist government convicted 14,932 out of more than 45,000 individuals accused of being *hanjian*.[7] Women were included, foremost among them being Chen Bijun (1891–1959), wife of Wang Jingwei (1883–1944). Wang was a Nationalist Party veteran who defected to the Japanese and became the head of China's collaboration regime in 1940. Some women were imprisoned by association with their *hanjian* husbands. Others, though not convicted, were attacked by government and literary circles such as Su Qing (1917–82) and Zhang Ailing (1920–95). Both published during the occupation in Shanghai and were targeted as *hanjian* writers after 1945. They were also found guilty because of their association with Chen Gongbo and Hu Lancheng, respectively, who were tried as *hanjian* by the Nationalist government.[8] In the 1950s, the Communist government accused writers, both men and women, who published under the puppet Manchukuo regime of collaborating with the Japanese. Except for those who left Manchuria by 1935, their works were condemned, dismissed, and ignored as *hanjian* literature in mainland China for decades, until the early 1980s.[9]

This chapter deals mainly with common, apolitical women in the occupied areas, referred to as "slaves in a lost nation" living in the "lost regions" (*lunxian qu*) by the contemporary mass media, periodicals, literary works, political speeches, and essays. The phrase "slaves in a lost nation" powerfully conveyed the sense of national humiliation. "The March of the Volunteers," a theme song in the film *Sons and Daughters of the Time of Storm* (*Fengyun ernü*, 1935), called on the Chinese to fight against the Japanese invaders:

> Arise, we who refuse to be slaves!
> With our very flesh and blood,
> Let us build our new Great Wall!

The song became the national anthem of the People's Republic of China in 1949.[10] In her first novel, *The Field of Life and Death* (*Shengsi chang*), published in 1935, the young writer Xiao Hong (1911–42) from Manchuria depicted how the Japanese occupation there affected ordinary individuals.[11] Through a peasant man, the author voiced the common political message: "In prior days he [Zhao San, a male peasant] hadn't understood what a nation was. In prior days he could even have forgotten his own nationality." Now he gave up his passive life and spoke before all the villagers: "I don't want to be a nationless slave [*wangguo nu*]. Alive I'm Chinese, and when I'm dead, I'll be a Chinese ghost."[12] In postwar China, the term *wangguo nu* has continued in common use. In collections of oral histories published in the 2000s, those from occupied Manchuria often describe their despair and explain that their resistance was driven by their unwillingness to be slaves in a lost nation.[13]

In the Cold War political climate, the Communist master narrative neglected the experiences of everyday life of the common people in the Japanese-occupied areas. In the post-Mao reform era, most academic works in China about those areas were devoted to the victims of the atrocities committed by the Japanese army, particularly the Nanjing Massacre and the "comfort women." The activities of writers, politicians, and collaborators became another focus. This scholarship has paid insufficient attention to how the occupation affected ordinary urban civilians' mental and material lives.[14] The general depiction is that people in occupied China lived in misery and suffering, in "a dark world of sadness."[15]

Recent English-language studies have turned to the complexity in the history of different regions in occupied China in local contexts.[16] In his work on a group of Chinese male writers in occupied Shanghai, Poshek Fu maintains that historians of China and other occupied countries have too often defined the moral choices of people during wartime by a Manichean division into heroes or villains, fighters or collaborators. Rejecting this view as too simplistic, Fu argues that the occupied areas were, in fact, a "grey zone" in which weakness and compromise were mixed with striving for dignity and displaying moral courage in the face of the enemy.[17] Timothy Brook reiterates that to understand the complexity of the War of Resistance, one must understand "the terrible ambivalences of living under war regimes and the tremendous ambiguities involved in making sense of everyday social conditions."[18] Keith Schoppa's study of war refugees in Zhejiang also illustrates the ambiguity. He argues that the chief goal of war refugees was to protect their families and ensure their survival, not nationalism and nationalist feelings.[19]

In the studies of the daily lives of women in occupied China, scholars explore the extra hardships they experienced and their everyday tactics for survival and resistance. Emily Honig notes that for the Shanghai cotton mill female workers during the war period, it was not the working class or gender consciousness or membership in trade unions or the Chinese Communist Party that offered major support to these suffering women; rather, it was the sisterhoods, the traditional women's own community, that helped them survive.[20] Zhao Ma's work sheds light on how lower-class women in occupied Beijing devised a wide array of everyday tactics to cope with the terrible war and occupation.[21] Susan Glosser, in her study of the magazine *Shanghai Women* (*Shanghai funü*), argues that by reporting on the lives of women in occupied Shanghai, the editors of the magazine "promoted psychological resistance" under the wartime circumstances. Their attaching of importance to women's domestic activities gave significance to the pursuit of everyday life as "itself heroic."[22] Nicole Huang's analysis of Shanghai women's print culture under the occupation holds that through their publications, women writers, Zhang Ailing and Su Qing included, and editors and publishers attributed meanings to everyday existence and offered a sense of stability in turbulent times. She maintains that "their shared attempt to come to terms with their experiences of war and turbulence must be regarded as a form of cultural resistance."[23] Huang goes further to argue that this women's print culture, with its imaginative and creative effects, transformed modern literature. Similarly, Chen Yan, in her examination of how the war affected gender dynamics in the lives of mostly middle-class women and men, challenges the view that those who remained in the occupied areas were unpatriotic. She shows how Yang Yinyu (1884–1938), a famous female educator, refused to collaborate with the Japanese and was murdered; and how Yang Jiang (1911–2016), a schoolteacher and playwright in occupied Shanghai, reflected years later about her plays: "The laughter in these two comedies shows that in the dark, long, nights, we did not lose confidence; in the harshness of life, we kept our optimism."[24]

R. Keith Schoppa observes that "collaboration and resistance are not necessarily dichotomous activities," that "collaborating in one way or another was simply the pragmatic choice of action."[25] Women could work within the occupation establishment to advance their own agendas. In *Resisting Manchukuo,* Norman Smith discusses the career and works of seven women writers of Manchukuo who were labelled as collaborators and traitors in the Mao era. He argues that these women continued the May Fourth tradition and produced anti-patriarchal literature, presenting women's sufferings, condemning the "male chauvinist" society, and revealing the darkness and destitution of colonial Manchukuo.[26] Wenwen Wang makes the point that whereas colonial Manchukuo promoted the conservative ideology of "good wives and wise mothers" (*liangqi xianmu*), female students, through essays written in their school journals argued for female emancipation.[27]

The middle-class women in the Morality Society in Manchukuo worked with the occupation regime to carve out a space for themselves, contends Prasenjit Duara. A redemptive society originated in 1918 in Shandong, drawing inspiration from Confucianism, Buddhism, and Daoism; under the Japanese occupation in Manchuria, the Morality Society enjoyed a wide audience of men and women, both rich and poor, through its "righteous" and virtuous schools, public lectures, classes, and clinics. Its resistance took complex forms. In pursuing their ideal of women of "tradition within modernity," the women in the society were able to find a spiritual means of coping with difficulties in life, derive moral autonomy, and carve out a public space for exerting their own influence. Although they were used by the Manchukuo regime, the women also used the regime for their religious mission.[28]

Condemned and dissolved by the Communist government on the mainland, the Morality Society continued under the Nationalist government in the post-1949 years, first on the mainland and then in Taiwan. In their published oral accounts, some members recalled their wartime experiences. Yuan Runlan (b. 1910) insisted that she joined the society because it promoted education, and education was a way to save the nation. She argued that in Manchukuo, the society "had its influence throughout the Northeast. It had developed to a phenomenal extent not entirely because of cooperation with the Japanese. In reality, the two sides maintained a sort of harmony only on the surface. The society's own influence had already been impressive; it was not just due to the assistance of the Japanese power."[29]

Jiang Yunzhong (b. 1916) joined the Morality Society in 1934. Her father, as head of the village, had been tortured by the Japanese for assisting anti-Japanese activists. He joined the society after his release. Discussing not politics but traditional Confucian morality, Jiang explained that "we made the Japanese agree with us, give us special exemption of labour service, and offer us a ration of rice."[30] The society appealed to both Yuan Runlan and Jiang Yunzhong because its agenda included women's education, self-cultivation, and self-reliance. More importantly, the society offered women opportunities to take on public roles in working outside the home as teachers and lecturers, helping women in their lives.[31]

Wartime China was different from occupied France under the Germans, but studies of daily life in occupied France offer insights on the complexity and ambiguity of history.[32] The documentary *The Sorrow and the Pity* argues for the existence of several "truths" of France under occupation: the truth of resistance, of collaboration, and of the majority of people struggling for self-preservation.[33] Robert Gildea proves that the history of occupied France was not a simple story of cold, hunger, absence of freedom, and fear, nor of good French and bad French, but rather one of multiple experiences. When the occupation disrupted the lives of the people, the French found solidarity in families, churches, trades, villages, towns, and regions. "What is most striking about the French under the Occupation is not how heroic or villainous they were but how imaginative, creative, and resourceful they were in pursuit of a better life."³⁴ Similarly, the Chinese story shows the multiple truths and people's resourceful ways of coping with reality under their circumstances.

My interviews provide opportunities for women who have been previously silenced to be heard. Like the French in Robert Gildea's work, "with the passage of time those who witnessed the Occupation are willing to talk about it candidly, as never before."³⁵ And when they talked, while many chose to tell their stories in alignment with the collective memories and political discourse, others expressed their own views and deviated from the dominant ones.³⁶ All of these can help us understand the complexity and richness of the history of the time. The Chinese women I met all agreed to be interviewed, perhaps because there was a basic trust, as I had met them through introductions from relatives and friends. An eager listener, I was welcomed with open hearts. Like those French people who lived through the German occupation interviewed by Gildea, these women felt that their experiences had not been taken seriously. Now, at this late stage of their lives, all wanted to release their suppressed memories to reflect on their lives and to come to terms with their wartime past.

These women's oral accounts of survival reveal a sense of uncertainty and of fear, but they do not perceive life at that time as just one of sadness and darkness. Their stories show that the Japanese occupation enhanced their national consciousness. From their perspective, they carried out their own everyday forms of resistance to gender inequality and to the Japanese aggression against China. As James Scott has argued, everyday resistance may have limited impact, but "what may be accomplished within this symbolic straitjacket is nonetheless something of a testament to human persistence and inventiveness."³⁷

Gender Consciousness within Middle-Class Families

The May Fourth and New Culture Movement of the 1910s to 1920s attacked traditional Chinese family values and institutions as imprisoning and crippling Chinese youth. China's transformation effected impressive changes in families. Many still maintained traditional patriarchal practices and values, but they also had the means and willingness to provide their girls with a modern education in the new schools, where they studied mathematics, language, geography, and history instead of only the traditional Confucian works. In sharing their stories, these six women evaluated and analyzed their parents' behaviour, particularly that of their mothers, demonstrating sympathy as well as voicing criticism. Their families had cultivated their gender consciousness and nurtured their determination to secure an education as a means of attaining independence.

Both Wang Yao (1913–2008) and Shang Pu (1917–2006) grew up in Shenyang, the capital of Liaoning Province in the Northeast. Known also as Manchuria, the Northeast was a land of forests, mountains, and plains, the homeland of the Manchus who established the Qing dynasty (1644–1911). This non-Han dynasty implemented anti–foot-binding laws, however ineffective, as they forbade their own women to bind their feet. In Manchuria, foot-binding was not as prevalent as in inner China. On the frontiers of China, Manchuria was politically unstable. Its fertile land had been a target and a battlefield for imperial expansion for the Russian and Japanese empires. The land attracted bandit groups. From 1918, Manchuria was under the warlord Zhang Zuolin (1875–1928), who was assassinated by the Japanese in 1928 when he deviated from his pro-Japan policy. His son Zhang Xueliang (1901–2001) succeeded him and recognized the Nationalist regime as the ruling government of China. To strengthen its power, the Zhang regime strove for modernization, with cities such as Shenyang establishing universities, schools, movies theatres, trolley buses, and vibrant commerce.

Wang Yao's description of her early life begins with the Manchurian Incident of September 18, 1931 (mentioned in the Introduction to this book), the day that turned her life upside down and disrupted her education. Born in 1913 in a village near Shenyang, she reflected that while growing up, "I was both unfortunate and fortunate." She was unfortunate because of the uneasy relationship between her parents. Her father had passed the initial level of the traditional civil service examinations and become a licentiate (*shengyuan*). With the abolition of the examination system in 1905, he went on to a modern education by studying economics at Japan's Tokyo Imperial University after an arranged marriage to a daughter of a scholarly family who had also received a modern school education. While her father was studying in Japan, her mother worked as a schoolteacher and then as an elementary school principal in a small town. When her father returned, the family lived in Shenyang and her mother stopped working. Yao's hope for a stable family life did not come true. Her mother had given birth to six children, including three boys, but all the boys died in infancy. Yao was the only child who survived. "A baby girl is like grass, so I could survive," she said, meaning that grass is hardy, unlike flowers, which are delicate. Giving birth to a child was difficult for a woman, and the death of infants was common in those days without modern medical care. In their son-less family, the couple's relationship grew tense: "One day hearing that they were fighting again in their room, I was so scared that I went in and kneeled down on my knees begging them to stop."

A woman who bore no son was considered to have failed in her responsibility to produce an heir. At the age of forty-two, Yao's mother had to agree to her husband's request to take a concubine in order to produce a son and continue the family line. She even held a ceremony to have the concubine into the family in order to show that she herself was a good wife. The concubine was young, only four years older than Yao. After she moved in, the parents' relationship deteriorated. Although the stress caused her mother to have a mental breakdown, Yao did not blame her father. To Yao, he was an "open-minded man" because he was willing to provide for her education all the way to university. She therefore considered herself fortunate. From an early age, she had loved to read both traditional literature and new stories and novels by female and male writers of the May Fourth era. Her dream was to go to university and to study abroad, where she would major in medicine. Also, perhaps unsurprisingly given her background, Wang Yao's hope as a teenager was to remain celibate for fear of repeating her mother's miseries in marriage. Many young women in those days had an idealistic vision of celibacy.

Shang Pu described her father as a "feudal-minded man" who remained a cold authority figure. "We had little emotional feelings for each other. He would call me to his room if he had something to say. I just stood straight with fear." Her father had gone to a traditional school before enrolling in a modern law school. After serving as a county official for a few years, he retired to Shenyang. The family lived in a traditional courtyard surrounded by walls. The huge compound consisted of front, middle, and rear courtyards. Shang Pu's feudal father had a principal wife who bore him thirteen children, but none survived. Her mother was his concubine. With little education, she had "married at the age of seventeen for the sole purpose of producing a son," but gave birth only to Shang Pu and another daughter, who died in infancy. Shang Pu's father then took another concubine, who bore three daughters and finally a son. "My family was so feudal. Those feudal relatives and family friends had wives and concubines. Nowadays, husbands and wives help and care for each other, but not back then. Women were oppressed, were treated as machines to produce children." To Shang Pu, marriage was a trap. At an early age, she made up her mind never to marry. Indeed, she remained single throughout her life.

Her father forbade all his girls to go to school for fear that a modern education would make them "unwomanly." Under his surveillance, Shang Pu's early education was a traditional one. From the age of seven, she studied Confucian works with a private tutor at home. In 1929, her father died, thereby liberating her from the confines of home. Going to a public school and cutting her long braid into bobbed hair like the other schoolgirls, now for the first time Shang Pu had an official name. She had not been given one at birth because her father had believed that once a child had an official name, he or she might not live long. The new school thus gave her not only a new education but also a new identity. At the new school, Shang Pu "didn't read much new literature" and "had not heard about the May Fourth Movement ... Heard about the Nationalists but not about the Communist Party."

At the time of my interview with Yu Jian (1917–2009), she had been disabled by a stroke and was unable to provide a detailed narrative of her life. She was able to give only short answers to my questions. Her daughter, also present, prompted her with some questions and details. Jian was born and raised in the city of Dalian, Liaoning, a port city leased to Russia in 1898 and then occupied by Japan in 1905 following the Japanese victory in the Russo-Japanese War. Her father was a businessman who engaged in commerce with the Chinese and Japanese. Her mother had some education. Mother gave birth to boys, but all died in infancy, so Jian was the only surviving child. Her father did not take a concubine. Growing up, Jian did not experience much gender discrimination at home. Her father dressed his only daughter in boy's clothing, sent her to a modern school, and even made her learn boxing with boys. The boxing class was tough: "My hands hurt so much that I didn't want to go ... didn't understand why he wanted me to learn. Not to be bullied? Maybe. I was the only girl in that [boxing] class."

She remembered that sometime before 1931, her father moved the whole family to Yantai, Shandong Province, because "he didn't want me to continue to have a Japanese education." Also, the Japanese made him act as a go-between to purchase some land. When he refused, he was imprisoned. After his release, he left Dalian for fear of more trouble. The news of the Manchurian Incident was known to her: "Yes, of course I heard it." At this point in our conversation, she began singing a few lines of a famous song, "On the Songhua River" ("Songhuajiang shang"): "September 18! September 18! Since that miserable moment, I have left my home and the countless treasure ..."[38] "We hated the Japanese!" she said in a clear voice.

Wang Bo (1915–2003) was from Huai'an, Jiangsu Province, where traditions ran deep and new ideas and Christian missionaries were active. Her father was a doctor of traditional Chinese medicine, while her mother came from a scholarly family but received no education. Among the six women interviewed, she was the only one who had had her feet bound as a child and unbound later. She did not mention the footbinding during the interview. Only later did her husband reveal this fact. Her avoidance of this topic may have been due to a sense of shame at having had to undergo such a "barbaric" practice. What she chose to stress was not her feet but how her parents had strongly supported her education. She explained:

> In those days, girls were discriminated against, and hardly any went to school. We were the early ones to go [in the local area]. In my class, many came from big landlord families. My family was not that wealthy ... Ours has been a scholarly family for several generations. Therefore, Father said, "Who cares if others hold the idea that men are superior and women inferior [*nanzun nübei*] – I want to send you to school."

Wang Bo "did not believe in the idea of women being inferior and men superior. At school, men and women were in the same class." When asked whether she had any idea of what she would do when she was growing up, she answered, "Not really; it would be best to continue my education." As a teenager, she often went to the local church. Since its introduction to China in the sixteenth century, Christianity had had a long and localized influence in her area. An American missionary recommended her for a nurse training program of the Christian Renci Hospital (Love and Mercy Hospital), founded in Huai'an by the Presbyterian Church of the United States. The four-year training offered her a good opportunity to pursue her education and her life-long career in medicine.

Both Zhang Shu (b. 1923) and Wang Zhen (b. 1926) were born and grew up in Beiping, the capital of China for most of the period since 1271. An old city of rich culture and history, it was a centre for the iconoclastic May Fourth Movement. Christianity also had a strong presence here. Zhang Shu believed that it was the Christian faith that nurtured the concept of gender equality in her family. She started her narrative by saying:

> Because I was born in a Christian family, Christianity had a strong impact on me. I went to the Peiyuan elementary school, the Beiman All-Girls School, and the Yanjing University. All of them were missionary schools.

And for four years, I went to a missionary middle school in Shanghai. Both my parents were Christians ... [In her family of four girls and two boys] there was gender equality absolutely ... No girls were looked down upon. On the contrary, Father treated us girls better than the boys. Mother was a traditional woman but because she turned to Christianity ... she had progressive ideas.

Her Christian father had received a modern education and worked at the customs office, while her mother was a strong supporter of female education. When Zhang Shu was only eight years old, her father died. Although their relatives urged her mother to remarry to have a man as the head of the family, she refused. Instead, she made up her mind to bring up her children on her own and to give all of them a good education. "Mother said, 'All my daughters will have no dowry. They each will have a college graduate certificate. This will be her dowry.'" From early on, Zhang Shu reported, she "loved school. Although I did not know why, I just did. I knew women were entitled to an education." In her family, all four girls went to college and married only after graduation. One brother joined the Nationalist air force. The other brother worked at the custom office after training in the customs school.

Wang Zhen began her narrative by noting that "ours was an intellectual [*zhishi fenzi*] family," and thus valued education highly. The term "intellectual" as she used it also implied one who often engaged in academic pursuits only and lacked social skills and political interest. "The Nationalist government had asked Father to be a member of the Nationalist Party but he never did ... Not interested in politics. This influenced us as well." Wang Zhen held that her father "was patriotic and believed in the idea 'of saving the country by science' [*kexue jiuguo*]." This was a popular idea in those days, when people hotly debated ways to save the country. Her father had majored in astrometeorology and studied in Japan. "He held a mixture of traditional and modern views of gender. He assumed that 'Men are superior, and women are inferior.' Perhaps this was the influence of Japan." He believed in education for girls, but only till high school and not college. He was a stern, authoritarian figure in the family. "If we did not have a good grade at school, we would be shaking with fear at the dinner table ... He would slap my brothers if they did not do well at school."

Wang Zhen was full of admiration for her mother, a strong-minded woman who was a graduate of the first class of the Suzhou Women's Normal School, famous for being a modern school of high academic quality. "Grandma was very open minded. Otherwise, women would have bound feet and could not go out. She sent my mother to school. Mother urged us to study hard ... She herself was educated ... She wanted us girls to be independent, financially independent." Under the influence of both parents, Wang Zhen developed a passion for education: "We studied hard with the motive of patriotism and for acquiring the ability to become independent and to serve the Chinese nation eventually. Another motive was to win honour for my mother. Mother said, So what you are girls? You should be good as well." Making their mother proud, she and her siblings all graduated from college.

Pursuing Education for Self-Reliance

The current Chinese historical narrative insists that Japanese colonial education in occupied China was a cultural invasion, aimed at enslaving the people. In contrast, Western missionary education in early twentieth-century China had benefited China's modernization.[39] The women featured in this chapter did not appear to worry much about ideological views, however. Instead, they were proud that they pursued education for their own economic, and thereby personal, independence. Three of them – Wang Yao, Shang Pu, and Wang Zhen – even sought out this education under the Japanese.

After the Manchurian Incident, schools in Shenyang were closed for a year or so. With no school and faced with the Japanese occupation, Wang Yao "felt lost, depressed, confused, not knowing what to do." All she knew was that she did not want to give up her education. In the summer of 1932, she and her uncle joined the estimated 100,000 students who left Manchuria for Beiping (a gesture symbolizing their refusal to live and study under the Japanese), which was still under Chinese rule.[40] Arriving in Beiping, she took the entrance examination for Beijing University, hoping to enter the Department of Chinese, but failed. She went to a school set up for refugees from the Northeast hoping to take another examination for Beijing University the following year. Japanese aggression once again crushed her dream. One day, she received a telegram from her father urging her and her uncle to return home immediately. In order not to place the family in danger, they went back.

> The situation seemed tense ... On the ship from Tianjin to Dalian, the surveillance was tight. The authorities asked us when we had gone to Beiping,

and what we had done there. We did not participate in any resistance activities. A couple of days after getting home ... [the authorities] interrogated my father whether my uncle and I had anti-Manchukuo and anti-Japanese thought. They forbade us to leave for Beiping again.

Her uncle managed to leave but Yao stayed: "I couldn't run away for fear this would cause trouble for my family." She explained that her father had worked at the Bank of Eastern Three Provinces (Dongsansheng guanyinhao), which had been brought under Japanese authority in 1932. Having to take care of a large family, he decided to stay in Shenyang even though some of his friends left to join the resistance.

Yao's father hired a female Japanese-language tutor for her. Soon, she decided to go to Japan to continue her education. The downsides of receiving an education from the colonial power did not come up during her account. Many Chinese students, including one close female friend, had already gone to study there.

After thinking back and forth, I told my father that I would like to go to Japan to study. I could not just sit at home doing nothing. From middle school, I had wanted to go to senior high, then college and then study abroad. My father had studied in Japan ... I asked another female friend to go together. Her father agreed too ... Going to Japan seemed to be my only choice.

In September 1933, she left for Japan to continue her education, with financial support from her father. In a time of uncertainty, she believed that education for a young woman was a worthy cause. After half a year of learning Japanese in a preparatory school in Tokyo, she and a dozen other Chinese students enrolled in the Japan Women's University in that city, with a concentration in education. From 1933 onward, the Japanese puppet regime, Manchukuo, awarded scholarships for study in Japan for the stated purpose of "training persons with talent for integration of the Japanese and Manchus."[41] Wang Yao took the exam in Tokyo in the spring of 1934, finished 19th out 1,200 applicants, and was awarded a government scholarship.[42]

In Manchukuo, the authorities established their general education policy to "promote thoroughly the spirit of nation-building for the Kingly Way, ethnic harmony, and the integration of Japanese and Manchus."[43] Severe censorship forbade the use of words such as *Zhongguo* (China) or *Zhonghua* (Chinese).[44] The schools referred to Japanese as the "national" language, and designated Chinese as the language of Manchukuo.

In middle schools, the "national morality" curriculum consisted of such Japanese valued concepts as "the way of the emperor," "the way of the gods," and the "union of nationalities/ethnic harmony" (*minzu xiehe*). All schools had to perform the daily morning ritual of raising the Japanese national flag and bowing in the direction of the Japanese emperor's palace and of the emperor of Manchukuo.[45] The national history and national geography taught in schools were confined to Manchuria only.[46] Education for women was for the purpose of cultivating "virtuous wives and good mothers."[47] In his study of education in Manchuria, historian Qi Hongshen has opposed the notion that Japanese-occupied Manchuria promoted modernization, trained professionals, and helped develop the economy. He contends that the Japanese colonial education as a cultural invasion was more vicious than military occupation because it aimed at stripping the Chinese of their national identity.[48]

Shang Pu continued her schooling in occupied Shenyang. In September 1931, the fourteen-year-old had just begun studying at the Affiliated Middle School of the Fengtian Women's Normal School. Then came the Manchurian Incident. "Gunshots went on throughout that night. Mother was so scared that she just stood there, not knowing what to do. The next morning, my sister (from another concubine of father) and I went to school as usual. When we approached the Eastern Gate [of the city walls], there were soldiers everywhere." All schools closed. Shang Pu was in despair. She had very much looked forward to going to school as a way of becoming a teacher so she could support her mother: "For a woman in the Northeast [that is, Manchuria], to be a teacher, a good teacher, was the best I could have hoped for." As her mother's only surviving daughter, she felt the need to take care of her widowed mother and her grandmother. After a year, her school reopened. The previous school principal had been imprisoned for his anti-Japanese views and replaced by an old-fashioned gentleman. Shang Pu was clear: The Japanese "wanted to impose on us the old Chinese idea of 'men being superior and women inferior' and the Japanese concept of 'wise wife and good mother.'" For her, these traditional values implied conservatism.

In 1940, when she was a schoolteacher, the Manchukuo regime selected Shang Pu, through examination, together with over a hundred schoolteachers to receive scholarships to study in Japan. "I hated the Japanese," she said, but she went to study in Japan because

> in Manchuria, there was no other way for a woman to receive higher education except by going to Japan. One had to study abroad. Some families

had money so they could simply go by applying for a travel pass, but they could not go to good schools. I was on the government funding and could go to public schools in Japan. The best was in Tokyo.

She noted, however, that schools in Tokyo did not accept people from Manchuria as they were considered to be of an inferior race. She and three other women from Manchuria went to Nara and studied for two years in the Women's Normal School, sharing a room together. Nara was a beautiful, ancient city with temples and a lot of deer, she remembered. She also remembered the effect of the war on Japan.

Many families had sons to go to the war and had ashes to receive from the front. At first, Japan was wealthy but when our Resistance War was winning, Japan was on the decline. The men went to the front. Businesses closed down. There was not much learning in school. The school organized supporting teams, learning military medical care, but did not require us to learn. We did not have much to do; did not learn much later.

Returning to Shenyang in the spring of 1943, she was assigned by the city's education bureau to teach in a high school. With her salary, she became the sole support of her mother and grandmother.

Wang Zhen had just graduated from elementary school when the Japanese occupied Beiping in July 1937. During the war, the family (except for her elder brother, a professional working for a Nationalist military factory) stayed in Beiping under the Japanese occupation. At first, her father refused to work for the Japanese and stayed home in defiance, like many others. Later, however, hard-pressed economically, he took up a job. The occupation brought a deep sense of insecurity and humiliation. The family lived in a traditional Chinese courtyard compound in the western section of the city. "Next door to us was a brothel for the Japanese, playing Japanese music and dance. Therefore, every day there were drunkards in and out. We were scared," Wang Zhen remembered. She enrolled in the Beiping First All-Girls School. Founded in 1913, the school enjoyed a lofty reputation. During the occupation, it had Japanese instructors. Wang Zhen recalled: "The school had Japanese language courses and we did not want to take them. Come to think of it now, it would have been useful to learn Japanese. However, back then we were all disgusted; we didn't want to learn Japanese; no one did ... Flower arrangement or tea ceremony, we did not want to learn any of it." The refusal was one way for them to resist.

In 1943, she passed the university entrance examination and was accepted by both Beijing University and Furen University. She chose Beijing University because the latter, a private, Catholic university, charged higher tuition. This Beijing University was not the "real" one as the original university had moved to the interior. After occupying Beiping, the Japanese took over the campus, and for some time used the "red building" of the university as the headquarters of their military police corps, turning the building's basement into a prison.[49] Later, the collaboration government established the "new" Beijing University. Wang Zhen's strong resentment of the Japanese did not prevent her from attending this university. The ability to go into higher education was something she did not want to give up.

She majored in chemistry at the Science College of the university. "Why chemistry? The college had only the departments of architecture and chemistry open for female students. I did not like architecture. When I went, there were only seven female students in the whole college." She rode a bicycle to school each day, and spent six hours in class. Believing that science could save the nation, she buried herself in books. "I was known as a bookworm, spending all my time in the university library … Never bored by reading academic works." She had a strong thirst to learn, and she wanted to make her mother proud.

In college, male students were interested in her, but "I was not interested … because I did not want to waste my time … Later I did have a boyfriend and brought him home. My father gave him a [math] test that really scared him, but he figured it out! … I am from this kind of family!" She reiterated that the family focused a lot on academic studies and lacked an interest in politics and social skills. That young man became her husband after the war.

Keeping Christian Faith for Self-Strength

While Wang Yao, Shang Pu, and Wang Zhen accepted education under the Japanese, three others – Wang Bo, Yu Jian, and Zhang Shu – received their education in Christian schools and were devoted to the Christian faith. In her early teens, Wang Bo converted to Christianity and remained faithful throughout her life. In 1936, at the age of twenty-one, she married a man she met at the Christian Renci Hospital. During the war years, Huai'an was first attacked by the Japanese and then subjected to the influence of the collaboration region, the Nationalists, and the Communists. When the situation permitted, Wang Bo operated her own small clinic as a midwife with the help of her husband, using the modern medical knowledge she had acquired. They managed to get medical supplies through connections in big cities. There was no church to attend, but she kept reading her Bible, grateful that her nurse training program at the Renci Hospital had enabled her to have an independent profession. "Christianity taught compassion ... It gave me spiritual strength," she said. At the time of our conversation, she showed me her Chinese Bible with pictures of pine trees in the Chinese painting style, and said that she had never given up her faith despite the government's discouragement and the banning of religion during the Mao era.

Growing up in Dalian, Yu Jian received an elementary school education under the Japanese occupation. Resentful of the Japanese and not wanting his daughter to be educated under them, her father took the whole family to Yantai, Shandong, a port city opened to foreign trade in 1858 and where Western missionaries had been active. Yu Jian went to the Chinese-run Chongde All-Girls School, which had French Catholic nuns as teachers. The school was conservative and strict in discipline. "The school gates were closed. Students were not permitted to go outside. We had classes on Chinese history and politics ... In physical education class, we played tennis ... Not much about gender equality. Students were mostly from wealthy families." Two years into senior middle school, she had to quit when her father became ill and could no longer afford her education. She found a teaching job at an elementary school.

Yu Jian did not convert to Catholicism until after leaving senior middle school. She could not remember the year but recalled that during a serious illness, "Catholic nuns and priests gave me books to read, so I converted after the illness." Yantai was occupied by the Japanese from February 1938 to 1945. Attending church during the war brought her peace and comfort, where "we just kneeled and prayed. Priests gave no sermons. Just prayed with us. The nuns would sing so beautifully accompanied by the organ." After 1949, she and her husband moved to Beijing. Her daughter, who was present at our interview, was surprised to learn for the first time that her mother had been a Catholic. Yu Jian had kept this a secret because adherence to any religion was dangerous under the Communist government until the 1980s. She claimed with a smile, "I have held on to my faith till now. Sometimes I went to church. I just didn't want to tell you [her three children] for fear you would object."

Among the six women interviewed, only Zhang Shu was born into a Christian family, and only she strongly refused an education under the Japanese. The eight years of war were a constant struggle to obtain an education. When the war broke out in the summer of 1937, she was studying at a missionary school in Shanghai financially supported by her second-eldest sister. In 1941, she returned home to enrol at the American missionary-operated Yanjing University in Beiping. Only a few months later, the Pacific War broke out and the Japanese closed the university.[50] Yanjing University moved into the interior with the Nationalists. Zhang Shu transferred to Beijing Normal University, which was administered under the collaboration regime. Strongly resentful of the Japanese educators there, she decided to leave for the Nationalist-controlled areas in the interior. In late 1942, she, her younger sister, and five other students made the arduous journey to the Nationalist-controlled city of Xi'an. The journey was arranged by Nationalist agents who were recruiting young people to their side. Her mother prepared seven suitcases of clothes for all seasons for her two daughters and repeated once again: "You must graduate from college."

Zhang Shu gave a long description of her hazardous journey. After taking the train from Beiping to Zhengzhou, Henan, and crossing Japanese blockades in the occupied area on foot, one day they were robbed by local bandits who took all their money and belongings, and when they took shelter before dark in a small village of only a few households, they were caught by the Japanese:

> With swords in hand, the Japanese asked us who were the Communists. No one dared to say anything. All were scared to death ... They took us on foot to police headquarters. It was getting dark. When we were near a rice field, all of a sudden, machine guns strafed from the opposite small hill ... Such a dangerous, life and death moment. We all lay on the ground ... The Japanese ran and the gunshots followed them ... We did not know who attacked the Japanese, the Eighth Route Army, or the local militia ... We didn't move until they all left.

Thanks to the resistance force, they managed to escape and took shelter in another village.

> I was a Christian from childhood but was not a very serious one. That night we had nowhere to go, had nothing left, and with the Japanese forces nearby ... I led a prayer with a small candle asking for God's protection for a safe crossing of the Yellow River ... It was the Nationalist-controlled area on the other side of the river.

From that night on, she reported, she became a firm believer in God. With the help of a local guide, she and her companions walked the whole night and then crossed the Yellow River. These penniless students continued on foot for another ten days or so before finally arriving in Xi'an. On the road, "I had no more clothes so I was unable to change. A male student gave me his big shirt. Had to borrow a man's shoes too ... We had to beg for food. Our determination to go on for education was never weakened."

In Xi'an, she enrolled in the Nationalist government–sponsored Northwest Music Conservatory, where students enjoyed free tuition and room and board, and her sister enrolled in a middle school. However, Zhang Shu disliked the Northwest Music Conservatory because "it was too much under the censorship" of the Nationalist government. In 1944, she and her sister undertook yet another arduous journey, hitchhiking their way to Chengdu in Nationalist-controlled Sichuan Province. "So hard, you could never imagine ... Once I was sick, running high fever ... In a small village ... drinking a lot of hot water I got better ... God was with us all the way, protecting us through all the hardships. Every step, God guided us. I prayed all the way."

In Chengdu, she entered Yanjing University, majoring in Western literature. A year later, while she was still in college, a young man proposed to her: "That was a crossroad for me: To continue school or to get married? That boyfriend had a job with a stable income. I would not have to work. But I was influenced by my mother. She said all my daughters must have a college degree certificate." She turned down the proposal and continued her schooling. In those days, she said lightheartedly, female students were a minority in college, "so I had several men to choose from ... I didn't feel gender discrimination. This sense of superiority may not be healthy, actually, but one had quite a few men to choose from ... I wanted someone outstanding in his profession." She married a young man of her choice after her graduation in 1948.

Enhanced Nationalist Consciousness and Everyday Forms of Resistance

Asked why they did not participate in organized resistance, these six women explained the circumstances that they believed made it impossible for them to become involved with political issues. Although none used such words as "women's liberation," "nationalism," "motherland," "citizen's responsibility," or "serving society," no one could be free of politics when living under the occupation. Japanese aggression had destroyed the stability of their lives, and in their narratives they cited examples of their own everyday forms of resistance. In their stories, their intense, deeply buried feelings against the invaders showed in expressions such as "slaves in a lost nation," "humiliation," "hatred," "Japanese devils," and "Japanese robbers." These were part of a common vocabulary employed by the Chinese during wartime and in Communist China's narratives, when propaganda demonized the Japanese aggressors, intensifying national hatred toward them.

Wang Bo of Jiangsu recalled:

When the Japanese came, we [she and her family] hid in a village. The Japanese devils were everywhere ... In those days we were first afraid of bandits, and then of the Japanese ... We often had to run from them. The Japanese did not treat people as humans. I had a relative who did not flee fast enough so she was raped.

Although she and her husband operated a small clinic, her medical skills could not save her two daughters in the harsh living conditions. One died of amoebic dysentery when she was little, the other of tuberculosis at the age of thirteen. Before her death, the latter, a Christian, asked: "Mom, shall I see you again after my death?" Wang Bo was in tears when recalling this. Antibiotics were available but too expensive to afford.

Yu Jian made a special point of not being much concerned with political affairs in occupied Yantai, Shandong. In her school, gender equality was hardly mentioned. She did not read newspapers published by the occupation and collaboration regimes "because they were not interesting." Regarding the Nationalist Party, she said, "I did not think much whether the party was good or not. It did not matter who was in power." She had heard from a schoolmate about the Communists and Mao Zedong and how great they were. One day, this schoolmate told Yu Jian that she planned to go to Yan'an. Yu Jian recalled: "I said to her I would like to go with you. Are you going to regret it? She asked me. No, I said. But she simply disappeared the next day." It is not clear why her schoolmate left without her. During our interview, Yu Jian remarked: "I do not have much regret about not going to Yan'an." The Communist Party's record of persecuting its own members from 1942 onward, especially during the Cultural Revolution, was still fresh in her mind. In fact, her daughter later told me that Yu Jian had been briefly labelled a "rightist" during the 1957 Anti-Rightist Campaign. She was working as an elementary school teacher then but some of her remarks got her into trouble. The cruelty of politics silenced her from then onward.

During the war, Yu Jian had held a teaching position at an elementary school in Yantai, and she and others had to perform Japanese rituals at a Japanese shrine: "I just stood at the last line, did not want to do anything." To exercise control over the education of the Chinese, the collaboration authorities administered "thought examinations" to schoolteachers.[51] Yu Jian was required to take such a test. To the question "Are the Japanese good?" her reply was a bold "No." To the question "What is your nationality?" her reply was "I am Chinese." Afraid that her replies would cause trouble, Yu Jian quit her position at the urging of her friends. Through a female friend, she found a job in the Zhangyu Wine Company in Yantai. It was also under the Japanese authorities but there was no direct contact with the Japanese. The pay was sufficient to support herself and her parents. Economic independence was precious to her. After her father passed away, her mother moved to Yantai to live with her. As the only child, she took care of her mother and did not want to marry so as to have "no one to control me ... Why should one marry? Why should one not be independent?" Social pressure for marriage was strong, however, and in 1948 she married a young technician in the same company who was introduced by a friend. She was twenty-nine by then, quite late for marriage at that time. An open-minded man, Yu Jian's husband helped with domestic duties, so she continued to work even after childbirth. Her mother was a great help too.

Shang Pu, who lived in Shenyang, explained that she knew that some people went to the interior to join the resistance. Even her younger sister wanted to go, but Shang Pu felt it was too dangerous: "The school principal was thrown into prison because he was anti-Japanese. We heard that his daughter was eaten up by the Japanese wolfdog ... We were scared ... Whichever family had someone to leave, that family would be caught and fed to wolfdogs." The reality was that "some spies are running dogs of the Japanese, some the toes of the running dogs. People did not dare to speak openly, for they did not know who the spies were among themselves." It was not just the fear; a sense of responsibility was important to her as well: "We felt we had to be loyal and filial to my mother, a value Mother had taught us since we were small ... My father died. Mother was a widow ... Had I left, they [her family members] might be imprisoned. We could not leave. Mother had only me. My younger sister was born by another concubine." Under the occupation, not interested in reading any newspapers or magazines, hardly having heard about the Communist Party and with only a little knowledge of the Nationalist Party, Shang Pu spent her spare time reading classical Chinese literature and Buddhist and Christian works. Although she never became a believer of either faith, she continued to draw strength from reading those works throughout her life.

Deep down, Shang Pu harboured resentment against the occupiers, which led to open defiance. Not long after she began working as an elementary school teacher, one day at lunchtime, as the female and male teachers were sitting down at their separate tables, the male Japanese school principal at the head table asked Shang Pu, the new female teacher, to fill his rice bowl. She refused, seeing in this request his way of imposing his authority and trying to humiliate the new teacher:

> I was furious. I was a teacher here, not a servant girl ... Sitting in my seat, tears running down my face, I did not move. A senior male teacher took the bowl of the Japanese to serve him some rice. The principal insisted, "I don't want you; let that young woman teacher serve. If she doesn't, she will not be able to serve her future husband well!" ... I wept and left the dining room without any lunch.

After the incident, she did not return to school for awhile. In 1940, she went to study in Japan on a Manchukuo government scholarship. Upon her return to Shenyang in 1943, she taught at a middle school under Japanese administrators, earning thirty yuan a month, five yuan less than a male teacher with the same qualifications. Life was hard.

> I got up early every morning, around five o'clock. Went to school after breakfast. Began the class at eight. Four classes in the morning, and two in the afternoon. My mother prepared meals at home. Sometimes I brought a lunchbox to school. The Chinese had to eat sorghum and were not allowed to eat rice. If they did, they would be treated as criminals of "national affairs," or economic criminals ... The food was rationed, very coarse sorghum or soya bean dregs. People say these were not for humans ... They were for draft animals. The Chinese were treated like animals!

From late 1943, when the Japanese were having severe military and economic difficulties, she and her colleagues and students had to work as labourers in either a textile factory or a cigarette factory. They did this until the Japanese surrender in August 1945.

Wang Yao admitted to lacking the courage to join the resistance while also stressing her own autonomy. From her father, she had heard about communism, socialism, the Chinese Communist Party, and ideas about striving for social equality. While studying in Tokyo in 1934, she met other Chinese students, men and women, for social gatherings on weekends and joined their socially progressive reading club. It was there that she met her future husband, who was from southern China. They fell in love. When her Japanese teacher warned her, a subject of Manchukuo, against marrying someone from the Republic of China because she should serve Manchukuo after graduation, she refused to yield to the pressure: "First, I believed in freedom of choice. Second, I had some anti-Manchukuo ideas. I wanted to be socially progressive. After some thinking, I came to see that there would be no other way to leave Manchuria [except to marry a man from then unoccupied China]." They were married in August 1936, and the war broke out the following July. Wang Yao, now pregnant, made the long and difficult journey with her husband back to his home village.

In the southern mountainous village, away from the battlefields, they thought of joining the Communist resistance since her husband's older brother was a Communist Party member. Yao explained that the plan did not work out as they already had a small family and she was in poor health, having been crippled by a foot injury at the age of eighteen. In 1941, she and her husband again planned to go to Yan'an, but first they paid a visit to her mother in Manchuria. Suffering from mental illness, her mother pleaded with them to stay in Manchuria. As she was the only child, Wang Yao and her husband stayed. Her husband found a job at a private non-Japanese-run bank while she ran the household. She admitted: "I was afraid of difficulties and did not have the strength to overcome them ... he was not so strong either." In Manchuria, she turned down an offer of a teaching position because

> at the Manchukuo schools, there was a morning ritual to bow to the Japanese emperor and sing the Japanese anthem. I said that I'd rather be a housewife than serving the occupation regime ... Back then it was *nuhua jiaoyu* [education to enslave], teaching Japanese language and practising Japanese rituals – morning salute to the Japanese emperor. So, I'd rather stay at home taking care of children, serving my husband ... To be a wise wife and good mother.

To her, to be a daughter, a wife, and a mother at home was meaningful. In a reminiscence written for her children, she summarized her life from July 1937 to July 1949: "These twelve years were not long, but the experience was rich. I came to understand hardship, the meaning and value of life; I took up the duties and responsibilities of a daughter, a wife, and a mother." Her father retired in 1942, so he stopped working for the Japanese before the war was over. He passed away in early 1949 before the Communist takeover. Wang Yao commented: "I do not know how to evaluate him. Working for the Japanese ... but he had friends who were anti-Japanese." In spite of everything, she had deep feelings for him.

Zhang Shu, who had spent the war years trying to continue her education, discussed how the war taught her about nationalism. She characterized herself as a person who did not care about politics at all throughout her life. "My second elder sister went to Yanjing University ... She was radical." After graduation, the sister went to Shanghai, where she worked at the YWCA and joined the underground Communist Party. Zhang Shu attended an American missionary school in the International Concession in Shanghai, financially supported by her sister. However, "my sister did not ask me to join any political activities ... perhaps because it was too dangerous. I knew they sometimes held meetings, but she never said anything to me." In the concession, free from the Japanese occupation, "the war was going on around me, but I seldom read the newspapers, hardly knew anything about the resistance against Japan, or about any of the battles, although the situation was serious." In the fall of 1941, she enrolled at Yanjing University. In this American-run university, still not taken by the Japanese in the occupied Beiping, the Pacific War changed her.

> Who would expect only three months after, Pearl Harbor happened? When it happened, we were in the classroom. That morning in December. Pearl Harbor left a deep impression on me, carved into my memory. We were in class when the Japanese soldiers arrived on motorcycles. It was a geology class. Until then, I had no idea about what went on in the outside world. I was, then and now, not interested in politics, and had no interest in current affairs. Suddenly, Japanese soldiers appeared. I was shocked ... Within a few days, we were driven out of the campus. I realized then that the Japanese were truly robbers ...
>
> Life had been peaceful for three months at the university, and I met a young man ... A life of excitement was disrupted by the Japanese. I did not have much idea of national hatred, had not that level of knowledge. I just felt that the Japanese were truly hateful. I hated them! The invasion disrupted my study, my schooling. Schools were closed down. Our life was turned upside down ...
>
> Leaving my sheltered dorm at Yanjing and going back into the city[52] ... I saw Japanese all over the streets. In our neighbourhood opposite to our

> house was a residence compound of Japanese families ... Although they did not mistreat us ... I did not think much of them.

Yanjing University relocated to the interior. Zhang Shu had no school to go to. At that time, the family depended on the income of her eldest sister, a nurse at the Union Hospital. Her older brother went to serve in the Nationalist air force. Zhang Shu went to Beiping Normal University, majoring in music.

> I felt keenly what it meant to be a slave in a lost nation. Why? The wife of the head of our department was Japanese ... Japanese language was compulsory. My piano professor was Japanese, and so was the voice professor. There were a few Chinese professors for music history. Ours was a Japanese-run university ... A female Japanese professor was so arrogant ... Seemed she was so superior ... I resented her.

When she went home from school on weekends, "there were Japanese everywhere. Drunken soldiers ... following female students around and talking nonsense." The political situation motivated Zhang to leave for the Nationalist-controlled areas in the interior. Her determination to refuse Japanese education sustained her on the long journey.

Wang Zhen, who stayed in occupied Beiping as a student throughout the war, commented that her father's apolitical views made all of her family uninterested in politics. Deep down, she was sure that "I loved my country" with "perhaps a blind love," an evaluation that implied that she was not sure what to do for the resistance. Yet, more often than the other five women I interviewed, she used the term "hate" or "hatred" (at least fifteen times) to describe how she had felt toward the Japanese. This language of hatred was in the official narrative of the war during the Mao era. Wang Zhen's feeling was shared by many since they have not yet gained a sense of closure. The war has remained an important issue between China and Japan to the present day.

Her home in Beiping's downtown area was near a brothel run for Japanese soldiers. She recalled that "we hated the Japanese so much that we wanted to beat them up. Hated them whenever I saw a Japanese flag." She remembered that some Japanese soldiers had robbed her younger brother of his skates and beaten him. "The Japanese didn't treat Chinese as humans." Although she repeated several times that she did not understand much about politics, "Father cultivated in us anti-Japanese feelings. Also, we saw how the Japanese bullied the Chinese. It was miserable to live as a slave in a lost nation. No self-esteem. All this made us hate the Japanese. We felt that the Chinese themselves were weak, as Father often lamented that we ourselves were too weak." During eight years of living under Japanese occupation, the hardest part for her was "the mental distress. I did not go hungry. The food was scarce ... but we did not feel the material life was too hard. The hardest was the mental distress under the Japanese oppression."

Her strong feelings inspired a sense of resistance. Excitedly, she described "our ways of resistance," one of which was refusing to learn the Japanese language. In military training, students would sing a song with ambiguous lyrics to defy the Japanese authorities. One winter's day, the students had a snowball fight but they targeted a Japanese teacher. Wang Zhen later realized that these activities were organized by underground Communist Party members. At Beijing University, she joined a reading club for progressive works of literature and philosophy organized also by the underground Communist Party, but the party did not recruit her as she was hesitant about becoming involved in politics. In the interview at her small apartment in Beijing, she reflected:

> Come to think of it now, had China not had revolution, China could not be saved. Science alone could not save the country. With no ruling power, how could you save the country? Therefore, Mao Zedong's seizing political power [from the Nationalist government] is right ... That is how I came to understand. Those who wanted to save the country by science did not succeed.

So she drew the conclusion that the fundamental way to save China was through revolution. In the late 1940s, many Chinese intellectuals took this view as the Communist Party and the Nationalist Party engaged in a brutal civil war.

******

Six middle-class women in the occupied areas were forced to engage in moral and survival struggles. In their reflections, they confronted the issues of fear, passivity, and their lack of interest in politics and of knowledge of current affairs. They encountered hardships in their everyday lives during the war, but they did not describe themselves merely as "slaves in a lost nation" or as victims consumed by fear and hatred. Their stories and reflections are accounts of personal striving for self-preservation and self-respect. Wang Yao, Shang Pu, Yu Jian, and Wang Bo were proud of how they had attained education, made choices for marriage or celibacy, and cared for parents and families, which they saw as important obligations and duties. Wang Zhen and Zhang Shu had persisted in their efforts to obtain an education during the war, which would have enormous implications for their lives. The narratives are testimonies of personal tenacity and everyday forms of resistance shaped by their gender consciousness, patriotic emotions, and concepts of independence. Deep down, these women maintained their dignity and refused to submit to patriarchal and foreign aggressors.

With the founding of the People's Republic of China in 1949, Wang Bo worked as a nurse in a hospital in Huai'an. The other five women were all in Beijing. Shang Pu worked as a schoolteacher until her retirement. Never married, she enjoyed respect and care from her students all the way to her old age, in sickness and until her death. Wang Yao changed from a housewife to a research staff member at a government office, aided by her Japanese-language proficiency and college education. Wang Zhen served as a research staff member at the Academy of Natural Sciences, reaching the senior level by the time she retired. Yu Jian taught in an elementary school until 1957, when the Anti-Rightist Campaign accused her of being a rightist. The label was dropped a couple of years later, but she never worked again. At first Zhang Shu stayed at home as a housewife for fear that her working in the US Information Service in Tianjin in 1948–49 would cause political trouble for her, but after the Cultural Revolution she took a position as a middle school teacher and a translator of English novels and went on to study for a degree in the United States.

Life had been hard for them. In spite of it all, these educated women tried to live a more fulfilling life than their mothers.

6
I Want to Speak Up before I Die: The Testimonies of China's "Comfort Women" and the Oral Narratives of Working-Class Women

In August 2017, a Chinese documentary, *Twenty-Two*, was publicly released in Beijing.[1] The film provided glimpses into the daily lives of the remaining twenty-two Chinese "comfort women," who had spoken up publicly about the sexual violence inflicted upon them by the Japanese Imperial Army. I watched this film in a Beijing cinema. The two-hundred-seat theatre was almost full. It was unusually quiet for a Chinese theatre throughout the entire show. The documentary's poster advertises it as the "last gaze" at these "comfort women" survivors. Yet, these elderly women are not there just to be gazed at but dominate the film. Their stories are so powerful that they forced the audience to confront the harsh reality of the past and present, and see that the traumas suffered by these women are a part of the history of the entire nation, and of the entire human race.

"Comfort women" (*weianfu*), a euphemism used by the Japanese military during the war, were in effect sex slaves, detained in comfort stations, at Japanese blockhouses, or in temporary places under the Japanese Imperial Army. An estimated 200,000 Chinese were forced to become comfort women during the war.[2] For those Chinese women under the Japanese occupation who were not sexually assaulted, the constant fear of sexual and other types of violence exacerbated the effects of economic poverty and the patriarchal system on their daily lives.

This chapter begins with an analysis of the published oral testimonies of the former Chinese sex slaves. This is followed by a discussion of the interviews I conducted with five working-class women.[3] During the fourteen years of the War of Resistance, all of these women suffered. Unlike the women associated with the Nationalists or the Communists, most had limited access to education and little knowledge of political ideology or connections to power. They underwent multiple layers of suffering not just during the war but also in the postwar era, when their miseries were met with public silence. In the narrative that merely condemned the victimizers or glorified the nation's sacrifice, the multiple forms of suffering were nearly forgotten.[4] The act of remembering by the former Chinese comfort women was a process of demanding justice. It led these women in a transformation from victim-survivors to "survivor activists."[5] Similarly, speaking of their bitterness in life empowered the five working-class women I interviewed who had survived the years of Japanese aggression. Because their sufferings and life experiences were significant to them, each was willing to tell her story.

Multi-Layered Sufferings and Breaking the Silence

Sexual violence against women, whether spontaneous or officially sanctioned, has been a part of all wars from ancient times all the way to the First World War, the Second World War, and to the present. Rape was a weapon of terror and revenge, and a way of inflicting the "ultimate humiliation" on the men of the conquered nation.[6] From the 1930s to 1945, sexual violence was inflicted by the Japanese aggressors in China through the comfort women system and other means of sexual torture. The gendered violence imposed "multi-layered injuries" on women,[7] subjecting them to abuses of "sexism, classism, racism, colonialism, imperialism, and capitalist imperialism."[8] Although the atrocities of the Japanese army in China were widely known and recorded during the war,[9] their horrors were largely ignored in public during the postwar period. At the Nuremberg and Tokyo war crimes trials following the Second World War, rape was not seen as a war crime. The Tokyo trial completely ignored the sexual enslavement of women by the Japanese Imperial Army.[10] In the Cold War climate, public memory of Japanese sexual violence was suppressed in China. The governments of Japan, the United States, South Korea, and China – both Communist and Nationalist – kept silent about Japanese atrocities to a large extent. The Maoist government denied Chinese victims any opportunity to demand financial compensation from the Japanese government. While many in Japan have recognized their country's war crimes, the denialists still constitute a strong force in the public sphere.[11] In the United States, a controversial article by

Harvard University professor J. Mark Ramseyer has argued that Korean women were willing sex workers.[12]

The victims who survived the wartime sexual violence were forced to endure years of isolation and alienation through the public silence. Psychological trauma would have made them unwilling to speak, although none ever forgot the suffering.[13] In a male-dominated political and social environment, the survivors, who were mostly poor, uneducated, and with little influence in society, were unable to accuse their abusers. Both men and women believed losing one's chastity as a woman was a crime to be condemned under Confucian moral values. Their deeply felt shame made the victims remain silent themselves. What was done to them brought not just personal shame but also shame upon the whole family, so they kept silent to protect both their own and their family's reputation.[14] To the nation, these women were reminders of the collective shame of being conquered by the Japanese, and of the failure of the community and the nation to protect women.[15] In China, society often viewed the surviving victims as collaborators, as public enemies. The nationalistic prejudice further reinforced the public silence about their sufferings.[16]

Since the 1980s, the concerted efforts of victims of the sexual violence, journalists, feminist academics and activists, and human rights groups in South Korea and Japan have pushed the issue onto the domestic and international platform. The United Nations addressed the issue of the comfort women in 1992. An international redress movement arose, demanding that the Japanese government accept its full responsibility and offer compensation to the surviving comfort women.[17]

In China, government-sponsored projects, academic research, and journalists' historical accounts since the 1980s have addressed the Japanese use of terror and atrocities against Chinese civilians in order to rescue history from its silence and to respond directly to the Japanese right wing's denial of their country's responsibility for, and cover-up of, war crimes. Studies have publicized horrific data on the mass killing and bombing of civilians, the forced labourers, the 731 Imperial Army's experiments with viruses on Chinese, and the sexual violence. During the Nanjing Massacre from December 1937 to early 1938, an estimated 300,000 Chinese were murdered by the Japanese Imperial Army, and 80,000 women were raped. Although denialists in Japan refuse to acknowledge the occurrence of the massacre, and there are controversies regarding the specific numbers of victims, numerous reports during the war, eyewitness testimonies, and recent studies constitute a large body of evidence.[18]

Concerns about gendered violence and comfort women in China began through journalist research and at the grassroots level.[19] Zhang Shuangbing, a schoolteacher of Yu County, Shanxi Province, was one of the local researchers. Since the 1980s, he has identified and interviewed over a hundred former comfort women in several counties in Shanxi. He offered assistance to research projects by Chinese scholars and filmmakers and by Japanese scholars, and published his interviews in 2011.[20]

The first monograph on Chinese comfort women was an emotionally charged work of reportage literature published in 1993.[21] In 1999, historian Su Zhiliang published his research exploring the formation and operation of the Japanese military sex slave system in China.[22] In the same year, the Research Center for Comfort Women was established at the Shanghai Normal University, where Su taught. The following year witnessed the convening of the first international conference on the study of the Chinese comfort women in Shanghai.[23] Su's second book on comfort women reports on the lives of the survivors in postwar China, how they lived in poverty and ill health, and how some suffered persecution in the series of political campaigns from 1949 onward.[24] Since then, Su and other scholars have continued the research and organized financial and legal assistance for the victims.[25] The first academic research monograph in the English language on Chinese comfort women was published in 2013 by Peipei Qiu in collaboration with Su Zhiliang and Chen Lifei. The work contains oral accounts of twelve former comfort women from three different areas of China: the eastern coastal region, central and northern China, and the southern frontiers – to show women's diverse experiences. The book demonstrates convincingly that the comfort women issue "is not simply a historical matter: they pose a fundamental challenge to those contemporary institutions that have perpetuated their sufferings."[26]

Among studies by Japanese scholars, one in-depth work on Chinese victims of sexual violence is by historian Ishida Yoneko. From October 1996 to March 2003, Ishida and her team conducted eighteen investigation trips in Yu County, Shanxi Province, where they interviewed former comfort women through collaboration with Chinese researchers, local government, the relatives of the victims, and local activists. Ishida's published work contains testimonies of nine victims and the adopted daughter of one victim, plus ten witnesses. It includes detailed contextual research on sexual violence in the area, which occurred not just in the "comfort station" but also in Chinese villages or Japanese military strongholds. It confronts the wartime responsibility of the Japanese army as victimizers.[27]

Besides offering their testimonies to the public, the survivors of sexual violence themselves courageously appeared in front of cameras to share their experiences.[28] Film director Guo Ke's documentary *Thirty-Two* was released in 2014.[29] The tittle indicates the number of comfort women who spoke out publicly and were still alive when the director began making the documentary. It focuses on one woman, Wei Shaolan, of Yao ethnicity, in Guangxi, and her son fathered by a Japanese who had raped her. In 2017, Guo Ke released another documentary, *Twenty-Two* (mentioned at the beginning of this chapter). Memorial museums such as the Nanjing Museum of the Site of the Lijixiang Comfort Stations (opened in 2015), the Chinese Comfort Women History Museum in Shanghai (opened in 2016), and the AMA Museum for Peace and Women's Human Rights in Taipei (opened in 2016) have brought the "painful and secret history" to the public in order to remember the past.[30]

"I Would Never Rest in Peace If I Did Not Speak Up": From Victim-Survivors to Survivor Activists

In the documentary *Twenty-Two,* Zhang Shuangbing laments:

> When I started investigating, there were 123 victims in Shanxi Province. Now [2014], only twelve here are still alive. I was very naïve at that time and just wanted to bring justice to them. I wanted the Japanese government to apologize and to compensate them. But in the end, after more than 30 years, they didn't receive a single cent or any apology from the Japanese government. They spoke out publicly about their past, which caused them disgrace. Now all the people around them and even the entire country know about them. It is not a good thing to them. So I regret very much. If I had known it would turn out like this I would have never disturbed them.

Indeed, as these poor and powerless women provided their own accounts of previously repressed memories of atrocities, they suffered once again the devastating pain. Burdened by painful memories and neglected by society for so long, they had endured mental and physical injuries and a deep sense of shame and self-blame. Each time they talked about the horrible experience, it was "as if they were going through the hell again."[31] Interviews caused them severe physical pain and psychological breakdown. Often after speaking out, they were haunted by distress.[32]

Academic research has recognized that it was a heroic confrontation of their bitter experiences when the victims told the public about their sufferings. Speaking in public also served "a cathartic function," for it helped relieve the oppression that had silenced these women for half a century.[33] Because of their inherent limitations, international law and legal process have failed the comfort women, but their testimonies are not futile for they demonstrate to the wider public the gross human rights violations that occurred.[34] The process of speaking up enabled them to see that their sufferings were not caused by themselves, that they must fight in order to wipe out the shame that society had imposed upon them.[35] It helped transform these women from victim-survivors to survivor activists in the redress movement for justice and dignity. The self-narrative established their own agency.

Zhang Shuangbing's investigation illustrates the transformation. In 1982, he learned from others that Hou Dong'e (1921–94) of Yu County had been one of the women taken to the Japanese blockhouse to be raped. In 1982, at the age of sixty-one, she lived with her seventy-year-old husband who was bedridden due to illness. Zhang began to help the couple in their daily life, and also wanted to learn more about Hou's past. Every time he brought up the topic, Hou would be evasive. Ten years later, in June 1992, after learning from the media about the Chinese war victims' efforts to claim compensation from the Japanese government, Zhang went to tell her the news. She responded:

> I trust you but I simply do not dare to believe this news because I know that twenty years ago, China and Japan became friendly. When hearing the news from the radio that China and Japan established diplomatic relations and issued a joint communique, people like us, who had suffered so much, were deeply saddened. No one would mention any revenge when China and Japan had no diplomatic relations. Now that the two countries are friendly, people have mentioned the revenge. I simply do not believe that there are people who would care for us suffering common people.[36]

After Zhang's repeated explanations, Hou agreed to talk. The first day, she cried so hard that she could hardly utter any complete sentences. When Zhang came again the following day, Hou told him that all the crying had released her pent-up bitterness, that she had had a good sleep. Thus, she began telling him her story. Not merely recalling the past, she also took action. In July 1992, with the assistance of Zhang Shuangbing and legal specialists, Hou Dong'e and four other victims of sex slavery and two former male forced labourers submitted their letter of appeal to the Japanese government requesting an apology and compensation. Hou was prepared to go to Tokyo for the public hearings at the end of that year, but was unable to make the trip due to a complication in communication and transportation.[37] She expressed no regret for her fight because "I finally had a chance to let out my grievances that had been buried in my heart all these years, and to make people see the shameless act of the Japanese aggressors and that I had been wronged."[38]

Similar to Hou, Liu Mianhuan (b. 1927) overcame her hesitation and let Zhang Shuangbing interview her in 1992–99 in order to prepare testimony for a lawsuit against the Japanese government. In 1992, she made her demand for Japan's official apology and compensation, and appeared as a witness in a Tokyo court five times from 1996 to 2004. She was determined: "I would fight for the lawsuit all the way to the end. I am in the right. This is a justified lawsuit; it is not a shameful and unspeakable matter. It was the Japanese soldiers who forced us at gun point into their blockhouse."[39] Hou Qiaoliang (1928–99), another victim, first met Zhang Shuangbing in 1992. She could not bring herself to come forward until two years later, when she saw progress in the redress movement and realized the importance of her own testimony. She began to talk and appeared at the court in Tokyo in 1996 and 1998.[40] In Zhang's decades of investigation, many other women approached him and were willing to speak up because they saw hope for attaining justice. Toward the end of their lives, these downtrodden women, who had lost so much during and after the war, refused to yield any longer. They left their records of sufferings because they came to see that their own words could provide evidence of Japanese war crimes, and their sufferings should not be in vain.

In their research in Yu County, Ishida Yoneko and her team did not initiate the interviews with the purpose of assisting litigation but informed the surviving victims that this would be an option. In the process of breaking their silence, the women developed trust in the researchers. In March 1998, ten of them expressed willingness to file lawsuits demanding apologies and financial compensation from the Japanese government. They were also motivated by the aspiration to regain personal honour, to "live with my back straight in the village," and to die in peace. They came to see meaning in their sufferings.[41] Yang Xihe said to the researchers:

> I want to speak up before I die no matter what. I might be a person with no power or influence, but today the reason why I have spoken to you about the bitter experience, mentioned to no one before and buried in my heart

for so long, is because I want an apology from the Japanese government. I would never rest in peace if I did not speak up. Please verify the crimes of the Japanese army that imposed humiliation not just upon me alone, but on many Chinese women. Help us prove that we were innocent victims of their sexual violence; help us restore our dignity.[42]

After Yang Xihe's death in 1998, her daughter continued the fight. In October that year, she and nine other women from Yu County filed lawsuits against the government of Japan with the assistance of Chinese and Japanese legal, civic, and academic organizations.[43]

These Chinese victims of the Japanese army's sexual slavery had their consciousness raised and their sense of responsibility to speak the truth enhanced. Yin Yulin (1929–2012) of Yu County voiced her feelings: "China won the Resistance War, and the Japanese troops fled back home in 1945. However, my misery did not disappear with them."[44] She had to speak out to expose the war crimes against women:

> The lower back pain that has bothered me for years has become worse, as has the trembling in my hands and legs. I am also suffering from acute psychological problems, such as intense fear and nightmares in which I relive those past experiences. I am trembling right now as I recall the past horror. These unspeakable things are really hard to talk about, but I can no longer keep silent. If I don't speak out, people will not know how evil those Japanese troops are.[45]

Li Lianchun (1924–2004) of Longling County, Yunnan Province, said:

> I've suffered my entire life, and I have been poor my whole life, but I have one thing that is priceless to me. That is my body, my dignity. My body is the most valuable thing to me. The damage to it cannot be compensated for with money, no matter how much money they pay. I am not seeking money, and I am not trying to get revenge. I just want to see justice done.[46]

Pain, Resilience, and the Aspirations of the Comfort Women

Through their own words, the former comfort women revealed their intense emotions. Each word is a meaning-making unit of discourse. As Maki Kimura has pointed out, "the very act of testifying to their experiences, regardless of what is considered to be 'inconsistency' or 'inaccuracy' in their accounts, also proved indispensable to the women's subject-formation."[47]

Once they broke their silence, they bravely confronted the hellish experiences that only they could describe. Frequently used words for expressing feelings were "fear," "horror," "agony," "pains," "misery," "humiliation," "nightmares," "bitterness," or "wish to die." In the women's descriptions, the Japanese aggressors did not treat them as humans, and they too saw the Japanese as beasts. The feelings of hatred, resentment, and being wronged were deeply buried in their memories.[48] Words such as "non-human," "beasts" (*chusheng*), or "no different from beasts" were often used to describe the aggressors.[49] It was a common practice in China during and after the war to refer to the Japanese soldiers as "devils" (*guizi*). In the testimonies in Ishida's collection and in the Chinese version of Peipei Qiu's work, the word "*guizi*" is often used.[50] In Qiu's English version, this word has been rendered as "Japanese soldier/s," "Japanese troop," "Japanese army," or "Japanese." It might have been the author's intention to be less emotional, but the feeling of hatred was lost in translation.

Providing testimonies gave women a chance to defend themselves by pointing out that they were coerced into sex slavery through abduction or deception, and any resistance would have led to beating, starvation, or death. Moreover, many endured the humiliation in order not to cause suffering for their families and communities. Self-sacrifice was highly expected of women in Chinese tradition. They identified with the traditional expectation that one should take care of the family through one's own sacrifice. Huang Youliang (b. 1927), of Li ethnicity in Hainan Island, Guangdong Province, was raped and kept as a sex slave by the Japanese for two years, from 1941 to 1943, first at her home – "If I hid, he would torture my parents" – then at a "comfort station." Escape would mean severe beating or death. Huang gave up hope of escaping and "submitted myself to fate."[51]

When the Japanese occupied an area, the army often forced the local collaboration regime to provide women as sex slaves.[52] In Yu County, Shanxi Province, Yang Shitong, a male witness reported that when the Japanese army stationed in Hedong Village built a blockhouse at the end of 1940, several villages established an "association for maintaining order" (*weichihui*). In order to maintain some level of security, the association had to supply men as labourers and women as sex slaves. Families that sent women might receive some financial compensation from villagers. In 1942, the association submitted five women to the Japanese army.

One of them, Nan Erpu (1912–67), was kept as a sex slave for more than a year and a half. She was chosen because she did not get along with her husband, who was twenty years older; her family did not receive compensation from the village.[53] Yang Baogui, another male eyewitness, commented that Nan Erpu and other women "were taken there to protect the villages."[54] Her younger brother, Nan Shuancheng (b. 1931), recalled:

> My elder sister ran away back home ... The Japanese devils could not find her so they tied me, a small boy, up to the horse saddle and let the horse drag me in the village for several rounds in order to force my elder sister out of hiding. My belly had cuts and wounds were all over. The villagers just looked on helplessly.
>
> I was dragged until the rope was broken ... When my sister learned what the Japanese devils had done to me, she came out and was taken again to the Hedong stronghold.[55]

Like many others, Nan Erpu continued to suffer after the war. In the Anti-counter-revolutionaries Movement in 1950 under the Communist government, she was accused of "living with the Japanese devil and giving birth to a child [who died soon after] for the Japanese devil." She was labelled as a "historical counter-revolutionary," and was imprisoned for three years. Although she received early release after two years, she was persecuted again in the early days of the Cultural Revolution (1966–76), and died by suicide in 1967.

It is difficult to imagine the horrible conditions that led to the death of so many sex slaves from starvation, illness, exhaustion, torture, or suicide. Many survived, and their families supported them. In Shanxi, payment of ransom seems to have been a common practice. For example, in Ishida's study, eight women were released after being ransomed with silver coins. Many did whatever they could to survive. Hou Dong'e recalled being locked up alone in a room and raped:

> I had no will to live any more. Thinking I should kill myself before the red-faced captain returned. But then I thought this was a Japanese place and if I died here, no one would know how I died and I would not leave a good reputation. I would not die at the Japanese place. People would laugh at me. Besides, I have a baby boy and a two-month-old girl. No one would care for them if I died. I have an elderly mother and a husband who was fighting at the front [a soldier in the Nationalist army]. I should not abandon them.[56]

For the sake of her family, she decided she must live even if it meant a life of humiliation.

Lin Ailan (1925–2015) of Hainan Island was locked up by the Japanese army for two years, and suffered torture and rape. When telling her story, she stressed that she was a war veteran in anti-Japanese activities, not just a victim of sexual violence: "When I was seventeen or eighteen, I began to follow the Communist Party, and fought battles ... I killed the Japanese devils." She wanted people to remember her as a fighter, not a victim. In her later years, living in a small, sparsely furnished room in a home for the aged, what she cherished the most were the medals awarded to her by the government for the sixtieth anniversary of victory in the War of Resistance against Japan.[57] Similarly, Wan Aihua of Yu County talked about her membership in the Communist Party in 1942 and her activities in the Communist-led resistance. In 1942–43, she was caught by the Japanese three times, interrogated about the Communists, and tortured and raped. During this period, she lost contact with the party. Fighter that she was, in 1992, with the assistance of concerned people, she became the first Chinese comfort woman to speak out in Tokyo at the International Public Hearing Concerning Postwar Compensation of Japan. In 1994, she succeeded in getting her party membership reinstated. She was determined to prove to her adopted daughter that she was "a good mother who was a fighter during the Resistance War."[58] She joined other women of Yu County in the redress movement, and went to Tokyo to testify in 1996, 1998, and 1999. In 2000, she attended the Women's International War Crimes Tribunal on Japan's Military Sexual Slavery in Tokyo organized by Asian women and human rights organizations. Her strong will kept her going in the fight to get the Japanese government to admit their wrongdoing and to "protect future generations from the kind of torture I suffered."[59]

Life treated these women with cruelty but they had inner strength and never lost the kindness in their hearts. In the documentary *Twenty-Two*, Komeda Mai, a female student from Japan who has been helping former sex slaves in Hainan Island since 2009, comments: "The wounds in their hearts are huge and deep but they are still being nice to us, whether we are from Japan or elsewhere." One of the women in *Twenty-Two*, Chen Lintao of Shanxi Province, expresses a hope for lasting peace: "I hope China and Japan can make peace with each other. No more wars. Once the war begins, a lot of people would die."

The documentary *Thirty-Two*, by Guo Ke, features one woman, Wei Shaolan of Guangxi Zhuang Autonomous Region. A peasant's wife, she was captured in 1944 and locked up as a sex slave for three months before she escaped. By then she was pregnant with the child of a Japanese. Her husband hated her but her mother-in-law showed understanding. When Shaolan tried to kill herself but was saved by her neighbour, her mother-in-law encouraged her to live. In July 1945, she gave birth to a boy. Her son grew up but was never able to marry since no one wanted a "Japanese." "No one suffered more than me," Wei Shaolan said. Yet, she believes: "The world is so wonderful. I will live to witness it even if it means eating only wild vegetables."[60] In December 2010, Wei Shaolan and her son, Luo Shanxue, participated in the Public Hearings for the Asian Victims of "Comfort Women" held in Tokyo. They submitted a petition for compensation, but received no reply before Wei Shaolan's death on May 5, 2019, at the age of ninety-nine.[61]

The Oral Narratives of Five Working-Class Women

In the effort to rescue history, Chinese government-history offices and academics have collected and published oral histories. Valuable as these are, there is still a lack of women's voices in them.[62] In the oral history of Shanxi Province about the War of Resistance, there are accounts of 665 people; more than 40 are women, among whom more than 10 are female Communist Party members. The accounts are organized under topics such as the fighting between the Communists and Nationalists; violence and crimes against people and the environment; how the Chinese Communist Party aroused the political consciousness of the people; and how the war affected everyday life, health, and education.[63] Chen Xuqing, one of the researchers in this project, notes that compared to male villagers, peasant women seldom provided clear answers regarding "political ideology, social conditions, commerce and economy, or ecological damages" in the war.[64] He observes that the peasant women's memories seem "often scattered and confused, with no specific time and clear logic." However, this does not mean they were incapable telling their stories. What is important, he concludes, is that these women remembered the Japanese aggressors out of lived experiences of suffering by them and their families, and not primarily out of political understanding of the nation.[65] Zhao Ma, in his study of lower-class women in occupied Beijing, observes that these women's lives were not marked by political changes but were part of a repeating cycle of crisis and survival.[66] Indeed, women's memories are shaped more by gender, as Gail Hershatter has shown in her study of rural peasant women who lived under Maoist socialism.[67]

During my research trip to China, I interviewed five working-class women who lived in Japanese-occupied Shanghai and in semi-occupied areas in Jiangsu and Shanxi Provinces. All were of poor family backgrounds and three had worked as child-labourers before the war. Wang Hong (1922–2010) was the only one who spoke Mandarin. The others – Bai Ai (b. 1919) from Shanxi, and Shao He (b. 1919), Yang Lai (b. 1920), and Ying Di (b. 1912) from Shanghai – spoke only local dialects that were difficult for me to follow, so I relied on interpreters. In contrast to victims of sexual violence at the hands of the Japanese Imperial Army, these women needed no encouragement to speak; all were willing to tell their stories. As with the peasant women in Shanxi in Chen Xuqing's study, specific times and places were not clear in these narratives, and the sequence of events was often confusing. Speeches were repetitive. Memories were fragmentary. The women were unfamiliar with political concepts. Nevertheless, they were able to reveal what was important to them, and they gave vivid descriptions of events from their own wartime experiences. Common themes were the cruelty of the Japanese army and the humiliations they inflicted on the Chinese, and the hardships the women endured: hunger, miseries, uncertainty, and anxiety under the Japanese. Most remarkable were their resilience and strength in mitigating hardships, working hard daily to contribute to the family income and to survive, and doing whatever they could to survive and keep their families together. Their courage and strength helped them persevere. They were among the many Chinese, as Timothy Brook notes, who, simply by surviving, kept their nation alive and ensured that it was not swallowed up by the Japanese Empire.[68]

Bitterness, Humiliation, and the Struggle for Survival

In the narrative of Shao He, two words that occurred often were "bitterness" and "poverty." Born into a poor family in Shanghai with no education, Shao He started working in the silk filature run by the Japanese at the young age of twelve, and then in a cigarette factory. Shanghai was the most industrialized city in early twentieth-century China, and women made up almost two-thirds of total industrial labour force there before 1949.[69] As a child-labourer, Shao He was "small and was often beaten." She said that she had not heard about the Communist Party during the war. Her family in Zhabei suffered in the heavy bombing by the Japanese in August 1937. Her grandmother was killed. The rest of the family and many others fled to the foreign concessions. In 1938, at the age of eighteen, she entered an arranged marriage, without seeing her future husband before the wedding. They moved to the Ningbo rural area, where they worked the land. Shao He confused the Japanese surrender in 1945 with the founding of the People's Republic of China in 1949. It seems that the years of the anti-Japanese war and the civil war up to 1949 were filled with similar days of hard work and hardship. Political events did not mark much of a turning point in her life-long struggle to survive.

Ying Di, born in Shanghai to a poor family, also worked as a child-labourer, first in a cigarette factory at the age of ten and then at an egg factory. Bitterness was a central theme of her narrative. Her husband through an arranged marriage died of tuberculosis when she was only twenty-two years old. She lost their only baby in a miscarriage. "So miserably bitter. My mother-in-law forced me to remarry. I refused so she beat me up ... I didn't want to be a concubine in that family," Ying wept. Never remarried, she just "swallowed up the bitterness" and worked for a wealthy Chinese family living in the concession. She did housework, taking care of babies and other chores and knitting to earn cash. The lady of the house, an obstetrician, taught her to read and write, and the family's belief in Buddhism influenced Ying to become a Buddhist. "Buddhism doesn't talk about politics. Only chanting scriptures ... Buddhism taught you not to desire for good food or clothes, or just personal pleasure. It is about being a good person. I believe in Buddhism out of my heart. Unlike some people nowadays who are just there for personal gains."

Japanese rule brought humiliation and instilled lasting resentment in her:

> The Japanese were so cruel. You had to lower your head when you saw them on the street. If you raised your head to look at them, they would beat you up. You had to bow to them. Otherwise, they would drag you over and give you a beating. The Japanese were brutal. If you walked fast, they would think you were up to no good ... They wanted to check your pass, "good subjects" [*liangmin*] card. If the photo was not good, they would ask for more ... If they think you are sick with some contagious disease, they would lock you up ... I have heard that the Japanese raped women. Women suffered [more than men] in the hands of the Japanese. Men would be dragged to do labour.
>
> I still hate the Japanese even now. See ten, hate ten!

Ying Di later worked as a vendor of cigarettes, candies, and other small items. She remained a firm adherent of Buddhism.

Yang Lai was born in Longhua Township near Shanghai, into a family that owned some land and ran a small business, and could even afford to give her (one of three siblings) an education. She began by saying: "In the 'the old society' (*jiu shehui*), women were looked down upon. Men were superior and women inferior. Young girls had little opportunity for education ... I received education for six years. Even men of the family could no longer afford education. Education cost ... My uncle said sending girls to school was useless!" The coming of the Japanese to Shanghai meant danger and humiliation:

> The bombs were dropping like rain. We had to run into the shelters. Once we were under a tree, a bomb dropped near us. It did not explode. Otherwise, we all would have died! ...
> My father had a small business. He was beaten by the Japanese. Had to bow to the Japanese. This was already "kind" of them to ask you to bow. In the worse situation they would just beat people up.

During the Japanese occupation, still unmarried, she supported the family by knitting. Sometimes, together with other women, she would travel by train, smuggling cigarettes, soap, candles, and other small items from Shanghai to rural villages, and bringing rice back to Shanghai. The Japanese controlled the railways and major transportation routes between Shanghai and other occupied areas with check stations. The police guarded the city entrances. Many Shanghainese, ranging from professional smugglers to common people like Yang, took up the risky business of smuggling.[70] For Yang:

> We would wrap all the small items in a cloth and hide them underneath our clothes. If found out by the Japanese, they would ask men to slap each other, and women to flick each other's forehead [as punishment]. They would laugh at us ... [I heard] someone smuggled rice into the concession and was found out. He was beaten by the dogs of the Japanese, wounded and disabled ... It was dangerous but we had to run the risk ... We had to survive.

Yang had heard about the Communist New Fourth Army, but "our area was far away [from the Communist-influenced area] and not many from the local area went to join the resistance. I was afraid." Unlike many other women, who had to marry early, she did not get married until after the war, when she was already in her early thirties, because "I did not want to get married. The family was doing OK [so that a woman did not have to marry a man for economic reasons]." This late marriage was not uncommon among Shanghai women workers. Emily Honig observes that the primary reason for a woman's late marriage was that parents wanted to keep their daughters at home so that the family would keep the financial income.[71] Yang's tone, however, revealed a sense of pride in her independence and her contribution to her own family.

Bai Ai was from Wutai County, Shanxi Province. The Japanese seized the county seat in October 1938, extending their control over part of the county. Of a poor peasant family, she had her feet bound in early childhood, and entered into an arranged marriage at the age of sixteen in a village not too far away from her natal home. A mountainous village, it had houses and traditional earthen caves built on slopes carved into terraces. A river down in the valley was the main source of water even in the 1990s. The main crops were wheat, millet, potatoes, and corn. Jujube trees dotted nearby residences and mountains. All her life, Bai seldom left her county. With no education, she spoke only the local dialect, which was unintelligible to me. We had to communicate through a relative of mine who acted as an interpreter.

Her story in the local dialect was vivid and lively. Although politics was not a familiar topic, she remembered the war clearly. She began by talking about fleeing the Japanese in the fall of 1938, when she was in her parents' village for a visit:

> So miserable. We had to run to hide into the mountains, very high. Aunty had bound feet. She had to use her hands to climb. The hands were bleeding. When we heard the sound of cannons, we all ran to hide into the mountains. I was only nineteen years old. My older brother ... was in the mountain valley. He dug a pit that three people could sit in and be covered by straw. We three were hiding there. Under the straw, we saw the Japanese marching.

Faced with this frightful situation, her brother even thought of killing Bai and his wife and himself. She recalled: "My sister-in-law had some opium. My brother said let the girl (me) take the opium to die [rather than be raped by the Japanese]. Then he said let's all die together."

About a hundred Japanese stayed in her parents' village. Her father was beaten to death by the Japanese: "The Japanese beat up my father so hard on his belly that he spit out food he had eaten. I didn't know why they hit him ... He died for nothing!" In her husband's village, the Japanese burned everything. Nothing was left. The house was burned to ashes. We built *yaodong* [a cave dwelling along the mountainside; a traditional style of housing in that area]; did not dare to build houses. We stayed in the dark cave ...

One day the Japanese came. They stabbed open my pants with a bayonet. I thought I would die at that moment ... The Japanese did not beat women but harassed them. Took away whoever was pretty.

Fortunately, she was not raped.

From 1938 to 1945, Wutai County was divided: part was under the occupation regime, part was under the Communists, and the area in between was the guerrilla zone.[72] Bai's husband's village became a "double-faced" (*liangmian*) village, subject to the Japanese occupation while also under the influence of the Communist Eighth Route Army and the guerrilla forces and lending support to their anti-Japanese activities. Bai Ai remembered that the Eighth Route Army organized women to make shoes for the army and to hold meetings. While several male villagers joined the guerrilla forces, "I understood nothing. Had heard about the Communist Party but did not know much." Her life was one of hunger, a struggle to survive: "Nothing much to eat. The dog food nowadays is better than what we ate then. Even corn was for guests only."

Bai Ai did remember Yan Xishan (1883–1960), a native of Wutai County who was the provincial head of Shanxi most of the time from 1917 to 1949. "I had my feet bound when I was little. Then the inspector sent by Yan Xishan came here to ask us women to unbind the feet." During his rule, Yan Xishan implemented policies for local improvements, including an anti–foot-binding policy.

"That Was No Life for Humans!" The Story of Wang Hong

Wang Hong was born in Liyang, Jiangsu Province, in southeastern China, an agricultural area with rice as the main crop. She was the most articulate of the five women I interviewed. Her granddaughter, a friend and academic colleague of mine in the United States, introduced me to her and told me that her grandmother liked telling stories of her past. Wang Hong's memories remained fresh, and her stories were vivid, with climax and dramatic effects, about how a young woman, not weak or dependent, lived through the war. She began: "My family was not doing well. My father had owned a small convenience store.

Gradually, he took up opium smoking, got addicted, and smoked away the family wealth. I was little then, only ten or eleven years old. No money to go to school. Went to school for a while but then life became miserable. Could not afford tuition." The family was in a small town that was exposed to modern ideas. Although Wang's grandmother insisted that girls should have bound feet and Wang's elder sister did, when grandmother died, Wang Hong's mother did not bind Hong's feet, nor did she make Wang Hong pierce her ears, an act defying tradition. Wang Hong and her three siblings all had elementary school educations. For three years, she attended a modern school where Mandarin was the medium of instruction.

When her parents went to work at a factory in Shanghai, Wang Hong went with them. A child-labourer at a camel hair textile factory, she worked a twelve-hour night shift: "The headman was so awful. I was little, only twelve or thirteen. Terrified when I saw him. Working in the night, I felt so sleepy. I would fall asleep even standing."

By the time the war broke out, Wang Hong and her parents were back in Liyang. During the war, Liyang was a complex area. After heavy bombing, the Japanese army took control of the county seat in December 1937. They lost and reoccupied the seat two more times, bombed the county thirty-four times, and carried out mopping-up campaigns in the Liyang area. In the absence of Japanese and the collaboration regime, the Nationalists ran their government there. The Communist New Fourth Army (N4A) also established its base in Liyang from the summer of 1938 to June 1940. The Japanese and the collaboration force, the Nationalists, and the Communists continued to battle in the area.[73]

The coming of the Japanese in 1937 pushed Wang Hong into an arranged marriage:

> At the bride price of several *dan* [one *dan* equals fifty kilograms] of rice, I was married off ... Rushed into my husband's family as people did not want to keep unmarried girls at home for fear they would be taken away by the Japanese to be raped ...
>
> His family had four sons. He was the second ... eleven years older than I since the family had no money to get a wife for him [earlier]. The matchmaker lied to us saying that he was six years older. I did not know that till later.

Japanese bombing was frequent. Once, "the Japanese came up [from the river near the village] without making much noise. We were all home having our meal. As soon as we saw them, we ran to hide in the rice field." Another time:

> A Japanese was killed, not by the Communists but by a peasant. The common people hated the Japanese. The Japanese bombed the area for fifteen days [for retaliation]. Some bombs dropped into our village. The village is long and narrow with a river at the front and rice fields behind. So the bombs would either drop into the river or hit the rice field ... it was such a torture.

Rape of local women by Japanese soldiers caused deep anxiety. She had a near-escape from the horror:

> The four of us young women were of similar age. I and another were newlywed, and two others about to get married. We went out to dig wild vegetables. From the river, came the Japanese from their boat with guns in hands onto the banks. They did not see us at first, but when the other three girls started running away, the Japanese saw them and caught them. A town girl as I was, I could not run as fast as others, so I was left behind. I saw the bayonet of the Japanese, so brightly shining. They took the three onto the boat. I ran quickly down into the rice field to hide. The water was up to my knees. I lay down in the water with only my head above the water. Those three girls struggled but were tied up by the Japanese and dragged away. I watched them from afar. Hid there for almost two hours.

Wang Hong escaped capture but the other three young women were kept by the Japanese for half a month. "They did not come back until after the *baozhang* [the head of the local administration] sent chickens and eggs to the Japanese. I never dared to go out to dig wild vegetables again." She remembered that after their release, the two engaged girls were married. Their husbands' families knew what had happened to them but "those were two good women; it was not their fault that they were caught by the Japanese." The married woman gave birth to a boy. During the interview, Wang Hong's grandnephew added that the boy was of the Japanese since he did not share a resemblance with his younger siblings. After growing up, he left the village for remote Qinghai in the northwest of China, where people would not know the circumstances of his birth. "That past was full of bitterness."

In the complex political situation in her area during the war, Wang Hong, like other common people in the area, witnessed and heard about the activities of the New Fourth Army, the Japanese, and the *hepingjun* (literally, the peace army, a term referring to the collaboration army), and the local bandits: "The bandits did not rob things. They only wanted money ... They were not afraid of the New Fourth Army, and the New Fourth Army were not afraid of them either. The bandits carried guns on them, guns with red or green silk ribbons." "Of course, I heard about the New Fourth Army ... On Sundays they often came to put on a performance at the ancestral hall ... The art troupe sang and danced for propaganda." "I saw Chen Yi [the general of the New Fourth Army], who was not very tall. He looked young. Not even thirty years old."[74]

Wang Hong recalled her near-death experience in one horrific military conflict:

> One night, the New Fourth Army quietly arrived in our village, getting ready to attack the blockhouse of the *heping* army. We were all terrified ... The New Fourth Army collected cotton quilts from us, wet them with water and placed them on tables to get into the blockhouse. Then we heard *kuang, kuang, kuang,* loud noises. The *heping* army surrendered. There were no Japanese among them. Those *heping* army soldiers were running dogs of the Japanese.

The New Fourth Army stayed in the village for some time. Then came Chinese New Year's Day. Wang Hong had just given birth to her firstborn boy. The Japanese came:

> We didn't know but the New Fourth Army knew that the Japanese would come. The Japanese laid a siege here ... I had just given birth the day before. In the afternoon. In the old society when giving birth one had to sit for 24 hours ...
> The morning of the New Year's Day, we heard noise. Villagers came out to pay a New Year's visit, and burning incense [to gods and ancestors] as usual, but as soon as one came out of the house, one was killed. The Japanese thought they were killing the New Fourth Army soldiers.

Faced with such danger, her husband and mother-in-law took the newborn son and fled the village, leaving Wang Hong alone in hiding in the house since she was too weak to walk. Her husband covered the door of the house with some bricks and firewood. Soon the Japanese bombing ignited the firewood and heavy smoke quickly filled the house.

The smoke was choking. I could not stay inside. I said to myself I must get out even if I were to be killed. I crept out the small opening [of the window] and saw some Japanese devils in front of another house, saying something and searching the house ...

[She ran away from the village.] It was raining heavily. It rained for the whole day. I ran into the fields and fell thirteen times ... I narrowly escaped death. I had to go across so many dead bodies, one here and one there. I was no longer in fear, just running for my life ...

That was no life for humans! ...

Falling and getting up, I got to a small village of seven or eight households. I asked for going inside but they did not want to take me in saying that you just gave birth so you were a "red person."

This means she was polluted by birth and would bring in bad luck. They did put her up in a pigsty. After the Japanese left her area, she and her family reunited. Wang Hong was unable to bear any more children. She believed that it was because of that horrible escape just after the birth of the first baby.

She described her relationship with her husband as not one of women being inferior but of mutual dependence, where even she was the stronger one: "I wasn't oppressed ... I was more forceful than my husband."

My husband was a kind person, good at Chinese acupuncture. One year when cholera erupted, he saved many people. However, I had even wanted to divorce him ...

After I gave birth I returned to the village for two years, and during that time, he alone was running a store at the town. He fooled around with another woman or several women. My older brother heard of this and urged me to divorce him. My mother told my mother-in-law about his behaviour and blamed him for neglecting his family. In those days, divorce did not need to go to any office. One just published an announcement in a newspaper. My mother-in-law was so worried that she went to town and told her son: "Do you want to die? If you continued to fool around, your wife would leave you. She wants a divorce! Where else could you find such a good woman like her?" Mother-in-law arranged a boat with some luggage and wanted to send me to town to join him. I insisted that we must have an agreement that if I go to be with him, all the money I earn would belong to me, and I should have a say in the family. Or else I would not go.

The deal worked out. Wang Hong alone managed a small vendor's table selling cigarettes and other items. Her husband was a co-owner of a convenience store. "My business was better than those of others because I was polite to everyone. Treating all with politeness." Later she and her husband opened their own store. Both worked hard and business was not bad.

When I asked whether she had any religious belief, she replied, "I believed nothing at all." Not religious faith but belief in kindness, in doing the right thing – that was Wang Hong's faith.

> I do not believe in anything, don't like that kind of nonsense. In those days, there were fortune tellers who were blind. There was this old man in our village ... he only wanted money from us ... I have been tough, not shy, and am fearless because I know what the right thing is to do. I would never do anything that would be harmful to others. I live with a good conscience.

At the time of the interview, she was in her late seventies, survived by her husband and their only son. She had helped bring up all four granddaughters when her son and daughter-in-law worked in another place. All four had university degrees. Wang Hong said with pride: "The neighbours in town respect me. Later when I was taking care of my four granddaughters, people all called me *shimu* [teacher's wife] since my husband was a Chinese medicine doctor." An ordinary woman, her strength has gained for her pride and respect.

******

Sexual violence throughout human history has inflicted multiple injuries on women. The atrocities suffered by Chinese women at the hands of the Japanese subjected them to abuses of sexism, classism, racism, and imperialism. Postwar silence imposed a further layer of injury due to social stigma and political persecution. Collective feminist and legal efforts have brought about changes since the 1980s. They forced the legal system to recognize that war rape is a crime against humanity. Victims of sexual violence during the Second World War participated in the process. The Chinese survivors of Japanese sexual violence spoke out. Their life stories reveal their inner voices on the multi-layered violence and the physical and psychological pain. Speaking out in public was powerful. It transformed them from victim-survivors to "survivor activists" in the international redress movement. Their testimonies do not ask for pity but demonstrate their inner strength and resilience, winning them personal dignity and public support.

Through the interviews, the five working-class women described how hard and bitter life was under the patriarchy and foreign imperialism. Specific incidents of Japanese aggression remained in their memories. Their stories speak not just about bitterness but about the women's own struggles to live, adapt, and do whatever they could in their lives of suffering.

All these powerless, marginalized women have created their own gendered version of the war they had lived through. Their stories provide another textured component of common people's lives in China's War of Resistance against Japan.

Epilogue

On August 15, 1945, the Emperor of Japan announced his country's unconditional surrender to the Allies. Japan's official surrender to China took place at a ceremony in Nanjing on September 9. The horrific human suffering, which had lasted fourteen years and was among the worst of the twentieth century, was finally over. China won back its lost sovereignty. The unequal treaties with the West were nullified. Manchuria and Taiwan were returned to China.

The victory came as a surprise to many Chinese, such as Shang Pu, the teacher in occupied Shenyang:

> On August 15, 1945, we were still doing manual labor in the factory [for the Japanese] ... We wondered why no Koreans [supervisors in the factory] had come ... Someone on the bus to work had heard that the Japanese had surrendered ... The following day, our Chinese school principal, cautious as always, asked us to still go to work. Others said: haven't you had enough as slaves in a lost nation? Why still go? ... Students threw their Japanese language textbooks on the track field and burned them all.[1]

The victory was a bright memory for Ying Di in occupied Shanghai: "Under the Japanese there was a lights-out curfew in the evenings. After their surrender, we were so happy. Now we could have our lights back on in the evenings!"[2] Yu Jian, in occupied Yantai, recalled with a tremulous voice and tears in her eyes: "Celebrations. Firecrackers on the street. Everyone was so happy. The Japanese were gone. We were overjoyed."[3]

Epilogue

Nationalist Party member Chen Meiquan, the director of the Female Students Army in 1945, described the celebration parade with her students held in Chongqing in August 1945:

> We prepared our parade float. On its platform were the Statue of Liberty, the Freedom Bell, our national flag, and portraits of Sun Yat-sen and Mr. Chiang. The female student soldiers followed ... People flashed the V for victory ... They gave us applause and cheers everywhere. This heartfelt scene is the most unforgettable in my life. So happy, so ecstatic![4]

With the end of the war, the students army was disbanded. Many young people returned to school. For Chen Meiquan, going home was the top priority. Returning to their old homes to be united with their families was the shared wish of so many Chinese civilians who had gone into exile in the interior with the Nationalists. Chen quit her job and went back to her home in Manchuria. During the eight years she had been away, her father had died of illness in 1943, her mother had aged and become frail, and the family-owned land and business were in poor condition due to lack of management. She accepted a teaching position at the Northeast Campus of the Central Police Academy in Shenyang, and was determined to care for her mother.[5]

Chi Pang-yuan expressed her reaction to the victory over Japan:

> When Japan surrendered, Chongqing was ecstatic, the only time I have seen anything like it in my life. Following Chiang's broadcast, the miserable earth erupted in joy, as people dropped their accustomed reserve and embraced in the streets, and jumped, laughed, and sang patriotic songs such as "beautiful mountains and river, the national flag waves ..." until they were hoarse.[6]

In the evening, torch in hand, Chi joined the parade. As it approached her middle school, she remembered Zhang Dafei, her hero, the young Christian pilot killed in the war. "At that moment, I suddenly felt everything go silent and could no longer stand being in the crowd." Running back home, "I spent victory night weeping bitterly in the dark."[7]

China had won a bitter victory. The long war had cost fifteen to twenty million lives. The economy was devastated. As historian Diana Lary observes: "At the end of the war, few Chinese looked back on the past eight years with much sense of excitement or triumph, nor did they feel, to use an English expression, that they 'had a good war.'"[8] The war had caused staggering social disruption. So many families had been destroyed and hopes for reunion shattered that many felt "defeat at the time of victory."[9] The postwar peace did not last long, as China was once again rent by the civil war between the Nationalists and the Communists (1946–49), which ended with the defeat of the Nationalists and their retreat to Taiwan. Years of tears and blood were followed by another period of tears and blood.

The experiences of the civil war were so painful that the joy of victory did not leave much of an impression on the memories of many. "The Japanese surrendered. Of course, we were happy but then, the Northeast was in chaos," Wang Yao, who had lived in occupied Shenyang, recalled.[10] The Japanese surrender did not mean much to Wang Hong of Liyang County, Jiangsu Province, either: "The Japanese surrendered but there came the Nationalists. They were hurting us."[11]

For the Communist women, the end of the War of Resistance against Japan meant the beginning of another conflict with the Nationalist army and government. They had to continue the mission of building a new, socialist China. Guo Lian, of the Communist Party in Shanxi, recalled: "We could hardly believe that we won the victory of the Resistance War ... The Japanese surrendered. However, our fight had to go on."[12] Luo Ying remembered: "We had a parade in Yan'an. Drums and flags. We were so happy. Never thought there would be a civil war. Not at all." She married her first love, who was also a Communist comrade, soon after the victory. Her husband then left to fight the Nationalists and was killed in action in 1947 at the age of twenty-five. Before he died, he had asked his comrades to give Luo Ying a new notebook as a token of his love, "the only legacy a husband left for his wife."[13] Wu Zhiying of the New Fourth Army recalled: "The Japanese aggressors had surrendered in August 1945. We were hoping to move into a new stage of peaceful and democratic reconstruction, but soon the Nationalist army was pressing us and instigated the civil war."[14] In their reminiscences collected in *Women Soldiers of the Central Plain* (*Zhongyuan nüzhanshi*), many New Fourth Army women soldiers recalled a fateful event in 1946 in which the Nationalist army laid siege to the Communist army in Henan and Hubei Provinces, with the aim of eliminating them. The women had to overcome hellish obstacles to break out of the siege and escape into Communist-controlled regions.

As seen in the oral accounts in *20th Century Wartime Experiences of Chinese Women* (*Fenghuo suiyue xia de Zhongguo funü fangwen jilu*), for women associated with the Nationalists, the word "victory" often served as a mere phrase marking the beginning of another period of turmoil and then exile across the strait to Taiwan. When Pei-Wang Zhihong in Beiping heard the news of Japan's surrender over the radio, she recalled: "Everyone was happy, saying that when the Nationalist army came, we would all go out to welcome Generalissimo Chiang ... The Nationalists came and were planning to bring order to the city, but then the Communists arrived ... After the Japanese left, there was more chaos." She left for Taiwan in late 1948 with her husband, who served in the Nationalist air force.[15] Mang Yuqin described: "We had expected that after the Japanese surrender and the return of the Northeast to the motherland, everyone would be able to enjoy a peaceful life. Who knew that chaotic times would come one after another?"[16] Several narrators spent pages recalling the miseries of family separation and the extreme hardships in fleeing to Taiwan in 1948–49.[17]

In 1948, when the Nationalist general Sun Liren (1900–90) mobilized the Women's Corps (Nü qingnian dadui) for the anti-Communist and anti–Soviet Union cause, many young women joined. *The Reminiscences of Women's Corps* (*Nü qingnian dadui fangwen jilu*) consists of accounts of former members. Several claimed that what had pushed them into the corps was the chance to escape the post-1945 chaos and the Communist class struggle against their families. You Huaiyan (b. 1929) had stayed with her family in the Japanese-occupied area in Yancheng, Jiangsu Province, during the War of Resistance. In 1945, the Communists established power there. She recalled: "As soon as they arrived, the Communists began the struggle of settling scores, declaring that 'the local tyrants and evil gentry exploit the poor,' so our family could not escape the struggle ... The Communists were terrible to us."[18] In 1948, she applied to join the Women's Corps. Xiao Wenyan (b. 1932 in Dalian, Liaoning) recalled that her father was the vice mayor in occupied Dalian. In 1945, soon after the war, the Communists came: "My family overnight fell from heaven to hell."[19] Her father was buried alive by the Communists two years later, and her family scattered. She herself joined the Women's Corps and went to Taiwan.

Post-1949 Transformations

The victory of the Chinese Communist Party and the founding of the People's Republic of China brought dramatic changes for women, changes that, in the words of many, "turned the world upside down" (*fantian fudi*). As outlined in Chapter 1, the government carried out a state-led women's liberation, or state feminism. Its effects were complex and paradoxical. This state feminism was accompanied by endless mass campaigns from the early 1950s. The government urged all women to work outside the home. However, Zhang Shu, one of the middle-class women featured in Chapter 5, decided to stay home for fear that her work for the US Information Service in Tianjin in 1948–49 would reflect poorly in any examination of her background and drag her into political trouble. Guo Zhenyi, the Communist Party member persecuted during the Yan'an Rectification Movement of 1942 (Chapter 3) was deprived of the opportunity to work because of her political record and the fact that she had refused to admit her "wrongs." During the 1951 Campaign to Suppress Counterrevolutionaries, Zhang Wei's husband (Chapter 4), an officer in the Nationalist propaganda ministry, was imprisoned and then sent to a labour camp for five years. In the Anti-Rightist Campaign of 1957, when many Communist members and intellectuals were accused of working against the party, Yu Jian (Chapter 5) and many others, including the famous writer Ding Ling, were labelled as rightists. Then the disastrous failure of the Great Leap Forward (1958) and the famine (1959–62) that followed caused tremendous economic hardship to women and their families in both rural and urban areas. During the Cultural Revolution (1966–76), almost all the Communist New Fourth Army women veterans and the five Communist women discussed in this book were accused of being "capitalist roaders," or "traitors," or "spies," and suffered attacks to different degrees. Some were driven to suicide by the persecution. They, along with middle-class women intellectuals, were forced to undergo reform through labour in rural areas for varying lengths of time.

The death of Mao Zedong in 1976 and the government's decision under Deng Xiaoping to initiate economic reforms and open up China to the West in 1978 inaugurated another era in the history of the People's Republic of China. The government carried out modernization in accordance with "Chinese characteristics." "China's Second Revolution," as Deng Xiaoping later called this new phase,[20] with its relaxation of political control, globalization, marketization, industrialization, and massive changes in all aspects, led to the commodification of women's bodies, discrimination against women, and intensified sexism and misogyny. The government continued interfering in women's lives, such as with the one-child policy. At the same time, the reforms led to the decline of state feminism and opened up space for women to pursue self-liberation and the development of a feminist public sphere for addressing women's culture, psychology, sexuality, and discourse. Different feminisms have emerged.[21] Under Xi Jinping, the government has from 2012 embarked on what is called

"China's Third Revolution" with Xi's promotion of a new nationalism and centralization of more power in his own hands.[22] Although Xi has affirmed gender equality, not a single woman was promoted to his Politburo at the Party Congress in 2022, and the Communist Party remains a patriarchal institution.[23]

Just as the War of Resistance had different implications and meanings for women of different geographical locations and backgrounds, it is important to explore how these successive changes from Mao to the present were experienced by women themselves using their own narratives and taking into consideration geographical location, age, education, and family background. Many studies have made important contributions in this respect.[24] When China in the 1990s and early 2000s engaged in the new remembering and reinterpretation of history as addressed in the Introduction and Chapter 1, those women in mainland China discussed in this book added their voices through self-writing and self-narrations about the War of Resistance. The war did not kill them. Hunger and hardship did not destroy them. Approaching the latter years of their lives, they expressed a strong wish to remember the past and to be remembered. Within the greater context in which their lives unfolded, they as individuals had their own motivations for and concerns about recounting their past experiences.

Those women who had moved to Taiwan with the Nationalists underwent political, economic, and social changes drastically different from those in the mainland. From 1949 to 1975, the Nationalist government remained in the hands of Chiang Kai-shek (d. 1975) and under martial law. Taiwan's economy was transformed from a rural to an industrialized society. Since 1987, when martial law was lifted, Taiwan has evolved from one-party rule under the Nationalist Party to a multi-party democracy. In the process of democratization, autonomous women's movements independent from the state have flourished.[25] Women entered politics. Tsai Ing-wen (b. 1956), who holds a doctorate in law from the University of London and is a member of the Democratic Progressive Party, served as president of Taiwan from 2016 to 2018, and from 2020 to 2024.

In remembering the past, historians in Taiwan have collected oral histories since the late 1950s. For women, this began in the 1980s, and since then a series of women's oral histories have appeared. The rich life stories told by these women about the long road from the mainland to Taiwan and from childhood to old age are an invaluable source for the study of twentieth-century China.

The Power of Women's Remembering

When the voices and memories of women of various backgrounds take centre stage, the history of the War of Resistance against Japan becomes richer in texture, and more diverse and inclusive in perspective. It demonstrates that the war had various implications and meanings for women and men, and for women in different contexts. Together, these women's self-narratives address the many ways women were affected by the war, how they endured, and the strategies they used. They are a testimonial to the universal fact that war is crueller for women than for men. They collectively challenge the traditional concept of what is historically important, affirming that women's roles on various fronts and in their everyday lives are a crucial part of the history of the war.[26]

The desire to reclaim the crucial roles of the New Fourth Army and women's contributions to the war, both of which were neglected in the master narrative under Mao, was the principal driver behind the publication of reminiscences from the Communist New Fourth Army. Although the women's writings do not openly challenge the inequalities within the party leadership, their reflections on those years demonstrate in effect a strong gendered stance. Determined to be free of the bonds of class oppression and patriarchy as well as to save the nation, these women chose to join the Communist-led resistance. Their collective memories celebrate their commitment to the Communist ideology and the virtues of heroic self-sacrifice. The collective community transformed them into Communist fighters and enabled them to exert agency in effecting political and social change. They fought for the nation and worked among the common people during a period of heroic struggle. The collective community also gave them a sense of belonging to a large family, in which they fulfilled their duties as wives and mothers, and in which they subordinated their own interests to those of the community since self-sacrifice was a moral ethos for them.

At the same time, beneath the collective identity, one can witness their attempt to stress their own agency. The Chinese Communist women fought with "quiet devotion"; the publication of their memories has now broken that silence. Their war stories depict them as ordinary soldiers who made heroic sacrifices and contributions to expand the party's base areas, mobilize rural Chinese for the war effort, and carry out social reform in the rural areas, all of which played a crucial part in victory in the War of Resistance and in the Communist Party's assumption of national power in 1949. The thrust of their remembrance is that women deserve a place in the history of the Chinese revolution. In the late 1980s, the party's reputation came under assault as intellectuals and the younger generation openly raised doubts concerning the party's legitimacy. In tandem with these trends, popular culture generated its images of Communist women, some for commercial motives. This impelled the women who fought in the Communist-led resistance during the war to tell their own stories.

Although public memory of the war was suppressed during the Mao era, these women proved that the state was never capable of destroying individual memory. The interviews with the five Communist women in Chapter 3 reveal clearly how they cherished these memories and how the women were now ready to tell their stories to the younger generation, including their children. Each interview took both the speaker and the interviewer through time and space back to the war years. The private setting and a younger, eager listener enabled the women to open up and speak with spontaneity. Compared with the written, published reminiscences of the New Fourth Army women, these interviews eschew the tales of self-sacrifice typical of party narratives and instead reveal details of daily lives, the women's inner thoughts, and their personal views about families, mother-daughter relations, love, marriage, and childrearing.

The five women were from relatively well-to-do families, which, according to Communist ideology, positioned them within the exploiting class or petty bourgeois class. In remembering their families, however, there were tender feelings more than harsh political criticisms. The narratives, sometimes diverging from the party line, reveal their own perspectives, expressing their complex and ambiguous views and varied experiences. This shows them to be real, flesh-and-blood human beings rather than "communists made of steel." As mothers, instead of glorifying the sacrifice of self so emphasized in Communist ideology, they emphasized the agonizing internal conflict they experienced in leaving their children to the care of peasants. Personally affected during the Yan'an Rectification Movement, they, as well as many other Communist Party members, did not forget the movement's damaging effects. Despite these adversities, they professed a strong belief in the people and faith that the party would correct its missteps. Their stories confirm that the party's political identity was empowering to them since such identity lent their work nationalist, revolutionary meanings and raised their political, social, and gendered status. What they affirmed as most important in their war experience was their youth and idealism, and their devotion to a cause that would strengthen China and help the next generation lead a better life.

During the Mao era, the People's Republic of China continued to treat the Nationalist Party as deadly enemies. Its historiography either erased the Nationalists' role in the War of Resistance or portrayed it negatively. This has changed since the late 1980s. In-depth studies have addressed the positive and important roles of the Nationalists in the War of Resistance. The published recollections of women associated with the Nationalist Party are valuable for enriching the history of the war on many levels. As in the case of the Communist women, the conflicts between the Nationalists and the Communists during the War of Resistance and the civil war were a major part of the Nationalist women's experiences. Defeated in the civil war, they went into exile on Taiwan. In their reminiscences, some raise the question of "what if?" What if they had remained on the mainland? For those who did remain and who suffered political persecution at the hands of the Communist government, the question is, what if they had left? Underlying these questions is these women's recognition of the complex entanglement of politics in individual lives.

Nationalist women's memories of the War of Resistance offer different perspectives from those of Communist women soldiers. To the Nationalist women, the war was not a good war. Running through their memories is a keen sense of grief over dislocation and the loss of home and loved ones. Privileged though these women's families may have been, the suffering associated with the war spared no one. Fleeing from Japanese aggression and then from mainland China after the Nationalists' defeat deeply affected individual families such as theirs. In describing their suffering during those years, however, they also shed light on how they refused to be crushed by all that these wars had imposed on them. The Nationalist government's mobilization of citizens for the anti-Japanese war effort enticed many women to offer their service in the military, the medical field, and the mobilization of common people. The conviction that "the rise and fall of all-under-heaven is the responsibility of everyone" was a strong motiving force. Their own way of serving was an example of how women were historical actors in bringing about change. Other women, such as Chi Pang-yuan, Huang Yun, and Zhang Wei, persisted in their quest for education as students, and Shao Menglan as a teacher, because they believed that education could save the nation and was also a way to achieve personal independence.

In contrast to Communist Party discourse, which held that China's wealthy and powerful were corrupt and ruthless exploiters of the working class and only radical class struggle could bring about women's liberation, Nationalist women valued the family as an anchor of strength. Such a standpoint was particularly poignant when the war was threatening to destroy all stability. These women perceived themselves as a link that preserved family relations. As the country became increasingly fragmented, they endeavoured to keep families together. Many such women took their obligations as daughter, wife, and mother seriously. They held to Confucian views on women's domestic roles as a means of self-empowerment. It was in the domestic sphere where many of these women exercised their influence.

During the war, while many people headed to Nationalist or Communist-controlled areas, the majority of the population remained in regions under Japanese occupation. These women and men were seen in the public eye and in subsequent mainstream histories as pathetic and pitiful "slaves of a lost nation." The urban middle-class women interviewed for this book who lived in the Japanese-occupied areas did not entirely accept this depiction, however. They kept their memories as a personal treasure, for they saw that their experiences in the war, however terrible, constituted a valuable shaping force in their lives. Born during the 1910s and 1920s, these women were from families characterized by the mixture of tradition and modernity typical of China's drastic transition from premodern empire to modern nation. Their memories of their family relationships reveal a mixture of views regarding gender and progress. Although their education in schools did not radicalize them, they all held a strong belief in education as a means of breaking out of the bonds of patriarchy and viewed financial independence as important for women's status.

They professed no political ideology and generally characterized themselves as apolitical. Their families were not closely affiliated with any political party or organization before or during the war. Yet their experiences under the Japanese occupation shaped their memories. They did not portray themselves as victims consumed by fear and insecurity but as resourceful and tenacious individuals pursuing education, even if that education was administered by so-called foreign imperialists. With respect to marriage, of all the women who were interviewed, one remained single all her life, viewing marriage as something that simply reduced women to machines for producing babies. The rest chose their own spouses. In daily life, they persevered in fulfilling their obligations as daughter, wife, and mother, and in holding jobs outside the home out of self-reliance and to support their families. Faith in Christianity, Buddhism, and the merits of Chinese tradition were sources of their strength. Apolitical though they were, the brutality and humiliation of the Japanese occupation enhanced their national consciousness. From their perspective, they strove for equality with men and struggled against Japanese aggression through their own everyday forms of resistance.

Former Chinese "comfort women," the most downtrodden social group, had endured a vast array of suffering during the Japanese invasion. The Japanese military employed sexual violence against Chinese women as a symbolic weapon to break the spirit of the Chinese. During the Cold War, the Chinese victims of this violence endured continued social isolation and alienation. From the late 1980s, however, the concerted efforts of journalists, scholars, feminist, and humanitarian and legal organizations in China and overseas assisted the former comfort women in speaking up. It was remarkable how they broke their silence to present their powerful testimonies. Though not successful in efforts to win compensation from Japan for their sufferings, they nevertheless became "survivor activists." Their participation in the redress movement aroused their sense of responsibility to speak the truth to the public before they died.

The interviews of the five working-poor women in this book recall the war years as particularly difficult ones replete with suffering. The women did not just complain about how miserable life had been but rather described how they had dealt with the bitterness of their lives and the perceived inequalities, and worked hard daily in order to survive. Their resilience helped them persevere. For them, remembering was a process of coming to terms with grief, resentment, humiliation, and their hatred of the Japanese. Such hatred was born in the hearts of many Chinese who experienced the war and its brutality. Despite official policies attempting to lessen such ill will, China and Japan have yet to come to reconciliation over the war.[27]

With self-narratives, in writing and through oral form, women validate their life experiences.[28] They affirm their agency as actors in history. The Chinese women in my book rarely used the word "feminism" (*nüquan zhuyi; nüxing zhuyi*). In China, feminism remains entangled from 1895 to the present in country's political, cultural, and social transformations. Of course, "women's rights" (*funü quanli; quanyi*), "equality between men and women" (*nannü pingdeng*), and "women's liberation" (*funü jiefang*) have been prevalent in public discourse. Indeed, equality between women and men has been at the centre of China's struggle for modernity.[29] In reflecting on their life paths, these women described the various strategies they employed to make changes in their lives no matter what the hardships or the political ideologies of the era involved.[30] Each of the stories here is unique. Together, they are a history of women's perseverance, agency, and impact. These women survived the turbulence of twentieth-century China and made their own contributions. To them and to us, their ordinary lives were extraordinary.

Appendix: Interviews

At the time of the interviews, I obtained from each interviewee oral permission to use the contents and their words from the interviews in my writings. All the interviews except one were recorded on tape. I use pseudonyms in the text as I promised anonymity to protect the interviewees' privacy and to encourage their openness.

The following short biographies cover the period up to 1945.

Bai Ai 白愛 (b. 1919)

Interviewed on October 2, 2001, at her home in Guodu Village, Wutai County, Shanxi Province.

Of a poor peasant family, her feet were bound in childhood, she had no education, and she entered into an arranged marriage. Her native Wutai County was often under attack by the Japanese during the war.

Gu Mei 顧梅 (1923–2011)

Interviewed on September 9 and 10, 2001, at her home in Jinan, Shandong.

Born in Shanghai. Her father ran a small fabrics store and her mother was a factory worker with no education. Gu Mei participated in the salvation association at her middle school in 1939, joined the Chinese Communist Party in 1940, worked for the resistance in the guise of a student in Shanghai, and went to the New Fourth Army in Anhui in 1942. She did not marry until after the War of Resistance.

Guo Lian 郭蓮 (1921–2012)

Interviewed on October 13 and 17, 2001, at her home in Beijing.

Born in Heilongjiang Province. Her father used to be a military officer and left the military around 1932. Her mother had no education. Guo Lian had an elementary school education during the Japanese occupation. In 1936, she joined her sister in Beiping, where she enrolled in night school taught by students and teachers from Beijing University. In late 1937, she arrived at the Taihang mountainous region in northern China to work for the Communist-led resistance, and she became a Communist Party member in December that year. She worked in propaganda, education, and later as the head of a district in Shanxi. She married during the war.

Guo Zhenyi 郭箴一 (her real name) (1902–76)

Her son talked to me on several occasions. The most recent was on July 21, 2021, via Skype, when he was at his home in Beijing while I was at my home in the United States.

Guo Zhenyi was from a wealthy family in Hubei Province. Both parents were educated. She graduated from Fudan University in Shanghai and was an activist for women's rights. She joined the Communist Party in 1939 and went to Yan'an with her husband, whom she had married of her own choice instead of through an arrangement. She and her husband were senior research staff members at the Yan'an Central Research Institute when both were accused of being members of the so-called Wang Shiwei anti-party group of five in 1942.

Huang Yun 黃雲 (1922–2006)

Interviewed on September 17, 2001, at her home in Shanghai. Her daughter and husband were present too.

Born in Baoshan, near Shanghai. Her father was a writer and bookstore owner in Shanghai. Her mother died of cholera when Huang Yun was only five years old. Her father remarried. During the war, she went with her parents to Sichuan, which was under Nationalist control and where she continued her education in middle school and at the Northeast University. She met her future husband, a fellow student, while at the university. They married in 1944.

Li Guang 李光 (b. 1922)

Interviewed on January 6 and 8, 2002, at her home in Beijing.

Born into a family of land and business owners in Wan County, Hebei Province. Her mother had several years of education. In the summer of 1937,

Li Guang was a student at the Baoding Women's Normal School. She joined the anti-Japanese work in her native Hebei in late 1937, and the Communist Party in 1938. She was in charge of women's work in the Jin-Cha-Ji Border Region during the war. She married a senior Communist leader in 1940.

Lu Nan 鲁南 (1923–2006)

Interviewed on October 15, 2001, at her home in Beijing.

Born in Kaifeng, Henan Province. Her father was a train engineer. Her mother was from a landowner's family and attended an old-style private school with Confucian learning. In middle school, Lu Nan was active in the student movement in Kaifeng in 1935. She went to Yan'an and became a member of the Communist Party in 1938. She worked as a stenographer and then as an elementary school teacher in Yan'an. She married a senior Communist leader in 1940.

Luo Ying 骆英 (1924–2019)

Interviewed on October 12, 2001, at her home in Beijing.

Born in Weinan County, Shaanxi Province. Her father worked as a senior staff member in a business firm in Sichuan. Her mother had no education. Luo Ying was active in anti-Japanese activities in middle school, and joined the Communist Party in March 1940. She went to Yan'an in 1942 and worked as a nurse in the Central Hospital. She did not marry until after the War of Resistance.

Shang Pu 尚樸 (1917–2006)

Interviewed on August 24, 2001, at the Beijing First Health Care Home.

Born in Shenyang, Liaoning Province. Her father had a law degree and worked as a county magistrate. Her mother had no education. Shang Pu received a two-year college education and taught in elementary and middle schools in Shenyang under the Japanese occupation in Manchukuo. She never married.

Shao He 邵荷 (b. 1919)

Interviewed on September 21, 2001, at her neighbourhood committee centre in Shanghai.

Born into a poor family, she worked as a child-labourer in Shanghai. She and her husband moved to the rural area of Ningbo, Zhejiang Province, after Shanghai was occupied by the Japanese. She worked on the land during the war.

WANG BO 汪波 (1915–2003)

Interviewed on September 14, 2001, at her home in Yangzhou, Jiangsu Province.

Born in Huai'an, Jiangsu Province. Her father was a doctor of traditional Chinese medicine. Her mother had no education. Wang Bo received nursing training for about four years at the Renci missionary hospital and was a Christian all her life. She married a man she met at the hospital in 1936. During the war, she had a midwifery business in her home area, assisted by her husband.

WANG HONG 王紅 (1922–2010)

Interviewed on September 15, and 16, 2001, at her home in Liyang, Jiangsu Province.

Born in Liyang. Her parents worked in factories in Shanghai before the war. Both had some education. She was educated for three years and worked as a child-labourer in Shanghai. Back in Liyang, she entered into an arranged marriage not long after the war broke out in 1937. Later in the war, the couple ran a small business in Liyang, an area often attacked by the Japanese.

WANG YAO 王瑤 (1913–2008)

Interviewed on August 21 and 23, 2001, at her home in Beijing.

Born in a village near Shenyang, Liaoning Province. Her father received a university education and worked in the banking business. Her mother was a schoolteacher and principal for some time. Wang Yao received a college education. She married a man of her choosing in 1936. From 1941 to 1945, the couple lived in Shenyang with her parents under the Japanese occupation. Her husband worked at a private bank while she stayed at home to care for the family.

WANG ZHEN 王珍 (B. 1926)

Interviewed on November 14, 2001, at her home in Beijing.

Born in Beiping. Her father was a scientist, while her mother, who was educated at the Suzhou Women's Normal School, stayed at home after marriage. Wang Zhen continued her education from middle school to university in occupied Beiping. She married after the war.

YANG LAI 楊來 (B. 1920)

Interviewed on September 21, 2001, at her neighbourhood committee centre in Shanghai.

Yang Lai was from a family with some land and a small business in Longhua, near Shanghai. She was educated for six years. She did knitting and other chores to support the family income, and smuggled goods in occupied Shanghai. She did not marry until after the war.

Ying Di 應娣 (b. 1912)

Interviewed on September 21, 2001, at her neighbourhood committee centre in Shanghai.

Born in Shanghai. Both parents worked as labourers, and she worked as a child-labourer. She was widowed a couple of years after an arranged marriage, and worked as a house servant in occupied Shanghai during the war.

Yu Jian 于健 (1917–2009)

Interviewed on September 7, 2001, at her home in Beijing. One of her daughters was present.

Born in Dalian, Liaoning Province. Her father was a businessman, and her mother, who had some education, stayed at home. Yu Jian received her education from a missionary senior middle school and worked in occupied Yantai, Shandong. She turned to Catholicism during the war, and married after the war.

Zhang Wei 張瑋 (1915–2002)

On February 9, 1990, Zhang Wei was videotaped at her son's home in North Carolina during her visit there. In addition to the videotape, I also obtained some background information from her son through several telephone conversations in the United States.

Zhang Wei was born in Baoshan County, near Shanghai. The family had some land and ran a small shop. Her mother received no education. After three years of traditional education, Zhang Wei pursued education in a modern school. During the war, she left Shanghai to study at the famous National Southwest Associated University, in Kunming, Yunnan Province. There she married of her own choice and raised a family.

Zhang Shu 張舒 (b. 1923)

Interviewed on January 9, 2002, at her home in Beijing.

Zhang Shu was born in Beiping. Her father worked in the customs office and her mother, who had some education, stayed at home. Both parents were Christians, as was Zhang Shu herself. She was a university student in occupied Beiping in 1937. In 1942, she went to the Nationalist-controlled interior to continue her university education. She did not marry until after the war.

Glossary

baozhang	保長	head of the local administration
chao xianqi liangmu	超賢妻良母	super wise wife and good mother
chusheng	畜生	beasts
da houfang	大後方	great rear area
dushu jiuguo	讀書救國	saving the country by book learning
fanggong, xiangong, fangong	防共限共反共	guarding against, restricting, and combating the Communists
fantian fudi	翻天覆地	turned the world upside down
funü jiefang	婦女解放	women's liberation
funü quanli	婦女權力	women's rights
gao, da, quan	高，大，全	tall, great, perfect
guan taitai	官太太	madam officer
guizi	鬼子	devils
guopo jiawang	國破家亡	the country destroyed, the family shattered

Glossary

hong erdai	紅二代	red second-generation
jishi wenxue	紀實文學	realistic piece of literature
jiushehui	舊社會	old society
kangzhan furen	抗戰夫人	resistance war wives
kangzhan gaoyu yiqie	抗戰高於一切	resistance above all
kangzhan	抗戰	resistance
kexue jiuguo	科學救國	to save the country by science
kuilei	傀儡	puppets
li, yi, lian, chi	禮義廉恥	propriety, righteousness, integrity, sense of shame
liangmian	兩面	double-faced
liangmin	良民	"good subjects"
lienü zhuan	列女傳	biographies of women
lunxian qu	淪陷區	lost regions
minzu xiehe	民族協和	union of nationalities/ethnic harmony
nannü pingdeng	男女平等	equality between men and women
nanzun nübei	男尊女卑	men are superior; women are inferior
nuhua jiaoyu	奴化教育	education to enslave
nüquan zhuyi	女權主義	feminism
nüquan	女權	women's rights
nüxing zhuyi	女性主義	feminism
qin Ri	親日	close to the Japanese
quanyi	權益	rights
sanqing tuan	三青團	Three People's Principles Youth Corps
shimu	師母	teacher's wife
tianxia xingwang, pifu youze	天下興亡匹夫有責	the rise and fall of all-under-heaven is the responsibility of every man

tongchou dikai	同仇敵愾	sharing the bitter hatred against the enemy
tongdi fenzi	通敵份子	people consorting with the enemy
Tongj	同濟	university
Wa	完	county
wangguo nu	亡國奴	slaves in a lost nation
wanjun	頑軍	anti-Communist army
wanzhong yixin	萬眾一心	one million hearts beating as one
xiange buchuo	弦歌不輟	schooling must go on with no interruption
xin xianqi liangmu zhuyi	新賢妻良母主義	"new-wise-wife-good mother-ism"
xuelei liuli	血淚流離	journey of blood and tears
yaodong	窰洞	cave dwelling
Yu	盂	county
zhandi fuwu tuan	戰地服務團	battlefield service troupe
zhishi fenzi	知識份子	intellectual
ziyou zhuyi	自由主義	liberal

Notes

Introduction

1 Interview with Wang Yao on August 21 and 23, 2001, at her home in Beijing.
2 Diana Lary, "Introduction: The Context of the War," in *China at War: Regions of China, 1937–1945,* ed. Stephen R. MacKinnon, Diana Lary, and Ezra F. Vogel (Stanford, CA: Stanford University Press, 2007), 7–13.
3 Rana Mitter, *China's Good War: How World War II Is Shaping a New Nationalism* (Cambridge, MA: Belknap Press of Harvard University Press, 2020), 3.
4 Elizabeth C. Economy, introduction to *The Third Revolution: Xi Jinping and the New Chinese State* (Oxford: Oxford University Press, 2018).
5 Rana Mitter and Aaron William Moore, "China in World War II, 1937–1945: Experience, Memory, and Legacy," *Modern Asian Studies* 45, 2 (March 2011): 225–40; Diana Lary, "War and Remembering: Memories of China at War," in *Beyond Suffering: Recounting War in Modern China,* ed. James Flath and Norman Smith (Vancouver: UBC Press, 2011), 262–87; Carol Gluck, "Operations of Memory: 'Comfort Women' and the World," in *Ruptured Histories: War, Memory, and the Post-Cold War in Asia,* ed. Sheila Miyoshi Jager and Rana Mitter (Cambridge, MA: Harvard University Press, 2007), 47–76; Mitter, *China's Good War.*
6 Joan Tumblety, "Introduction: Working with Memory as Source and Subject," in *Memory and History: Understanding Memory as Source and Subject,* ed. Joan Tumblety (London: Routledge, 2013), 1–16.
7 Kathryn Anderson and Dana C. Jack, "Learning to Listen: Interview Techniques and Analyses," in *Women's Words: The Feminist Practice of Oral History,* ed. Sherna Berger Gluck and Daphne Patai (New York: Routledge, 1991), 11; Tess Cosslett, Celia Lury, and Penny Summerfield, eds., introduction to *Feminism and Autobiography: Texts, Theories, Methods* (New York: Routledge, 2000).
8 See, for example, Bonnie S. Anderson and Judith P. Zinsser, *A History of Their Own: Women in Europe from Prehistory to the Present,* rev. ed. (Oxford: Oxford University Press, 2000).

9 Joan W. Scott, "Rewriting History," in *Behind the Lines: Gender and the Two World Wars*, ed. Margaret Randolph Higonnet, Jane Jenson, Sonya Michel, and Margaret Collins Weitz (New Haven, CT: Yale University Press, 1987), 19–30.
10 Personal Narratives Group, Joy Webster Barbre, et al., eds. *Interpreting Women's Lives: Feminist Theory and Personal Narratives* (Bloomington: Indiana University Press, 1989); Sherna Berger Gluck and Daphne Patai, eds., *Women's Words: The Feminist Practice of Oral History* (New York: Routledge, 1991); Susan H. Armitage with Patricia Hart and Karen Weathermon, eds., *Women's Oral History: The Frontiers Reader* (Lincoln: University of Nebraska Press, 2002).
11 Penny Summerfield, *Reconstructing Women's Wartime Lives: Discourse and Subjectivity in Oral Histories of the Second World War* (Manchester and New York: Manchester University Press, 1998), 5, 8.
12 Gail Hershatter, *The Gender of Memory: Rural Women and China's Collective Past* (Berkeley: University of California Press, 2011), 24–31.
13 This phrase has its origin in the work of Gu Yanwu (1613–82), a philosopher of the Ming dynasty.
14 Liu Jucai, *Zhongguo jindai funü yundongshi* [Modern history of Chinese women's movement] (Beijing: Zhongguo funü chubanshe, 1989), 103.
15 Joan Judge, "Talent, Virtue, and the Nation: Chinese Nationalisms and Female Subjectivities in the Early Twentieth Century," *American Historical Review* 106, 3 (June 2001): 765–66.
16 Li Youning, "Zhongguo xinnüjie zazhi de chuangkan ji neihan" [The creation and perceptions of the journal of Chinese New Women's Circle], in *Zhongguo funüshi lunwenji* [A collection of essays on Chinese women's history], ed. Li Youning and Zhang Yufa (Taipei: Commercial Press, 1981), 1: 182–83; Zheng Wang, introduction to *Women in the Chinese Enlightenment: Oral and Textual Histories* (Berkeley: University of California Press, 1999); Li Xiaojiang, chief ed., *Rang nüren ziji shuohua: qinli zhanzheng* [Let women speak for themselves: experiencing the wars] (Beijing: Shenghuo, dushu, xinzhi sanlian shudian, 2003), 1–4.
17 Song Meiling, "Xin shenghuo yu funü" [New life and women], *Funü xin shenghuo yuekan* 1 (November 1936): 2–5.
18 Elisabeth Croll, *Feminism and Socialism in China* (London: Routledge and Kegan Paul, 1978), 153–76; Susan L. Glosser, *Chinese Visions of Family and State, 1915–1953* (Berkeley: University of California Press, 2003), ch. 2.
19 Rana Mitter, "Classifying Citizens in Nationalist China during World War II, 1937–1941," *Modern Asian Studies* 45, 2 (2011): 249.
20 Merle Goldman and Elizabeth J. Perry, "Introduction: Political Citizenship in Modern China," in *Changing Meanings of Citizenship in Modern China*, ed. Merle Goldman and Elizabeth J. Perry (Cambridge, MA: Harvard University Press, 2002), 6.
21 Helen M. Schneider, *Keeping the Nation's House: Domestic Management and the Making of Modern China* (Vancouver: UBC Press, 2011), 39–42.
22 The notion of "good wife and wise mother" (*liangqi xianmu*) was conceptualized by the Meiji Japanese reformers and was introduced to China around 1905. In China, it was reworded as "wise wife and good mother" (*xianqi liangmu*). Scholars have debated about the order of the words, whether it was Confucian in origin or a product of modernity, and the effects of the concept. See Joan Judge, *The Precious Raft of History: The Past, the West, and the Woman Question in China* (Stanford, CA: Stanford University Press, 2008),

110–15. For an introduction to the debates on this concept in the 1930s, see Xia Rong, *Funü zhidao weiyuanhui yu kangRi zhanzheng* [Women's advisory committee of the New Life Movement and the War of Resistance] (Beijing: Renmin chubanshe, 2010), 52–70.
23 Zhenzhuang, "Funü xinyun yu 'xianqi liangmu' zhuyi" [New Life Movement for women and 'wise-wife-good-mother'-ism], *Funü xin shenghuo yuekan* 7 (May 1937): 16–17.
24 Zhou Hong, *Xingbie, zhengzhi yu guozu shiye xia nüxing jiefang de yanshuo – Funü gongming yanjiu (1929–1944)* [The narratives of women's liberation through the lens of gender, politics, and nation: the study of *Women's Resonance* (1929–1944)] (Xinbei, Taiwan: Huamulan chubanshe, 2013), 1–3. The journal was first published in Shanghai in March 1929 and continued to 1944.
25 See essays in *Funü gongming* 4, 11 (November 1936), a special issue on the wise wives and good mothers.
26 Theresa Kelleher, "Confucianism," in *Women in World Religions*, ed. Arvind Sharma (Albany: State University of New York Press, 1987), 135–60; Chenyang Li, "Introduction: Can Confucianism Come to Terms with Feminism?" in *The Sage and the Second Sex: Confucianism, Ethics, and Gender*, ed. Chenyang Li (Chicago and La Salle, IL: Open Court, 2000), 1–21.
27 Patricia B. Ebrey, *Confucianism and Family Rituals in Imperial China* (Princeton, NJ: Princeton University Press, 1991); Patricia B. Ebrey, *The Inner Quarters: Marriage and the Lives of Chinese Women in the Sung Period* (Berkeley: University of California Press, 1993); Dorothy Ko, *Teachers of the Inner Chambers: Women and Culture in Seventeenth-Century China* (Stanford, CA: Stanford University Press, 1994).
28 Monica E. Neugebauer, "Domestic Activism and Nationalist Struggle," in *The Women and War Reader*, ed. Lois Ann Lorentzen and Jennifer E. Turpin (New York: New York University Press, 1998), 177.
29 Kay Ann Johnson, *Women, the Family, and Peasant Revolution in China* (Chicago: University of Chicago Press, 1983), 40.
30 Wang, *Women in the Chinese Enlightenment*, 1.
31 Chong-Sik Lee, *Revolutionary Struggle in Manchuria: Chinese Communism and Soviet Interest, 1922–1945* (Berkeley: University of California Press, 1983), 131.
32 Ibid., 237–41.
33 Patricia Stranahan, *Underground: The Shanghai Communist Party and the Politics of Survival, 1927–1937* (Lanham, MD: Rowman and Littlefield, 1998), 1–5, chs. 4 and 5.
34 Robert Chi, "'The March of the Volunteers': From Movie Theme Song to National Anthem," in *Re-envisioning the Chinese Revolution: The Politics and Poetics of Collective Memories in Reform China*, ed. Ching Kwan Lee and Guobin Yang (Stanford, CA: Stanford University Press, 2007), 217–44.
35 The journal was published from July 1935 to January 1941, first in Shanghai, later in Wuhan, and then in Chongqing. Ding Mingjing, "The Female and the Country during the Anti-Japanese War – Analyses of the *Women's Lives* Magazine," MA thesis (in Chinese with English title) (Shanghai: Huadong shifan daxue, Shanghai, 2006).
36 Junhui, "Pingbo He Ziheng jun zhi nüzi jiaoyu lun" [Refuting Mr. He Ziheng's ideas on women's education], *Funü shenghuo* 1, 5 (November 1935). Included in Zhonghua quanguo funü lianhehui funü yundong lishi yanjiushi, comp., *Cong "Yier jiu" yundong kan nüxing de rensheng jiazhi* [Perception of women's life values through the December Ninth Movement] (Beijing: Zhongguo funü chubanshe, 1988), 226–31 [hereafter CYEJ].
37 Shen Zijiu, "Jinnian zenyang jinian 'sanba'?" [How to commemorate March Eighth this year?], *Funü shenghuo* 2, 2 (February 1936). Included in CYEJ, 91–93.

38 Parks M. Coble, *Facing Japan: Chinese Politics and Japanese Imperialism* (Cambridge, MA: Harvard University Press, 1991), 8, *passim*.
39 Ibid., 99.
40 Lily Xiao Hong Lee and A.D. Stefanowska, eds., *Biographical Dictionary of Chinese Women: The Twentieth Century 1912–2000* (Armonk, NY: M.E., Sharpe, 2003), 466–74.
41 Ibid., 200–4.
42 John Israel, *Student Nationalism in China, 1927–1937* (Stanford, CA: Stanford University Press/Hoover Institution on War, Revolution, and Peace, 1966), ch. 5; John Israel and Donald W. Klein, *Rebels and Bureaucrats: China's December 9ers* (Berkeley: University of California Press, 1976), ch. 3.
43 Elizabeth A. Littell-Lamb, "Ding Shujing: The YWCA Pathway for China's 'New Women,'" in *Salt and Light: Lives of Faith That Shaped Modern China*, ed. Carol Lee Hamrin and Stacey Bieler (Eugene, OR: Pickwick, 2009), 79–97.
44 Niu Shengni, "Ling yizhong funü yundong – yi Zhonghua jidujiao nüqingnian hui de nonggong shiye weili (1904–1933)" [An alternative women's movement: a case study of the Chinese YWCA's peasant-worker movement (1904–1933)], in *Xingbie yu lishi: jindai Zhongguo funü yu jidujiao* [Gender and history: modern Chinese women and Christianity], ed. Tao Feiya (Shanghai: Renmin chubanshe, 2006), 234–82.
45 Emily Honig, *Sisters and Strangers: Women in the Shanghai Cotton Mills, 1919–1949* (Stanford, CA: Stanford University Press, 1986), 223–24.
46 T'ien-wei Wu, "The Chinese Communist Movement," in *China's Bitter Victory: The War with Japan, 1937–1945*, ed. James C. Hsiung and Steven I. Levine (Armonk, NY: M.E. Sharpe, 1992), 80.
47 Hong Yizhen, *Zhongguo Guomindang funü gongzuo zhi yanjiu, 1924–1949* [English title given by the publisher: *The Kuomintang and Women's Affairs, 1924–1949*] (Taipei: Guoshiguan, 2010), 237–54; Xia Rong, *Funü zhidao weiyuanhui yu kangRi zhanzheng*, 152.
48 Zhonghua quanguo funü lianhehui funü yundong lishi yanjiushi, comp., *Zhongguo funü yundong lishi ziliao, 1937–1945* [Historical materials of Chinese women's movement, 1937–1945] (Beijing: Zhongguo funü chubanshe, 1991), 58–65 [hereafter ZFYLZ (1937–45)].
49 Hong Yizhen, *Zhongguo Guomindang funü gongzuo zhi yanjiu*, 285.
50 Song Meiling, "Zhongguo funü kangzhan de shiming" [The mission of Chinese women in the War of Resistance] (July 1, 1941), in *Jiang furen yanlun ji* [Collection of speeches and works by Madame Jiang], by Song Meiling (Taipei: Zhonghua funü fangong lianhehui, 1977), 2: 741–42.
51 Croll, *Feminism and Socialism in China*, 176–84; Hong Yizhen, *Zhongguo Guomindang funü gongzuo zhi yanjiu*, 286–88.
52 Hong Yizhen, ibid., 286–88.
53 Ibid., ch. 4; Zhou Lei and Liu Ningyuan, *Kangzhan shiqi Zhongguo funü yundong yanjiu (1931–1945)* [Study of Chinese women's movement in the War of Resistance (1931–1945)] (Beijing: Shoudu jingji maoyi daxue chubanshe, 2016); Ke Huiling, "Kangzhan chuqi de zhishi nüqingnian xiaxiang – yi Jiangxi weili de yanjiu" [Women intellectual youth in the countryside during the early Sino-Japanese war: the case of Jiangxi], *Jindai Zhongguo funüshi yanjiu* 19 (December 2011): 33–73.
54 Lü Fangshang, "Kangzhan shiqi Zhongguo de fuyun gongzuo" [The women's work during the War of Resistance], in Li Youning and Zhang Yufa, *Zhongguo funüshi lunwenji*, 1: 378–412.
55 Liang Huijin, "Kangzhan shiqi de funü zuzhi" [Women's organizations in the War of Resistance against Japan], in *Zhongguo funüshi lunji xuji* [A collection of articles on Chinese women's history, sequel], ed. Bao Jialin (Taipei: Daoxiang chubanshe, 1991), 380.

56 Mary Jo Waelchli, "Wu Yifang: Abundant Life in Training Women for Service," in Hamrin and Bieler, *Salt and Light*, 152–70. For a short biography of Wu Yifang, see Lee and Stefanowska, *Biographical Dictionary of Chinese Women: The Twentieth Century, 1912–2000*, 561–64.
57 Chen Xiuping, *Chenfu lu: Zhongguo qingyun yu jidujiao nannu qingnianhui* [Records of upheavals: China's youth movement and the YMCA and YWCA] (Shanghai: Tongji daxue chubanshe, 1989), ch. 4.
58 Isabel Brown Crook and Christina K. Gilmartin with Yu Xiji, *Prosperity's Predicament: Identity, Reform, and Resistance in Rural Wartime China*, comp. and ed. Gail Hershatter and Emily Honig (Lanham, MD: Rowman and Littlefield, 2013), pt. 2.
59 Louise Edwards, *Gender, Politics, and Democracy: Women's Suffrage in China* (Stanford, CA: Stanford University Press, 2008), 3–4.
60 Ibid., ch. 7.
61 Danke Li, *Echoes of Chongqing: Women in Wartime China* (Urbana: University of Illinois Press, 2010), 2–3.
62 Joshua H. Howard, "The Politicization of Women Workers at War: Labour in Chongqing's Cotton Mills during the Anti-Japanese War," *Modern Asian Studies* 47, 6 (November 2013): 1888–1940.
63 Schneider, *Keeping the Nation's House*, ch. 5.
64 Johnson, *Women, the Family, and Peasant Revolution in China*, 75.
65 Tani E. Barlow, *The Question of Women in Chinese Feminism* (Durham, NC: Duke University Press, 2004), chs. 4 and 5; Jin Feng, *The New Woman in Early Twentieth-Century Chinese Fiction* (West Lafayette, IN: Purdue University Press, 2004), chs. 7 and 8, and Epilogue; Haiping Yan, *Chinese Women Writers and the Feminist Imagination, 1905–1948* (London: Routledge, 2006), chs. 6 and 7.
66 Yuan Liangjun, ed., *Ding Ling yanju ziliao* [Research materials on Ding Ling] (Tianjin: Tianjin renmin chubanshe, 1982), 9–41.
67 Johnson, *Women, the Family, and Peasant Revolution in China*, 72–75.
68 Nora is the liberated heroine in the Norwegian playwright Henrik Ibsen's play *A Doll's House*, which premiered in Copenhagen in 1879. Nora became a model of a new woman who left her husband and family. It was extremely popular in urban areas of early twentieth-century China. In 1923, the leading Chinese writer Lu Xun gave a speech titled "What Happens after Nora Leaves Home?" at Beijing Women's Normal College, which warned women of the severe social obstacles once they left their homes to go into society. See Ying-Ying Chien, "Feminism and China's New 'Nora': Ibsen, Hu Shi and Lu Xun," *Comparatist* 19 (May 1995): 97–113.
69 Ding Ling, *Ding Ling wenji* [Works of Ding Ling] (Changsha: Hunan renmin chubanshe, 1983–84), 4: 388–92.
70 Patricia Stranahan, *Yan'an Women and the Communist Party*, China Research Monograph no. 26 (Institute of East Asian Studies, University of California, Center for Chinese Studies, 1976), 54–58; Patricia Stranahan, *Molding the Medium: The Chinese Communist Party and the Liberation Daily* (Armonk, NY: M. E. Sharpe, 1990), 54–81; Mark Selden, *China in Revolution: The Yenan Way Revisited* (Armonk, NY: M.E. Sharpe, 1995), 152–65.
71 Johnson, *Women, the Family, and Peasant Revolution in China*, 74.
72 Ding Ling, "Jieda sange wenti – zai Beijing yuyan xueyuan waiguo liuxuesheng zuotanhui shang de jianghua" [Answer to three questions – a talk to foreign students at the Beijing Language Institute], in Ding Ling, *Ding Ling wenji*, 4: 171–84.
73 ZFYLZ (1937–45), 647–49.
74 Croll, *Feminism and Socialism in China*, 210.
75 Stranahan, *Yan'an Women and the Communist Party*, 3, 4.

76 Chang-ming Hua, "Peasants, Women and Revolution – CCP Marriage Reforms in the Shaan-Gan-Ning Border Area," *Republican China* 10 (November 1984): 1–24.
77 Judith Stacey, *Patriarchy and Socialist Revolution in China* (Berkeley: University of California Press, 1983), Introduction, chs. 4 and 5.
78 Ibid., 170.
79 Helen Praeger Young, "Threads from Long March Stories: The Political, Economic and Social Experience of Women Soldiers," in *Women in China: The Republican Period in Historical Perspective,* ed. Mechthild Leutner and Nicola Spakowski (Münster, Germany: Lit Verlag, 2005), 182.
80 Francine D'Amico, "Feminist Perspectives on Women Warriors," in Lorentzen and Turpin, *The Women and War Reader,* 120.
81 Jane L. Price, "Women and Leadership in the Chinese Communist Movement, 1921–1945," *Bulletin of Concerned Asian Scholars* 7, 1 (January-March 1975): 19–24.
82 See their essays in Zhonghua quanguo funü lianhehui, ed., *Cai Chang, Deng Yingchao, Kang Keqing funü jiefang wenti wenxuan, 1938–1987* [Selected works by Cai Chang, Deng Yingchao, and Kang Keqing on the issue of women's liberation, 1938–1987] (Beijing: Renmin chubanshe, 1983), 16–41, 45–61, 82–86, 95–98.
83 See Chapter 1 of this book.
84 Christina K. Gilmartin, *Engendering the Chinese Revolution: Radical Women, Communist Politics, and Mass Movements in the 1920s* (Berkeley: University of California Press, 1995), 204–5.
85 Helen P. Young, *Choosing Revolution: Chinese Women Soldiers on the Long March* (Urbana: University of Illinois Press, 2001).
86 Nicola Spakowski, "Women's Military Participation in the Communist Movement of the 1930s and 1940s: Patterns of Inclusion and Exclusion," in Leutner and Spakowski, *Women in China: The Republican Period in Historical Perspective,* 160.
87 David S.G. Goodman, "Revolutionary Women and Women in the Revolution: The Chinese Communist Party and Women in the War of Resistance to Japan, 1937–1945," *China Quarterly* 164 (December 2000): 915–42.
88 Xiaoping Cong, *Marriage, Law, and Gender in Revolutionary China, 1940–1960* (Cambridge: Cambridge University Press, 2016).
89 Zheng Wang, *Finding Women in the State: A Socialist Feminist Revolution in the People's Republic of China, 1949–1964* (Berkeley: University of California Press, 2017).
90 Maki Kimura, *Unfolding the "Comfort Women" Debates: Modernity, Violence, Women's Voices* (New York: Palgrave Macmillan, 2016), ch. 8.
91 Jennifer Turpin, "Many Faces: Women Confronting War," in Lorentzen and Turpin, *The Women and War Reader,* 3–18.
92 Robert Gildea, *Marianne in Chains: Everyday Life in the French Heartland under the German Occupation* (New York: Metropolitan Books/Henry Holt, 2002).
93 Svetlana Alexievich, *The Unwomanly Face of War: An Oral History of Women in World War II,* trans. Richard Pevear and Larissa Volokhonsky (New York: Random House, 2017), xvi.

CHAPTER 1: REPRESENTATIONS OF WARTIME
WOMEN IN THE PEOPLE'S REPUBLIC OF CHINA

1 Deng Yingchao, "Zhongguo funü yundong dangqian de fangzhen renwu baogao" [Report on current policy and tasks of Chinese women's movement], in *Deng Yingchao wenji* [Collection of Deng Yinchao's works], by Deng Yichao (Beijing: Renmin chubanshe, 1994), 66–75.

2 Ling Zifeng and Zhai Qiang, dirs., *Zhonghua nüer* [Daughters of China] (1949; Changchun, Jilin: Dongbei dianying zhipianchang).
3 Sha Meng, dir., *Zhao Yiman* (1950; Changchun, Jilin: Dongbei dianying zhipianchang).
4 See, for example, Agnes Smedley, *Battle Hymn of China* (New York: Alfred A Knopf, 1943); Agnes Smedley, *Portraits of Chinese Women in Revolution* (Old Westbury, NY: Feminist Press, 1976); Helen Foster Snow [Nym Wales, pseud.], *The Chinese Communists: Sketches and Autobiographies of the Old Guard* (Westport, CT: Greenwood Press, 1972); Helen Foster Snow, *Women in Modern China* (Paris: Monton, 1967); Mary Sheridan, "Yenan Women in Revolution," in *Lives: Chinese Working Women*, ed. Mary Sheridan and Janet W. Salaff (Bloomington: Indiana University Press, 1984), 180–96.
5 Ding Weiping, *Zhongguo funü kangzhanshi yanjiu, 1937–1945* [A study of Chinese women in the War of Resistance against Japan, 1937–1945] (Changchun, Jilin: Jilin renmin chubanshe, 1999), 192–96; Mark Selden, *China in Revolution: The Yenan Way Revisited* (Armonk, NY: M.E. Sharpe, 1995).
6 Lu Ban, *Xin funü duben* [Reader for the new women] (Hong Kong: Xin minzhu chubanshe, 1949), 8–9.
7 Jonathan Unger, "Introduction," in *Using the Past to Serve the Present: Historiography and Politics in Contemporary China*, ed. Jonathan Unger (Armonk, NY: M. E. Sharpe, 1993), 7.
8 Susanne Weigelin-Schwiedrzik, "Party Historiography," in Unger, *Using the Past to Serve the Present*, 157, 164.
9 Yinan He, "Remembering and Forgetting the War: Elite Mythmaking, Mass Reaction, and Sino-Japanese Relations, 1950–2006," *History and Memory* 19, 2 (September 2007): 46–48; Kirk Denton, "Introduction," in *Exhibiting the Past: Historical Memory and the Politics of Museums in Postsocialist China* (Honolulu: University of Hawaii Press, 2014); Chan Yang, *World War Two Legacies in East Asia: China Remembers the War* (New York: Routledge, 2018), 31–35.
10 Gregor Benton, *New Fourth Army: Communist Resistance along the Yangtze and the Huai, 1938–1941* (Surrey, UK: Curzon 1999), 6–7; David S.G. Goodman, *Social and Political Change in Revolutionary China: The Taihang Base Area in the War of Resistance to Japan, 1937–1945* (Lanham, MD: Rowman and Littlefield, 2000), x.
11 Chan Yang, *World War Two Legacies in East Asia*, ch. 4.
12 Rana Mitter and Aaron William Moore, "China in World War II, 1937–1945: Experience, Memory, and Legacy," *Modern Asian Studies* 45, 2 (March 2011): 238.
13 Barbara Alpern Engel, "The Womanly Face of War: Soviet Women Remember World War II," in *Women and War in the Twentieth Century: Enlist with or without Consent*, ed. Nicole Ann Dombrowski (New York: Garland, 1999), 138–39.
14 Mayfair Mei-hui Yang, "From Gender Erasure to Gender Difference," in *Spaces of Their Own: Women's Public Sphere in Transnational China*, ed. Mayfair Mei-hui Yang (Minneapolis: University of Minnesota Press, 1999), 35–67; Yue Meng, "Female Images and National Myth," in *Gender Politics in Modern China: Writing and Feminism*, ed. Tani E. Barlow (Durham, NC: Duke University Press, 1993), 118–36; Dai Jinhua, *Xieta liaowang: Zhongguo dianying wenhua, 1978–1998* [Perspectives from the slanted tower: Chinese cinema culture 1978–1998] (Taipei: Yuanliu chuban gongsi, 1999), 89–118.
15 Harriet Evans, *Women and Sexuality in China: Female Sexuality and Gender since 1949* (New York: Continuum, 1997), 4–10.
16 Hung-Yok Ip, "Fashioning Appearances: Feminine Beauty in Chinese Communist Revolutionary Culture," *Modern China* 29, 3 (July 2003): 329–61.

17 Zheng Wang, "'State Feminist'? Gender and Socialist State Formation in Maoist China," *Feminist Studies* 31, 3 (Fall 2005): 519–51.
18 Dorothy Ko and Wang Zheng, "Introduction: Translating Feminism in China," in *Translating Feminisms in China: A Special Issue of Gender and History,* ed. Dorothy Ko and Wang Zheng (Malden, MA: Blackwell, 2007), 9. See also Zhong Xueping, Wang Zheng, and Bai Di, eds., *Some of Us: Chinese Women Growing Up in the Mao Era* (London: Rutgers University Press, 2001).
19 Zhong, Wang and Bai, *Some of Us.*
20 Deng Yingchao, "Yi Mao Zedong sixiang wei zhidao, yanjiu funü yundong lishi ziliao" [Conducting research on historical documents of women's movement under the guidance of Mao Zedong thought], in *Deng Yingchao wenji,* 145–49.
21 Zhao Xian, "Souji Shanghai funü yundong lishi ziliao de gongzuo huibao" [Work report on collecting documents for the history of Shanghai women's movement], in *Fuyunshi yanjiu ziliao* [Research materials for the study of the history of women's movement], comp. Quanguo fulian fuyun lishi yanjiushi, 2: 21–23 (December 10, 1981) [hereafter FYSYJZL]. This journal was published four times a year for internal circulation only. I have an incomplete personal collection of the journal, given by a Chinese friend. His mother received these materials due to her veteran Communist position. I am grateful for his trust and generosity.
22 In the Mao era, China's academia produced a few studies of women in the traditional period. See Du Fangqin, *Faxian funü de lishi – Zhongguo funüshi lunji* [The discovery of women's history – collection of essays on Chinese women's history] (Tianjin: Tianjin shehui kexueyuan chubanshe, 1996), 195–97.
23 Joan Judge, "Introduction," in *The Precious Raft of History: The Past, the West, and the Woman Question in China* (Stanford, CA: Stanford University Press, 2008); Joan Judge and Hu Ying, eds., "Introduction," in *Beyond Exemplar Tales: Women's Biography in Chinese History* (Berkeley: University of California Press, 2011).
24 Tina Mai Chen, "Propagating the Propaganda Film: The Meaning of Film in Chinese Communist Party Writings, 1949–1965," *Modern Chinese Literature and Culture* 15, 2 (2003): 154–93.
25 Wu Qiong, *Zhongguo dianying de leixing yanjiu* [A study of Chinese film genres] (Beijing: Zhongguo dianying chubanshe, 2005), 103n3.
26 Cai Chang et al., "Jinian Xiang Jingyu tongzhi xunnan sanshi zhounian" [On the thirtieth anniversary of comrade Xiang Jingyu's death for the revolution], *Zhongguo funü* 1958: 5, 16–20; 1958: 6, 25–27.
27 For the mother of Mencius, see Lily Xiao Hong Lee and A.D. Stefanowska, eds., *Biographical Dictionary of Chinese Women: Antiquity through Sui, 1600 B.C.E.–618 C.E.* (Armonk, NY: M.E, Sharpe, 2007), 46–47. For Ban Zhao, see ibid., 103–6. For Mu Guiying, see Lily Xiao Hong Lee and Sue Wiles, eds., *Biographical Dictionary of Chinese Women: Tang through Ming, 618–1644* (Armonk, NY: M.E. Sharpe, 2014), 341–44.
28 For Mulan, see Lily Xiao Hong Lee and A.D. Stefanowska, eds., *Biographical Dictionary of Chinese Women: Antiquity through Sui, 1600 B.C.E.–618 C.E.* (Armonk, NY: M.E, Sharpe, 2007), 324–29.
29 Louise Edwards, *Women Warriors and Wartime Spies of China* (New York: Cambridge University Press, 2016), 117–36.
30 Yin Hong and Leng Yan, *Xin Zhongguo dianyingshi (1949–2000)* [A history of new China's cinema (1949–2000)] (Changsha, Hunan: Hunan meishu chubanshe, 2002), 8–9.

31 Ibid., 40.
32 Paul Ropp, "Passionate Women: Female Suicide in Late Imperial China – Introduction," *Nan Nü* 3, 1 (2001): 3–21.
33 Dai Jinhua, *Xieta liaowang*, 106–12.
34 Xu Yunqing, *Yingxiong de jiemei – Kanglian huiyi lu* [Heroic sisters – recollections of the Kanglian] (Changchun, Jilin: Jilin renmin chubanshe, 1960; 2nd ed., 1978). In the epilogue of the second edition, Xu Yunqing wrote that her book was banned during the Cultural Revolution, and many of the Kanglian leaders and comrades were accused of being traitors and spies. The second edition was published, in her words, in order to right the wrongs, and to honour those in the Kanglian.
35 Ibid., 28.
36 Ibid., 126.
37 Yang Mo, *Qingchun zhi ge* [The song of youth] (Beijing: Zuojia chubanshe, 1958).
38 Cui Gui and Chen Huaikai, dirs., *Qingchun zhi ge* [The song of youth] (1959; Beijing: Beijing diangying chipianchang).
39 Yin Hong and Leng Yan, *Xin Zhongguo dianyingshi*, 39.
40 Chan Yang, *World War Two Legacies in East Asia*, 154–56.
41 Yue Meng, "Female Images and National Myth," 130.
42 Beijingshi jiaoyuju: Beijingshi gaoji zhongxue shiyong keben, *Yuwen 4* [Beijing senior middle school provisional textbook, Chinese 4]. (Beijing: Beijing chubanshe, 1962), 39.
43 Dai Jinhua, *Xieta liaowang*, 110.
44 Rong Guanxiu bianjizu, *Rong Guanxiu* (Beijing: Xinhua chubanshe, 1990). This biography includes newspaper articles in the 1940s and, 1960s, and in the post-Mao period.
45 Feng Yifu and Li Jun, dirs., *Huimin zhidui* [The detachment of the Hui people] (1959; Beijing: Bayi dianying zhipianchang). For Bai Wenguan's story, see Chen Jingbo, "Huimin zhi mu: ji Huimin zhidui Ma Benzhai zhi mu yingyong xunguo" [Mother of the Hui people: an account of the mother of Ma Benzhai of the Hui detachment and her heroic death for the nation], *Hongqi piaopiao* 10 (January 1959): 159–75.
46 Nancy Scheper-Hughes, "Maternal Thinking and the Politics of War," in *The Women and War Reader*, ed. Lois Ann Lorentzen and Jennifer E. Turpin (New York: New York University Press, 1998), 227.
47 Hai Mo, "Si saozi" [Sister four], *Hongqi piaopiao* 2 (July 1957): 207–25.
48 Luo Ya, "Wei chujia de mama" [An unwed mother], *Zhongguo funü* (1958): 8, 16–19.
49 Bell Yung, "Model Opera as Model: From Shajiabang to Sagabong," in *Popular Chinese Literature and Performing Arts in the People's Republic of China 1949–1979*, ed. Bonnie S. McDougall (Berkeley: University of California Press, 1984), 144–64.
50 *Sha Village* (*Shajiabang*) and *The Red Lantern* (*Hongdeng ji*).
51 Yue Meng, "Female Images and National Myth"; Yang, "From Gender Erasure to Gender Difference," 35–67.
52 Carol Gluck, "Operations of Memory: 'Comfort Women' and the World," in *Ruptured Histories: War, Memory, and the Post–Cold War in Asia*, ed. Sheila Miyoshi Jager and Rana Mitter (Cambridge, MA: Harvard University Press, 2007), 47–76; James Reilly, "Remember History, Not Hatred: Collective Remembrance of China's War of Resistance to Japan," *Modern Asian Studies* 45, 2 (2011): 463–90.
53 Arthur Waldron, "China's New Remembering of World War II: The Case of Zhang Zizhong," *Modern Asian Studies* 30, 4 (October 1996): 945–78; Denton, *Exhibiting the Past*, ch. 6; Fengqi Qian and Guo-Qiang Liu, "Remembrance of the Nanjing Massacre

in the Globalised Era: The Memory of Victimisation, Emotions and the Rise of China," *China Report* 55, 2 (2019): 81–101.
54 Rana Mitter, *China's Good War: How World War II Is Shaping a New Nationalism* (Cambridge, MA: Belknap Press of Harvard University Press, 2020).
55 Geremie Barmé, "History for the Masses," in *Using the Past to Serve the Present*, ed. Jonathan Unger (Armonk, NY: M.E. Sharpe, 1993), 260–86; Rana Mitter, "Old Ghosts, New Memories: China's Changing War History in the Era of Post-Mao Politics," *Journal of Contemporary History* 38, 1 (January 2003): 117–31; Diana Lary, "War and Remembering: Memories of China at War," in *Beyond Suffering: Recounting War in Modern China*, ed. James Flath and Norman Smith (Vancouver: UBC Press, 2011), 262–87.
56 Kang Liu, "Reinventing the 'Red Classics' in the Age of Globalization," *Neohelicon* 37 (2010): 329–47; Rosemary Roberts and Li Li, eds., "Introduction," in *The Making and Remaking of China's "Red Classics": Politics, Aesthetics, and Mass Culture* (Hong Kong: Hong Kong University Press, 2017).
57 Zhen Zhang, "'Never Abandon, Never Give Up': Soldiers Sortie as a New Red Classic of the Reform Era," *ASIANetwork Exchange* 26, 1 (2019): 96–115.
58 The fifth generation of film directors challenge the Communist hero myth by going to war topics. See Dai Jinhua, *Xieta liaowang*, 35–71.
59 Wu Qiong, *Zhongguo dianying de leixing yanjiu*, 94–98.
60 Evans, *Women and Sexuality in China;* Wendy Larson, "Never This Wild: Sexing the Cultural Revolution," *Modern China* 25, 4 (1999): 423–50.
61 Edwards, *Women Warriors and Wartime Spies of China*, 117–36.
62 Yibin diwei dangshi gongzuo weiyuanhui, Sichuansheng fulian Yibin dique banshichu, *KangRi yingxiong Zhao Yiman* [Anti-Japanese heroine Zhao Yiman] (Chengdu: Sichuan daxue chubanshe, 1989). For the two letters, see 216–17.
63 Sun Tie, dir., *Wode muqin Zhao Yiman* [My mother Zhao Yiman] (2005; Fuzhou: Fujian dianying zhipianchang, 2005).
64 Ding Hei, dir., *Xinsijun nübing* [Women soldiers of the New Fourth Army] (first aired 2011; Shanghai: Shanghai wenguang xinwen chuanmei jituan, Shanghai dianshi chuanmei gongsi).
65 Zhang Suzhou et al. *Wode muqin: sange Xinsijun nübing de gushi* [My mother: the stories of three women soldiers of the N4A] (2010; Shanghai: Shanghai zhonghang wenhua chuanbo youxian zeren gongsi; Anhui guangbo dianshitai).
66 Chen Danhuai and Ye Weiwei, *Sange Xinsijun nübing de duocai rensheng: huiyi muqin Zhang Qian, Wang Yugeng, Ling Ben* [Multicoloured lives of three women soldiers of the New Fourth Army: remembering mothers: Zhang Qian, Wang Yugeng, and Ling Ben] (Beijing: Renmin chubanshe, 2011).
67 Du Fangqin, *Faxian funü de lishi*, 33, 205.
68 Luo Qiong, "Xuexi Deng Yingchao dajie sanci jianghua de chubu tihui" [My preliminary thought on studying elder sister Deng Yingcho's three speeches]. FYSYJZL 2: 7–11 (December 10, 1981); Luo Qiong, "Zai disanci fuyun lishi bianzuan weiyuanhui, di erci quanguo fuyunshi gongzuo huiyi shang de jianghua" [Speech at the third meeting of the compilation committee for the history of women's movement and the second national meeting on the history of women's movement], FYSYJZL 3: 4–10 (1984).
69 Deng Yingchao, "Zai quanguo funü yundong lishi ziliao bianzuan weiyuanhui di yici huiyi shang de jianghua" [The speech at the first meeting of the committee for compilation of historical materials of the Chinese women's movement], FYSYJZL 2: 5–6 (December 10, 1981).

70 Deng Yingchao, "Zhenfen geming jingshen, zuohao fuyunshi gongzuo" [Inspire revolutionary enthusiasm and conduct well the work on the history of women's movement], FYSYJZL 3: 14–17 (March 10, 1982).
71 Wang Youqiao, "Zai quanguo fulian xuanjiao gongzuo zuotanhui shang de baogao" [Lecture on the ACWF seminar of propaganda and education work], May 30, 1980. This document is internally circulated. Total pages: 26. I have a copy given by a Chinese friend. His mother received these materials due to her veteran CCP position.
72 Deng Yingchao, "Zai Quanguo funü yundong lishi ziliao bianzuan weiyuanhui di yici huiyi shang de jianghua."
73 Sun Sibai, "Tantan 'Zhongguo funü yundongshi' de bianxie wenti" [On some issues of compilation of the history of Chinese women's movement] FYSYJZL 2: 16–20 (December 10, 1981).
74 Luo Qiong, "Zai disanci fuyun lishi bianzuan weiyuanhui, di erci quanguo fuyunshi gongzuo huiyi shang de jianghua," 4–10.
75 Edwards, *Women Warriors and Wartime Spies of China*, 118–19.
76 Wang Youqiao, "Zai quanguo fulian xuanjiao gongzuo zuotanhui shang de baogao."
77 Luo Qiong, "Zai disanci fuyun lishi bianzuan weiyuanhui, di erci quanguo fuyunshi gongzuo huiyi shang de jianghua," 6.
78 Dong Bian, "Zai fuyunshi gongzuo zuotanhui shang de xiaojie" [A brief summary at the seminar on the work for the history of women's movement], FYSYJZL 2: 12–15 (December 10, 1981).
79 Zhonghua quanguo funü lianhehui funü yundong lishi yanjiushi, *Zhongguo funü yundonshi (xin minzhu zhuyi shiqi)* [History of Chinese women's movement, new democratic period]. (Beijing: Chunqiu chubanshe, 1989).
80 For example, Zhonghua quanguo funü lianhehui, ed., *Cai Chang, Deng Yingchao, Kang Keqing funü jiefang wenti wenxuan, 1938–1987* [Selected works by Cai Chang, Deng Yingchao, and Kang Keqing on the issue of women's liberation, 1938–1987] (Beijing: Renmin chubanshe, 1983); Quanguo fulian funü yundong lishi yanjiushi, ed., *Cong "Yier jiu" yundong kan nüxing de rensheng jiazhi* [Perception of women's life values through the December Ninth Movement] (Beijing: Zhongguo funü chubanshe, 1988) [hereafter CYEJ]; Zhonghua quanguo funü lianhehui funü yundong lishi yanjiushi, ed., *Zhongguo funü yundong lishi ziliao* [Historical materials of Chinese women's movement], 5 vols. (Beijing: Zhongguo funü chubanshe, 1986–91); Luo Guangda, chief ed., *Jinguo yinghao – kangRi zhanzheng zhong de Jin-Cha-Ji funü ertong sheyingzhan* [Heroic women: photograph exhibition of women and children of Jin-Cha-Ji in the Anti-Japanese War] (Shenyang, Liaoning: Liaoning meishu chubanshe, 1989).
81 Tani E. Barlow, *The Question of Women in Chinese Feminism* (Durham, NC: Duke University Press, 2004), ch. 6.
82 Ibid., ch. 7; Du Fangqin, *Faxian funü de lishi;* Ye Hanming, "Funü, xingbie ji qita: jin niannian Zhongguo dalu he Xianggang de jindai Zhongguo funüshi yanjiu jiqi fazhan qianjing" [Women, gender, and others: research on modern Chinese women's history in mainland China and Hong Kong during recent twenty years and its prospective development], *Jindai Zhongguo funushi yanjiu* 13 (December 2005): 107–65.
83 Li Xiaojiang, chief ed., *Rang nüren ziji shuohua: qinli zhanzheng* [Let women speak for themselves: experiencing the wars] (Beijing: Shenhuo, dushu, xinzhi sanlian shudian, 2003).
84 For more on this, see Chapter 6.
85 Ding Weiping, *Zhongguo funü kangzhanshi yanjiu, 1937–1945* [A study of Chinese women in the War of Resistance against Japan, 1937–1945] (Changchun: Jilin renmin chubanshe, 1999).

86 Zhou Lei and Liu Ningyuan, *Kangzhan shiqi Zhongguo funü yundong yanjiu (1931–1945)* [Study of Chinese women's movement in the War of Resistance (1931–1945)] (Beijing: Shoudu jingji maoyi daxue chubanshe, 2016).
87 Xia Rong, *Funü zhidao weiyuanhui yu kangRi zhanzheng* [Women's advisory committee of the New Life Movement and the War of Resistance] (Beijing: Renmin chubanshe, 2010).
88 Chen Yan, *Xingbei yu zhanzheng: Shanghai 1932–1945* [Gender and war: Shanghai 1932–1945] (Beijing: Shehui kexue wenxian chubanshe, 2014).
89 Luo Jiurong, "Jindai Zhonguo nüxing zizhuan shuxie zhong de aiqing, hunyin yu zhengzhi" [English title given by the author: "Love, Marriage and Politics in Modern Chinese Women's Autobiographical Writings"], *Jindai Zhongguo funüshi yanjiu* 15 (December 2007): 77–140; Jing M. Wang, *When "I" Was Born: Women's Autobiography in Modern China* (Madison: University of Wisconsin Press, 2008).
90 Roxane Witke, *Comrade Chiang Ch'ing* (Boston: Little, Brown, 1977), 4.
91 For book-length biographies about early CCP women, see, for example, Jin Feng, *Deng Yingchao zhuan* [A biography of Deng Yingchao] (Beijing: Renmin chubanshe, 1993); Wang Xingjuan, *Jinggang dujuan hong – He Zizhen fengyu rensheng* [The red azalea of the Jinggang mountains – the stormy life of He Zizhen] (Shenyang: Liaoning renmin chubanshe, 2000).
92 For example, Li Jianzhen, *Li Jianzhen huiyilu* [Memoirs by Li Jianzhen] (Beijing: Zhonggong dangshi chubanshe, 1991); Kang Keqing, *Kang Keqing huiyilu* [Memoirs by Kang Keqing] (Beijing: Jiefangjun chubanshe, 1993); Zeng Zhi, *Yige geming de xingcunzhe* [A survivor of the revolution] (Guangzhou: Guangdong renmin chubanshe, 1999); Wei Junyi, *Sitong lu and Lu Sha de lu* [Reflections of pains and *The Road of Lu Sha*], rev. ed. (Beijing: Wenhua yishu chubanshe, 2003); Wang Yugeng, *Wangshi zhuozhuo* [Brilliant moments in memories], 2nd ed. (Beijing: Renmin chubanshe, 2012).

Taiwan scholar Ke Huiling has a study of the memoirs of five women who belong to the first generation of the Chinese Communist Party: Hu Lanqi, Huang Mulan, Qin Deyun, Chen Bilan, and Yang Zilie. See Ke Huiling, "Yishi yu xushi: zuopai funü huiyilu zhong de geming zhanyan yu shenghuo liudong (1920s–1950s)" [Legends and narratives: the revolutionary displaying and life fluctuation in the left women's memoirs, 1920s–1950s], *Jindai Zhongguo funü yanjiu* 15 (December 2007): 141–62.
93 See, for example, Liaowang banjibu, *Hongjun nü yingxiong zhuan* [Biographies of Red Army heroines] (Beijing: Xinhua chubanshe, 1986); Han Zi, chief ed., *Nübing liezhuan* [Biographies of women soldiers], 3 vols. (Shanghai: Shanghai wenyi chubanshe, 1985–87); Jiangxisheng fulian, ed., *Nüying zishu* [Self-narratives of heroines] (Nanchang: Jiangxi renmin chubanshe, 1988).
94 Jinian Yan'an nüda wushi zhounian chouweihui, ed., *Yan'an nüda: 1939–1989* [The Yan'an Women's University: 1939–1989] (Beijing: n.p., 1989); Yan'an Zhongguo nüzi daxue Beijing xiaoyouhui, ed., *Yanshui qing* [Love for the Yan River] (Beijing: Zhongguo funü chubanshe, 1999); E-Yu bianqu gemingshi bianjibu; Hubeisheng funü lianhehui, eds., *Zhongyuan nüzhanshi* [Women soldiers of the central plain], 3 vols. (Beijing: Zhongguo funü chubanshe, 1991–94) [hereafter ZYNZS]; Beijing xinsijun yanjiuhui ji huazhong kangRi genjudi yanjiuhui, ed., *Tieliu: Tiejun jinguopu* [Iron currents: accounts of heroines of the ironsides] (Beijing: Jiefanjun chubanshe, 2003) [hereafter TL]; Shi Deqing, ed., *Fenghuo Taihang banbiantian* [Half of the sky in the wartime Taihang] (Beijing: Zhongyang wenxian chubanshe, 2005); Jin-Cha-Ji bianqu beiyuequ funü kangRi douzheng shiliao bianjizu, ed., *Fenghuo jinguo* [Women in the battle fire] (Beijing: Zhongguo funü chubanshe, 1990).

95 ZYNZS, 1: 3.
96 Jin Yihong, *Nüxing xushi yu jiyi* [Women's narrative and memory] (Beijing: Jiuzhou chubanshe, 2007).
97 Zhang Xi, *Kangzhan nüxing dang'an* [Archives of women in the War of Resistance against Japan] (Beijing: Qingnian chubanshe, 2007).
98 Liu Ying, *Dongbei Kanglian nübing* [Women soldiers of Northeast Anti-Japanese Allied Forces] (Ha'erbin: Heilongjiang renmin chubanshe, 2015).
99 Qi Hongshen, ed., *Liuwang: kangzhan shiqi dongbei liuwang xuesheng koushu* [Exiles: oral narratives by refugee students of northeast during the War of Resistance] (Zhengzhou, Henan: Daxiang chubanshe, 2008). In this collection, all narrators are men. Qi Hongshen, ed., *Mosha buliao de zuizheng: Riben qinHua jiaoyu koushushi* [Non-erasable evidence of crime: oral history of education under Japanese aggression of China] (Beijing: Renmin jiaoyu chubanshe, 2005). This work consists of forty-four oral accounts, among which six were by women. Qi Hongshen, *Riben duiHua jiaoyu qinlue: dui Riben qinHua jiaoyu de yanjiu yu pipan* [Japan's educational invasion of China: study and criticism of Japan's educational invasion of China] (Beijing: Kunlun chubanshe, 2005). The second half of this work has oral accounts by eleven people who lived in occupied Manchuria, one of them a woman.
100 Cui Yongyuan, planner; Zeng Hairuo, dir., *Wo de kangzhan* [My war of resistance] (2011; Beijing: Beijing wuxing chuanqi wenhua chuanmei youxian gongsi), DVD. A book was published based on the documentary: Zhongguo chuanqi 2010 zhi wode kangzhan jiemuzu, ed., *Wode kangzhan – 300 wei qinlizhe koushu lish* [My war of resistance: an oral history of 300 witnesses] (Beijing: Zhongguo youyi chuban gongsi, 2010). On Cui Yongyuan's project, see Paul Thompson, "Changing Encounters with Chinese Oral History," *Oral History* 45, 2 (Autumn 2017): 96–105; Mitter, *China's Good War*, 145–50.
101 Zhang Jun, chief ed., *Zhanzheng yinyun xia de nianqingren, 1931–1945; Zhongguo wangshi* [Youth under the dark clouds of the war; China's memory] (Guilin: Guangxi shifan daxue chubanshe, 2016). There are oral accounts by twenty-one people, one of them a woman.
102 See, for example, Li Bingxin, ed. *QinHua Rijun baoxing shilu* [Records of violence of Japanese invading troops in China] (Shijiazhuang: Hebei renmin chubanshe, 1995); Yin Shihong and Fu Xiuyan, chief eds., *Yongyuan de cantong: Jiangxisheng qiangjiu kangzhan shiqi zaoshou Rijun qinhai shiliao: koushu shilu* [The lasting pain: rescued historical records of the suffering of violence committed by the invading Japanese army in Jiangxi province during the resistance war period: oral histories], 2 vols. (Beijing: Remin chubanshe, 2010).
103 Su Zhiliang, Yao Fei, and Chen Lifei, *QinHua Rijun "weian fu" wenti yanjiu* [On the issue of "comfort women" by the Japanese invading troops of China] (Beijing: Zhonggong dangshi chubanshe, 2016), 4.
104 Wang Siyi, "Memorials and Memory: The Curation and Interpretation of Trauma Narratives – Using the Examples of Exhibitions on the Theme of 'Comfort Women' in East Asian Society," *Chinese Studies in History* 53, 1 (2020): 56–71.

CHAPTER 2: SELF-WRITING BY THE WOMEN SOLDIERS OF
THE COMMUNIST NEW FOURTH ARMY

1 Beijing xinsijun yanjiuhui ji huazhong kangRi genjudi yanjiuhui, ed., *Tieliu: Tiejun jinguopu* [Iron currents: accounts of heroines of the ironsides] (Beijing: Jiefanjun chubanshe, 2003), 174–76 [hereafter TL]. I do not find this particular interview in Agnes Smedley's *Battle Hymn of China* (New York: Alfred A Knopf, 1943).

2 Chen Danhuai and Ye Weiwei, *Sange Xinsijun nübing de duocai rensheng: huiyi muqin Zhang Qian, Wang Yugeng, Ling Ben* [Multicoloured lives of three women soldiers of the New Fourth Army: remembering mothers: Zhang Qian, Wang Yugeng, and Ling Ben] (Beijing: Renmin chubanshe, 2011), 146–52, 186–94.
3 E-Yu bianqu gemingshi bianjibu; Hubeisheng funü lianhehui, eds. *Zhongyuan nüzhanshi* [Women soldiers of the central plain], 3 vols. (Beijing: Zhongguo funü chubanshe, 1991–94) [hereafter ZYNZS].
4 TL.
5 Wang Yugeng, *Wangshi zhuozhuo* [Brilliant moments in memories], 2nd ed. (Beijing: Renmin chubanshe, 2012).
6 Ding Hei, dir., *Xinsijun nübing* [Women soldiers of the New Fourth Army] (first aired 2011; Shanghai: Shanghai wenguang xinwen chuanmei jituan, Shanghai dianshi chuanmei gongsi).
7 Zhang Suzhou, Chen Danhuai, and Ye Weiwei, planners; Chen Xiaojin and Zhao Hongmei, producers, *Wode muqin: sange Xinsijun nübing de gushi* [My mother: the stories of three women soldiers of the N4A] (2010; Shanghai: Shanghai zhonghang wenhua chuanbo youxian zeren gongsi; Anhui guangbo dianshitai).
8 Chen and Ye, *Sange Xinsijun nübing de duocai rensheng*.
9 Zhu Qiangdi, *Xinsijun nübing* [Women soldiers of the New Fourth Army] (Jinan, Shandong: Jinan chubanshe, 2004).
10 Yue Siping, chief ed., *Balujun* [The Eighth Route Army] (Beijing: Zhonggong dangshi chubanshe, 2005), 19–24; T'ien-wei Wu, "The Chinese Communist Movement," in *China's Bitter Victory: The War with Japan, 1937–1945*, ed. James C. Hsiung and Steven I. Levine (Armonk, NY: M.E. Sharpe, 1992), 80.
11 Gregor Benton, *New Fourth Army: Communist Resistance along the Yangtze and the Huai, 1938–1941* (Surrey, UK: Curzon 1999), ch. 13; Yung-fa Chen, *Making Revolution: The Communist Movement in Eastern and Central China, 1937–1945* (Berkeley: University of California Press, 1986), 64–69; Lanxin Xiang, *Mao's Generals: Chen Yi and the New Fourth Army* (Lanham, MD: University Press of America, 1998), 92–95.
12 Ding Xing, ed., *Xinsijun cidian* [Dictionary of the New Fourth Army] (Shanghai: Shanghai cishu chubanshe, 1997), 1–3.
13 Benton, *New Fourth Army*, 6.
14 TL, 16–17.
15 Chen and Ye, *Sange Xinsijun nübing de duocai rensheng*, 274–77.
16 ZYNZS, 3: 613, 3: 641–43. For the list of the names, see 3: 630–40.
17 Ibid., 3: 642.
18 Ibid., 1: 2.
19 Ibid., 1: 259.
20 Chen and Ye, *Sange Xinsijun nübing de duocai rensheng*, 2.
21 ZYNZS, 1: 3.
22 Ibid., 1: 2–3.
23 Rana Mitter, *China's Good War: How World War II Is Shaping a New Nationalism* (Cambridge, MA: Belknap Press of Harvard University Press, 2020), 6.
24 ZYNZS, 2: 3–4. For Zeng Zhi's autobiography, see Zeng Zhi, *Yige geming de xingcunzhe* [A survivor of the revolution] (Guangzhou: Guangdong renmin chubanshe, 1999).
25 On Xiang Ying in the CCP power struggle, see Benton, *New Fourth Army*, 678–97.
26 Ibid., ch. 15.
27 TL, 280.

28 Ibid., 235–62. This is a long essay written by a group of authors named only as "some old comrades in the team of women prisoners." See also two other essays: 263–76, 310–30.
29 On the CCP's requirement for autobiography writing, see Chen Yongfa, *Yan'an de yinying* [The English title given by the publisher: Yenan's shadow], Monograph Series no. 60 (Taipei: Institute of Modern History, Academia Sinica, 1990), 27–30.
30 TL, 353–57.
31 Ibid., 137–45.
32 Wang Yugeng, "Changjiang de nüer – ji Yang Ruinian tongzhi" [Daughter of the Yangzi River – the account of comrade Yang Ruinian], in Wang, *Wangshi zhuozhuo*, 124–48.
33 Ding Hei, *Xin Sijun nübing*.
34 Hans van de Ven, *China at War: Triumph and Tragedy in the Emergence of the New China* (Cambridge, MA: Harvard University Press, 2018), 4.
35 T'ien-wei Wu, "The Chinese Communist Movement," 86–87, 95–102.
36 Benton, *New Fourth Army*, ch. 5.
37 ZYNZS, 1: 58–59, 1: 164–66, 1: 185–87, 1: 212–21.
38 TL, 235–62, 263–76, 276–97, 310–30, 353–64, 649–52.
39 ZYNZS, 1: 317–21.
40 Diana Lary, *China's Civil War: A Social History, 1945–1949* (Cambridge: Cambridge University Press, 2015), 105–6.
41 Benton, *New Fourth Army*, 66.
42 Zeng Ke, ed., *Chunhua qiushi* [Spring flowers, autumn harvest] (Zhengzhou: Henan renmin chubanshe, 1985). This book is a collection of reminiscences of the Beicang All-Women's Middle School by its students and staff.
43 Ibid., 333–35.
44 Ibid., 168.
45 Ibid., 1.
46 TL, 427–37.
47 Benton, *New Fourth Army*, 54.
48 Helen P. Young, "Why We Joined the Revolution: Voices of Chinese Women Soldiers," in *Women and War in the Twentieth Century: Enlisted with or without Consent*, ed. Nicole Ann Dombrowski (New York: Garland, 1999), 92–111.
49 ZYNZS, 3: 219–27.
50 Ibid., 2: 66–77.
51 Zhang Wenqing, "Shensui yuanyuan, teshu jidi – Shanghai yu Xinsijun xieshou kang-Ri [Deep roots, special base – the joint efforts in the resistance against Japan by Shanghai and the New Fourth Army], in *Xinsijun yu Shanghai* [The New Fourth Army and Shanghai], ed. Zhang Yun (Shanghai: Shanghai renmin chubanshe, 2003), 8–9; Yan Weiqing, "Shanghai dui Xinsijun de renli zhiyuan" [Supply of manpower of Shanghai to the New Fourth Army], in Zhang Yun, *Xinsijun yu Shanghai*, 138–43.
52 Benton, *New Fourth Army*, 50.
53 Ibid., 68–69.
54 TL, 64–77.
55 Benton, *New Fourth Army*, 85–87.
56 Ibid., 68.
57 TL, 365–67.
58 ZYNZS, 3: 439–40.
59 Ibid., 3: 431–35.

60 Ibid., 1: 45.
61 Chen and Ye, *Sange Xinsijun nübing*, 17.
62 TL, 343–52.
63 Ibid., 78–84.
64 Ibid., 64–70.
65 Jane Price, "Women and Leadership in the Chinese Communist Movement, 1921–1945," *Bulletin of Concerned Asian Scholars* 7, 1 (January-March 1975): 19–24; Zhou Lei and Liu Ningyuan, *Kangzhan shiqi Zhongguo funü yundong yanjiu (1931–1945)* [Study of Chinese women's movement in the War of Resistance (1931–1945)] (Beijing: Shoudu jingji maoyi daxue chubanshe, 2016), 56–61.
66 Liang Yi, "Yan'an nüzi daxue pingjie" [On the Yan'an Women's University], *KangRi Zhanzheng yanjiu* 2 (1992): 91–104.
67 TL, 12–13, 163–69.
68 Benton, *New Fourth Army*, 84.
69 TL, 201–9. Agnes Smedley mentions the hospital and that a "Doctor Chang" (Zhang Yangfen?) was the only woman medical doctor. *Battle Hymn of China*, 267. See also Zhu Qiangdi, *Xinsijun nübing*, 98–109. Zhu mentions that Zhang joined the N4A with a fellow student, Wu Zhili, her future husband.
70 See, for example, TL, 386–91.
71 ZYNZS, 1: 258–69.
72 Chang-tai Hung, *War and Popular Culture: Resistance in Modern China, 1937–1945* (Berkeley: University of California Press, 1994), ch. 6.
73 TL, 467–80.
74 Ibid., 483.
75 Chen and Ye, *Sange Xinsijun nübing*, 19–24.
76 Ibid., 175.
77 Ibid., 175–76.
78 TL, 15.
79 TL, 179–84.
80 Ibid., 210–16; ZYNZS, 2: 217–32.
81 ZYNZS, 1: 2, 1: 6–7.
82 TL, 549–53.
83 Zhonghua quanguo funü lianhehui funü yundong lishi yanjiushi, comp., *Zhongguo funü yundong lishi ziliao, 1937–1945* [Historical materials of Chinese women's movement, 1937–1945] (Beijing: Zhongguo funü chubanshe, 1991), 404–11 [hereafter ZFYLZ (1937–45)].
84 ZYNZS, 1: 12–15.
85 TL, 8–9.
86 Ibid., 557.
87 Ibid., 176.
88 Ibid., 177, 179.
89 Ibid., 365–85.
90 For example, see the experience of Zhang Qian, the wife of General Chen Yi. Chen and Ye, *Sange Xinsijun nübing*, 43–46.
91 Nicole Ann Dombrowski, "Soldiers, Saints, or Sacrificial Lamb? Women's Relationship to Combat and the Fortification of the Home Front in the Twentieth Century," in *Women and War in the Twentieth Century*, ed. Nicole Ann Dombrowski (New York: Garland, 1999), 18.

92. Christina K. Gilmartin, *Engendering the Chinese Revolution: Radical Women, Communist Politics, and Mass Movements in the 1920s* (Berkeley: University of California Press, 1995), 113.
93. ZFYLZ (1937–45), 157. For Liang Hongyu, see Lily Xiao Hong Lee and Sue Wiles, eds., *Biographical Dictionary of Chinese Women: Tang through Ming, 618–1644* (Armonk, NY: M.E. Sharpe, 2014), 238–39.
94. Zhu Hongzhao, *Yan'an richang shenghuo zhong de lishi* [History of daily life in Yan'an] (Guiling: Guangxi shifan daxue chubanshe, 2007), 213.
95. Zeng Zhi, *Yige geming de xingcunzhe*, 327–28.
96. ZYNZS, 3: 385–86.
97. Ibid., 1: 43, 1: 60–65, 3: 17–18.
98. Ibid., 1: 63.
99. Zhu Hongzhao, *Yan'an richang shenghuo zhong de lishi*, 243. His sources for this are reminiscences. In my interview of an N4A couple, they told me this rule too, but said it was "28-5-*tuan*," that is, one spouse should be aged twenty-eight and have five years of service.
100. Chen and Ye, *Sange Xinsijun nübing*, 194.
101. ZYNZS, 2: 135.
102. Ibid., 3: 125.
103. Ibid., 3: 364.
104. Ibid., 3: 237.
105. Ibid., 3: 236–39.
106. Ibid., 1: 327.
107. In *Yan'an richang shenghuo zhong de lishi*, 246, Zhu Hongzhao mentions that it was possible to have an abortion in the hospital. Song Qingling, the director of the Alliance of Protecting China (Baowei Zhongguo tongmeng), sent women's contraceptive devices to the New Fourth Army. See Shen Qizhen, "Zai Song Qingling danchen 95 zhounian jinianhui shang de jianghua" [Speech at the memorial conference on Song Qingling's ninety-fifth birthday]," in *Jinian Song Qingling wenji* [Essays in memory of Song Qingling], ed. Song Qingling jinianhui bangongshi (Beijing: Zhongguo heping chubanshe, 1992), 46.
108. ZYNZS, 1: 262.
109. Ibid., 1: 262–63.
110. Nancy Scheper-Hughes, "Maternal Thinking and the Politics of War," in *The Women and War Reader*, ed. Lois Ann Lorentzen and Jennifer E. Turpin (New York: New York University Press, 1998), 229.
111. ZYNZS, 3: 470.
112. Ibid., 1: 311.
113. Ibid., 2: 167.

Chapter 3: My Journey of the Revolution

1. These words are from her written reminiscence. See Luo Xing, *Xinlu siyu* [Journey of heart; threads of words], 31. This is in her self-published collection of essays and poems. The preface is dated 2016. No place of publisher. I was given a copy by the author.
2. See Appendix for times and places of interviews, and brief biographies of each woman.
3. His mother, Guo Zhenyi (1902–76), was one of the five "anti-party clique" in the 1942 Rectification Movement.

4 Women's narratives of their own lives are often motivated by the inner urge to reconstruct the self in the male-dominated social structure. See Personal Narratives Group, "Origins," in *Interpreting Women's Lives: Feminist Theory and Personal Narratives*, ed. Personal Narratives Group, Joy Webster Barbre, et al. (Bloomington: Indiana University Press, 1989), 3–15; Liz Stanley, "From 'Self-Made Women' to 'Women's Made-Selves'? Audit Selves, Simulation and Surveillance in the Rise of Public Woman," in *Feminism and Autobiography: Texts, Theories, Methods*, ed. Tess Cosslett, Celia Lury, and Penny Summerfield (London: Routledge, 2000), 40–60.
5 Svetlana Alexievich, *The Unwomanly Face of War: An Oral History of Women in World War II*, trans. Richard Pevear and Larissa Volokhonsky (New York: Random House, 2017), xvii.
6 Michal Bosworth, "'Let Me Tell You …': Memory and the Practice of Oral History," in *Memory and History: Understanding Memory as Source and Subject*, ed. Joan Tumblety (London: Routledge, 2013), 31–32.
7 Luo Xing, *Xinlu siyu*, preface.
8 Chen Yongfa, *Yan'an de yinying* [Yenan's shadow], Monograph Series no. 60 (Taipei: Institute of Modern History, Academia Sinica, 1990), 27–30.
9 Yung-fa Chen, *Making Revolution: The Communist Movement in Eastern and Central China, 1937–1945* (Berkeley: University of California Press, 1986), 324–64; Gao Hua, *How the Red Sun Rose: The Origins and Development of the Yan'an Rectification Movement, 1930–1945*, trans. Stacy Mosher and Guo Jian (Hong Kong: Chinese University Press, 2018), chs. 10, 11, and 12.
10 Mark Selden, *China in Revolution: The Yenan Way Revisited* (Armonk, NY: M.E. Sharpe, 1995), 156.
11 Gao Hua, *How the Red Sun Rose*, 651–52; Yudi Wu, "Yan'an Iron Bodhisattva: Hunting Spies in the Rectification Campaign," in *1943: China at the Crossroads*, ed. Joseph W. Esherick and Matthew T. Combs (Ithaca, NY: East Asian Program, Cornell University, 2015), 203–41.
12 Diana Lary, *The Chinese People at War: Human Suffering and Social Transformation, 1937–1945* (Cambridge: Cambridge University Press, 2010), 22.
13 Gao Hua, *How the Red Sun Rose*, 221–23.
14 See her reminiscences by Guo Li in Shi Deqing, ed., *Fenghuo Taihang banbiantian* [Half of the sky in the wartime Taihang] (Beijing: Zhongyang wenxian chubanshe, 2005), 368–74.
15 Gao Hua, *How the Red Sun Rose*, 602–4.
16 Ibid., 651–52.
17 Yan'an Zhongguo nüzi daxue Beijing xiaoyouhui, ed., *Yanshui qing* [Love for the Yan River] (Beijing: Zhongguo funü chubanshe, 1999), 441–48.
18 Ibid., 259–61.
19 Gao Hua, *How the Red Sun Rose*, 591.
20 Chen Yongfa, *Yan'an de yinying*, 4.
21 Gao Hua, *How the Red Sun Rose*, 445; 656.
22 For a brief introduction to Wang Ruqi, see "Zhongyang yanjiuyuan, jindaishi yanjiusuo" funü qikan zuozhe yanjiu pingtai" [Research platform of authors of women's journals], https://mhdb.mh.sinica.edu.tw/magazine/web/acwp_author.php?no=1795.
For a brief introduction of Guo Zhenyi, see Ibid., https://mhdb.mh.sinica.edu.tw/magazine/web/acwp_author.php?no=1215.
23 Guo Zhenyi, *Zhongguo funü wenti* [Issues of Chinese women] (Shanghai: Commercial Press, 1937).
24 Wei Junyi, *Sitong lu and Lu Sha de lu* [Reflections of pains and *The Road of Lu Sha*], rev. ed. (Beijing: Wenhua yishu chubanshe, 2003), 19.

25 Ibid., 6.
26 Ibid., 207–391.
27 Helen Praeger Young, *Choosing Revolution: Chinese Women Soldiers on the Long March* (Urbana: University of Illinois Press, 2001), 242.
28 This joke is also mentioned in a slightly different version in Wei, *Sitong lu and Lu Sha de lu*, 221–22.

Chapter 4: Those Turbulent Years

1 Chi Pang-yuan, *Juliu he* [The great flowing river] (Taipei: Tianxia yuanjian chuban gufen youxian gongsi, 2009). Her book was published in Beijing: Chi Pang-yuan [Qi Bangyuan], *Juliu he* [The great flowing river] (Beijing: Shenghuo dushu xinzhi sanlian shudian, 2011). The Beijing edition eliminates sections deemed politically unsuitable. Her book has an English translation: Chi Pang-yuan, *The Great Flowing River: A Memoir of China, from Manchuria to Taiwan*, ed. and trans. John Balcom (New York: Columbia University Press, 2018).
2 Chi Pang-yuan, *The Great Flowing River*, vii.
3 Wang Dewei, "Houji" [Epilogue], in *Juliu he*, by Chi Pang-yuan (Beijing: Shenghuo dushu xinzhi sanlian shudian, 2011), 385.
4 Virginia C. Li [Chinese name: Li Zhen], *From One Root Many Flowers: A Century of Family Life in China and America* (Amherst, NY: Prometheus Books, 2003); Yang Huimin, *Babai zhuangshi yu wo* [The eight hundred heroes and I] (Taipei: Fozhiguang chubanshe, 1979).
5 In this study, I use oral accounts in Luo Jiurong, You Jianming, Qu Haiyuan, interviewers, *Fenghuo suiyue xia de Zhongguo funü fangwen jilu* [English title given by the publisher: *20th Century Wartime Experiences of Chinese Women: An Oral History*] (Taipei: Institute of Modern History, Academia Sinica, 2004) [hereafter FHSY], and Chen Sanjing, Zhu Hongyuan, Wu Meihui, interviewers, *Nü qingnian dadui fangwen jilu* [English title by the publisher: *The Reminiscences of Women's Corps*] (Taipei: Institute of Modern History, Academia Sinica, 1995) [hereafter NQNDD].

Also used are: Chen Meiquan, *Chen Meiquan xiansheng fangwen jilu* [English title given by the publisher: *The Reminiscences of Policewoman Chen Mei-chyuan*] (Taipei: Institute of Modern History, Academia Sinica, 1996); Shao Menglan, *Chuncan daosi si fangjin: Shao Menglan nüshi fengwen jilu* [English title given by the publisher: *Spring Silkworm Spins Silk Till Its Death: The Reminiscences of Ms. Shao Meng-lan*] (Taipei: Institute of Modern History, Academia Sinica, 2005); Zhou Meiyu, *Zhou Meiyu xiansheng fangwen jilu* [English title given by the publisher: *The Reminiscences of Prof. Chow Mei Yu*] (Taipei: Institute of Modern History, Academia Sinica, 1993).
6 See the Appendix.
7 Wang Zheng, *Women in the Chinese Enlightenment: Oral and Textual Histories* (Berkeley: University of California Press, 1999). This work has interviews of five women. One of them, Zhu Su'e, was a GMD member. Li Danke, *Echoes of Chongqing: Women in Wartime China* (Urbana: University of Illinois Press, 2010). Li's work includes interviews of twenty women who lived in Chongqing during the war. They were of different socio-economic and political backgrounds. One of them had a husband who worked in the military hospital during the war, and one worked in the Wartime Child Welfare Protection Association, headed by Song Meiling.

8 Yu Chien-Ming, "Beyond Rewriting Life History: Three Female Interviewees' Personal Experiences of War," in *Beyond Exemplar Tales: Women's Biography in Chinese History*, ed. Joan Judge and Hu Ying (Berkeley: University of California Press, 2011), 278.
9 Lily Xiao Hong Lee and A.D. Stefanowska, eds., *Biographical Dictionary of Chinese Women: The Twentieth Century 1912–2000* (Armonk, NY: M.E, Sharpe, 2003), 226–30.
10 Lü Fangshang, "Kangzhan shiqi Zhongguo de fuyun gongzuo" [The women's work during the War of Resistance], in *Zhongguo funüshi lunwenji*, ed. Li Youning and Zhang Yufa (Taipei: Shangwu yishuguan, 1981), 1:383; Zhang Yufa, "Zhanzheng dui Zhongguo funü de yingxiang (1937–1949)" [The impact on the wars on Chinese women (1937–1949)], *Jindai Zhongguo funüshi yanjiu* 17 (December 2009): 160. Zhang has the number as 126 in the Zhenjiang women's battalion.
11 Pingchao Zhu, *Wartime Culture in Guilin, 1938–1944* (Lanham, MD: Lexington Books, 2015), 4–14.
12 Liang Huijin, "Kangzhan shiqi de funü zuzhi" [Women's organizations in the War of Resistance against Japan], in *Zhongguo funüshi lunji xuji* [A collection of articles on Chinese women's history, sequel], ed. Bao Jialin (Taipei: Daoxiang chubanshen, 1991), 372.
13 Shen Zijiu, "Guangxi nüxuesheng jun" [The Guangxi women students army], in *Kangzhan zhong de nüzhanshi*, ed. Shen Zijiu [Women soldiers in the resistance war] (n.p.: Zhanshi chubanshen, n.d.), 76–80. This was published during the war but the place and dates are unknown.
14 Yan Zhaofen, "Chufa qianhou: Guangxi nüxuesheng jun tongxun" [Before and after the departure: report on the Guangxi women students army] in Shen Zijiu, *Kangzhan zhong de nüzhanshi*, 80–83.
15 Yang Huilin, "Guangxi niangzijun huijianji [Meeting the Guangxi women students army] in Shen Zijiu, *Kangzhan zhong de nüzhanshi*, 83–88.
16 Zhonghua quanguo funü lianhehui funü yundong lishi yanjiushi, comp., *Zhongguo funü yundong lishi ziliao, 1937–1945* [Historical materials of Chinese women's movement, 1937–1945] (Beijing: Zhongguo funü chubanshe, 1991), 248–51 [hereafter ZFYLZ (1937–45)]. For the militia and women's mobilization in Guangxi, see also Diana Lary, "One Province's Experience of War: Guangxi, 1937–1945," in *China at War: Regions of China, 1937–1945*, ed. Stephen R. MacKinnon, Diana Lary, and Ezra F. Vogel (Stanford, CA: Stanford University Press, 2007), 314–34.
17 The student army dissolved in December 1939. Her younger sister returned home while she remained in Anhui to continue the propaganda work. See Zhou Lei and Liu Ningyuan, *Kangzhan shiqi Zhongguo funü yundong yanjiu (1931–1945)* [Study of Chinese women's movement in the War of Resistance (1931–1945)] (Beijing: Shoudu jingji maoyi daxue chubanshe, 2016), 93–95.
18 Ibid., 95–96.
19 Ibid., 96; Wu Xiangxiang, *Dierci Zhong-Ri Zhanzhengshi, 1931–1945* [History of the second Sino-Japanese War, 1931–1945] (Taipei: Tsung Ho Book, 1973), 2: 611.
20 Zhang Yufa, "Zhanzheng dui Zhongguo funü de yingxiang (1937–1949)," 160–61.
21 NQNDD, 427–28.
22 Mo Yan, *Hong gaoliang jiazu* [The red sorghum family] (Beijing: Jiefangjun wenyi chubanshe, 1987).
23 NQNDD, 428.
24 Ibid., 430–31.
25 Ibid., 333–37.
26 Ibid., 335.

27 Ibid., 341.
28 Ibid., 391–92.
29 Zhou Meiyu, *Zhou Meiyu xiansheng fangwen jilu*, 83.
30 For more on her, see also Zhou Chunyan, "Funü yu kangzhan shiqi de zhandi jiuhu" [Women and battlefield first aid during the second Sino-Japanese War], *Jindai Zhongguo funüshi yanjiu* 24 (December 2014): 133–218.
31 Sonya Grypma and Cheng Zhen, "The Development of Modern Nursing in China," in *Medical Transitions in Twentieth-Century China*, ed. Mary Brown Bullock and Bridie Andrews (Bloomington: Indiana University Press, 2014), 306.
32 Zhou Meiyu, *Zhou Meiyu xiansheng fangwen jilu*, 42.
33 Ibid., 48–49.
34 Ibid., 54–55.
35 Ibid., 151–52.
36 Grypma and Cheng Zhen, "The Development of Modern Nursing in China," 307.
37 Hong Yizhen, *Zhongguo Guomindang funü gongzuo zhi yanjiu 1924–1949* [English title given by the publisher: *The Kuomintang and Women's Affairs, 1924–1949*] (Taipei: Guoshiguan, 2010), 241.
38 Zhou Meiyu, *Zhou Meiyu xiansheng fangwen jilu*, 2–3.
39 For the section on her life before and during the War of Resistance, NQNDD, 1–8.
40 Ibid., 5–6.
41 Yang Huimin, *Babai zhuangshi yu wo*.
42 Ibid., 43–44.
43 Margaret Mih Tillman, "Engendering Children of the Resistance: Models for Gender and Scouting in China, 1919–1937," *Cross-Currents: East Asian History and Culture Review*, E-Journal no. 13 (December 2014), 134–73. https://escholarship.org/uc/item/9501x9cd.
44 Yang Huimin, *Babai zhuangshi yu wo*, chs. 7 and 9.
45 Ying Yunwei, dir., *Babai zhuangshi* [Eight hundred heroes] (1938; Hong Kong: Zhongnan guangrong yingpian gongsi, 1938).
46 Ding Shanxi, dir., *Babai zhuangshi* [Eight hundred heroes] (1975; Taipei: Zhongying gongsi).
47 Guan Hu, dir., *Babai* [Eight hundred] (2020; Shenzhen: Huayi xiongdi dianying gongsi).
48 Yang Huimin, "Xianqi zai babai zhuangshi zhi qian" [Delivering flag to the eight hundred heroes], in *Shanghai yiri* [One day in Shanghai], ed. Zhu Zuotong and Mei Yi (Shanghai: Huamei chuban gongsi, 1938), pt. 1, 53–54.
49 *Li bao*, October 29, 1937: "Sihang gujun" [Lone army in Sihang], in *"Ba yisan" kangzhan shiliao xuanbian* [Selected historical materials on the "August 13" resistance], comp. Shanghai shehui kexueyuan lishi yanjiusuo (Shanghai: Renmin chubanshe, 1986), 70–71.
50 Tillman, "Engendering Children of the Resistance"; Su Zhiliang and Hu Haolei, "Sihang gujun de guang yu ying" [Lights and shadows of the lone army of Sihang warehouse], *Dang'an chunqiu* 7 (2015): 13–16; 8 (2015): 37–38; 9 (2015): 27–30; 10 (2015): 32–35.
51 Tillman, "Engendering Children of the Resistance," 159; Yang, Huimin *Babai zhuangshi yu wo*, ch. 10.
52 Yang Huimin, *Babai zhuangshi yu wo*, 147–50.
53 Ibid., *zixu* [self-introduction].
54 Wang Zheng, *Women in the Chinese Enlightenment*, 187–220.
55 Ibid., 201.
56 Chi Pang-yuan, *The Great Flowing River*, 58.
57 NQNDD, 248.

58 FHSY, 188, 189.
59 Ibid., 189–92.
60 Li, *From One Root Many Flowers*, 120.
61 Ibid., 136.
62 FHSY, 409.
63 Stephen MacKinnon, "Refugee Flight at the Outset of the Anti-Japanese War," in *Scars of War: The Impact of Warfare on Modern China*, ed. Diana Lary and Stephen MacKinnon (Vancouver: UBC Press, 2001), 118–22; Diana Lary, *The Chinese People at War, 1937–1945* (Cambridge: Cambridge University Press, 2010), 24–29.
64 Stephen R. MacKinnon, *Wuhan, 1938: War, Refugees, and the Making of Modern China* (Berkeley: University of California Press, 2008), 44–54.
65 FHSY, 171.
66 Ibid., 153–66.
67 Rana Mitter, "Classifying Citizens in Nationalist China during World War II, 1937–1941," *Modern Asian Studies* 45, 2 (2011): 254.
68 NQNDD, 302–3.
69 Pan Xun et al., *KangRi zhanzheng shiqi Chongqing da hongzha yanjiu* [English title given by the publisher: *Research on Japan's Bombing Raid to Chongqing during the Anti-Japanese War*] (Beijing: Commercial Press, 2013), 11.
70 FHSY, 75.
71 Ibid., 83–84.
72 Chi Pang-yuan, *The Great Flowing River*, 51.
73 Ibid., 113.
74 Ibid., 126.
75 Ibid., 173.
76 Ibid., 168–74.
77 Pan Xun et al., *KangRi zhanzheng shiqi Chongqing da hongzha yanjiu*, 14.
78 Jui-te Chang, "Bombs Don't Discriminate? Class, Gender, and Ethnicity in the Air-Raid-Shelter Experiences of the Wartime Chongqing Population," in *Beyond Suffering: Recounting War in Modern China*, ed. James Flath and Norman Smith (Vancouver: UBC Press, 2011), 59–79.
79 Li, *Echoes of Chongqing*, 86–87.
80 Ibid., 99–100.
81 John Israel, *Lianda: A Chinese University in War and Revolution* (Stanford, CA: Stanford University Press, 1998), 10–13.
82 Mark Selden, *China in Revolution: The Yenan Way Revisited* (Armonk, NY: M.E. Sharpe, 1995), 115–17, 208–12.
83 Zhang Yufa, "Zhanzheng dui Zhongguo funü de yingxiang (1937–1949)," 158.
84 Israel, *Lianda*, 28–29; Lary, *The Chinese People at War*, 90.
85 Israel, *Lianda*, 27–28.
86 Israel, *Lianda*; Su Zhiliang et al., *Zhongguo kangzhan neiqian shilu* [The record of the exodus into the interior in China's War of Resistance] (Shanghai: Renmin chubanshe, 2015), ch. 4.
87 Israel, *Lianda*, 14–15.
88 Jennifer Liu, "Defiant Retreat: The Relocation of Middle Schools to China's Interior, 1937–1945," *Frontiers of History in China* 8, 4 (2013): 558–84.
89 Zhuangzi, "Qiushui" [Autumn floods], in *Chuang Tzu: Basic Teachings*, trans. Burton Watson (New York: Columbia University Press, 1964), 105–6.
90 Chi Pang-yuan, *The Great Flowing River*, 74.

91 Ibid., ch. 3.
92 NQNDD, 169.
93 R. Keith Schoppa, *In a Sea of Bitterness: Refugees during the Sino-Japanese War* (Cambridge, MA: Harvard University Press, 2011), ch. 8.
94 Shao Menglan, *Chuncan daosi si fangjin*.
95 Ibid., 127.
96 Ibid., 122.
97 Ibid., 130–32.
98 Wang Zheng, *Women in the Chinese Enlightenment*, ch. 4.
99 For student loan and financial assistance, see Wu Xiangxiang, *Dierci Zhong-Ri Zhanzhengshi*, 1: 684. See also Su Zhiliang et al., *Zhongguo kangzhan neiqian shilu*, 186.
100 Chen Meiquan, *Chen Meiquan xiansheng fangwen jilu*, 9.
101 Ibid., 18.
102 Ibid., 68.
103 Ibid., 37–53.
104 Ibid., 39.
105 Ibid., 51–52.
106 FHSY, 235–83.
107 Lü Fangshang, "Ling yizhong 'wei zuzhi': kangzhan shiqi hunyin yu jiating wenti chutan" [Another "illegitimate organization": an initial study of marriage and family issues in the resistance war], *Jindai Zhongguo funüshi yanjiu* 3 (August 1995): 97–121.
108 FHSY, 262.
109 Ibid., 276.
110 Ibid., 134.
111 Ibid., 344.
112 Ibid., 354.
113 Ibid., 398–99.
114 Ibid., 401.
115 Ibid., 19.
116 Ibid., 25.
117 Ibid., 39.
118 Ibid., 567–68.
119 Zhou Meiyu, *Zhou Meiyu xiansheng fangwen jilu*, 65.
120 NQNDD, 336–37.
121 Ibid., 339.
122 Ibid., 41–47.
123 Li, *Echoes of Chongqing*, 73–78.
124 Ibid., 74–75.
125 Zhou Meiyu, *Zhou Meiyu xiansheng fangwen jilu*, 82–84.
126 Chen Meiquan, *Chen Meiquan xiansheng fangwen jilu*, 60.
127 Ibid., 69.
128 NQNDD, 31.

Chapter 5: Surviving under the Enemy

1 Lo Jiu-jung, "Survival as Justification for Collaboration 1937–1945," in *Chinese Collaboration with Japan, 1932–1945: The Limits of Accommodation*, ed. David P. Barrett and Lawrence N. Shyu (Stanford, CA: Stanford University Press, 2001), 116–32.

2 David P. Barrett, "Introduction: Occupied China and the Limits of Accommodation," in Barrett and Shyu, *Chinese Collaboration with Japan 1932–1945*, 10.
3 Diana Lary, "War and Remembering: Memories of China at War," in *Beyond Suffering: Recounting War in Modern China*, ed. James Flath and Norman Smith (Vancouver: UBC Press, 2011), 263.
4 R. Keith Schoppa, "Book Review: Christian Henriot and Wen-hsin Yeh, editors. In the Shadow of the Rising Sun: Shanghai under the Japanese Occupation," *China Review International* 11, 2 (Fall 2004): 378–81.
5 See the Appendix.
6 Diana Lary, *The Chinese People at War: Human Suffering and Social Transformation, 1937–1945* (Cambridge: Cambridge University Press, 2010), 68.
7 Yun Xia, *Down with Traitors: Justice and Nationalism in Wartime China* (Seattle: University of Washington Press, 2017), 6.
8 Ibid., 129–40.
9 Norman Smith, *Resisting Manchukuo: Chinese Women Writers and the Japanese Occupation* (Vancouver: UBC Press, 2007), 11, 132–37.
10 Robert Chi, "'The March of the Volunteers': From Movie Theme Song to National Anthem," in *Re-envisioning the Chinese Revolution: The Politics and Poetics of Collective Memories in Reform China,* ed. Ching Kwan Lee and Guobin Yang (Stanford, CA: Stanford University Press, 2007), 217–44.
11 Xiao Hong, *The Field of Life and Death and Tales of Hulan River,* trans. Howard Goldblatt (Boston: Cheng and Tsui, 2002).
12 Ibid., 72, 73.
13 See, for example, Qi Hongshen, ed., *Liuwang: kangzhan shiqi dongbei liuwang xuesheng koushu* [Exiles: oral narratives by refugee students of northeast during the War of Resistance] (Zhengzhou, Henan: Daxiang chubanshe, 2008); Qi Hongshen, ed., *Heian xia de xinghuo: wei Manzhouguo wenxue qingnian ji Riben dangshiren koushu* [Sparks in the darkness: oral narratives by literary youth and Japanese litigants under the pseudo-Manchu regime] (Zhengzhou, Henan: Daxiang chubanshe, 2011).
14 Rong Weimu *et al.*, "Bitan kangRi zhanzheng yu lunxianqu yanjiu" [Written discussion of the studies of the anti-Japanese war and the occupied areas], *KangRi zhanzheng yanjiu* 1 (2010): 126–49. This is a collection of essays by twenty-four historians.
15 Zhang Xianwen and Zhang Yufa, chief eds., *Zhonghua minguo zhuantishi* [Topical history of the Republic of China], vol. 12, *Kangzhan shiqi de lunxianqu yu wei zhengquan* [Occupied regions and illegitimate regimes in the anti-Japanese war] (Nanjing: Nanjing daxue chubanshe, 2015), 507.
16 See, for example, Barrett and Shyu, *Chinese Collaboration with Japan, 1932–1945;* Christian Henriot and Wen-Hsin Yeh, *In the Shadow of the Rising Sun: Shanghai under Japanese Occupation* (Cambridge: Cambridge University Press, 2004); Timothy Brook, *Collaboration: Japanese Agents and Local Elites in Wartime China* (Cambridge, MA: Harvard University Press, 2005); Stephen R. MacKinnon, Diana Lary, and Ezra F. Vogel, eds., *China at War: Regions of China, 1937–1945* (Stanford, CA: Stanford University Press, 2007); Jonathan Henshaw, Craig A. Smith, and Norman Smith, eds., *Translating the Occupation: The Japanese Invasion of China, 1931–45* (Vancouver: UBC Press, 2021).
17 Poshek Fu, *Passivity, Resistance, and Collaboration: Intellectual Choices in Occupied Shanghai, 1937–1945* (Stanford, CA: Stanford University Press, 1993), xiv, xv. Fu borrows the grey zone concept from Primo Levi's *The Drowned and the Saved.* Trans. Raymond Rosenthal (New York: Vintage International, 1989).
18 Brook, *Collaboration*, 11.

19 R. Keith Schoppa, *In a Sea of Bitterness: Refugees during the Sino-Japanese War* (Cambridge, MA: Harvard University Press, 2011), 310.
20 Emily Honig, *Sisters and Strangers: Women in the Shanghai Cotton Mills, 1919–1949* (Stanford, CA: Stanford University Press, 1986); Emily Honig, "Burning Incense, Pledging Sisterhood: Community of Women Workers in the Shanghai Cotton Mills, 1919–1949," in *Feminism and Community*, ed. Penny A. Weiss and Marilyn Friedman (Philadelphia: Temple University Press, 1995), 59–75.
21 Zhao Ma, *Runaway Wives, Urban Crimes, and Survival Tactics in Wartime Beijing, 1937–1949* (Cambridge, MA: Harvard University Asia Center, 2015).
22 Susan Glosser, "'Women's Culture of Resistance': An Ordinary Response to Extraordinary Circumstances," in Henriot and Yeh, *In the Shadow of the Rising Sun*, 302–24.
23 Nicole Huang, *Women, War, Domesticity: Shanghai Literature and Popular Culture of the 1940s* (Leiden: Brill, 2005), 31; Nicole Huang, "Fashioning Public Intellectuals: Women's Print Culture in Occupied Shanghai (1941–1945)," in Henriot and Yeh, *In the Shadow of the Rising Sun*, 325–45.
24 Chen Yan, *Xingbei yu zhanzheng: Shanghai 1932–1945* [Gender and war: Shanghai 1932–1945] (Beijing: Shehui kexue wenxian chubanshe, 2014), 267–82.
25 Schoppa, "Book Review."
26 Smith, *Resisting Manchukuo*, 85, chs. 5 and 6.
27 Wenwen Wang, "Beyond 'Good Wives and Wise Mothers': Feminism as Anticolonialism in Manchukuo Schools," *Twentieth-Century China* 45, 3 (October 2020): 285–307.
28 Prasenjit Duara, "Of Authenticity and Woman: Personal Narratives of Middle-Class Women in Modern China," in *Becoming Chinese: Passages to Modernity and Beyond*, ed. Wen-hsin Yeh (Berkeley: University of California Press, 2000), 342–64; Prasenjit Duara, *Sovereignty and Authenticity: Manchukuo and the East Asian Modern* (Lanham, MD: Rowman and Littlefield, 2003), ch. 4.
29 Yuan Runlan, "Yuan Runlan nüshi fangwen jilu" [The interview of Yuan Runlan], in *Cong dongbei dao Taiwan: Wanguo daodehui xiangguan renwu fangwen jilu* [From the Northeast to Taiwan: interviews of people related with the Wan'guo daodehui], ed. Luo Jiurong et al. (Taipei: Institute of Modern History, Academia Sinica, 2006), 72.
30 Jiang Yunzhong, *Jiang Yunzhong nüshi fangwen jilu* [English title given by the publisher: *The Reminiscences of Mme. Jiang Yun-jung*] (Taipei: Institute of Modern History, Academia Sinica, 2005), 27.
31 Jiang Yunzhong, *Jiang Yunzhong nüshi fangwen jilu*; Yuan Runlan, "Yuan Runlan nüshi fangwen jilu," 69–94.
32 Xia, *Down with Traitors*, 8–12.
33 Stanley Hoffmann, "Introduction," in *The Sorrow and the Pity: A Film*, by Marcel Ophuls (New York: Outerbridge and Lazard, 1972), 7–26.
34 Robert Gildea, *Marianne in Chains: Everyday Life in the French Heartland under the German Occupation* (New York: Metropolitan Books/Henry Holt, 2002), 16.
35 Ibid., 10.
36 Ibid., 10–11.
37 James C. Scott, *Weapons of the Weak: Everyday Forms of Peasant Resistance* (New Haven, CT: Yale University Press, 1985), 33.
38 The song was composed by Zhang Hanhui in 1935.
39 Qi Hongshen, ed., *Mosha buliao de zuizheng: Riben qinHua jiaoyu koushushi* [Non-erasable evidence of crime: oral history of education under Japanese aggression of China] (Beijing: Renmin jiaoyu chubanshe, 2005), 5, 6; Song Enrong and Yu Zixia, chief eds.,

Riben qinHua jiaoyu quanshi [A general history of education under Japanese aggression of China] (Beijing: Renmin jiaoyu chubanshe, 2005), 1: 1, 1: 18–19.
40 The number is from Qi Hongshen, *Liuwang*, 1–2.
41 Song and Yu, *Riben qinHua jiaoyu quanshi*, 1: 303–15.
42 She told me in the interview that the local newspaper had published the list of recipients, and that was how her father learned about the award. I was unable to verify the specifics of the paper.
43 Song and Yu, *Riben qinHua jiaoyu quanshi*, 1: 91.
44 Qi Hongshen, *Heian xia de xinghuo*, 11.
45 Qi Hongshen, *Riben duihua jiaoyu qinlue: dui Riben qinhua jiaoyu de yanjiu yu pipan* [Japan's educational invasion of China: study and criticism of Japan's educational invasion of China] (Beijing: Kunlun chubanshe, 2005), 55–60.
46 Qi Hongshen, *Heian xia de xinghuo*, 127.
47 Song and Yu, *Riben qinHua jiaoyu quanshi*, 1: 105.
48 Qi Hongshen, *Mosha buliao de zuizheng*, 5, 6.
49 Qi Hongshen, *Riben duihua jiaoyu qinlue*, 79–80.
50 Song and Yu, *Riben qinHua jiaoyu quanshi*, 2: 282–83.
51 Zhejiang was the first province where this was done. See Song and Yu, *Riben qinHua jiaoyu quanshi*, 2: 183–84; Qi Hongshen, *Riben duihua jiaoyu qinlue*, 87–88.
52 Yanjing University was outside the old the city walls of Beiping.

Chapter 6: I Want to Speak Up before I Die

1 Guo Ke, dir., *Ershier* [Twenty-two] (2017; Chengdu: Sichuan guangying shenchu wenhua chuanbo youxian gongsi).
2 Su Zhiliang, *Weianfu yanjiu* [A study of the comfort women] (Shanghai: Shanghai shudian chubanshe, 1999), 285. See Peipei Qiu, with Su Zhiliang and Chen Lifei, *Chinese Comfort Women: Testimonies from Imperial Japan's Sex Slaves* (Vancouver: UBC Press, 2013), 38.
3 See the Appendix.
4 Timothy Brook, "Preface: Lisbon, Xuzhou, Auschwitz: Suffering as History," in *Beyond Suffering: Recounting War in Modern China*, ed. James Flath and Norman Smith (Vancouver: UBC Press, 2011), xv; Diana Lary and Stephen MacKinnon, "Introduction," in *Scars of War: The Impact of Warfare on Modern China*, ed. Diana Lary and Stephen MacKinnon (Vancouver: UBC Press, 2001), 3–15.
5 In her research on the comfort women system, Maki Kimura examines how the comfort women outside China transformed from "social stigma to survivor-activists." See Maki Kimura, *Unfolding the "Comfort Women" Debates: Modernity, Violence, Women's Voices* (New York: Palgrave Macmillan, 2016), ch. 8.
6 Susan Brownmiller, *Against Our Will: Men, Women and Rape* (New York: Simon and Schuster, 1975), 32.
7 Egami Sachiko, "Rijun funü baoxing he zhanshi Zhongguo funü zazhi" [Japanese army's sexual violence and Chinese women magazines during the war], in *Taotian zuinie: erzhan shiqi de Rijun "weianfu" yanjiu* [Monstrous atrocities: the Japanese military comfort women system during the Second World War], ed. Su Zhiliang, Rong Weimu, and Chen Lifei (Shanghai: Xuelin chubanshe, 2000), 56–57.
8 C. Sarah Soh, *The Comfort Women: Sexual Violence and Postcolonial Memory in Korea and Japan* (Chicago: University of Chicago Press, 2008), xiii.

9. Egami Sachiko, "Rijun funü baoxing he zhanshi Zhongguo funü zazhi"; Daqing Yang, "Atrocities in Nanjing: Searching for Explanations," in Lary and MacKinnon, *Scars of War*, 76–96; Wang Xiaokui, "Historical Shifts in Remembering China's Nanjing Massacre," *Chinese Studies in History* 50, 4 (2017): 324–34.
10. Nicola Henry, *War and Rape: Law, Memory, and Justice* (New York: Routledge, 2011), 7–8.
11. Perry Link, "Foreword," in *Nanking 1937: Memory and Healing*, ed. Feifei Li, Robert Sabella, and David Liu (Armonk, NY: M.E. Sharpe, 2002), ix–xx.
12. Professor J. Mark Ramseyer of Harvard University is a well-known denier. In his paper of 2021, he argues that Korean women were willing sex workers recruited through a contract in brothels/"comfort stations" across East Asia in the 1930s and 1940s. See J. Mark Ramseyer, "Contracting for Sex in the Pacific War," *International Review of Law and Economics* 65 (March 2021).
13. Carol Gluck, "Operations of Memory: 'Comfort Women' and the World," in *Ruptured Histories: War, Memory, and the Post-Cold War in Asia*, ed. Sheila Miyoshi Jager and Rana Mitter (Cambridge, MA: Harvard University Press, 2007), 47–76.
14. Bonnie B.C. Oh, "The Japanese Imperial System and the Korean 'Comfort Women' of World War II," in *Legacies of the Comfort Women of World War II*, ed. Margaret Stetz and Bonnie B.C. Oh (Armonk, NY: M.E. Sharpe, 2001), 13; George Hicks, *The Comfort Women: Japan's Brutal Regime of Enforced Prostitution in the Second World War* (New York: W.W. Norton, 1995), 21; Qiu et al., *Chinese Comfort Women*, 151–59.
15. Margaret Stetz and Bonnie B.C. Oh, "Introduction," in Stetz and Oh, *Legacies of the Comfort Women of World War II*, xii.
16. Qiu et al., *Chinese Comfort Women*, 195–96.
17. Oh, "The Japanese Imperial System and the Korean 'Comfort Women' of World War II," 13–20; Kimura, *Unfolding the "Comfort Women" Debates*, 4–5; Gluck, "Operations of Memory: 'Comfort Women' and the World," 47–76; Qiu et al., *Chinese Comfort Women*, 1–3, ch. 9.
18. Numerous works have appeared. See, for example, En-Han Lee, "The Nanking Massacre Reassessed: A Study of the Sino-Japanese Controversy over the Factual Number of Massacred Victims," in Li, Sabella, and Liu, *Nanking 1937: Memory and Healing*, 47–74; Fengqi Qian and Guo-Qiang Liu, "Remembrance of the Nanjing Massacre in the Globalised Era: The Memory of Victimisation, Emotions and the Rise of China," *China Report* 55, 2 (2019): 81–101.
19. Su Zhiliang, *Weianfu yanjiu*, 370–74; Qiu et al., *Chinese Comfort Women*, ch. 9.
20. Zhang Shuangbing, *Paoluo li de nüren: Shanxi Rijun xing nuli diaocha shilu* [Women in the blockhouse: the investigation record of the sex slaves under the Japanese army in Shanxi] (Nanjing: Jiangsu renmin chubanshe, 2011). The interviews were edited by Zhang.
21. Jiang Hao, *Zhaoshi: Zhongguo weianfu* [Expose: Chinese comfort women] (Beijing: Zuojia chubanshe, 1993).
22. Su Zhiliang, *Weianfu yanjiu*.
23. Su Zhiliang, Rong Weimu, and Chen Lifei, *Taotian zuinie*, 1.
24. Su Zhiliang, *Rijun xingnuli: Zhongguo "weianfu" zhenxiang* [Sex slaves of the Japanese troops: a true account of Chinese "comfort women"] (Beijing: Renmin chubanshe, 2000).
25. Su Zhiliang, Rong Weimu, and Chen Lifei, *Taotian zuinie*, 1; Su Zhiliang, Yao Fei, and Chen Lifei. *QinHua Rijun "weianfu" wenti yanjiu* [Study of issues of the "comfort women" under the Japanese invading army] (Beijing: Zhonggong dangshi chubanshe, 2016).
26. Qiu et al., *Chinese Comfort Women*, 196.

27 Ishida Yoneko and Uchida Tomoyuki, *Koodo no mura no seibooryoku: Da'nyan tachi no sensoo wa owaranai* [Sexual violence in the villages located in the area of the yellow earth: the war is not over to these aged women] (Tokyo: Soodosha, 2004). I use the Chinese translation of this work, titled *Fasheng zai huangtu cunzhuang li de Rijun xingbaoli – daniangmen de zhanzheng shangwei jiushu* [English title given by the publisher: *Sexual Violence in YuXian: Their War Is Not Over*], trans. Zhao Jingui (Beijing: Shehui kexue wenxian chubanshe, 2008).
28 Li Xiaofang, *Shiji nahan: 67 wei xingcun weianfu shilu* [Cries of the century: testimonies of sixty-seven surviving comfort women] (Beijing: Zhonggong dangshi chubanshe, 2008). From 2004 to 2006, Li Xiaofang, a photojournalist, visited survivors of Chinese, Korean, Miao, Li, and Yao ethnicities in different parts of China and in South Korea.
29 Guo Ke, dir., *Sanshier* [Thirty-two] (2014; Chengdu: Sichuan guangying shenchu wenhua chuanbo youxian gongsi).
30 Wang Siyi, "Memorials and Memory: The Curation and Interpretation of Trauma Narratives – Using the Examples of Exhibitions on the Theme of 'Comfort Women' in East Asian Society," *Chinese Studies in History* 53, 1 (2020): 56–71.
31 Qiu et al., *Chinese Comfort Women*, 78.
32 Ibid., 77.
33 Keith Howard, ed., *True Stories of the Korean Comfort Women* (London: Cassell, 1995), vii.
34 Henry, *War and Rape*, 115.
35 Ishida Yoneko and Uchida Tomoyuki, *Fasheng zai huangtu cunzhuang li de Rijun xingbaoli*, 6.
36 Zhang Shuangbing, *Paoluo li de nüren*, 5.
37 Ibid., 3–16; Qiu et al., *Chinese Comfort Women*, 168.
38 Zhang Shuangbing, *Paoluo li de nüren*, 16.
39 Ibid., 38–39.
40 Ibid., 64–73.
41 Ishida Yoneko and Uchida Tomoyuki, *Fasheng zai huangtu cunzhuang li de Rijun xingbaoli*, 10–11.
42 Ibid., 44.
43 Ibid., 24–25.
44 Qiu et al., *Chinese Comfort Women*, 117.
45 Ibid., 117–18.
46 Ibid., 147.
47 Kimura, *Unfolding the "Comfort Women" Debates*, 197.
48 Zhang Shuangbing, *Paoluo li de nüren*, 2.
49 Ibid.
50 Qiu, Peipei, with Su Zhiliang and Chen Lifei, *Riben diguo de xing nuli: Zhongguo "weianfu" zhengyan* [Sexual slaves under the Japanese imperialism: testimonies of the Chinese "comfort women"] (Hong Kong: Hong Kong University Press, 2017.)
51 Qiu et al., *Chinese Comfort Women*, 127–28.
52 Egami Sachiko, "Rijun funü baoxing he zhanshi Zhongguo funü zazhi," 66.
53 Ishida Yoneko and Uchida Tomoyuki, *Fasheng zai huangtu cunzhuang li de Rijun xingbaoli*, 52–53.
54 Ibid., 62.
55 Ibid., 66.
56 Zhang Shuangbing, *Paoluo li de nüren*, 9–10.

57 Guo Ke, *Ershier*.
58 Qiu et al., *Chinese Comfort Women*, 124, 125.
59 Several versions of Wan Aihua's interview exist. See Qiu et al., *Chinese Comfort Women*, 119–25; Ishida Yoneko and Uchida Tomoyuki, *Fasheng zai huangtu cunzhuang li de Rijun xingbaoli*, 83–99; Zhang Shuangbing, *Paolou li de nüren*, 47–49. The Women's International War Crimes Tribunal on Japan's Military Sexual Slavery in Tokyo in the year 2000 was organized by Asian women and human rights organizations. See Qiu et al., *Chinese Comfort Women*, 182.
60 Guo Ke, *Sanshier* (the documentary has English subtitles).
61 Zhao Linlu, "Jiushijiu sui 'weianfu' Wei Shaolan cishi: yizhi meiyou dengdao Riben de daoqian" [Ninety-nine-year-old "comfort woman" Wei Shaolan passed away: never received a Japanese apology before her death], *China News Network*, May 6, 2019, http://www.xinhuanet.com/politics/2019-05/06/c_1124454995.htm.
62 See, for example, Yin Shihong and Fu Xiuyan, chief eds., *Yongyuan de cantong: Jiangxisheng qiangjiu kangzhan shiqi zaoshou Rijun qinhai shiliao: koushu shilu* [The lasting pains: rescued historical records of the suffering of violence committed by the invading Japanese army in Jiangxi province during the resistance war period: oral histories], 2 vols. (Beijing: Remin chubanshe, 2010). The Jiangxi provincial Academy of Social Science organized research teams in all counties and municipalities to collect oral accounts of violence and crimes committed by the Japanese military. The work includes sixty-seven people's accounts, among which fifteen were by women.
63 Zhang Chengde and Sun Liping, eds., *Shanxi kangzhan koushushi* [The oral histories of resistance war in Shanxi]. (Taiyuan: Shanxi renmin chubanshe, 2005).
64 Chen Xuqing, "Xinling de jiyi: ku'nan yu kangzheng – Shanxi kangzhan koushushi" [Memories of the heart: sufferings and resistance – oral histories of the resistance war in Shanxi] (PhD diss., Zhejiang University, 2005), 86.
65 Ibid., 92–93.
66 Zhao Ma, *Runaway Wives, Urban Crimes, and Survival Tactics in Wartime Beijing, 1937–1949* (Cambridge, MA: Harvard University Asia Center, 2015), 11.
67 Gail Hershatter, *The Gender of Memory: Rural Women and China's Collective Past* (Berkeley: University of California Press, 2011), 24–31.
68 Brook, "Preface: Lisbon, Xuzhou, Auschwitz: Suffering as History," xvii.
69 Emily Honig, *Sisters and Strangers: Women in the Shanghai Cotton Mills, 1919–1949* (Stanford, CA: Stanford University Press, 1986), 1.
70 Frederic Wakeman Jr., "Shanghai Smuggling," in *In the Shadow of the Rising Sun: Shanghai under Japanese Occupation*, ed. Christian Henriot and Wen-Hsin Yeh (Cambridge: Cambridge University Press, 2004), 116–53.
71 Honig, *Sisters and Strangers*, 182–83.
72 Zhonggong Wutai xianwei dangshi yanjiushi, ed., *Wutai renmin kangRi douzhengshi* [The history of the Wutai people's anti-Japanese struggle] (Internal circulation, 1985), 7–8. I received a copy from Zhao Peicheng, a member of the committee of compilation.
73 Zhonggong Liyangshi weiyuanhui, dangshi ziliao zhengli yanjiu lingdao xiaozu, ed., *Liyang geming douzhengshi* [The history of Liyang's revolutionary struggle] (Nanjing: Jiangsu renmin chubanshe, 1995), 25–35. See also the Chronology, 118–31.
74 General Chen Yi was born in 1901. The New Fourth Army headquarters in Jiangnan at Shuixi Village, Liyang, was established in November 1939.

Epilogue

1. For my interview with her, see Chapter 5.
2. For my interview with her, see Chapter 6.
3. For my interview with her, see Chapter 5.
4. Chen Meiquan, *Chen Meiquan xiansheng fangwen jilu* [English title given by the publisher: *The Reminiscences of Policewoman Chen Mei-chyuan*] (Taipei: Institute of Modern History, Academia Sinica, 1996), 55.
5. Ibid., 58–59.
6. Chi Pang-yuan, *The Great Flowing River: A Memoir of China, from Manchuria to Taiwan*, ed. and trans. John Balcom (New York: Columbia University Press, 2018), 176.
7. Ibid.
8. Diana Lary, "War and Remembering: Memories of China at War," in *Beyond Suffering: Recounting War in Modern China*, ed. James Flath and Norman Smith (Vancouver: UBC Press, 2011), 263.
9. Paul G. Pickowicz, "Victory as Defeat: Postwar Visualizations of China's War of Resistance," in *Becoming Chinese: Passages to Modernity and Beyond*, ed. Wen-hsin Yeh (Berkeley: University of California Press, 2000), 365–98.
10. For my interview with her, see Chapter 5.
11. For my interview with her, see Chapter 6.
12. For my interview with her, see Chapter 3.
13. For my interview with her, see Chapter 3.
14. E-Yu bianqu gemingshi bianjibu; Hubeisheng funü lianhehui, eds., *Zhongyuan nüzhanshi* [Women soldiers of the central plain], 3 vols. (Beijing: Zhongguo funü chubanshe, 1991–94), 1: 327 [hereafter ZYNZS].
15. Luo Jiurong, You Jianming, Qu Haiyuan, interviewers, *Fenghuo suiyue xia de Zhongguo funü fangwen jilu* [English title given by the publisher: *20th Century Wartime Experiences of Chinese Women: An Oral History*] (Taipei: Institute of Modern History, Academia Sinica, 2004), 197–98 [hereafter FHSY].
16. Ibid., 358.
17. See also Yu Chien-ming, "Beyond Rewriting Life History: Three Female Interviewees' Personal Experiences of War," in *Beyond Exemplar Tales: Women's Biography in Chinese History*, ed. Joan Judge and Hu Ying (Berkeley: University of California Press, 2011), 262–80.
18. Chen Sanjing, Zhu Hongyuan, Wu Meihui, interviewers, *Nü qingnian dadui fangwen jilu* [English title by the publisher: *The Reminiscences of Women's Corps*] (Taipei: Institute of Modern History, Academia Sinica, 1995), 194 [hereafter NQNDD].
19. Ibid., 507.
20. Elizabeth C. Economy, *The Third Revolution: Xi Jinping and the New Chinese State* (Oxford: Oxford University Press, 2018), 6.
21. Mayfair Mei-hui Yang, ed., *Spaces of Their Own: Women's Public Sphere in Transnational China* (Minneapolis: University of Minnesota Press, 1999); Tani E. Barlow, *The Question of Women in Chinese Feminism* (Durham, NC: Duke University Press, 2004).
22. Economy, *The Third Revolution*, 10 passim.
23. Alexandra Stevenson, "Leadership Changes Reveal That in China, Men Still Rule," *New York Times*, October 23, 2022.
24. See for example, Arianne M. Gaetano and Tamara Jacka, eds., *On the Move: Women and Rural-to-Urban Migration in Contemporary China* (New York: Columbia University Press,

2004); Gail Hershatter, *The Gender of Memory: Rural Women and China's Collective Past* (Berkeley: University of California Press, 2011).
25 Doris T. Chang, *Women's Movements in Twentieth-Century Taiwan* (Chicago: University of Illinois Press, 2009); Catherine S.P. Farris, "Women's Liberation under 'East Asian Modernity' in China and Taiwan," in *Women in the New Taiwan: Gender Roles and Gender Consciousness in a Changing Society*, ed. Catherine S.P. Farris, Anru Lee, and Murray Rubinstein (Armonk, NY: M.E. Sharpe, 2004), 325–77.
26 Sherna Berger Gluck, "What's So Special about Women? Women's Oral History," in *Women's Oral History: The* Frontiers *Reader*, ed. Susan H. Armitage, with Patricia Hart and Karen Weathermon (Lincoln: University of Nebraska Press, 2002), 3–4.
27 Arthur Waldron, "China's New Remembering of World War II: The Case of Zhang Zizhong." *Modern Asian Studies* 30, 4 (October 1996): 949.
28 On the power of oral history, see Sherna Berger Gluck and Daphne Patai, "Introduction," in *Women's Words: The Feminist Practice of Oral History*, ed. Sherna Berger Gluck and Daphne Patai (New York: Routledge, 1991), 1–5.
29 Dorothy Ko and Wang Zheng, "Introduction: Translating Feminism in China," in *Translating Feminisms in China: A Special Issue of Gender and History*, ed. Dorothy Ko and Wang Zheng (Malden, MA: Blackwell, 2007), 1–12.
30 While working on this project, I came to share some of the views of the feminist historian Sherna B. Gluck. Her interviews with American women in Second World War have made her appreciate "the subtle and incremental nature of change and understand that changes in consciousness are not necessarily or immediately reflected in dramatic alternations in the public world. They may be very quietly played out in the private world of women yet expressed in a fashion that can both affect future generations and eventually be expressed more openly when the social climate is right." See Sherna Berger Gluck, *Rosie the Riveter Revisited: Women, the War, and Social Change* (Boston: Twayne, 1987), x. The Chinese women in my book made incremental changes that affected future generations.

Bibliography

ABBREVIATIONS

CYEJ Zhonghua quanguo funü lianhehui funü yundong lishi yanjiushi, comp. *Cong "Yier jiu" yundong kan nüxing de rensheng jiazhi* [Perception of women's life values through the December Ninth movement]. Beijing: Zhongguo funü chubanshe, 1988.

FHSY Luo Jiurong, You Jianming, Qu Haiyuan, interviewers. *Fenghuo suiyue xia de Zhongguo funü fangwen jilu* [English title by the publisher: *20th Century Wartime Experiences of Chinese Women: An Oral History*]. Taipei: Institute of Modern History, Academia Sinica, 2004.

FYSYJZL Quanguo fulian fuyun lishi yanjiushi, comp. *Fuyunshi yanjiu ziliao* [Research materials for the study of the history of women's movement]. For internal circulation only, 1981–86.

NQNDD Chen Sanjing, Zhu Hongyuan, Wu Meihui, interviewers. *Nü qingnian dadui fangwen jilu* [English title by the publisher: *The Reminiscences of Women's Corps*]. Taipei: Institute of Modern History, Academia Sinica, 1995.

TL Beijing xinsijun yanjiuhui ji huazhong kangRi genjudi yanjiuhui, ed. *Tieliu: tiejun jinguopu* [Iron currents: accounts of heroines of the ironsides]. Beijing: Jiefanjun chubanshe, 2003.

ZFYLZ (1937–45) Zhonghua quanguo funü lianhehui funü yundong lishi yanjiushi, comp. *Zhongguo funü yundong lishi ziliao, 1937–1945* [Historical materials of Chinese women's movement, 1937–1945]. Beijing: Zhongguo funü chubanshe, 1991.

ZYNZS   E-Yu bianqu gemingshi bianjibu; Hubeisheng funü lianhehui, eds. *Zhongyuan nüzhanshi* [Women soldiers of the central plain]. 3 vols. Beijing: Zhongguo funü chubanshe, 1991–94.

Alexievich, Svetlana. *The Unwomanly Face of War: An Oral History of Women in World War II*. Translated by Richard Pevear and Larissa Volokhonsky. New York: Random House, 2017.

Armitage, Susan H., with Patricia Hart and Karen Weathermon, eds. *Women's Oral History: The* Frontiers *Reader*. Lincoln: University of Nebraska Press, 2002.

Anderson, Bonnie S., and Judith P. Zinsser. *A History of Their Own: Women in Europe from Prehistory to the Present*. Rev. ed. Oxford: Oxford University Press, 2000.

Anderson, Kathryn, and Dana C. Jack. "Learning to Listen: Interview Techniques and Analyses." In *Women's Words: The Feminist Practice of Oral History*, edited by Sherna Berger Gluck and Daphne Patai, 11–26. New York: Routledge, 1991.

Bao Jialin, ed. *Zhongguo funüshi lunji xuji* [A collection of articles on Chinese women's history, sequel]. Taipei: Daoxiang chubanshe, 1999.

Barlow, Tani E., ed. *Gender Politics in Modern China: Writing and Feminism*. Durham, NC: Duke University Press, 1993.

–. *The Question of Women in Chinese Feminism*. Durham NC: Duke University Press, 2004.

Barmé, Geremie. "History for the Masses." In *Using the Past to Serve the Present*, edited by Jonathan Unger, 260–86. Armonk, NY: M.E. Sharpe, 1993.

Barrett, David, and Larry N. Shyu, eds. *Chinese Collaboration with Japan, 1932–1945*. Stanford, CA: Stanford University Press, 2001.

Beijingshi jiaoyuju: Beijingshi gaoji zhongxue shiyong keben, *Yuwen 4* [Beijing senior middle school provisional textbook: Chinese 4]. Beijing: Beijing chubanshe, 1962.

Benton, Gregor. *New Fourth Army: Communist Resistance along the Yangtze and the Huai, 1938–1941*. Surrey, UK: Curzon, 1999.

Bosworth, Michal. "'Let Me Tell You ...': Memory and the Practice of Oral History." In *Memory and History: Understanding Memory as Source and Subject*, edited by Joan Tumblety, 19–33. London: Routledge, 2013.

Brook, Timothy. *Collaboration: Japanese Agents and Local Elites in Wartime China*. Cambridge, MA: Harvard University Press, 2005.

–. "Preface: Lisbon, Xuzhou, Auschwitz: Suffering as History." In *Beyond Suffering: Recounting War in Modern China*, edited by James Flath and Norman Smith, xi–xix. Vancouver: UBC Press, 2011.

Brownmiller, Susan. *Against Our Will: Men, Women and Rape*. New York: Simon and Schuster, 1975.

Bullock, Mary Brown, and Bridie Andrews, eds. *Medical Transitions in Twentieth-Century China*. Bloomington: Indiana University Press, 2014.

Cai Chang et al. "Jinian Xiang Jingyu tongzhi xunnan sanshi zhounian" [On the thirtieth anniversary of comrade Xiang Jingyu's death for the revolution]. *Zhongguo funü* (1958): 5, 6, 16–20, 25–27.

Chang, Doris T. *Women's Movements in Twentieth-Century Taiwan*. Chicago: University of Illinois Press, 2009.

Chang, Jui-te. "Bombs Don't Discriminate? Class, Gender, and Ethnicity in the Air-Raid-Shelter Experiences of the Wartime Chongqing Population." In *Beyond Suffering: Recounting War in Modern China*, edited by James Flath and Norman Smith, 59–79. Vancouver: UBC Press, 2011.

Chen Danhuai and Ye Weiwei. *Sange Xinsijun nübing de duocai rensheng: huiyi muqin Zhang Qian, Wang Yugeng, Ling Ben* [Multicoloured lives of three women soldiers of the New Fourth Army: remembering mothers: Zhang Qian, Wang Yugeng, and Ling Ben]. Beijing: Renmin chubanshe, 2011.

Chen Jingbo. "Huimin zhi mu: ji Huimin zhidui Ma Benzhai zhi mu yingyong xunguo" [Mother of the Hui people: an account of the mother of Ma Benzhai of the Hui detachment and her heroic death for the nation]. *Hongqi piaopiao* 10 (January 1959): 159–75.

Chen Meiquan. *Chen Meiquan xiansheng fangwen jilu* [English title given by the publisher: *The Reminiscences of Policewoman Chen Mei-chyuan*]. Taipei: Institute of Modern History, Academia Sinica, 1996.

Chen, Tina Mai. "Propagating the Propaganda Film: The Meaning of Film in Chinese Communist Party Writings, 1949–1965." *Modern Chinese Literature and Culture* 15, 2 (2003): 154–93.

Chen Xiuping. *Chenfu lu: Zhongguo qingyun yu jidujiao nannü qingnianhui* [Records of upheavals: China's youth movement and the YMCA and YWCA]. Shanghai: Tongji daxue chubanshe, 1989.

Chen Xuqing. "Xinling de jiyi: ku'nan yu kangzheng – Shanxi kangzhan koushushi" [Memories of the heart: sufferings and resistance – oral histories of the resistance war in Shanxi]. PhD dissertation, Zhejiang University, 2005.

Chen Yan. *Xingbei yu zhanzheng: Shanghai 1932–1945* [Gender and war: Shanghai 1932–1945]. Beijing: Shehui kexue wenxian chubanshe, 2014.

Chen Yongfa. *Yan'an de yinying* [The Shadow of Yan'an]. Taipei: Institute of Modern History, Academia Sinica, 1990.

Chen, Yung-fa. *Making Revolution: The Communist Movement in Eastern and Central China, 1937–1945*. Berkeley: University of California Press, 1986.

Chi Pang-yuan. *The Great Flowing River: A Memoir of China, from Manchuria to Taiwan*. Edited and translated by John Balcom. New York: Columbia University Press, 2018.

–. *Juliu he* [The great flowing river]. Beijing: Shenghuo dushu xinzhi sanlian shudian, 2011.

–. *Juliu he* [The great flowing river]. Taipei: Tianxia yuanjian chuban gufen youxian gongsi, 2009.

Chi, Robert. "'The March of the Volunteers': From Movie Theme Song to National Anthem." In *Re-envisioning the Chinese Revolution: The Politics and Poetics of Collective Memories in Reform China*, edited by Ching Kwan Lee and Guobin Yang, 217–44. Stanford, CA: Stanford University Press, 2007.

Chien, Ying-Ying. "Feminism and China's New 'Nora': Ibsen, Hu Shi and Lu Xun." *Comparatist* 19 (May 1995): 97–113.

Coble, Parks M. *Facing Japan: Chinese Politics and Japanese Imperialism*. Cambridge, MA: Harvard University Press, 1991.

Cong, Xiaoping. *Marriage, Law and Gender in Revolutionary China, 1940–1960*. Cambridge: Cambridge University Press, 2016.

Cosslett, Tess, Celia Lury, and Penny Summerfield, eds. *Feminism and Autobiography: Texts, Theories, Methods*. New York: Routledge, 2000.

Croll, Elisabeth. *Feminism and Socialism in China*. London: Routledge and Kegan Paul, 1978.

Crook, Isabel Brown, and Christina K. Gilmartin with Yu Xiji. *Prosperity's Predicament: Identity, Reform, and Resistance in Rural Wartime China*, compiled and edited by Gail Hershatter and Emily Honig. Lanham, MD: Rowman and Littlefield, 2013.

Cui Gui and Chen Huaikai, dirs., *Qingchun zhi ge* [The song of youth]. 1959; Beijing: Beijing dianying zhipianchang.

Cui Yongyuan, planner; Zeng Hairuo, dir. *Wo de kangzhan* [My war of resistance]. 2011; Beijing: Beijing wuxing chuanqi wenhua chuanmei youxian gongsi. DVD.

D'Amico, Francine. "Feminist Perspectives on Women Warriors." In *The Women and War Reader*, edited by Lois Ann Lorentzen and Jennifer E. Turpin, 119–25. New York: New York University Press, 1998.

Dai Jinhua. *Xieta liaowang: Zhongguo dianying wenhua, 1978–1998* [Perspectives from the slanted tower: Chinese cinema culture, 1978–1998]. Taipei: Yuanliu chuban gongsi, 1999.

Deng Yingchao. *Deng Yingchao wenji* [Collection of Deng Yinchao's works]. Beijing: Renmin chubanshe, 1994.

–. "Yi Mao Zedong sixiang wei zhidao, yanjiu funü yundong lishi ziliao" [Conducting research on historical documents of women's movement under the guidance of Mao Zedong thought]. In *Deng Yingchao wenji* [Collection of Deng Yinchao's works], by Deng Yingchao, 145–49. Beijing: Renmin chubanshe, 1994.

–. "Zai quanguo funü yundong lishi ziliao bianzuan weiyuanhui di yici huiyi shang de jianghua" [The speech at the first meeting of the committee for compilation of historical materials of the Chinese women's movement]. FYSYJZL 2: 5–6 (December 10, 1981).

–. "Zhenfen geming jingshen, zuohao fuyunshi gongzuo" [Inspire revolutionary enthusiasm and conduct well the work on the history of women's movement]. FYSYJZL 3: 14–17 (March 10, 1982).

Denton, Kirk. *Exhibiting the Past: Historical Memory and the Politics of Museums in Postsocialist China*. Honolulu: University of Hawaii Press, 2014.

Ding Hei, dir. *Xinsijun nübing* [Women soldiers of the New Fourth Army]. First aired 2011; Shanghai: Shanghai wenguang xinwen chuanmei jituan, Shanghai dianshi chuanmei gongsi.

Ding Ling. *Ding Ling wenji* [Works of Ding Ling]. Changsha: Hunan renmin chubanshe, 1983–84.

–. "Jieda sange wenti – zai Beijing yuyan xueyuan waiguo liuxuesheng zuotanhui shang de jianghua" [Answer to three questions – a talk to foreign students as the Beijing Language Institute]. In *Ding Ling wenji* [Works of Ding Ling], by Ding Ling, 4: 171–84. Changsha: Hunan renmin chubanshe, 1984.

Ding Mingjing. "The Female and the Country during the Anti-Japanese War – Analyses of the *Women's Lives* Magazine." MA thesis (in Chinese with English title), Huadong shifan daxue, Shanghai, 2006.

Ding Shanxi, dir. *Babai zhuangshi* [Eight hundred heroes]. 1975; Taipei: Zhongying gongsi.

Ding Weiping. *Zhongguo funü kangzhanshi yanjiu, 1937–1945* [A study of Chinese women in the War of Resistance against Japan, 1937–1945]. Changchun: Jilin renmin chubanshe, 1999.

Ding Xing, ed. *Xinsijun cidian* [Dictionary of the New Fourth Army]. Shanghai: Shanghai cishu chubanshe, 1997.

Dombrowski, Nicole Ann. "Soldiers, Saints, or Sacrificial Lamb? Women's Relationship to Combat and the Fortification of the Home Front in the Twentieth Century." In *Women and War in the Twentieth Century: Enlisted with or without Consent*, edited by Nicole Ann Dombrowski, 2–37. New York: Garland, 1999.

–, ed. *Women and War in the Twentieth Century: Enlisted with or without Consent*. New York: Garland, 1999.

Dong Bian. "Zai fuyunshi gongzuo zuotanhui shang de xiaojie" [A brief summary at the seminar on the work for the history of women's movement]. FYSYJZL 2: 12–15 (December 10, 1981).

Du Fangqin. *Faxian funü de lishi – Zhongguo funüshi lunji* [The discovery of women's history – collection of essays on Chinese women's history]. Tianjin: Tianjin shehui kexueyuan chubanshe, 1996.

Duara, Prasenjit. "Of Authenticity and Woman: Personal Narratives of Middle-Class Women in Modern China." In *Becoming Chinese: Passages to Modernity and Beyond*, edited by Wen-hsin Yeh, 342–64. Berkeley: University of California Press, 2000.

—. *Sovereignty and Authenticity: Manchukuo and the East Asian Modern*. Lanham, MD: Rowman and Littlefield, 2003.

Ebrey, Patricia B. *Confucianism and Family Rituals in Imperial China*. Princeton, NJ: Princeton University Press, 1991.

—. *The Inner Quarters: Marriage and the Lives of Chinese Women in the Sung Period*. Berkeley: University of California Press, 1993.

Economy, Elizabeth C. *The Third Revolution: Xi Jinping and the New Chinese State*. Oxford: Oxford University Press, 2018.

Edwards, Louise. *Gender, Politics, and Democracy: Women's Suffrage in China*. Stanford, CA: Stanford University Press, 2008.

—. *Women Warriors and Wartime Spies of China*. New York: Cambridge University Press, 2016.

Egami Sachiko. "Rijun funü baoxing he zhanshi Zhongguo funü zazhi" [Japanese army's sexual violence and Chinese women magazines during the war]. In *Taotian zuinie: erzhan shiqi de Rijun "weianfu" yanjiu* [Monstrous atrocities: the Japanese military comfort women system during the Second World War], edited by Su Zhilinag, Rong Weimu, and Chen Lifei, 56–70. Shanghai: Xuelin chubanshe, 2000.

Engel, Barbara Alpern. "The Womanly Face of War: Soviet Women Remember World War II." In *Women and War in the Twentieth Century: Enlist with or without Consent*, edited by Nicole Ann Dombrowski, 138–59. New York: Garland, 1999.

Esherick, Joseph W., and Matthew T. Combs, eds. *1943: China at the Crossroads*. Ithaca, NY: East Asian Program, Cornell University, 2015.

Evans, Harriet. *Women and Sexuality in China: Female Sexuality and Gender since 1949*. New York: Continuum, 1997.

Farris, Catherine S.P. "Women's Liberation Under 'East Asian Modernity' in China and Taiwan." In *Women in the New Taiwan: Gender Roles and Gender Consciousness in a Changing Society*, edited by Catherine S.P. Farris, Anru Lee, and Murray Rubinstein, 325–76. Armonk, NY: M.E. Sharpe, 2004.

Farris, Catherine S.P., Anru Lee, and Murray Rubinstein, eds. *Women in the New Taiwan: Gender Roles and Gender Consciousness in a Changing Society*. Armonk, NY: M.E. Sharpe, 2004.

Feng, Jin. *The New Woman in Early Twentieth-Century Chinese Fiction*. West Lafayette, IN: Purdue University Press, 2004.

Feng Yifu and Li Jun, dirs., *Huimin zhidui* [The detachment of the Hui people]. 1959; Beijing: Bayi dianying zhipianchang.

Flath, James, and Norman Smith, eds. *Beyond Suffering: Recounting War in Modern China*. Vancouver: UBC Press, 2011.

Fu, Poshek. *Passivity, Resistance, and Collaboration: Intellectual Choices in Occupied Shanghai, 1937–1945*. Stanford, CA: Stanford University Press, 1993.

Gaetano, Arianne M., and Tamara Jacka, eds. *On the Move: Women and Rural-to-Urban Migration in Contemporary China*. New York: Columbia University Press, 2004.

Gao Hua. *How the Red Sun Rose: The Origins and Development of the Yan'an Rectification Movement, 1930–1945*. Translated by Stacy Mosher and Guo Jian. Hong Kong: Chinese University Press, 2018.

Gildea, Robert. *Marianne in Chains: Everyday Life in the French Heartland under the German Occupation*. New York: Metropolitan Books/Henry Holt, 2002.

Gilmartin, Christina K. *Engendering the Chinese Revolution: Radical Women, Communist Politics, and Mass Movements in the 1920s*. Berkeley: University of California Press, 1995.

Glosser, Susan L. *Chinese Visions of Family and State, 1915–1953*. Berkeley: University of California Press, 2003.

–. "'Women's Culture of Resistance': An Ordinary Response to Extraordinary Circumstances." In *In the Shadow of the Rising Sun: Shanghai under Japanese Occupation*, edited by Christian Henriot and Wen-Hsin Yeh, 302–24. Cambridge: Cambridge University Press, 2004.

Gluck, Carol. "Operations of Memory: 'Comfort Women' and the World." In *Ruptured Histories: War, Memory, and the Post-Cold War in Asia*, edited by Sheila Miyoshi Jager and Rana Mitter, 47–76. Cambridge, MA: Harvard University Press, 2007.

Gluck, Sherna Berger. *Rosie the Riveter Revisited: Women, the War, and Social Change*. Boston: Twayne, 1987.

–. "What's So Special about Women? Women's Oral History." In *Women's Oral History: The Frontiers Reader*, edited by Susan H. Armitage with Patricia Hart and Karen Weathermon, 3–20. Lincoln: University of Nebraska Press, 2002.

Gluck, Sherna Berger, and Daphne Patai. "Introduction." In *Women's Words: The Feminist Practice of Oral History*, edited by Sherna Berger Gluck and Daphne Patai, 1–5. New York: Routledge, 1991.

–, eds. *Women's Words: The Feminist Practice of Oral History*. New York: Routledge, 1991.

Goldman, Merle, and Elizabeth J. Perry, eds. *Changing Meanings of Citizenship in Modern China*. Cambridge, MA: Harvard University Press, 2002.

–. "Introduction: Political Citizenship in Modern China." In *Changing Meanings of Citizenship in Modern China*, edited by Merle Goldman and Elizabeth J. Perry, 1–22. Cambridge, MA: Harvard University Press, 2002.

Goodman, David S.G. "Revolutionary Women and Women in the Revolution: The Chinese Communist Party and Women in the War of Resistance to Japan, 1937–1945." *China Quarterly* 164 (December 2000): 915–42.

–. *Social and Political Change in Revolutionary China: The Taihang Base Area in the War of Resistance to Japan, 1937–1945*. Lanham, MD: Rowman and Littlefield, 2000.

Grypma, Sonya, and Cheng Zhen. "The Development of Modern Nursing in China." In *Medical Transitions in Twentieth-Century China*, edited by Mary Brown Bullock and Bridie Andrews, 297–316. Bloomington: Indiana University Press, 2014.

Guan Hu, dir. *Babai* [Eight hundred]. 2020; Shenzhen: Huayi xiongdi dianying gongsi.

Guo Ke, dir. *Ershier* [Twenty-two]. 2017; Chengdu: Sichuan guangying shenchu wenhua chuanbo youxian gongsi.

–. *Sanshier* [Thirty-two]. 2014; Chengdu: Sichuan guangying shenchu wenhua chuanbo youxian gongsi.

Guo Zhenyi. *Zhongguo funü wenti* [Issues of Chinese women]. Shanghai: Commercial Press, 1937.

Hai Mo. "Si saozi" [Sister four]. *Hongqi piaopiao* 2 (July 1957): 207–25.
Hamrin, Carol Lee, and Stacey Bieler, eds. *Salt and Light: Lives of Faith That Shaped Modern China*. Eugene, OR: Pickwick, 2009.
Han Zi, chief ed. *Nübing liezhuan* [Biographies of women soldiers]. 3 vols. Shanghai: Shanghai wenyi chubanshe, 1985–87.
He, Yinan. "Remembering and Forgetting the War: Elite Mythmaking, Mass Reaction, and Sino-Japanese Relations, 1950–2006." *History and Memory* 19, 2 (September 2007): 43–74.
Henriot, Christian, and Wen-Hsin Yeh, eds. *In the Shadow of the Rising Sun: Shanghai under Japanese Occupation*. Cambridge: Cambridge University Press, 2004.
Henry, Nicola. *War and Rape: Law, Memory, and Justice*. New York: Routledge, 2011.
Henshaw, Jonathan, Craig A. Smith, and Norman Smith, eds. *Translating the Occupation: The Japanese Invasion of China, 1931–45*. Vancouver: UBC Press, 2021.
Hershatter, Gail. *The Gender of Memory: Rural Women and China's Collective Past*. Berkeley: University of California Press, 2011.
Hicks, George. *The Comfort Women: Japan's Brutal Regime of Enforced Prostitution in the Second World War*. New York: W.W. Norton, 1995.
Higonnet, Margaret Randolph, Jane Jenson, Sonya Michel, and Margaret Collins Weitz, eds. *Behind the Lines: Gender and the Two World Wars*. New Haven, CT: Yale University Press, 1987.
Hoffmann, Stanley. "Introduction." In *The Sorrow and the Pity: A Film*, by Marcel Ophuls, 7–26. Filmscript translated by Mireille Johnston. New York: Outerbridge and Lazard, 1972.
Hong Yizhen. *Zhongguo Guomindang funü gongzuo zhi yanjiu, 1924–1949* [English title given by the publisher: *The Kuomintang and Women's Affairs, 1924–1949*]. Taipei: Guoshiguan, 2010.
Honig, Emily. "Burning Incense, Pledging Sisterhood: Community of Women Workers in the Shanghai Cotton Mills, 1919–1949." In *Feminism and Community*, edited by Penny A. Weiss and Marilyn Friedman, 59–75. Philadelphia: Temple University Press, 1995.
–. *Sisters and Strangers: Women in the Shanghai Cotton Mills, 1919–1949*. Stanford, CA: Stanford University Press, 1986.
Howard, Joshua H. "The Politicization of Women Workers at War: Labour in Chongqing's Cotton Mills during the Anti-Japanese War." *Modern Asian Studies* 47, 6 (November 2013): 1888–1940.
Howard, Keith, ed. *True Stories of the Korean Comfort Women*. London: Cassell, 1995.
Hsiung, James C., and Steven I. Levine. *China's Bitter Victory: The War with Japan, 1937–1945*. Armonk, NY: M.E. Sharpe, 1992.
Hua, Chang-Ming. "Peasants, Women and Revolution – CCP Marriage Reform in the Shaan-Gan-Ning Border Area." *Republican China* 10 (November 1984): 1–24.
Huang, Nicole. "Fashioning Public Intellectuals: Women's Print Culture in Occupied Shanghai (1941–1945)." In *In the Shadow of the Rising Sun: Shanghai under Japanese Occupation*, edited by Christian Henriot and Wen-Hsin Yeh, 325–45. Cambridge: Cambridge University Press, 2004.
–. *Women, War, Domesticity: Shanghai Literature and Popular Culture of the 1940s*. Leiden: Brill, 2005.
Hung, Chang-tai. *War and Popular Culture: Resistance in Modern China, 1937–1945*. Berkeley: University of California Press, 1994.

Ip, Hung-Yok. "Fashioning Appearances: Feminine Beauty in Chinese Communist Revolutionary Culture." *Modern China* 29, 3 (July 2003): 329–61.
Ishida Yoneko and Uchida Tomoyuki. *Fasheng zai huangtu cunzhuang li de Rijun xingbaoli –daniangmen de zhanzheng shangwei jiushu* [English title given by the publisher: *Sexual Violence in YuXian: Their War Is Not Over*]. Translated by Zhao Jingui. Beijing: Shehui kexue wenxian chubanshe, 2008.
Israel, John. *Lianda: A Chinese University in War and Revolution*. Stanford, CA: Stanford University Press, 1998.
Israel, John, and Donald W. Klein. *Rebels and Bureaucrats: China's December 9ers*. Berkeley: University of California Press, 1976.
–. *Student Nationalism in China, 1927–1937*. Stanford, CA: Stanford University Press/ Hoover Institution on War, Revolution, and Peace, 1966.
Jager, Sheila Miyoshi, and Rana Mitter, eds. *Ruptured Histories: War, Memory, and the Post–Cold War in Asia*. Cambridge, MA: Harvard University Press, 2007.
Jiang Hao. *Zhaoshi: Zhongguo weianfu* [Expose: Chinese comfort women]. Beijing: Zuojia chubanshe, 1993.
Jiang Yunzhong. *Jiang Yunzhong nüshi fangwen jilu* [English title given by the publisher: *The Reminiscences of Mme. Jiang Yun-jung*]. Taipei: Institute of Modern History, Academia Sinica, 2005.
Jiangxisheng fulian, ed. *Nüying zishu* [Self-narratives of heroines]. Nanchang: Jiangxi renmin chubanshe, 1988.
Jin Feng. *Deng Yingchao zhuan* [A biography of Deng Yingchao]. Beijing: Renmin chubanshe, 1993.
Jin Yihong. *Nüxing xushi yu jiyi* [Women's narrative and memory]. Beijing: Jiuzhou chubanshe, 2007.
Jin-Cha-Ji bianqu beiyuequ funü kangRi douzheng shiliao bianjizu, ed. *Fenghuo jinguo* [Women in the battle fire]. Beijing: Zhongguo funü chubanshe, 1990.
Jinian Yan'an nüda wushi zhounian chouweihui, ed. *Yan'an nüda: 1939–1989* [The Yan'an Women's University: 1939–1989]. Beijing: n.p., 1989.
Johnson, Kay Ann. *Women, the Family, and Peasant Revolution in China*. Chicago: University of Chicago Press, 1983.
Judge, Joan. *The Precious Raft of History: The Past, the West, and the Woman Question in China*. Stanford, CA: Stanford University Press, 2008.
–. "Talent, Virtue, and the Nation: Chinese Nationalisms and Female Subjectivities in the Early Twentieth Century." *American Historical Review* 106, 3 (June 2001): 765–803.
Judge, Joan, and Hu Ying, eds. *Beyond Exemplar Tales: Women's Biography in Chinese History*. Berkeley: University of California Press, 2011.
Junhui. "Pingbo He Ziheng jun zhi nüzi jiaoyu lun" [Refuting Mr. He Ziheng's ideas on women's education], *Funü shenghuo* 1, 5 (November 1935). Included in CYEJ, 226–31.
Kang Keqing. *Kang Keqing huiyilu* [Memoirs by Kang Keqing]. Beijing: Jiefangjun chubanshe, 1993.
Ke Huiling. "Kangzhan chuqi de zhishi nüqingnian xiaxiang – yi Jiangxi weili de yanjiu" [Women intellectual youth in the countryside during the early Sino-Japanese war: the case of Jiangxi]. *Jindai Zhongguo funüshi yanjiu* 19 (December 2011): 33–73.
–. "Yishi yu xushi: zuopai funü huiyilu zhong de geming zhanyan yu shenghuo liudong (1920s–1950s)" [Legends and narratives: the revolutionary displaying and life fluctuation in the left women's memoirs (1920s–1950s)]. *Jindai Zhongguo funü yanjiu* 15 (December 2007): 141–62.

Kelleher, Theresa. "Confucianism." In *Women in World Religions*, edited by Arvind Sharma, 135–60. Albany: State University of New York Press, 1987.

Kimura, Maki. *Unfolding the "Comfort Women" Debates: Modernity, Violence, Women's Voices*. New York: Palgrave Macmillan, 2016.

Ko, Dorothy. *Teachers of the Inner Chambers: Women and Culture in Seventeenth-Century China*. Stanford, CA: Stanford University Press, 1994.

Ko, Dorothy, and Wang Zheng. "Introduction: Translating Feminism in China." In *Translating Feminisms in China: A Special Issue of Gender and History*, edited by Dorothy Ko and Wang Zheng, 1–12. Malden, MA: Blackwell, 2007.

–, eds. *Translating Feminisms in China: A Special Issue of Gender and History*. Malden, MA: Blackwell, 2007.

Larson, Wendy. "Never This Wild: Sexing the Cultural Revolution." *Modern China* 25, 4 (1999): 423–50.

Lary, Diana. *China's Civil War: A Social History, 1945–1949*, Cambridge: Cambridge University Press, 2015.

–. *The Chinese People at War: Human Suffering and Social Transformation, 1937–1945*. Cambridge: Cambridge University Press, 2010.

–. "Introduction: The Context of the War." In *China at War: Regions of China, 1937–1945*, edited by Stephen R. MacKinnon, Diana Lary, and Ezra F. Vogel, 1–14. Stanford, CA: Stanford University Press, 2007.

–. "One Province's Experience of War: Guangxi, 1937–1945." In *China at War: Regions of China, 1937–1945*, edited by Stephen R. MacKinnon, Diana Lary, and Ezra F. Vogel, 314–34. Stanford, CA: Stanford University Press, 2007.

–. "War and Remembering: Memories of China at War." In *Beyond Suffering: Recounting War in Modern China*, edited by James Flath and Norman Smith, 262–87. Vancouver: UBC Press, 2011.

Lary, Diana, and Stephen MacKinnon, eds. *Scars of War: The Impact of Warfare on Modern China*. Vancouver: UBC Press, 2001.

–. "Introduction." In *Scars of War: The Impact of Warfare on Modern China*, edited by Diana Lary and Stephen MacKinnon, 3–15. Vancouver: UBC Press, 2001.

Lee, Ching Kwan, and Guobin Yang, eds. *Re-envisioning the Chinese Revolution: The Politics and Poetics of Collective Memories in Reform China*. Stanford, CA: Stanford University Press, 2007.

Lee, Chong-Sik, *Revolutionary Struggle in Manchuria: Chinese Communism and Soviet Interest, 1922–1945*. Berkeley: University of California Press, 1983.

Lee, En-Han. "The Nanking Massacre Reassessed: A Study of the Sino-Japanese Controversy over the Factual Number of Massacred Victims." In *Nanking 1937: Memory and Healing*, edited by Feifei Li, Robert Sabella and David Liu, 47–74. Armonk, NY: M.E. Sharpe, 2002.

Lee, Lily Xiao Hong, and A.D. Stefanowska, eds. *Biographical Dictionary of Chinese Women: Antiquity through Sui, 1600 B.C.E.–618 C.E.* Armonk, NY: M.E, Sharpe, 2007.

–, eds. *Biographical Dictionary of Chinese Women: The Twentieth Century, 1912–2000*. Armonk, NY: M.E. Sharpe, 2003.

Lee, Lily Xiao Hong, and Sue Wiles, eds. *Biographical Dictionary of Chinese Women: Tang through Ming, 618–1644*. Armonk, NY: M.E. Sharpe, 2014.

Leutner, Mechthild, and Nicola Spakowski, eds. *Women in China: The Republican Period in Historical Perspective*. Münster, Germany: Lit Verlag, 2005.

Li bao, October 29, 1937: "Sihang gujun" [Lone army in Sihang]. In *"Ba yisan" kangzhan shiliao xuanbian* [Selected historical materials on the "August 13" resistance], compiled by Shanghai shehui kexueyuan lishi yanjiusuo, 70–71. Shanghai: Renmin chubanshe, 1986.

Li Bingxin, ed. *QinHua Rijun baoxing shilu* [Records of violence of Japanese invading troops in China]. Shijiazhuang: Hebei renmin chubanshe, 1995.

Li, Chenyang. "Introduction: Can Confucianism Come to Terms with Feminism?" In *The Sage and the Second Sex: Confucianism, Ethics, and Gender,* edited by Chenyang Li, 1–21. Chicago and La Salle, IL: Open Court, 2000.

–, ed. *The Sage and the Second Sex: Confucianism, Ethics, and Gender.* Chicago and La Salle, IL: Open Court, 2000.

Li, Danke. *Echoes of Chongqing: Women in Wartime China.* Urbana: University of Illinois Press, 2010.

Li, Feifei, Robert Sabella, and David Liu, eds. *Nanking 1937: Memory and Healing.* Armonk, NY: M.E. Sharpe, 2002.

Li Jianzhen. *Li Jianzhen huiyilu* [Memoirs by Li Jianzhen]. Beijing: Zhonggong dangshi chubanshe, 1991.

Li, Virginia C. *From One Root Many Flowers: A Century of Family Life in China and America.* Amherst, NY: Prometheus Books, 2003.

Li Xiaofang. *Shiji nahan: 67 wei xingcun weianfu shilu* [Cries of the century: testimonies of sixty-seven surviving comfort women]. Beijing: Zhonggong dangshi chubanshe, 2008.

Li Xiaojiang, chief ed. *Rang nüren ziji shuohua: qinli zhanzheng* [Let women speak for themselves: experiencing the wars]. Beijing: Shenhuo, dushu, xinzhi sanlian shudian, 2003.

Li Youning. "Zhongguo xinnüjie zazhi de chuangkan ji neihan" [The creation and perceptions of the journal of Chinese New Women's Circle]. In *Zhongguo funüshi lunwenji* [A collection of essays on Chinese women's history], edited by Li Youning and Zhang Yüfa, 1: 179–242. Taipei: Commercial Press, 1981.

Li Youning and Zhang Yüfa, eds., *Zhongguo funüshi lunwenji* [A collection of essays on Chinese women's history]. Taipei: Commercial Press, 1981.

Liang Huijin. "Kangzhan shiqi de funü zuzhi" [Women's organizations in the War of Resistance against Japan]. In *Zhongguo funüshi lunji xuji* [A collection of articles on Chinese women's history, sequel], edited by Bao Jialin, 359–90. Taipei: Daoxiang chubanshe, 1999.

Liang Yi. "Yan'an nüzi daxue pingjie" [On the Yan'an Women's University]. *KangRi Zhanzheng yanjiu* 2 (1992): 91–104.

Liaowang banjibu. *Hongjun nüyingxiong zhuan* [Biographies of Red Army heroines]. Beijing: Xinhua chubanshe, 1986.

Ling Zifeng and Zhai Qiang, dirs. *Zhonghua nüer* [Daughters of China]. 1949; Changchun, Jilin: Dongbei dianying zhipianchang.

Link, Perry. "Foreword." In *Nanking 1937: Memory and Healing,* edited by Feifei Li, Robert Sabella, and David Liu, ix–xx. Armonk, NY: M.E. Sharpe, 2002.

Littell-Lamb, Elizabeth A. "Ding Shujing: The YWCA Pathway for China's 'New Women.'" In *Salt and Light: Lives of Faith That Shaped Modern China,* edited by Carol Lee Hamrin and Stacey Bieler, 79–97. Eugene, OR: Pickwick, 2009.

Liu, Jennifer. "Defiant Retreat: The Relocation of Middle Schools to China's Interior, 1937–1945." *Frontiers of History in China* 8, 4 (2013): 558–84.

Liu Jucai. *Zhongguo jindai funü yundongshi* [Modern history of Chinese women's movement]. Beijing: Zhongguo funü chubanshe, 1989.
Liu, Kang. "Reinventing the 'Red Classics' in the Age of Globalization." *Neohelicon* 37 (2010): 329–47.
Liu Ying. *Dongbei Kanglian nübing* [Women soldiers of Northeast Anti-Japanese Allied Forces]. Ha'erbin: Heilongjiang renmin chubanshe, 2015.
Lo Jiu-jung. "Survival as Justification for Collaboration 1937–1945." In *Chinese Collaboration with Japan, 1932–1945: The Limits of Accommodation*, edited by David P. Barrett and Lawrence N. Shyu, 116–32. Stanford, CA: Stanford University Press, 2001.
Lorentzen, Lois Ann, and Jennifer E. Turpin, eds. *The Women and War Reader*. New York: New York University Press, 1998.
Lu Ban. *Xin funü duben* [Reader for the new women]. Hong Kong: Xin minzhu chubanshe, 1949.
Lü Fangshang. "Kangzhan shiqi Zhongguo de fuyun gongzuo" [The women's work during the War of Resistance]. In *Zhongguo funüshi lunwenji*, edited by Li Youning and Zhang Yüfa, 1: 378–412. Taipei: Commercial Press, 1981.
–. "Ling yizhong 'wei zuzhi': kangzhan shiqi hunyin yu jiating wenti chutan" [Another "illegitimate organization": an initial study of marriage and family issues in the resistance war]. *Jindai Zhongguo funüshi yanjiu* 3 (August 1995): 97–121.
Luo Guangda, chief ed. *Jinguo yinghao – kangRi zhanzheng zhong de Jin-Cha-Ji funü ertong sheyingzhan* [Heroic women: photograph exhibition of women and children of Jin-Cha-Ji in the Anti-Japanese War]. Shenyang, Liaoning: Liaoning meishu chubanshe, 1989.
Luo Jiurong, "Jindai Zhonguo nüxing zizhuan shuxie zhong de aiqing, hunyin yu zhengzhi" [English title given by the author: Love, marriage and politics in modern Chinese women's autobiographical writings]. *Jindai Zhongguo funüshi yanjiu* 15 (December 2007): 77–140.
Luo Jiurong et al. *Cong Dongbei dao Taiwan: Wanguo daodehui xiangguan renwu fangwen jilu* [From the Northeast to Taiwan: interviews of people related with the Wanguo daodehui]. Taipei: Institute of Modern History, Academia Sinica, 2006.
Luo Qiong. "Xuexi Deng Yingchao dajie sanci jianghua de chubu tihui" [My preliminary thought on studying elder sister Deng Yingcho's three speeches]. FYSYJZL 2: 7–11 (December 10, 1981).
–. "Zai disanci fuyun lishi bianzuan weiyuanhui, di erci quanguo fuyunshi gongzuo huiyi shang de jianghua" [Speech at the third meeting of the compilation committee for the history of women's movement and the second national meeting on the history of women's movement]. FYSYJZL 3: 4–10 (1984).
Luo Xing. *Xinlu siyu* [Journey of heart; threads of words]. Self-published, 2016.
Luo Ya. "Wei chujia de mama" [An unwed mother]. *Zhongguo funü* (1958): 8, 16–19.
Ma, Zhao. *Runaway Wives, Urban Crimes, and Survival Tactics in Wartime Beijing, 1937–1949*. Cambridge, MA: Harvard University Asia Center, 2015.
MacKinnon, Stephen R. "Refugee Flight at the Outset of the Anti-Japanese War." In *Scars of War: The Impact of Warfare on Modern China*, edited by Diana Lary and Stephen MacKinnon, 118–34. Vancouver: UBC Press, 2001.
–. *Wuhan, 1938: War, Refugees, and the Making of Modern China*. Berkeley: University of California Press, 2008.
MacKinnon, Stephen R., Diana Lary, and Ezra F. Vogel, eds. *China at War: Regions of China, 1937–1945*. Stanford, CA: Stanford University Press, 2007.

McDougall, Bonnie S., ed. *Popular Chinese Literature and Performing Arts in the People's Republic of China 1949–1979*. Berkeley: University of California Press, 1984.
Meng, Yue. "Female Images and National Myth." In *Gender Politics in Modern China: Writing and Feminism,* edited by Tani E. Barlow, 118–36. Durham, NC: Duke University Press, 1993.
Mitter, Rana. *China's Good War: How World War II Is Shaping a New Nationalism*. Cambridge, MA: Belknap Press of Harvard University Press, 2020.
–. "Classifying Citizens in Nationalist China during World War II, 1937–1941." *Modern Asian Studies* 45, 2 (2011): 243–75.
–. "Old Ghosts, New Memories: China's Changing War History in the Era of Post-Mao Politics." *Journal of Contemporary History* 38, 1 (January 2003): 117–31.
Mitter, Rana, and Aaron William Moore. "China in World War II, 1937–1945: Experience, Memory, and Legacy." *Modern Asian Studies* 45, 2 (March 2011): 225–40.
Mo Yan, *Hong gaoliang jiazu* [The red sorghum family]. Beijing: Jiefangjun wenyi chubanshe, 1987.
Neugebauer, Monica E. "Domestic Activism and Nationalist Struggle." In *The Women and War Reader,* edited by Lois Ann Lorentzen and Jennifer E. Turpin, 177–83. New York: New York University Press, 1998.
Niu Shengni. "Ling yizhong funü yundong – yi Zhonghua jidujiao nüqingnian hui de nonggong shiye weili (1904–1933)" [An alternative women's movement: a case study of the Chinese YWCA's peasant-worker movement (1904–1933)]. In *Xingbie yu lishi: jindai Zhongguo funü yu jidujiao* [Gender and history: modern Chinese women and Christianity], edited by Tao Feiya, 234–82. Shanghai: Renmin chubanshe, 2006.
Oh, Bonnie B.C. "The Japanese Imperial System and the Korean 'Comfort Women' of World War II." In *Legacies of the Comfort Women of World War II,* edited by Margaret Stetz and Bonnie B.C. Oh, 3–25. Armonk, NY: M.E. Sharpe, 2001.
Pan Xun et al. *KangRi zhanzheng shiqi Chongqing da hongzha yanjiu* [English title given by the publisher: *Research on Japan's Bombing Raid to Chongqing during the Anti-Japanese War*]. Beijing: Commercial Press, 2013.
Personal Narratives Group. "Origins." In *Interpreting Women's Lives: Feminist Theory and Personal Narratives,* edited by Personal Narratives Group, Joy Webster Barbre, et al., 3–15. Bloomington: Indiana University Press, 1989.
Personal Narratives Group, Joy Webster Barbre, et al., eds. *Interpreting Women's Lives: Feminist Theory and Personal Narratives*. Bloomington: Indiana University Press, 1989.
Pickowicz, Paul G. "Victory as Defeat: Postwar Visualizations of China's War of Resistance." In *Becoming Chinese: Passages to Modernity and Beyond,* edited by Wen-hsin Yeh, 365–98. Berkeley: University of California Press, 2000.
Price, Jane L. "Women and Leadership in the Chinese Communist Movement, 1921–1945." *Bulletin of Concerned Asian Scholars* 7, 1 (January-March 1975): 19–24.
Qi Hongshen, ed. *Heian xia de xinghuo: wei Manzhouguo wenxue qingnian ji Riben dangshiren koushu* [Sparks in the darkness: oral narratives by literary youth and Japanese litigants under the pseudo-Manchu regime]. Zhengzhou, Henan: Daxiang chubanshe, 2011.
–, ed. *Liuwang: kangzhan shiqi dongbei liuwang xuesheng koushu* [Exiles: oral narratives by refugee students of northeast during the War of Resistance]. Zhengzhou, Henan: Daxiang chubanshe, 2008.
–, ed. *Mosha buliao de zuizheng: Riben qinHua jiaoyu koushushi* [Non-erasable evidence of crime: oral history of education under Japanese aggression of China]. Beijing: Renmin jiaoyu chubanshe, 2005.

—. *Riben duiHua jiaoyu qinlue: dui Riben qinHua jiaoyu de yanjiu yu pipan* [Japan's educational invasion of China: study and criticism of Japan's educational invasion of China]. Beijing: Kunlun chubanshe, 2005.
Qian, Fengqi, and Guo-Qiang Liu. "Remembrance of the Nanjing Massacre in the Globalised Era: The Memory of Victimisation, Emotions and the Rise of China." *China Report* 55, 2 (2019): 81–101.
Qiu, Peipei, with Su Zhiliang and Chen Lifei. *Chinese Comfort Women: Testimonies from Imperials Japan's Sex Slaves*. Vancouver: UBC Press, 2013.
—. *Riben diguo de xing nuli: Zhongguo "weianfu" zhengyan* [Sexual slaves under the Japanese imperialism: testimonies of the Chinese "comfort women"]. Hong Kong: Hong Kong University Press, 2017.
Ramseyer, J. Mark. "Contracting for Sex in the Pacific War." *International Review of Law and Economics* 65 (March 2021). https://www.sciencedirect.com/science/article/pii/S0144818820301848.
Reilly, James. "Remember History, Not Hatred: Collective Remembrance of China's War of Resistance to Japan." *Modern Asian Studies* 45, 2 (2011): 463–90.
Roberts, Rosemary, and Li Li, eds. *The Making and Remaking of China's "Red Classics": Politics, Aesthetics, and Mass Culture*. Hong Kong: Hong Kong University Press, 2017.
Rong Guanxiu bianjizu. *Rong Guanxiu*. Beijing: Xinhua chubanshe, 1990.
Rong Weimu et al. "Bitan kangRi zhanzheng yu lunxianque yanjiu" [Written discussion of the studies of the anti-Japanese war and the occupied areas]. *KangRi zhanzheng yanjiu* 1 (2010): 126–49.
Ropp, Paul. "Passionate Women: Female Suicide in Late Imperial China – Introduction." *Nan Nü* 3, 1 (2001): 3–21.
Scheper-Hughes, Nancy. "Maternal Thinking and the Politics of War." In *The Women and War Reader*, edited by Lois Ann Lorentzen and Jennifer E. Turpin, 227–33. New York: New York University Press, 1998.
Schneider, Helen M. *Keeping the Nation's House: Domestic Management and the Making of Modern China*. Vancouver: UBC Press, 2011.
Schoppa, R. Keith. "Book Review: Christian Henriot and Wen-hsin Yeh, editors. In the Shadow of the Rising Sun: Shanghai under the Japanese Occupation." *China Review International* 11, 2 (Fall 2004): 378–81.
—. *In a Sea of Bitterness: Refugees during the Sino-Japanese War*. Cambridge, MA: Harvard University Press, 2011.
Scott, James C. *Weapons of the Weak: Everyday Forms of Peasant Resistance*. New Haven, CT: Yale University Press, 1985.
Scott, Joan W. "Rewriting History." In *Behind the Lines: Gender and the Two World Wars*, edited by Margaret Randolph Higonnet, Jane Jenson, Sonya Michel, and Margaret Collins Weitz, 19–30. New Haven, CT: Yale University Press, 1987.
Selden, Mark. *China in Revolution: The Yenan Way Revisited*. Armonk, NY: M.E. Sharpe, 1995.
Sha Meng, dir. *Zhao Yiman*. 1950; Changchun, Jilin: Dongbei dianying zhipianchang.
Shanghai shehui kexueyuan lishi yanjiusuo, comp. *"Ba yisan" kangzhan shiliao xuanbian* [Selected historical materials on the "August 13" resistance]. Shanghai: Renmin chubanshe, 1986.
Shao Menglan. *Chuncan daosi si fangjin: Shao Menglan nüshi fengwen jilu* [English title given by the publisher: *Spring Silkworm Spins Silk Till Its Death: The Reminiscences of Ms. Shao Meng-lan*]. Taipei: Institute of Modern History, Academia Sinica, 2005.

Sharma, Arvind, ed. *Women in World Religions*. Albany: State University of New York Press, 1987.
Shen Qizhen. "Zai Song Qingling danchen 95 zhounian jinianhui shang de jianghua" [Speech at the memorial conference on Song Qingling's ninety-fifth birthday]. In *Jinian Song Qingling wenji* [Essays in memory of Song Qingling], edited by Song Qingling jinianhui bangongshi, 45–47. Beijing: Zhongguo heping chubanshe, 1992.
Shen Zijiu. "Jinnian zenyang jinian 'sanba'?" [How to commemorate March Eighth this year?], *Funü shenghuo* 2, 2 (February 1936). Included in CYEJ, 91–93.
–. "Guangxi nüxuesheng jun" [The Guangxi women students army]. In *Kangzhan zhong de nüzhanshi* [Women soldiers in the resistance war], edited by Shen Zijiu, 76–80. N.p.: Zhanshi chubanshen, n.d.
–. *Kangzhan zhong de nüzhanshi* [Women soldiers in the resistance war]. N.p.: Zhanshi chubanshen, n.d.
Sheridan, Mary. "Yenan Women in Revolution." In *Lives: Chinese Working Women*, edited by Mary Sheridan and Janet W. Salaff, 180–96. Bloomington: Indiana University Press, 1984.
Sheridan, Mary, and Janet W. Salaff, eds. *Lives: Chinese Working Women*. Bloomington: Indiana University Press, 1984.
Shi Deqing, ed. *Fenghuo Taihang banbiantian* [Half of the sky in the wartime Taihang]. Beijing: Zhongyang wenxian chubanshe, 2005.
Smedley, Agnes. *Battle Hymn of China*. New York: Alfred A. Knopf, 1943.
–. *Portraits of Chinese Women in Revolution*. Old Westbury, NY: Feminist Press, 1976.
Smith, Norman. *Resisting Manchukuo: Chinese Women Writers and the Japanese Occupation*. Vancouver: UBC Press, 2007.
Snow, Helen Foster [Nym Wales, pseud.]. *The Chinese Communists: Sketches and Autobiographies of the Old Guard*. Westport, CT: Greenwood Press, 1972.
–. *Women in Modern China*. Paris: Monton, 1967.
Soh, C. Sarah. *The Comfort Women: Sexual Violence and Postcolonial Memory in Korea and Japan*. Chicago: University of Chicago Press, 2008.
Song Enrong and Yu Zixia, chief eds. *Riben qinHua jiaoyu quanshi* [A general history of education under Japanese aggression of China], 2 vols. Beijing: Renmin jiaoyu chubanshe, 2005.
Song Meiling. *Jiang furen yanlun ji* [Collection of speeches and works by Madame Jiang]. Taipei: Zhonghua funü fangong lianhehui, 1977.
–. "Xin shenghuo yu funü" [New life and women]. *Funü xin shenghuo yuekan* 1 (November 1936): 2–5.
–. "Zhongguo funü kangzhan de shiming" [The mission of Chinese women in the War of Resistance] (July 1, 1941). In *Jiang furen yanlun ji* [Collection of speeches and works by Madame Jiang], by Song Meiling, 2: 736–42. Taipei: Zhonghua funü fangong lianhehui, 1977.
Song Qingling jinianhui bangongshi, ed. *Jinian Song Qingling wenji* [Essays in memory of Song Qingling]. Beijing: Zhongguo heping chubanshe, 1992.
Spakowski, Nicola. "Women's Military Participation in the Communist Movement of the 1930s and 1940s: Patterns of Inclusion and Exclusion." In *Women in China: the Republican Period in Historical Perspective*, edited by Mechthild Leutner and Nicola Spakowski, 129–71. Münster, Germany: Lit Verlag, 2005.
Stacey, Judith. *Patriarchy and Socialist Revolution in China*. Berkeley: University of California Press, 1983.

Stanley, Liz. "From 'Self-Made Women' to 'Women's Made-Selves'? Audit Selves, Simulation and Surveillance in the Rise of Public Woman." In *Feminism and Autobiography: Texts, Theories, Methods,* edited by Tess Cosslett, Celia Lury, and Penny Summerfield, 40–60. London: Routledge 2000.

Stetz, Margaret, and Bonnie B.C. Oh. "Introduction." In *Legacies of the Comfort Women of World War II,* edited by Margaret Stetz and Bonnie B.C. Oh, xi–xvi. Armonk, NY: M.E. Sharpe, 2001.

–, eds. *Legacies of the Comfort Women of World War II.* Armonk, NY: M.E. Sharpe, 2001.

Stevenson, Alexandra. "Leadership Changes Reveal That in China, Men Still Rule." *New York Times,* October 23, 2022.

Stranahan, Patricia. *Molding the Medium: The Chinese Communist Party and the Liberation Daily.* Armonk, NY: M.E. Sharpe, 1990.

–. *Underground: The Shanghai Communist Party and the Politics of Survival, 1927–1937.* Lanham, MD: Rowman and Littlefield, 1998.

–. *Yan'an Women and the Communist Party.* China Research Monograph no. 26. Institute of East Asian Studies, University of California, Center for Chinese Studies, 1976.

Su Zhiliang. *Rijun xingnuli: Zhongguo "weianfu" zhenxiang* [Sex slaves of the Japanese troops: a true account of Chinese "comfort women"]. Beijing: Renmin chubanshe, 2000.

–. *Weianfu yanjiu* [A study of the comfort women]. Shanghai: Shanghai shudian chubanshe, 1999.

Su Zhiliang and Hu Haolei. "Sihang gujun de guang yu ying" [Lights and shadows of the lone army of Sihang warehouse]. *Dang'an chunqiu* 7 (2015): 13–16; 8 (2015): 37–38; 9 (2015): 27–30; 10 (2015): 32–35.

Su Zhiliang et al. *Zhongguo kangzhan neiqian shilu* [The record of the exodus into the interior in China's War of Resistance]. Shanghai: Renmin chubanshe, 2015.

Su Zhiliang, Yao Fei, and Chen Lifei. *QinHua Rijun "weianfu" wenti yanjiu* [Study of issues of the "comfort women" under the Japanese invading army]. Beijing: Zhonggong dangshi chubanshe, 2016.

Su Zhiling, Rong Weimu, and Chen Lifei, chief eds. *Taotian zuinie: erzhan shiqi de Rijun "weianfu" yanjiu* [Monstrous atrocities: the Japanese military comfort women system during the Second World War]. Shanghai: Xuelin chubanshe, 2000.

Summerfield, Penny. *Reconstructing Women's Wartime Lives: Discourse and Subjectivity in Oral Histories of the Second World War.* Manchester and New York: Manchester University Press, 1998.

Sun Sibai. "Tantan 'Zhongguo funü yundongshi' de bianxie wenti" [On some issues of compilation of the history of Chinese women's movement]. FYSYJZL 2: 16–20 (December 10, 1981).

Sun Tie, dir. *Wode muqin Zhao Yiman* [My mother Zhao Yiman]. 2005; Fuzhou: Fujian dianying zhipianchang.

Tao Feiya, ed. *Xingbie yu lishi: jindia Zhongguo funü yu jidujiao* [Gender and history: modern Chinese women and Christianity]. Shanghai: Renmin chubanshe, 2006.

Thompson, Paul. "Changing Encounters with Chinese Oral History." *Oral History* 45, 2 (Autumn 2017): 96–105.

Tillman, Margaret Mih. "Engendering Children of the Resistance: Models for Gender and Scouting in China, 1919–1937." *Cross-Currents: East Asian History and Culture Review.* E-Journal no. 13 (December 2014), 134–73. https://escholarship.org/uc/item/9501x9cd.

Tumblety, Joan. "Introduction: Working with Memory as Source and Subject." In *Memory and History: Understanding Memory as Source and Subject*, edited by Joan Tumblety, 1–16. London: Routledge, 2013.

–, ed. *Memory and History: Understanding Memory as Source and Subject*. London: Routledge, 2013.

Turpin, Jennifer. "Many Faces: Women Confronting War." In *The Women and War Reader*, edited by Lois Ann Lorentzen and Jennifer E. Turpin, 3–18. New York: New York University Press, 1998.

Unger, Jonathan. "Introduction." In *Using the Past to Serve the Present: Historiography and Politics in Contemporary China*, edited by Jonathan Unger, 1–8. Armonk, NY: M.E. Sharpe, 1993.

–, ed. *Using the Past to Serve the Present: Historiography and Politics in Contemporary China*. Armonk, NY: M.E. Sharpe, 1993.

Van de Ven, Hans. *China at War: Triumph and Tragedy in the Emergence of the New China*. Cambridge, MA: Harvard University Press, 2018.

Waelchli, Mary Jo. "Wu Yifang: Abundant Life in Training Women for Service." In *Salt and Light: Lives of Faith That Shaped Modern China*, edited by Carol Lee Hamrin and Stacey Bieler, 152–70. Eugene, OR: Pickwick, 2009.

Wakeman, Frederic Jr. "Hanjian (Traitor)! Collaboration and Retribution in Wartime Shanghai." In *Becoming Chinese: Passages to Modernity and Beyond*, edited by Wen-Hsin Yeh. Berkeley, CA: University of California Press, 2000, 298–341.

–. "Shanghai Smuggling." In *In the Shadow of the Rising Sun: Shanghai under Japanese Occupation*, edited by Christian Henriot and Wen-Hsin Yeh, 116–53. Cambridge: Cambridge University Press, 2004.

Waldron, Arthur. "China's New Remembering of World War II: The Case of Zhang Zizhong." *Modern Asian Studies* 30, 4 (October 1996): 945–78.

Wang Dewei. "Houji" [Epilogue]. In *Juliu he*, by Chi Pang-yuan, 375–88. Beijing: Shenghuo dushu xinzhi sanlian shudian, 2011.

Wang, Jing M. *When "I" Was Born: Women's Autobiography in Modern China*. Madison: University of Wisconsin Press, 2008.

Wang Siyi. "Memorials and Memory: The Curation and Interpretation of Trauma Narratives – Using the Examples of Exhibitions on the Theme of 'Comfort Women' in East Asian Society." *Chinese Studies in History* 53, 1 (2020): 56–71.

Wang, Wenwen. "Beyond 'Good Wives and Wise Mothers': Feminism as Anticolonialism in Manchukuo Schools." *Twentieth-Century China* 45, 3 (October 2020): 285–307.

Wang Xiaokui. "Historical Shifts in Remembering China's Nanjing Massacre." *Chinese Studies in History* 50, 4 (2017): 324–34.

Wang Xingjuan. *Jinggang dujuan hong – He Zizhen fengyu rensheng* [The red azalea of the Jinggang mountains – the stormy life of He Zizhen]. Shenyang: Liaoning renmin chubanshe, 2000.

Wang Youqiao. "Zai quanguo fulian xuanjiao gongzuo zuotanhui shang de baogao" [Lecture on the ACWF seminar of propaganda and education work], May 30, 1980. This document is internally circulated.

Wang Yugeng. "Changjiang de nüer – ji Yang Ruinian tongzhi" [Daughter of the Yangzi River – the account of comrade Yang Ruinian]. In *Wangshi zhuozhuo*, by Wang Yugeng, 124–48. 2nd ed. Beijing: Renmin chubanshe, 2012.

–. *Wangshi zhuozhuo* [Brilliant moments in memories]. 2nd ed. Beijing: Renmin chubanshe, 2012.
Wang, Zheng. *Finding Women in the State: A Socialist Feminist Revolution in the People's Republic of China, 1949–1964*. Berkeley: University of California Press, 2017.
–. "'State Feminist'? Gender and Socialist State Formation in Maoist China." *Feminist Studies* 31, 3 (Fall 2005): 519–51.
–. *Women in the Chinese Enlightenment: Oral and Textual Histories*. Berkeley: University of California Press, 1999.
Wei Junyi. *Sitong lu and Lu Sha de lu* [Reflections of pains and *The Road of Lu Sha*]. Revised ed. Beijing: Wenhua yishu chubanshe, 2003.
Weigelin-Schwiedrzik, Susanne. "Party Historiography." In *Using the Past to Serve the Present: Historiography and Politics in Contemporary China*, edited by Jonathan Unger, 151–73. Armonk, NY: M. E. Sharpe, 1993.
Weiss, Penny A., and Marilyn Friedman, eds. *Feminism and Community*. Philadelphia: Temple University Press, 1995.
Witke, Roxane. *Comrade Chiang Ch'ing*. Boston: Little, Brown, 1977.
Wu Qiong. *Zhongguo dianying de leixing yanjiu* [A study of Chinese film genres]. Beijing: Zhongguo dianying chubanshe, 2005.
Wu, T'ien-wei. "The Chinese Communist Movement." In *China's Bitter Victory: The War with Japan, 1937–1945*, edited by James C. Hsiung and Steven I. Levine, 79–106. Armonk, NY: M.E. Sharpe, 1992.
Wu Xiangxiang. *Dierci Zhong-Ri zhanzhengshi, 1931–1945* [History of the second Sino-Japanese War, 1931–1945]. Taipei: Tsung Ho Book, 1973.
Wu, Yudi. "Yan'an Iron Bodhisattva: Hunting Spies in the Rectification Campaign." In *1943: China at the Crossroads*, edited by Joseph W. Esherick and Matthew T. Combs, 203–41. Ithaca, NY: East Asian Program, Cornell University, 2015.
Xia Rong. *Funü zhidao weiyuanhui yu kangRi zhanzheng* [Women's advisory committee of the New Life Movement and the War of Resistance]. Beijing: Renmin chubanshe, 2010.
Xia, Yun. *Down with Traitors: Justice and Nationalism in Wartime China*. Seattle: University of Washington Press, 2017.
Xiang, Lanxin. *Mao's Generals: Chen Yi and the New Fourth Army*. Lanham, MD: University Press of America, 1998.
Xiao Hong. *The Field of Life and Death and Tales of Hulan River*. Translated by Howard Goldblatt. Boston: Cheng and Tsui, 2002.
Xu Yunqing. *Yingxiong de jiemei – Kanglian huiyi lu* [Heroic sisters – recollections of the Kanglian]. Changchun, Jilin: Jilin renmin chubanshe, 1960; 2nd ed., 1978.
Yan, Haiping, *Chinese Women Writers and the Feminist Imagination, 1905–1948*. London: Routledge, 2006.
Yan Weiqing. "Shanghai dui Xinsijun de renli zhiyuan" [Supply of manpower of Shanghai to the New Fourth Army]. In *Xinsijun yu Shanghai* [The New Fourth Army and Shanghai], edited by Zhang Yun, 138–43. Shanghai: Shanghai renmin chubanshe, 2003.
Yan Zhaofen. "Chufa qianhou: Guangxi nüxuesheng jun tongxun" [Before and after the departure: report on the Guangxi women students army] In *Kangzhan zhong de nüzhanshi* [Women soldiers in the resistance war], edited by Shen Zijiu, 80–83. N.p.: Zhanshi chubanshen, n.d.
Yan'an Zhongguo nüzi daxue Beijing xiaoyouhui, ed. *Yanshui qing* [Love for the Yan River]. Beijing: Zhongguo funü chubanshe, 1999.

Yang, Chan. *World War Two Legacies in East Asia: China Remembers the War*. New York: Routledge, 2018.
Yang, Daqing. "Atrocities in Nanjing: Searching for Explanations." In *Scars of War: The Impact of Warfare on Modern China*, edited by Diana Lary and Stephen MacKinnon, 76–96. Vancouver: UBC Press, 2001.
Yang Huilin. "Guangxi niangzijun huijianji" [Meeting the Guangxi women students army]. In *Kangzhan zhong de nüzhanshi* [Women soldiers in the resistance war], edited by Shen Zijiu, 83–88. N.p.: Zhanshi chubanshen, n.d.
Yang Huimin. *Babai zhuangshi yu wo* [The eight hundred heroes and I]. Taipei: Fozhiguang chubanshe, 1979.
—. "Xianqi zai babai zhuangshi zhi qian" [Delivering flag to the eight hundred heroes]. In *Shanghai yiri* [One day in Shanghai], edited by Zhu Zuotong and Mei Yi, pt. 1, 53–54. Shanghai: Huamei chuban gongsi, 1938.
Yang, Mayfair Mei-hui. "From Gender Erasure to Gender Difference." In *Spaces of Their Own: Women's Public Sphere in Transnational China*, edited by Mayfair Mei-hui Yang, 35–67. Minneapolis: University of Minnesota Press, 1999.
—, ed. *Spaces of Their Own: Women's Public Sphere in Transnational China*. Minneapolis: University of Minnesota Press, 1999.
Yang Mo. *Qingchun zhi ge* [The song of youth]. Beijing: Zuojia chubanshe, 1958.
Ye Hanming, "Funü, xingbie ji qita: jin niannian Zhongguo dalu he Xianggang de jindai Zhongguo funüshi yanjiu jiqi fazhan qianjing" [Women, gender, and others: research on modern Chinese women's history in mainland China and Hong Kong during recent twenty years and its prospective development]. *Jindai Zhongguo funushi yanjiu* 13 (December 2005): 107–65.
Yeh, Wen-hsin, ed. *Becoming Chinese: Passages to Modernity and Beyond*. Berkeley: University of California Press, 2000.
Yibin diwei dangshi gongzuo weiyuanhui, Sichuansheng fulian Yibin dique banshichu. *KangRi yingxiong Zhao Yiman* [Anti-Japanese heroine Zhao Yiman]. Chengdu: Sichuan daxue chubanshe, 1989.
Yin Hong and Leng Yan. *Xin Zhongguo dianyingshi (1949–2000)* [A history of new China's cinema (1949–2000)]. Changsha, Hunan: Hunan meishu chubanshe, 2002.
Yin Shihong and Fu Xiuyan, chief eds. *Yongyuan de cantong: Jiangxisheng qiangjiu kangzhan shiqi zaoshou Rijun qinhai shiliao: koushu shilu* [The lasting pain: rescued historical records of the suffering of violence committed by the invading Japanese army in Jiangxi province during the resistance war period: oral histories]. 2 vols. Beijing: Renmin chubanshe, 2010.
Ying Yunwei, dir. *Babai zhuangshi* [Eight hundred heroes]. 1938; Hong Kong: Zhongnan guangrong yingpian gongsi.
Young, Helen P. *Choosing Revolution: Chinese Women Soldiers on the Long March*. Urbana: University of Illinois Press, 2001.
—. "Threads from Long March Stories: The Political, Economic and Social Experience of Women Soldiers." In *Women in China: The Republican Period in Historical Perspective*, edited by Mechthild Leutner and Nicola Spakowski, 172–93. Münster, Germany: Lit Verlag, 2005.
—. "Why We Joined the Revolution: Voices of Chinese Women Soldiers." In *Women and War in the Twentieth Century: Enlisted with or without Consent*, edited by Nicole Ann Dombrowski, 92–111. New York: Garland, 1999.

Yu, Chien-ming. "Beyond Rewriting Life History: Three Female Interviewees' Personal Experiences of War." In *Beyond Exemplar Tales: Women's Biography in Chinese History*, edited by Joan Judge and Hu Ying, 262–79. Berkeley: University of California Press, 2011.

Yuan Liangjun, ed. *Ding Ling yanju ziliao* [Research materials on Ding Ling]. Tianjin: Tianjin renmin chubanshe, 1982.

Yuan Runlan. "Yuan Runlan nüshi fangwen jilu" [The interview of Yuan Runlan]. In *Cong dongbei dao Taiwan: wanguo daodehui xiangguan renwu fangwen jilu* [From the northeast to Taiwan: interviews of people related with the Wan'guo daodehui], edited by Luo Jiurong et al., 69–94. Taipei: Institute of Modern History, Academia Sinica, 2006.

Yue Siping, chief ed. *Balujun* [The Eighth Route Army]. Beijing: Zhonggong dangshi chubanshe, 2005.

Yung, Bell. "Model Opera as Model: From Shajiabang to Sagabong." In *Popular Chinese Literature and Performing Arts in the People's Republic of China 1949–1979*, edited by Bonnie S. McDougall, 144–64. Berkeley: University of California Press, 1984.

Zeng Ke, ed. *Chunhua qiushi* [Spring flowers, autumn harvest]. Zhengzhou: Henan renmin chubanshe, 1985.

Zeng Zhi. *Yige geming de xingcunzhe* [A survivor of the revolution]. Guangzhou: Guangdong renmin chubanshe, 1999.

Zhang Chengde and Sun Liping, eds. *Shanxi kangzhan koushushi* [The oral histories of resistance war in Shanxi]. Taiyuan: Shanxi renmin chubanshe, 2005.

Zhang Jun, chief ed. *Zhanzheng yinyun xia de nianqingren, 1931–1945; Zhongguo wangshi* [Youth under the dark clouds of the war; China's memory]. Guilin: Guangxi shifan daxue chubanshe, 2016.

Zhang Shuangbing. *Paoluo li de nüren: Shanxi Rijun xingnuli diaocha shilu* [Women in the blockhouse: the investigation record of the sex slaves under the Japanese army in Shanxi]. Nanjing: Jiangsu renmin chubanshe, 2011.

Zhang Suzhou, Chen Danhuai, and Ye Weiwei, planners; Chen Xiaojin and Zhao Hongmei, producers. *Wode muqin: sange Xinsijun nübing de gushi* [My mother: the stories of three women soldiers of the N4A]. 2010; Shanghai: Shanghai zhonghang wenhua chuanbo youxian zeren gongsi; Anhui guangbo dianshitai.

Zhang Wenqing. "Shensui yuanyuan, teshu jidi – Shanghai yu Xinsijun xieshou kangRi [Deep roots, special base – the joint efforts in the resistance against Japan by Shanghai and the New Fourth Army]. In *Xinsijun yu Shanghai* [The New Fourth Army and Shanghai], edited by Zhang Yun, 3–14. Shanghai: Shanghai renmin chubanshe, 2003.

Zhang Xi. *Kangzhan nüxing dang'an* [Archives of women in the War of Resistance against Japan]. Beijing: Qingnian chubanshe, 2007.

Zhang Xianwen and Zhang Yufa, chief eds. *Zhonghua minguo zhuantishi* [Topical history of the Republic of China], vol. 12, *Kangzhan shiqi de lunxianqu yu wei zhengquan* [Occupied regions and illegitimate regimes in the anti-Japanese war]. Nanjing: Nanjing daxue chubanshe, 2015.

Zhang Yufa. "Zhanzheng dui Zhongguo funü de yingxiang (1937–1949)" [The impact of the wars on Chinese women (1937–1949)]. *Jindai Zhongguo funüshi yanjiu* 17 (December 2009): 157–74.

Zhang Yun, ed. *Xinsijun yu Shanghai* [The New Fourth Army and Shanghai]. Shanghai: Shanghai renmin chubanshe, 2003.

Zhang, Zhen. "'Never Abandon, Never Give Up': Soldiers Sortie as a New Red Classic of the Reform Era." *ASIANetwork Exchange* 26, 1 (2019): 96–115.

Zhao Linlu, "Jiushijiu sui 'weianfu' Wei Shaolan cishi: yizhi meiyou dengdao Riben de daoqian" [Ninety-nine-year-old "comfort woman" Wei Shaolan passed away: never received a Japanese apology before her death], *China News Network*, May 6, 2019, http://www.xinhuanet.com/politics/2019–05/06/c_1124454995.htm.

Zhao Xian. "Souji Shanghai funü yundong lishi ziliao de gongzuo huibao" [Work report on collecting documents for the history of Shanghai women's movement]. FYSYJZ 2: 21–23 (December 10, 1981).

Zhenzhuang. "Funü xinyun yu 'xianqi liangmu' zhuyi" [New Life Movement for women and "wise-wife-good-mother"-ism]. *Funü xin shenghuo yuekan* 7 (May 1937): 16–17.

Zhong, Xueping, Wang Zheng, and Bai Di, eds. *Some of Us: Chinese Women Growing Up in the Mao Era*. London: Rutgers University Press, 2001.

Zhongguo chuanqi 2010 zhi wode kangzhan jiemuzu, ed. *Wode kangzhan – 300 wei qinlizhe koushu lish* [My war of resistance: an oral history of 300 witnesses]. Beijing: Zhongguo youyi chuban gongsi, 2010.

Zhonggong Liyangshi weiyuanhui, dangshi ziliao zhengli yanjiu lingdao xiaozu, ed. *Liyang geming douzhengshi* [The history of Liyang's revolutionary struggle]. Nanjing: Jiangsu renmin chubanshe, 1995.

Zhonggong Wutai xianwei dangshi yanjiushi, ed. *Wutai renmin kangRi douzhengshi* [The history of the Wutai people's anti-Japanese struggle]. Internal circulation, 1985.

Zhonghua quanguo funü lianhehui, ed. *Cai Chang, Deng Yingchao, Kang Keqing funü jiefang wenti wenxuan, 1938–1987* [Selected works by Cai Chang, Deng Yingchao, and Kang Keqing on the issue of women's liberation, 1938–1987]. Beijing: Renmin chubanshe, 1983.

Zhonghua quanguo funü lianhehui funü yundong lishi yanjiushi. *Zhongguo funü yundongshi (xin minzhu zhuyi shiqi)* [History of Chinese women's movement, new democratic period]. Beijing: Chunqiu chubanshe, 1989.

Zhonghua quanguo funü lianhehui funü yundong lishi yanjiushi, ed. *Zhongguo funü yundong lishi ziliao* [Historical materials of Chinese women's movement], 5 vols. Beijing: Zhongguo funü chubanshe, 1986–91.

"Zhongyang yanjiuyuan, jindaishi yanjiu suo: funü qikan zuozhe yanjiu pingtai [Research platform of authors of women's journals]," https://mhdb.mh.sinica.edu.tw/magazine/web/acwp_author.php?no=1795 and https://mhdb.mh.sinica.edu.tw/magazine/web/acwp_author.php?no=1215.

Zhou Chunyan. "Funü yu kangzhan shiqi de zhandi jiuhu" [Women and battlefield first aid during the second Sino-Japanese War]. *Jindai Zhongguo funüshi yanjiu* 24 (December 2014): 133–218.

Zhou Hong. *Xingbie, zhengzhi yu guozu shiye xia nüxing jiefang de yanshuo – Funü gongming yanjiu (1929–1944)* [The narratives of women's liberation through the lens of gender, politics, and nation: the study *Women's Resonance* (1929–1944)]. Xinbei, Taiwan: Huamulan chubanshe, 2013.

Zhou Lei and Liu Ningyuan. *Kangzhan shiqi Zhongguo funü yundong yanjiu (1931–1945)* [Study of Chinese women's movement in the War of Resistance (1931–1945)]. Beijing: Shoudu jingji maoyi daxue chubanshe, 2016.

Zhou Meiyu. *Zhou Meiyu xiansheng fangwen jilu* [English title given by the publisher:

The Reminiscences of Prof. Chow Mei Yu]. Taipei: Institute of Modern History, Academia Sinica, 1993.

Zhu Hongzhao. *Yan'an richang shenghuo zhong de lishi* [History of daily life in Yan'an]. Guiling: Guangxi shifan daxue chubanshe, 2007.

Zhu, Pingchao. *Wartime Culture in Guilin, 1938–1944*. Lanham, MD: Lexington Books, 2015.

Zhu Qiangdi. *Xinsijun nübing* [Women soldiers of the New Fourth Army]. Jinan, Shandong: Jinan chubanshe, 2004.

Zhu Zuotong and Mei Yi, eds. *Shanghai yiri* [One day in Shanghai]. Shanghai: Huamei chuban gongsi, 1938.

Zhuangzi. "Qiushui" [Autumn floods]. In *Chuang Tzu: Basic Teachings,* translated by Burton Watson, 96–110. New York: Columbia University Press, 1964.

Index

Note: "CCP" refers to the Chinese Communist Party.

activism: 14–15; comfort women redress, 19, 155, 157–59, 163, 223n59; historical studies in reform era, 37–38; in schools, 12, 51, 66, 76–80; YWCA programs, 11–12, 14, 51, 149. *See also* national salvation movement; women's movement (1890s–1945)
ACWF (All-China Women's Federation): 18, 23–24, 34–37, 40–41; in Cultural Revolution, 30, 35; historical studies by, 24–25, 34–38, 41; journals, 25, 34–35, 37; political agenda, 24–25, 35–36, 40; in reform era, 34–37
agency of women: 6–7, 15, 181–86; daily life of soldiers, 55; domestic sphere, 10, 15, 118–24, 184–85; memoirs on, 39; middle-class women, 129–31, 144–52; Nationalist-associated women, 15, 19, 106–7, 118–24, 184–85; occupied areas, 129–31, 148–49, 151–52; revolutionary paths, 55
All-China Women's Federation. *See* ACWF (All-China Women's Federation)
Anti-Japanese Military and Political University, 55, 113

Anti-Rightist Campaign, 145–46, 152, 180
arranged marriage. *See* marriage, arranged
the arts: 11, 21–22, 56–57; arts for political purposes, 11, 21–22, 30–34, 56–57, 86, 100–1, 113, 172; in Cultural Revolution, 30, 38–39, 203n34; historical trends, 21–22, 31; red themes in reform era, 31–34, 40–41. *See also* film; literature; music; television; theatre
autobiographies. *See* biographies and autobiographies
autonomy. *See* agency of women

Bai Ai, 165, 168–69, 187
Bai Wenguan, 29
Ban Zhao, 25
Bao Yousun, 58
The Battle of Fanchang (Wang Yugeng), 57
Beiping/Beijing: capital of China, vii, 135; May Fourth Movement centre, 135; museums, 40; occupation, 80, 108, 112–13, 140–41; universities, 112–13, 137, 141, 143; Yanjing University, 70, 135, 143, 149–50, 220n52

biographies and autobiographies: 24–25, 38–39, 182–86; autobiography, 38–39; CCP's requirement for autobiography, 69–70, 209n29; empowerment of self-articulation, 7, 212n4; fiction, 93; literary tradition of, 24–25, 38–39; in Mao era, 38–39; memoirs, 39; in reform era, 32–33, 38–39. *See also* oral history
bourgeois. *See* middle class
Brilliant Moments in Memories (Wang Yugeng), 43
Brook, Timothy, 128, 165
Buddhism, 129, 147, 166, 185

Cai Chang, 17
Cao Jingyi, 101–2, 122
Catholicism, 141–42
CCP. *See* Communist Party (CCP)
Central Party School, 113
Central Party School, Yan'an, 113
Chen Bijun, 126–27
Chen Gongbo, 127
Chen Lian, 50
Chen Lifei, 156
Chen Lintao, 163
Chen Meiquan, 118–19, 124, 177
Chen Shaomin, 58
Chen Xuqing, 164
Chen Yan, 38, 129
Chen Yi, 43, 54, 172, 223n74
Cheng Quan (Chen Chuangang), 92
Chi Pang-yuan: 19, 98–99, 123–24; education, 114–15, 184; memoirs, 98–99, 107, 111–12, 114, 213n1; Nationalists, 19, 98–99, 123–24, 177; spelling of name, vii; suffering and losses, 19, 99, 107, 111–12; on Zhang Dafei, 99, 111–12, 115, 177
Chiang Kai-shek: anti-Communist stance, 49–50; appeasement and nonresistance, 8, 10, 11, 51, 72–73, 76–77; Confucian ethics, 8–10; Nationalist government, 4, 8, 181; New Life Movement, 8–10, 11, 12–13, 38; Song Meiling's activism, 8–9, 12–14, 104, 123; Taiwan government (1949–75), 4, 181;

Xi'an Incident (1936), 72. *See also* Nationalist Party, government (1931–45); Taiwan
childbirth. *See* pregnancy and childbirth
children: child care, 16, 33, 61, 63–64, 183; child labour, 51, 165–66, 170; infant mortality, 64, 73, 132, 134; in-laws as caregivers, 33; one-child policy, 180; patrilineal culture, 71–72, 73; peasants as caregivers, 63–64, 94–97; of rape victims, 157, 162, 164, 171; refugee children's association, 123; separation of mothers and children, 33, 94–97, 183; sonless mothers, 71–72, 74, 75–76, 132–33; of women soldiers, 33–34, 63–64, 94–95. *See also* motherhood, Communist; motherhood, traditional; pregnancy and childbirth
Chinese Communist Party (CCP). *See* entries beginning with Communist Party (CCP)
Chinese Women's University, 55, 60, 89–90, 113
Chongqing: bombings and air raids, 110–12; Nationalist capital, 4, 13, 177; oral histories, 15, 213n7
Christianity: 141–44; Catholicism, 141–42; gender consciousness, 135–36; ideals of compassion and service, 104; medical training, 135; missionary schools, 104, 135–36, 137, 142–43, 149; occupied areas, 126, 135–36, 141–44, 147, 149, 185
citizenship and nationalism: 8–15; family values, 9–15; New Life Movement, 9–10; red-themed arts in reform era, 31–34; rise and fall of all-under-heaven, 8, 56, 102, 184, 198, 196n13; women's movements, 7–8. *See also* national salvation movement
civil war (1946–49): 4, 49–50, 178–79; narrative sources, 37, 44–45, 47, 178–79; as national salvation, 151, 178; rural areas, 22

class: 53–54; gender and class theory, 10, 23–24, 51–52, 53; vulnerability and class inequalities, 112; YWCA programs, 11–12, 51–52. *See also* middle class; peasants and villagers; upper class; working class

colleges. *See* universities and colleges

comfort women: 19, 153–57, 174–75, 186; children of, 157, 162, 164, 171; collaboration regimes, 161–62; denialists of violence, 154–55, 221*n*12; films, 153, 157, 163–64; gender consciousness, 160; hatred for Japanese, 161, 186; historical studies on, 37, 40, 156–58; museums, 40, 157; narrative sources, 40, 156–57, 223*n*62; political awareness of, 154–55, 160; political persecution, 156, 162; postwar public silences, 154–58, 174, 186; redress movement, 154–55, 157–60, 163–64, 174–75, 186; self-sacrifice for family, 161–63; statistics, 153, 155; survivor activists, 19, 155, 157–59, 163, 174–75, 186, 220*n*5, 223*n*59; working poor, 155, 156, 157

Communist Party (CCP): 4, 10–11; arts for political purposes, 11, 31–34, 56–57; autobiography requirement, 69–70, 209*n*29; founding (1921), 10; gender consciousness, 10, 15–18, 52, 54–55, 61; Marxist ideology, 10, 46; membership ceremony, 80, 82, 83; memoirs of women in early history of, 206*n*92; "red classics" of ideology, 31–34; war memory studies, 5. *See also* Cultural Revolution (1966–76); Mao Zedong, government (1949–76); Mao Zedong era, women; Rectification Movement (1942–44)

Communist Party (CCP), wartime: 4, 10–11; August First Declaration (1935), 10; civil war, 178–79; conflicts with Nationalists, 10–11, 49–50, 84–85, 102, 122–23; gender consciousness, 15–18, 52, 54–55, 61; Japanese surrender (1945), 176–79; national salvation movement, 10–11; opposition to appeasement, 11; United Front, 10, 44, 49–50. *See also* civil war (1946–49); Eighth Route Army; guerrilla forces; New Fourth Army (N4A); Northeast Anti-Japanese Allied Forces (Kanglian); Red Army; United Front; War of Resistance (1931–45)

Communist Party (CCP), wartime, women: 18–19; combat, 17, 58–59; gender consciousness, 10, 15–18, 52, 54–55, 61; metaphor of revolutionary family, 42, 47–48, 61–62, 90, 93; motives for joining, 52; revolutionary paths, 18–19, 42, 50–55. *See also* Mao Zedong era, women; New Fourth Army (N4A)

concessions in occupied areas, 81, 83, 106, 149, 166

concubines: feudal tradition, 133; filial duties, 146; sonless mothers, 71–72, 74, 75–76, 132–33

Confucianism: 8–10; celibacy, 155; Communist values, 17, 25–26; courage to go on, 114; education at home, 25, 114–15, 126, 131, 134; ethical concepts, 8–10, 25–26; family values, 8–10, 17, 25, 61, 86, 104, 121, 185; Morality Society, 129–30; Mulan as heroine, 25, 60, 72; Nationalist concerns, 8–13, 184–85; New Life Movement (NLM), 8–10, 11, 12–13, 38; opposition to, 8, 10, 15–16, 24, 129, 131, 135; patriarchy, 17; Three Obediences and Four Virtues, 121. *See also* good wives and wise mothers

Cong, Xiaoping, 17–18

Croll, Elisabeth, 16

Crook, Isabel Brown, 14

Cui Yongyuan, 39–40, 207*n*100

Cultural Revolution (1966–76): 30, 38–39, 180; autobiography requirement, 69–70, 209n29; ban on revolutionary arts, 30, 38–39, 210n34; damage to party, 35, 45; forgiveness for, 47–48; impact on historical research, 24, 30, 35, 45, 145; loyalty to Communist cause, 47–48; persecution victims, 30, 69, 162, 180
culture, traditional. *See* Confucianism; traditional culture

Daughters of China (film, 1949, 1987), 21, 26–27, 32
death: heroic revolutionaries, 29, 33, 81, 83; infant mortality, 64, 73, 132, 134; suicide, 27, 29, 162, 164, 180
Deng Xiaoping, 31, 180
Deng Yingchao, 17, 21, 24, 35, 123
Ding Ling, 15–16, 50, 60, 180
Ding Weiping, 37–38
A Doll's House (Ibsen), 16, 199n68
domestic life. *See* family life
drama. *See* theatre
Duara, Prasenjit, 129

education: 51, 112–18; Confucian education at home, 25, 114–15, 126, 131, 134; courage to go on, 114–17, 124; for economic independence, 115, 118, 126, 136–37; gender consciousness, 72, 97, 115–17, 131–32, 147, 185; Japanese education, 75, 108, 138–41, 146, 148, 150; Kaifeng middle school, 51, 76, 104–5, 189, 209n42; missionary schools, 104, 135–36, 137, 142–43; modernization (early 1900s), 72–73, 131, 137; Morality Society, 129–30; narrative sources, 39, 209n42; national salvation by science, 136, 141, 151; night schools, 12, 51–52, 58, 76, 113; political activism, 12, 51, 66, 76–83; refugee students, 114, 117, 137, 143–44; school curricula, 55, 57, 72–73, 113–15, 118, 131, 142; of soldiers, 54, 100, 104–5; study abroad in Japan, 138–40, 147, 148; temporary sites, 117; textbooks, 25, 29. *See also* universities and colleges
education, Communist: 112–13; anti-Japanese activities, 51–52; arts for political purposes, 56–57, 86, 113; curricula, 55, 57; literacy schools, 113; Mao on women's education, 55; N4A recruits, 51–53, 54; revolutionary ideals, 51, 54, 77–78, 81–82; "saving the country by book learning," 113; universities, 55, 76, 112–13; Yan'an as centre, 55, 113
education, Nationalist: 112–18, 124, 184; censorship, 144; curricula, 113–15, 118; financial support, 118; middle schools, 114–15; military training, 100, 120; as national salvation, 113, 115, 184; nonpartisan educators, 117–18; "schooling must go on," 114, 124; youth corps, 118
Education Brigade, 55
Edwards, Louise, 15
Eight Women Walking into the River (film, 1987), 32
the 800 heroes, 105–6
Eighth Route Army: conflicts with Nationalists, 49–50, 84–85; expansion of, 79; narrative sources, 39; peasant recruits, 52; student recruits, 43, 51, 79–80; United Front, 12, 44, 49–50
equality, women's, 186. *See also* gender consciousness

family life: 13–15, 61–65, 107–12, 124; agency of women, 15, 122–24, 182–83; class theory and gendered issues, 23–24; comfort women's self-sacrifice, 161–63; Communist values, 25–30, 122–23, 182–83; Confucian values, 9–10, 121; duties, 29, 60, 84, 118–19, 121, 146, 148–49, 152;

education at home, 115, 131, 134; gender consciousness, 52, 72–73; Ibsen's Nora as new woman, 16, 199*n*68; labour outside the home, 25, 36, 86; metaphor of revolutionary family, 42, 47–48, 61–62, 90, 93, 182; narrative sources, 119–20; national salvation movement, 9–15; Nationalist-associated women, 118–24, 184–85; peasants, 57–58; sacrifice for revolution, 25–26, 63–64, 78, 96–97, 182–83. *See also* concubines; gender consciousness; good wives and wise mothers; marriage; motherhood, Communist; motherhood, traditional; traditional culture

Fan Li, 63

feminism: feminist studies, 5–7; gender studies, 37–41; key questions, 6; Marxist ideology, 10, 46; recent modernization, 180–81; as term, 186. *See also* gender consciousness; women's movement (1890s–1945)

FHSY (*20th Century Wartime Experiences of Chinese Women*), 116–17, 119–22, 178

The Field of Life and Death (Xiao Hong), 127

film: 11, 21, 25–30; biographies of heroines, 24–30; comfort women, 153, 157, 163–64; in Cultural Revolution, 30; "the 800" and Yang Huimin, 106; historical trends, 21–22; Kanglian women soldiers, 21, 26–27, 32–34; patriotic songs, 70; popularity of, 25; portrayals of Japanese, 30, 33–34; propaganda tool, 11, 21, 25; red themes in reform era, 31–34, 40–41, 204*n*58; revolutionary history genre (1921–49), 25–26. *See also* television

footbinding: laws against, 132, 169; peasants, 168, 169; refusal of, 33, 77; unbound feet, 72, 135, 169

forced labour, 147, 159, 161

France, under occupation, 130–31

Fu, Poshek, 128, 118*n*17
Fudan University, 84, 92, 117

Ge Yu, 90

gender consciousness: 6–8, 186, 225*n*30; Communist women, 15–18, 52, 54–55, 61; conservative views, 196*n*22; education, 72–73, 97, 115–16, 131–32, 185; historical studies of, 37–38; Ibsen's Nora as new woman, 16, 199*n*68; incremental changes, 225*n*30; interviews as self-articulation, 67, 212*n*4; Morality Society, 129–30; Nationalist women, 9–10, 14, 19, 106–7, 119, 124; pay inequity, 147; rise and fall of all-under-heaven, 8, 56, 102, 184, 198, 196*n*13; rural areas, 86–88; sonless mothers, 71–72, 74, 75–76, 132–33; terminology, 186. *See also* feminism; gender studies; women's movement (1890s–1945)

gender studies: 5–6, 37–41; ACWF institute, 37; oral history projects, 37, 39–41. *See also* ACWF (All-China Women's Federation)

gendered violence. *See* comfort women; sexual violence

Gildea, Robert, 20, 130–31
Gilmartin, Christina, 17, 60
Glosser, Susan, 128–29
Gluck, Sherna, 231*n*30
GMD. *See* Nationalist Party, government (1931–45)

good wives and wise mothers: 9, 196*n*22; agency of women, 10, 15; inversion (wise wife and good mother), 196*n*22; Japanese curricula, 139; national salvation, 9, 13–14; occupied areas, 129, 148; opposition to ideology of, 9, 11, 129

Goodman, David, 17

The Great Flowing River (Chi Pang-yuan), 98–99, 220*n*1

Great Leap Forward (1958), 180

Gu Mei: 73–75, 97, 183, 187; education, 74, 81, 84; gender consciousness, 74, 84, 97; marriage, 95, 97; political autobiography, 69–70, 73–74, 84, 90; Rectification Movement, 90, 183; revolutionary path, 18–19, 69–70, 73–75, 81–82, 83–84, 95, 97, 183
Guangxi, 100–1, 157, 163–64
guerrilla forces: 101–2; medical care, 56; Northeast Anti-Japanese Allied Forces, 10, 21, 26–28, 32, 39, 203n34; support for anti-Japanese forces, 56, 58–59, 169; women fighters, 26–28, 33, 56, 101–2
Guo Dejie, 101
Guo Ke, 157, 163
Guo Lian: 68–69, 75–76, 96–97, 188; on civil war, 178; education, 75–76, 80–81; gender consciousness, 75–76, 84, 86–87, 97; interview, 68–69, 188; marriage, 80–81, 89, 96–97; motherhood, 96–97, 183; Rectification Movement, 88–89, 183; revolutionary path, 18–19, 68–69, 75–76, 80–81, 86–87, 88–89, 97, 183
Guo Wencui, 104–5, 124
Guo Zhenyi, 92, 180, 188, 211n3
Guomindang. *See* Nationalist Party, government (1931–45)

Harbin, 26, 27
He Junnan, 108
He Xiangning, 11–12
health care. *See* medical care
Henan University, 76
Heroic Sisters: Recollections of the Kanglian (booklet, 1960, 1978), 27–28
heroines: 18, 25–30; ACWF biographies, 25; bourgeois-miss-turned-Communist-fighter, 28–29, 30, 53–54; in Cultural Revolution, 30; heroic mothers, 29–30, 33, 35–36; martyrs, 25–27, 32; Mulan as heroine, 25, 58, 60, 72; narrative sources, 22–23, 27–28; peasant soldiers, 27–28; red-themed arts in reform era, 31–34; slaves to fighters, 26–28, 30; as stereotypes, 25–30, 46; stories of 8 women soldiers, 26–27, 32
Hershatter, Gail, 6, 164
higher education. *See* universities and colleges
historiography: 18, 22–30, 37–38, 40–41, 181–86; ACWF studies, 24–25, 34–38, 40–41; biographies of Communist heroines, 24–30; in civil war, 22; cult of Mao, 5, 18, 22–23, 40; Cultural Revolution's impact on, 24, 30, 35, 45; diverse narratives, 31; gender consciousness, 37–38; historical trends, 21–22, 31, 37–41; in Mao era, 18, 22–30; narrative sources, 18; national mythmaking, 22–23; oral history projects, 37–41; in reform era, 18, 31–41; suffering and losses, 23, 107–8; War of Resistance, 5, 18, 22–23; War of Resistance as a "good war," 31, 47, 124, 177–78; women's marginalization, 23–24, 40, 44–46, 65. *See also* heroines
The History of the Chinese Women's Movement (ACWF, 1989), 36–37
Honig, Emily, 128, 168
Hou Dong'e, 158–59, 162–63
Hou Qiaoliang, 159
Howard, Joshua H., 15
Hu Lancheng, 127
Hu Xiuzhi, 27
Hua Yixia, 53
Huang, Nicole, 129
Huang Youliang, 161
Huang Yu, 123
Huang Yun, 99, 109–10, 118, 184, 188
The Hui Muslim Detachment (film, 1959), 29

Ibsen, Henrik, 16, 199n68
interviews. *See* oral history; research project
Iron Currents (TL), 43, 48–49, 52–53
Ishida Yoneko, 156, 159

Index

Japan: Chinese students in, 138–40, 147, 148; film portrayals in reform era, 30, 33–34; war crimes, 155–56, 164; war's impact on, 140
Japan, war against. *See* War of Resistance (1931–1945)
Japan, wartime sexual violence. *See* comfort women; sexual violence
Japanese-occupied areas. *See* Manchuria, Manchukuo regime; middle-class women, occupied China; occupied China
Jiang Qing (Mao's wife), 30, 39
Jiang Yunzhong, 130
Jiang Zhonglin, 101, 214n17
Jin Yihong, 39
Jin-Cha-Ji region (Shanxi-Chahar-Hebei), 15, 29, 87–88, 90, 189
Johnson, Kay Ann, 15
Journal of Women's Studies (ACWF), 37
journals. *See* publishing
Judge, Joan, 8

Kaifeng, Henan, 51, 76–77, 82, 189
Kaifeng All-Girls Middle School, 51, 76, 104–5, 189
Kang Keqing, 17
Kang Youwei, 7
Kanglian. *See* Northeast Anti-Japanese Allied Forces (Kanglian)
Kangzhan. See War of Resistance (1931–1945)
Ke Huiling, 206n92
Kimura, Maki, 160–61, 227n5
Komeda Mai, 163

Lary, Diana, 177
Leng Yun, 26–27
Let women speak for themselves (Li Xiaojiang, ed.), 37
Li, Danke, 15, 213n7
Li, Virginia C. (Li Zhen), 108
Li Guang: 68, 87–88, 97, 183, 188–89; education, 68, 72–73, 79–80, 189; gender consciousness, 72–73, 84, 87–88, 97; interview, 68, 188; marriage, 94, 97, 189; motherhood, 94–95, 183; publications, 68, 87;

Rectification Movement, 90, 183; revolutionary path, 18–19, 72–73, 79–80, 87–88, 94–95, 97, 183
Li Hanhun, 108
Li Jianzhen, 58
Li Jinzhao, 89–90
Li Landing, 53, 59
Li Lianchun, 160
Li Xi, 51–52
Li Xiaojiang, 37
Li Zhen, 108
Li Zongren, 101
Lianda (National Southwest Associated University), 113, 115, 116
Liang Hongyu, 60
Liang Qichao, 7
Liaoning. *See* Shenyang, Liaoning
liberation, women's, 186. *See also* feminism; gender consciousness
Lin Ailan, 163
Lin Daojing (character), 28–29
Lin Juxian, 63
Lin Ke, 61
Ling Ben, 43
literature: first-person narration, 38; heroine as revolutionary, 28–29; novels and short stories, 28–30, 93; print culture, 128–29; red themes in reform era, 31; "traitor" writers, 126–27
Liu Jie, 59
Liu Mianhuan, 159
Liu Ningyuan, 38
Liu Ying, 39
Liyang, Jiangsu, 169–74, 178
love. *See* family life; marriage
lower class. *See* peasants and villagers; working class
Lü Fangshang, 14
Lu Lihua, 117–18
Lu Nan: 68, 76–77, 95–97, 183, 189; education, 76–77, 82–83, 189; gender consciousness, 76–77, 84, 97; interview, 68, 189; marriage, 95–97, 189; motherhood, 95–96, 183; nurse and teacher, 82, 86, 96; Rectification Movement, 90–91, 183; revolutionary path, 18–19, 76–77, 82–83, 85–86, 97, 183

Lu Xun Art College, Taihang, 86, 113
Luo Jiurong, 122
Luo Qiong, 36, 53–54
Luo Xing, 211*n*1
Luo Ying: 66–68, 77–79, 91, 97, 183, 189; education, 66, 71–72, 77–78, 84–85; gender consciousness, 71–72, 84, 85, 97; interviews, 66, 67–68, 189; marriages, 93, 97, 178; medical work, 66, 85, 91, 97; motherhood, 97; publications, 68; revolutionary path, 18–19, 66–68, 71–72, 77–79, 84–85, 91, 97, 178, 183
Lushan conference (1938), 12–13, 104

Ma, Zhao, 128
Ma Benzhai, 29
Mai, Komeda, 163
Manchuria: 3, 129–31; education, 129–30, 137–39; gender consciousness, 129; Japanese education, 75, 108, 138–41, 148; life under occupation, 127, 137–39, 148–49, 177; Manchurian Incident (1931), 3, 10, 38, 75, 132, 137, 139; modernization, 132; Morality Society, 129–30; narrative sources, 207*n*99; students in Japan, 138–40, 147, 148; women writers, 129. *See also* Northeast Anti-Japanese Allied Forces (Kanglian); Shenyang, Liaoning
Manchuria, Manchukuo regime: 3, 19, 125–26, 138–39; collaboration regimes, 125, 126–27, 129–31, 161–62; conservative ideology, 129
Mang Yuqin, 121, 179
Mao Weiqing, 48
Mao Zedong, government (1949–76): 4–5; apology for Rectification Movement, 71, 89–90, 93; cult of Mao, 5, 18, 22, 40; in Cultural Revolution, 30; on education of women, 55; founding of PRC, 4–5; historiography, 22, 184; Jiang Qing's activities, 30, 39; Nationalists' condemnation by, 5, 22, 99–100, 184; "red classics" of ideology, 31–34. *See also* Cultural Revolution (1966–76)
Mao Zedong era, women: 16, 22–25; AWCF projects, 23, 40–41; biographies of heroines, 24–30; class theory and gendered issues, 23–24; comfort women silences, 154; Cultural Revolution, 30; films on heroines, 26–27; gender consciousness, 16, 22–24; heroines as stereotypes, 30, 46; marginalization in histories, 5, 18, 22–25, 40, 44–46, 65, 183; martyrs, 25–27, 30, 32; red-themed arts in reform era, 31–34; state feminism, 23–24, 179–80; war as male experience, 23. *See also* Cultural Revolution (1966–76)
"The March of the Volunteers" (song), 11, 78, 117, 127
Marco Polo Bridge Incident (1937), 12, 44, 77
marriage: 62–65, 93–97; agency of women, 173–74; celibacy, 133; child brides, 52; class theory and gendered issues, 23–24; to collaborators, 126–27; Communist wives, 62–65; divorce, 16, 70, 89, 95–96, 173–74; free choice in marriage, 16, 17, 185; gender consciousness, 49, 52, 103, 185; N4A soldiers, 62–65; narrative sources, 52; Nationalist "war wives," 103, 120; patriarchal traditions, 17; romantic love, 49, 62–63, 93–96, 112; separate residences, 63; soldiers' rule (age, service, and status), 62, 211*n*99; working class, 168. *See also* concubines
marriage, arranged: for political purposes, 60–63, 94–95; to prevent rape by Japanese, 170; rejection of, 80–81; as traditional culture, 52, 60
martyrs, 25–27, 30, 32
Marxism, 10, 46, 54, 70–71

Index

mass media: 18, 40–41; commercialization, 31–32, 45–46; Communist heroines, 18, 25–30; in Cultural Revolution, 30; red themes in reform era, 31–34, 40–41. *See also* film; television

May Fourth Movement (New Culture Movement), 8, 10, 15–16, 24, 129, 131, 135

medical care: education, 103–4; guerrilla soldiers, 56; missionaries, 142; N4A medical care, 55–56, 59, 210*n*69; Nationalists, 82–83, 103–4; nurses, 82–83, 103–4, 124, 135; reproductive health, 56, 211*n*107; women staff, 55–56, 210*n*69

memoirs. *See* biographies and autobiographies

Meng Yue, 28–29

middle class: 4, 53–54; gender studies, 38, 129; heroine of bourgeois-miss-turned-Communist-fighter, 28–29, 30, 53–54; refugees, 108–10; revolutionary paths, 50–55. *See also* class

middle-class women, occupied China: 19, 125–28, 151–52, 185; agency of women, 19, 129, 185; education, 126, 137–41, 185; family survival, 126, 185; food shortages, 147, 151; gender consciousness, 126, 129, 131–37, 185; good wives and wise mothers, 129, 148, 196*n*22; grey zones in areas, 128, 218*n*17; hatred for Japanese, 134, 140, 145–52; loyalty tests of schoolteachers, 146; marriage to collaborators, 126–27; moral courage, 128; political awareness, 19, 126, 127, 128, 144–51, 185; religion and spirituality, 126, 129–30, 141–44, 185; resistance in, 144–51; theatre, 129; women's print culture, 128–29

middle/upper class, Communist women: 66–71, 97; interviews with five women, 66–68. *See also* Gu Mei; Guo Lian; Li Guang; Lu Nan; Luo Ying

military. *See* War of Resistance, military

Mitter, Rana, 31

Mo Yan, 101

Morality Society, 129–30

motherhood, Communist: 94–97, 183; arts in reform era, 33–34; biographies of heroines, 25–30; Cultural Revolution portrayals, 30; femininity of mother's body, 29; heroic mother, 29–30, 33; sacrifice for revolution, 25–26, 33, 63–64, 94–97; separation of mothers and children, 94–97, 183. *See also* children; pregnancy and childbirth

motherhood, traditional: as biologically determined roles, 60; childbirth customs, 172–73; Confucian values, 8–10, 25; education at home, 115, 126, 134; family values, 25, 124; heroic mother, 29–30; New Life Movement, 9–10; postnatal care, 96; sonless mothers, 71–72, 74, 75–76, 132–33; women's domestic roles, 185. *See also* children; pregnancy and childbirth

movies. *See* film

Mu Guiying, 25, 58

Mulan, 25, 58, 60, 72

museums, 31, 40, 157

music: conservatories, 121–22, 144; in Cultural Revolution, 30; "Graduation Song," 70; "The March of the Volunteers," 11, 78, 117, 127; "On the Songhua River," 134; operas, 30; for political purposes, 32, 70, 78, 87, 117, 177; theatre arts, 56–57, 86

My Mother: The Stories of Three Women Soldiers of the N4A (film, 2010), 34, 43

My Mother Zhao Yiman (film, 2005), 32–34

My War of Resistance (TV series, 2010), 39–40

N4A. *See* New Fourth Army (N4A)
names: changes to honour mothers, 71; changes to protect families, 54; delayed for fear of mortality, 134; as revolutionary identity, 54
Nan Erpu, 162
Nan Shuancheng, 162
Nanjing Massacre (1937–38), 40, 107–8, 128, 155
Nankai University, 114–15
narratives in self-writing. *See* biographies and autobiographies
national salvation movement: 11–15; Communists, 11, 15–18; by education, 113, 115, 130, 136, 141, 151, 184; family values, 9–15, 196*n*22; gender consciousness, 9–15; vs individual rights, 9, 14; motives for women soldiers, 42, 56; Nationalists, 11–15, 107, 184; not to be a "slave in a lost nation," 75, 87–88, 126, 127, 145; publishing industry, 11, 14; revolution and civil war as salvation, 151; student activism, 70, 76; women's emancipation, 9. *See also* citizenship and nationalism; good wives and wise mothers
National Southwest Associated University (Lianda), 113, 115
nationalism. *See* citizenship and nationalism; national salvation movement
Nationalist Party, government (1931–45): 4, 19, 184; appeasement and nonresistance, 8, 10, 11, 51, 72–73, 76–77; Chongqing as capital (1937–46), 13, 109; conflicts with CCP, 49–50, 84–85, 102, 122–23; "the 800" and Yang Huimin, 105–6; gender consciousness, 9–10, 14, 19, 119, 124; historiography in reform era, 31, 36, 38, 99, 184; Japanese surrender (1945), 176–79. *See also* Chiang Kai-shek; Nationalist Revolutionary Army
Nationalist Party, postwar in Taiwan: 99–100, 184; Chiang's government (1949–75), 4, 181; Morality Society, 129–30; social class, 99–100; sufferings and losses, 98–100, 184. *See also* Chi Pang-yuan; Chiang Kai-shek; Taiwan
Nationalist Party, postwar on mainland: 99–100; agency of women, 106–7; condemnation in the PRC discourse, 5, 22, 99–100; executions of "traitors" to China, 126–27; gender consciousness, 106–7; narrative sources, 100. *See also* Huang Yun; Zhang Wei
Nationalist Party, women (1931–): 19, 98–100, 112, 122–23, 184; agency of women, 10, 15, 19, 36, 106–7, 122–24; family duty, 118–22, 124, 184–85; family losses, 19, 98–100, 107–12; gender consciousness, 106–7; narrative sources, 19, 116–17, 119–20, 178–79, 213*n*5; national salvation movement, 11–15, 107, 184; New Life Movement (NLM), 8–10, 11, 12–13, 38; oral history projects, 38, 99; *Women's Resonance*, 197*n*24. *See also* Nationalist Revolutionary Army, women
Nationalist Revolutionary Army: 44, 100–7; arts for political purposes, 56, 100–1; civil war, 178–79; concentration camps, 50; corruption, 78–79, 82–83; Japanese surrender (1945), 177; medical care, 103–4; narrative sources, 117, 179; United Front, 12, 44, 49–50; Wan'nan Incident (1941), 48–50; Xi'an Incident, 72. *See also* United Front
Nationalist Revolutionary Army, women: 100–7; Burma road, expedition army, 101, 105; civil war, 178–79; gender consciousness, 14, 45–47, 100, 103; guerrilla warfare, 101–2; historiography in reform era, 31, 99; narrative sources, 98–99; "resistance war wives," 103; student army, 51, 100–3, 214*n*17

Index

New Culture Movement (May Fourth Movement), 8, 10, 15–16, 24, 129, 131, 135
New Fourth Army (N4A): 44–45, 52–53, 57–59, 65; arts, 56–57, 172; as CCP operation, 44; civil war, 178–79; conflicts with Nationalists, 44, 49–50, 84–85, 122–23; educated force, 53; marginalization in histories, 44; medical care, 55–56; peasant relations, 57–59, 172; statistics, 44, 52, 57; student recruits, 44, 51–53; United Front, 12, 44, 49–50; Wan'nan Incident (1941), 44, 48–50; Xiang Ying as commander, 48, 58
New Fourth Army, women: 18–19, 43, 44–47, 52–65, 182–83; civil war, 178–79; in combat, 58–59; daily life, 55–65; education, 52–55; film and TV series, 34, 43, 49; gender consciousness, 18, 43, 44–46, 54–55, 57–61, 182–83; guerrilla forces, 58–59; health workers, 55–56, 210n69; leadership positions, 58–59; marginalization in histories, 23–24, 44–46, 65, 182–83; metaphor of revolutionary family, 42, 47–48, 61–62, 90, 93; narrative sources, 18, 43, 48–49, 51–53, 178; new identity as Communist, 54; patriarchy, 55, 59–61; portrayals in reform era, 34, 45–46; revolutionary paths, 42, 45–48, 50–55, 61–62, 65, 182–83; social class, 52–54; student recruits, 51–52; training, 54–55. See also *Women Soldiers of the Central Plain* (ZYNZS, 3 vols., 1991–94)
New Life Movement (NLM), 8–10, 11, 12–13, 38
Niu Luogui, 64
Northeast Anti-Japanese Allied Forces (Kanglian): films on heroines, 21, 26–27, 32–34; formation, 10; narrative sources, 26–27, 39, 203n34; women peasants as slaves to fighters, 27–28
Northeast China. See Manchuria

Northeast University, 118
"not just a man's cause," 7. See also research project
NQNDD *(The Reminiscences of Women's Corps)*, 117, 179

occupied China: 4, 19, 125–26, 165, 185–86; collaboration with Japanese, 125, 129–31, 161–62; executions of "traitors" to China, 126–27; flight to interior, 109–11, 125, 146, 150; forced labour, 147, 159, 161; foreign concession areas, 81, 83, 106, 149, 166; grey zones, 128, 218n17; hatred for Japanese, 134, 140, 145–52, 165–69, 171, 186; heroines of guerrilla forces, 26; historical studies in reform era, 128; narrative sources, 126, 131; peasants, 168–69; refugees from, 108–9, 137, 143–44; regional control, 125; resistance, 129–31; silenced memories, 125, 131; "slaves in a lost nation," 75, 87–88, 126, 127, 145, 185; statistics, 125, 126; terms for people in, 126–27, 145. See also comfort women; Manchuria, Manchukuo regime; middle-class women, occupied China
oral history: 37–41, 67–68, 182–86; evidence of war atrocities, 40, 223n62; gender's influence, 164–65; interviews, 67–68; marginalization of women, 40, 164, 181; Nationalists, 99, 181; in reform era, 37, 39–41, 99, 181; research centres, 40

Pan Fang (Pan Huitian), 92
patriarchy: 60–61; child care as gendered work, 60–61; comfort women, 19; Nationalist army, 103; N4A women soldiers, 55, 59–61; patrilineal culture, 71–72, 73; peasant culture, 17, 58; resistance to, 52; sonless mothers, 71–72, 74, 75–76, 132–33; women's narratives as self-articulation, 67, 212n4; working class, 167

peasants and villagers: 22, 57–59, 86–87, 168–75; arranged marriages, 170, 173–74; arts for political purposes, 172; child care for soldiers, 63–64, 94–97; class inequalities, 112; Communist mobilization, 17, 22, 57–59, 86–88; education, 57–58, 168, 170; films, 26–27; gender consciousness, 17, 52, 57–59, 86–89; hatred for Japanese, 171; heroic mothers, 29–30; literacy and languages, 28, 58, 105, 168; narrative sources, 26–28, 164–65, 168; occupied China, 168–75; political awareness, 87, 127, 164, 169, 172; sexual violence by Japanese, 171; soldiers' relations with, 54, 57–58, 65, 84, 86, 105, 169; traditional culture, 17, 52, 58, 168–69; women's support for fighters, 27–30, 59, 63–64, 86–88, 169

Pei-Wang Zhihong, 108, 178–79

Peking Union Medical College (PUMC), 103

People's Republic of China (PRC): 4–5; constitutional equality for women, 23; national anthem (1949), 11, 117, 127. *See also* Cultural Revolution (1966–76); Mao Zedong, government (1949–76); Mao Zedong era, women

People's Republic of China, reforms (1980s–): 5, 31–41, 180–81; ACWF historical studies, 34–37; China's Third Revolution, 180–81; Deng Xiaoping reforms, 31, 180; gender studies, 37–41; new nationalism, 5; red-themed arts, 31–34; reinterpretations of war years, 5, 31–34; Xi Jinping reforms, 5, 32, 41, 180–81

plays. *See* theatre

Plunder of Peach and Plum (film, 1934), 70

policewomen, 119

poverty. *See* peasants and villagers; working class

PRC. *See* People's Republic of China (PRC)

pregnancy and childbirth: contraception, 64, 211n107; infant mortality, 64, 73, 109, 132, 134; N4A soldiers, 56, 63–65; patriarchal responses to, 60–61; traditional culture, 172–73

publishing: 11; ACWF studies, 25, 34–37; in Cultural Revolution, 30; gender consciousness, 11; heroines of Mao era, 27–30; journals in Mao era, 25; novels and short stories, 28–30; wartime, 14

Qi Hongshen, 39, 139, 207n99
Qian Zhengying, 54
Qin Yun, 62
Qiu, Peipei, 156, 161
Qiu Yihan, 48–49

Ramseyer, Mark, 155, 221n12
rape. *See* sexual violence
Reader for New Women (1949), 22
Rectification Movement (1942–44): 71, 88–93, 183; anti-party group of 5 (1942), 92–93, 211n3; forgiveness for, 47–48, 89–90, 93, 183; loyalty to Communist cause, 47–48, 70–71, 89–93, 183; Mao's apology, 71, 89–90, 93; persecution of party members, 16, 47–48, 66, 70–71, 88–91, 180; Yan'an as centre, 89

Red Army: gender consciousness, 17, 52, 62; narrative sources, 48; reorganization, 44, 58

Red Flag Floating in the Sky, 23
The Red Lantern (TV series, 2007), 30, 32
Red Sorghum series (Mo Yan), 101
red-themed arts in reform era, 31–34
reform era. *See* People's Republic of China, reforms (1980s–)
religion and spirituality: beliefs outside religion, 147, 174; Buddhism, 147, 166, 185; Morality Society, 129–30. *See also* Christianity; Confucianism
The Reminiscences of Women's Corps (NQNDD), 117, 179

research project: 4–7; ACWF sources, 34–37; agency of women, 6–7; feminist approach, 5–7; gender analysis, 6, 46; interviews, 4, 67–68, 109, 131, 165, 187; interviews, refusal, 70–71; key questions, 6, 42; narrative sources, 4–6, 34–37, 66–67; ordinary women, 5–7; published narratives, 43, 66–67, 99; videos, 99, 115, 191; war memory studies, 5–6
resistance. *See* agency of women
Resistance War. *See* War of Resistance (1931–45)
rights, women's, 186. *See also* gender consciousness
rise and fall of all-under-heaven, 8, 56, 102, 184, 198, 196*n*13
The Road of Lu Sha (Wei Junyi), 93
Rong Guanxiu, 29, 203*n*44
rural areas. *See* peasants and villagers

salvation, national. *See* national salvation movement
Schneider, Helen, 15
schools. *See* education
Schoppa, R. Keith, 128, 129
Scott, James, 131
Second World War: Japanese surrender (1945), 176–79; Tokyo war crimes trials, 154; US role in, 22, 149
self-writing. *See* biographies and autobiographies
sexual violence: 154–55, 174–75, 186; arranged marriages to prevent rape, 170; children of rape victims, 157, 162, 164, 171; fear of, 153, 171; fear of Japanese, 108, 145; oral history evidence, 40, 223*n*62; rape, 154, 155, 163, 171; war statistics, 155. *See also* comfort women
sexuality: celibacy, 94, 133, 155; in reform era, 31–32, 33. *See also* gender consciousness
Sha Village (opera), 30
Shaanxi, 66, 77, 84–85
Shajiabang (TV series, 2006), 32
Shang Pu: 133–34, 151–52, 189; early life, 132, 133; education, 134, 146–47, 189; gender consciousness, 139, 144, 147; Japanese education, 137, 139–41, 147; Manchurian Incident, 139; political awareness, 126, 144–45, 146–47; refusal to marry, 133, 152; teacher, 147, 152, 189
Shanghai: arts, 56; bombings (1937), 74; child labour, 165–66, 170; comfort women research, 156; daily life, 128–29, 167, 176; "the 800" and Yang Huimin, 105–6; historical studies on women, 24, 38, 202*n*21; missionary schools, 149; museums, 157; music conservatory, 121–22; N4A recruits, 52–53, 54, 56; occupation, 81, 83, 105–6, 128–29; women's print culture, 107, 128–29; working class women, 167–68; YWCA programs, 11–12
Shanxi-Chahar-Hebei (Jin-Cha-Ji) Border Region, 15, 29, 87–88, 90, 189
Shao He, 165–66, 189
Shao Menglan, 117, 123–24, 184
Shenyang, Liaoning: 132; education, 137, 177; Manchurian Incident, 3, 10, 38, 75, 132, 137, 139. *See also* Shang Pu; Wang Yao
Shunping (Wan), Hebei, 72, 188–89
Si Saozi (Sister Four), 29
A Single Spark Starts a Prairie Fire, 23
Sino-Japanese War. *See* War of Resistance (1931–45)
slaves, sex. *See* comfort women
"slaves in a lost nation," 75, 87–88, 126, 127, 145. *See also* occupied China
slaves to fighters as heroines, 26–28, 30
Smedley, Agnes, 42, 56, 207*n*1, 210*n*69
Smith, Norman, 129
social class. *See* class
Song Meiling (Madame Chiang Kai-shek), 8–9, 12–14, 104, 123
Song Qingling, 11–12, 211*n*107
The Song of Youth (film, 1959), 28–29, 30
The Song of Youth (novel, 1958), 28–29, 30
The Song of Youth (TV series, 2006), 32
songs. *See* music

Sons and Daughters of the Time of Storm (film, 1935), 11, 127
Spakowski, Nicola, 17
spirituality. *See* religion and spirituality
Stacey, Judith, 17
Stranahan, Patricia, 16
students. *See* education
Su Qing, 127, 129
Su Zhiliang, 37, 156
suicide, 27, 29, 162, 164, 180
Sun Liren, 179
Sun Yat-sen, 11–12, 72–73, 114, 177

Taihang Base Area, 88–89
Taiwan: 19, 98–100, 181, 184; agency of women, 19, 124, 181; democratization, 181; Morality Society, 129–30; museums, 157; narrative sources, 19, 99, 181; Nationalist government (1949–75), 4, 181; suffering and losses, 19, 98–100, 179, 184
Tao Zhu, 60–61
teachers. *See* education
television: in Cultural Revolution, 30; interviews with veterans, 39–40; N4A women soldiers (2011), 34, 43, 49; red themes in reform era, 31–32, 34, 40–41. *See also* film
theatre: comedies, 129; model plays in Mao era, 30; N4A arts, 56–57, 172; Nationalist women's army, 100–1; patriotic plays, 57, 100–1, 117; political purposes, 56–57, 78, 100–1, 172; school groups, 52, 78, 117
Thirty-Two (film, 2014), 157, 163–64
Tianjin, 80, 113, 114, 152, 180
TL (*Iron Currents: Accounts of Heroines of the Ironsides*), 43, 48–49, 52–53
traditional culture: 13, 16. *See also* concubines; Confucianism; footbinding; good wives and wise mothers; marriage, arranged; motherhood, traditional; New Life Movement (NLM); patriarchy
Tsai Ing-wen, vii, 181
TV. *See* television

20th Century Wartime Experiences of Chinese Women (FHSY), 116–17, 119–22, 178–79
Twenty-Two (film, 2017), 153, 157, 163

United Front: 12, 15–18, 44, 49–50; conflicts of Nationalists and CCP, 49–50, 84–85, 99–100, 102, 122–23; formation, 12, 44; gender consciousness, 17–18; women in combat, 17, 58–59
universities and colleges: 112–15; arts schools, 113, 121; curricula, 55, 113; gender consciousness, 117, 119, 126, 144; Japanese education, 112–13, 150; medical schools, 103; military academy in Wuhan, 33; missionary schools, 135; modernization, 118; music conservatories, 121–22, 144; national salvation movement, 70, 76; nonpartisan educators, 117–18; police colleges, 119; private schools, 117–18; relocation to interior, 113, 115, 118, 141; study abroad in Japan, 138–40, 147, 148; women students before wartime, 33; women's economic independence, 118, 126, 136–37, 144; youth organizations, 118
upper class: Communist women, 66–71, 97; education by peasants, 54; N4A recruits, 53–54; Nationalist-associated women, 99–100, 108, 121; as refugees, 108–10. *See also* class; middle/upper class, Communist women

van de Ven, Hans, 49
video. *See* film; television
villagers. *See* peasants and villagers
violence: portrayals of Japanese soldiers, 34. *See also* sexual violence

Wan (Shunping), Hebei, 72, 188–89
Wan Aihua, 163, 223n59
Wang, Wenwen, 129
Wang, Zheng, 18, 213n7

Index 261

Wang Bo: 135, 151–52, 190; Christian faith, 126, 135, 141–42, 190; education, 135, 141, 152; footbinding, 126; gender consciousness, 135, 144; marriage, 126, 141, 145; motherhood, 145–46; nursing, 135, 141–42, 145, 152, 190; political awareness, 126, 144–45
Wang Hong, 19, 165, 169–74, 178, 190
Wang Hongjiu, 101–2
Wang Jingwei, 126–27
Wang Jinwen, 53
Wang Ke, 102–3, 122–23
Wang Ming, 60
Wang Ruqi, 92
Wang Shiwei, 92
Wang Yao: 132–33, 147–49, 151–52, 190; early life, 132–33; education, 133, 137–38; gender consciousness, 133; Japanese education, 137–39, 141, 148, 152; Manchurian Incident, 3, 132; marriage, 133, 148–49, 151–52, 190; political awareness, 125–26, 144–45, 147–48
Wang Youqiao, 35, 205*n*71
Wang Yugeng: 42–43; marriage to Chen Yi, 43, 54, 223*n*74; marriage to Ye Fei, 43, 45; motherhood, 43; publications, 43, 45, 49, 57; revolutionary path, 42–43, 49, 57–59
Wang Zhen: 136–37, 150–52, 190; education, 136–37, 140–41, 152; gender consciousness, 136–37, 141, 144; hatred for Japanese, 140–41, 150–51; Japanese education, 137, 140–41, 151, 190; marriage, 141, 190; political awareness, 126, 140–41, 144–45, 150–51
Wan'nan Incident (1941), 44, 48–50
War of Resistance (1931–45): 4, 12–13, 125–26; Japanese surrender (1945), 176–79; Manchurian Incident (1931), 3, 139; Marco Polo Bridge Incident (1937), 12, 44, 77; museums, 40; "not just a man's cause," 7; oral history projects, 37–41; Pearl Harbor, 149; regional control, 125; statistics, 177; Wan'nan Incident (1941), 44, 48–50. *See also* national salvation movement
War of Resistance, historiography: 22–24, 37–38, 181; as a "good war," 31, 47, 124, 177–78; Mao's national mythmaking, 22–23; museums, 31, 40, 157; oral history projects, 37–41; suffering and losses, 23, 107–8; women's marginalization, 23–24, 40, 44–46, 65. *See also* historiography
War of Resistance, military: 12–13, 44–45, 125; Eighteenth Group Army, 44; regional control, 125; United Front, 12, 44, 49–50. *See also* Eighth Route Army; guerrilla forces; Nationalist Revolutionary Army; New Fourth Army (N4A); Red Army; United Front
Wartime Child Welfare Protection Association (ZZEB), 123, 213*n*7
Wei Gongzhi, 62
Wei Junyi, 92–93
Wei Shaolan, 157, 163–64
Weinan, Shaanxi, 66, 71–72, 77–78, 189
wise wives and mothers. *See* good wives and wise mothers
women: agency of women, 181–86; biographies and autobiographies, 182–86; feminist studies, 5–7; gender consciousness, 184–86; historiography, 37–41, 181–86; Marxist ideology, 10, 46; multiple identities, 97; national salvation movement, 10–11; oral history, 182–86; sexuality in reform era, 31–32; war memories, 5–7; work in reform era, 36. *See also* agency of women; gender consciousness; gender studies; historiography; women's movement (1890s–1945)
Women of China (ACWF journal), 25
Women of the Great Times (Wang Yugeng), 57

Women Soldiers of the Central Plain (ZYNZS, 3 vols., 1991–94), 39, 43, 45–50, 52, 53, 62
Women Soldiers of the New Fourth Army (book, 2004), 43
Women Soldiers of the New Fourth Army (TV series, 2011), 34, 43, 49
women's movement (1890s–1945): 7–8, 14–15; ACWF historical studies, 24, 34–37; Communists, 15–18; economic independence, 16, 115, 118, 126, 136–37; free choice in marriage, 16, 17; individual rights vs national salvation, 9, 14, 16; male allies, 7; May Fourth Movement, 8, 10, 15–16, 129, 131, 135; nationalism, 8–9, 15; New Life Movement (NLM), 8–10, 11, 12–13, 38; rise and fall of all-under-heaven, 8, 56, 102, 184, 198, 196n13; terminology, 186. *See also* activism; agency of women
Women's New Life Movement Monthly, 9
Women's Resonance (journal), 9, 197n24
working class: 51–52, 164–75, 186; child labour, 51, 165–66, 170; education of, 51–52, 55, 167; education of soldiers by, 54; hardships, 165, 166–69; hatred for Japanese, 165, 166–68, 186; late marriages, 168; narrative sources, 164–65; Nationalist concerns, 14; occupied China, 153–54, 164–75; patriarchal culture, 167; political awareness, 165, 166, 167–68; resilience, 165; revolutionary paths, 50, 51–52, 55; survival in occupied areas, 128, 165, 186; vulnerability and class inequalities, 112. *See also* peasants and villagers
Wu Jiaying, 123
Wu Jufang, 108
Wu Weijing, 109
Wu Yifang, 14
Wu Zhiying, 64, 178
Wuhan, 33, 56, 83, 115
Wutai County, Shanxi, 168–69

Xi Jinping, 5, 32, 41, 180–81
Xia Rong, 38
Xi'an, 84, 85
Xi'an Incident, 72
Xiang Jingyu, 25, 123
Xiang Ying, 48, 58
Xiao Hong, 127
Xiao Wenyan, 179
Xie Bingying, 100
Xie Fei, 58–59
Xu Liuyun, 120
Xu Yunqing, 27–28, 203n34
Xue Ping, 64

Yan Xishan, 169
Yan'an: 4, 85; Rectification Movement, 71, 88–93, 183; schools and universities, 55, 113
Yang Baogui, 162
Yang Huimin, 105–6
Yang Jiang, 129
Yang Lai, 165, 167–68, 190–91
Yang Mo, 28–29
Yang Ruinian, 49
Yang Shitong, 161
Yang Ti, 54
Yang Xianzhi, 123
Yang Xihe, 159–60
Yang Yinyu, 129
Yang Zheng, 52
Yanjing University, 70, 135, 143, 144, 149–50, 220n52
Ye Fei, 43, 45
Ye Hua, 56
Yi people, 105
Yi Qiping, 56
Yin Yulin, 160
Ying Di, 165, 166, 176, 191
YMCA (Young Men's Christian Association), 14
You Huaiyan, 179
Young, Helen, 17, 52
Yu Chien-ming, 100
Yu Guofang, 117
Yu Jian: 134, 151–52, 191; Christian faith, 141, 142, 191; education, 134, 141, 142, 191; gender consciousness, 134, 144–45;

hatred for Japanese, 134, 146, 176;
   interview, 134; marriage, 142, 146,
   152; motherhood, 146; political
   awareness, 126, 144–46, 152, 180
Yu Wenxiu, 120
Yuan Guoping, 48–49
Yuan Runlan, 130
Yuan Zhenwei, 48–49
Yue Fei, 60
Yunling, 42, 56
YWCA (Young Women's Christian
   Association), 11–12, 14, 51, 149

Zeng Kehong, 48
Zeng Zhi, 47–48, 60
Zhang Ailing, 127, 129
Zhang Boling, 114
Zhang Dafei, 99, 111–12, 115, 177
Zhang Jun, 207n101
Zhang Ming, 52
Zhang Qian (wife of Chen Yi), 43, 54
Zhang Rongzhen, 121–22
Zhang Shu: 143–44, 149–52, 191;
   Christian faith, 135–36, 141–44,
   149, 191; education, 135–36,
   141–44, 149–50, 152, 191; flight
   to interior, 143–44, 150, 191;
   gender consciousness, 135–36,
   144; hatred for Japanese, 149–50;
   Japanese education, 150; marriage,
   136, 144, 191; political awareness,
   126, 143–45, 149–50, 180

Zhang Shuangbing, 156–59
Zhang Wei: 99, 115–16, 191; education,
   115–16, 184; gender consciousness,
   115–16; marriage, 115, 116, 180;
   Nationalists, 99, 116, 180; videos,
   99, 115, 191
Zhang Xi, 39
Zhang Xueliang, 72, 132
Zhang Yangfen, 56, 210n69
Zhang Yuqin, 107–8
Zhang Zhangzhu, 54
Zhang Zuolin, 132
Zhang-Wang Mingxin, 111
Zhao Ma, 164
Zhao Yiman, 21, 26, 32–34
Zhao Yiman (film, 1950, 2005), 21, 26,
   32–34
Zhenzhuang, 9
Zhong Qiguang, 43
Zhou Lei, 38
Zhou Linbing, 48
Zhou Meiyu, 103–4, 122, 124
Zhou Zhifang, 63
Zhu Hong, 45–46
Zhu Hongzhao, 60, 211n99, 211n107
Zhu Juyi, 108–9
Zhu Su'e, 106–7, 213n7
Zhu Wenhua, 64
Zhugou tragedy (1939), 50
ZYNZS (*Women Soldiers of the Central
   Plain*) (3 vols., 1991–94), 39, 43,
   45–50, 52, 53, 62

Printed and bound in Canada by Friesens
Set in Adobe Garamond Pro by Apex CoVantage, LLC
Copy editor: Frank Chow
Proofreader: Sophie Pouyanne
Cover designer: Jess Sullivan
Cover images: *Top and bottom right*: Wiki Commons; *bottom left*: Zhao Yiman, from the film "Zhao Yiman," Changchun Film Studio, 1950.